ABOUT THE AUTHORS

D0507604

The author/co-author of 170 books, Brad Steiger wrote the paperback bestseller *Strangers from the Skies* about UFOs. His edited work *Project Bluebook* was hailed by *Omni* magazine as one of the best UFO books of the century. Steiger was inducted into the Hypnosis Hall of Fame for his work with UFO contactees, abductees, and past life regression. In Minneapolis, he received the Lifetime Achievement Award at the National UFO and Unexplained Phenomena Conference.

The author/co-author of 43 books, Brad's wife, Sherry Steiger, an ordained minister with a special interest in UFOs in the Bible and world religions, began working closely in 1985 with Dr. J. Allen Hynek, official scientific advisor for the U.S. Air Force's twenty-year study of UFOs. Sherry served as his publicist, and confidante at his nonprofit UFO research organization in Phoenix until his death in 1986. This position made her privy to unpublished research and more than 80,000 documented cases from 161 countries.

For many decades, the Steigers have researched and investigated UFOs and their cultural impact throughout world history, and they have lectured and conducted seminars on the phenomenon throughout the United States and overseas. Sherry and Brad were featured in twenty-two episodes of the television series *Could It Be a Miracle?*. Together, their television appearances and specials include: *The Joan Rivers Show, Entertainment Tonight, Inside Edition, Hard Copy, Hollywood Insider,* and specials on HBO, USA Network, The Learning Channel, The History Channel, and Arts and Entertainment (A&E), among others. They appear frequently as guests on numerous domestic and international radio talk shows.

REAL ALIENS, SPACE BEINGS, AND CREATURES FROM OTHER WORLDS

Brad Steiger and Sherry Hansen Steiger

VISIBLE INK PRESS

Detroit

REAL ALIENS, SPACE BEINGS, AND CREATURES FROM OTHER WORLDS

Visible Ink Press®
43311 Joy Rd., #414
Canton, MI 48187-2075

Visible Ink Press is a registered trademark of Visible Ink Press LLC.

Most Visible Ink Press books are available at special quantity discounts when purchased in bulk by corporations, organizations, or groups. Customized printings, special imprints, messages, and excerpts can be produced to meet your needs. For more information, contact Special Markets Director, Visible Ink Press, www.visibleink.com, or 734-667-3211.

Project Manager: Kevin S. Hile
Art Director: Mary Claire Krzewinski
Typesetting: Marco Di Vita
Proofreaders: Sarah Hermsen and Sharon Malinowski
Indexer: Larry Baker

ISBN 978-1-57859-333-0

Cover images: iStock

Library of Congress Cataloging-in-Publication Data

Steiger, Brad.
  Real aliens, space beings, and creatures from other worlds / by Brad Steiger.
    p. cm.
  Includes bibliographical references and index.
  ISBN 978-1-57859-333-0
  1. Human-alien encounters. I. Title.
  BF2050.S74 2011
  001.942—dc22
                                                    2011000563

Printed in the United States of America

10 9 8 7 6 5 4 3 2 1

Contents

CONTRIBUTORS

Ricardo Pustanio

Ricardo Pustanio is an enduring icon in the world of New Orleans Mardi Gras float design and local artistry. Today his phenomenal creative talents are witnessed by thousands upon thousands of locals and tourists who throng the streets of New Orleans each year to catch a glimpse of one of the oldest and most prestigious parades of the season, the Krewe of Mid-City. According to Ricardo, "The best is still to come!"

Born in New Orleans, Ricardo is the third son of local golfing legend Eddie "Blackie" Pustanio, a well-known icon of the sport. When Ricardo was baptized, the famous "Diamond Jim" Moran was hailed as his godfather and all the major golfing pros who visited the elder Pustanio at his City Park Golf Course digs bounced little Ricardo on their knees at one time or another.

Like nearly every child brought up in the city of New Orleans, Ricardo was taught by his parents to enjoy the pageantry and revelry of the great old-line Mardi Gras parades. These halcyon Mardi Gras days of his youth were Ricardo's first taste of the passion that would become the artistic inspiration of his later career. During the 1960s Ricardo's entries won first place awards and rode with the King of Mid-City three years in a row: a true precursor of things to come.

The winner of many art competitions throughout his life, his earliest prize-winning work was created while Ricardo was still in Kindergarten. From an early age, Ricardo's works were distinguished with prizes and praise. Many are now in private art collections in New Orleans and across the United States.

Ricardo's special style has been very visible in his work on numerous backdrops and displays for the 1984 New Orleans World's Fair; several of his original pieces from that Fair have garnered high prices at auctions throughout the United States and Europe.

Ricardo served Le Petit Theatre du Vieux Carré as technical director for its 1992 to 1993 season, during which he contributed his considerable artistic talents to the creation of scenery and backdrops for the season's major productions, including *West Side Story* and *The Baby Dance*, for which he created a giant sixty-foot by thirty-foot pâpier-maché pyramid, one of the highlights of the season. Ricardo's set designs for the

Ricardo Pustanio

productions of *King Midas and the Golden Touch* and *The Snow Queen* won him numerous awards.

In 1992 Ricardo began his long association with William Crumb and the Children's Educational Theatre. His work on scenery and backdrops has toured with the company in thirteen major productions across the United States, and he continues to contribute his talents to the organization to this day. Ricardo has also donated his time and talent to a number of nonprofit organizations, including the Save Our Lake Foundation and the March of Dimes.

Ricardo displayed his talent with scenic design in some of the best-known films produced in his area, including *Angel Heart*, starring Mickey Rourke; *The Big Easy*, starring Dennis Quaid and Ellen Barkin; Anne Rice's *Interview with the Vampire*, starring Tom Cruise and Brad Pitt; and most recently in the much-anticipated *A Love Song for Billy Long*, which stars John Travolta and was filmed in historic New Orleans.

Ricardo has conceptualized and designed numerous book covers and illustrations for major works of science fiction and fantasy: he was voted Best New Artist of the Year at World Cons held in New Orleans and in Amsterdam, Holland. Ricardo has also illustrated children's books, created portraits and artwork for private clients across the United States and in Europe, and has to his credit three original action comic books, the illustration and design of the long-running International Middle Eastern Dancer magazine, and several decks of personalized Tarot cards.

Reflecting on his artist achievements, Ricardo says: "I have paid my dues many times over the years and I am always in a constant state of expectation: I can't wait for the next challenge, the next thing to approach me. I am probably most proud of my work with the Krewe of Mid-City in recent years, because they have allowed me an unlimited palette to create with: the only limit is my imagination, and as you see, that has never had any limits!"

Ricardo Pustanio's hands have been busy creating artworks that have brought joy and pleasure to thousands of people over the years. It is no wonder that has been named one of The Hardest Working Mardi Gras Artists in the City of New Orleans and in the history of Mardi Gras design.

Bill Oliver

Bill Oliver

Artist Bill Oliver is also a musician, composer, and award-winning song writer. His music is sometimes reflective and moody, and his compositions, like his art, often act as "sound photographs" that capture a moment of life and freeze it in time for further contemplation—even if that moment of contemplation involves a vampire, zombie, UFO visitor, or a werewolf.

Oliver resides in Vancouver, British Columbia, where he has nourished a life-long interest in the paranormal, UFOs, the metaphysical, and all things esoteric that stems from many personal experiences. His enthusiasm for pursuing the unknown brought him into personal contact and interview opportunities with experiencers in all aspects of the paranormal. These encounters have had significant influences on much of Bill's work.

Brad Steiger first became familiar with Oliver's exciting artwork when the Canadian won the Christmas Art contest on the Jeff Rense Program in 2005. In the art contest for Halloween 2006, Bill won honorable mention.

As the two men became better acquainted, Steiger was honored to learn that he had been one of Oliver's boyhood heroes with his work on the paranormal, the esoteric, and things that go bump in the night.

"To be reading one of Brad's classic books one day and being asked to do some art for one of his new books another is truly paranormal," Oliver said.

Visit Bill Oliver's Website at http://www.boysoblue.com.

Alyne Pustanio

Folklorist and occultist Alyne Pustanio is a New Orleans native whose roots go deep into the local culture. It is from that proverbial "gumbo" that she draws her inspiration for most of her tales of terror and fascination.

A descendant of Portuguese and Sicilian immigrant families who trace their ancestry to European Gypsies, Alyne was exposed to the mysteries of the occult at an early age. Two great-grandmothers were gifted and sought out mediums, and another relative is a verified psychic. Alyne, however, credits her mother—an avid spiritualist—with inspiring her life-long interest in the supernatural and unexplained.

These interests, combined with her avocations in folklore and history, result in a validity and passion that is immediately obvious in all her writings. Learn more at www.hauntedamericatours.com.

Alyne Pustanio

Pastor Robin Swope

Pastor Robin Swope, known as the Paranormal Pastor, has been a Christian minister for more than fifteen years in both mainline and Evangelical denominations. He has served as a missionary to Burkina Faso, West Africa, and ministered to the homeless in New York City's Hell's Kitchen. He is the founder and chief officiant of Open Gate Ministerial Services and a member of St. Paul's United Church of Christ in Erie, Pennsylvania. Read more about Pastor Swope at Http://theparanormalpastor.blogspot.com.

William Michael Mott

William Michael (Mike) Mott has been creative director for a national toy and manufacturing company and a high-performance software company, the art director for a city newspaper, has worked as an artist/designer for Fortune 500 companies, as well as for an NSF engineering research center, and for a

Pastor Robin Swope

variety of freelance clients such as book and magazine publishers. A freelance artist and writer, he writes both fiction and nonfiction. His artwork and writing have appeared or been featured in many publications, such as *Computer Graphics World Magazine, DRAGON Magazine, FATE, NEXUS, World Explorer, Undaunted Press, Lost Continent Library Magazine,* and others.

Mike Mott

Mike has created artwork and graphic design for mass-market book covers, posters, brochures, packaging, CD-ROM covers and art collections, and digital/Web-based media, winning several design awards from regional Advertising Federation awards for printed material to awards for Website graphics and design. His artwork has been featured in the exhibition "In Dreams Awake: Art of Fantasy" at the Olympia and York Gallery, New York City, 1988, as well as at the 1987 World Fantasy Con, Con*stellation, the DragonCon 2001 art show, several one-man exhibits, and digital galleries in various venues. He researches and writes on Fortean, folklore, comparative religion, and paranormal topics.

Mike is the author of the satirical fantasy novel *Pulsifer: A Fable* and its sequel, *Land of Ice, a Velvet Knife*, both soon to be re-released in an omnibus edition from TGS Publishing. In addition, he has written the nonfiction books *Caverns, Cauldrons, and Concealed Creatures* and *This Tragic Earth: The Art and World of Richard Sharpe Shaver*. Mott's pulp fiction anthology of fiction, verse, and artwork, *PULP WINDS*, featuring an introduction by Brad Steiger, has recently been published by TGS (www.hiddenmysteries.com). Mike can be reached at admin@mottimorphic.com and at mottimorph@earthlink.net. His website is www.mottimorphic.com.

Chris Holly

Chris Holly

Chris Holly lives on Long Island in New York, where she presently writes and publishes the site Endless Journey with Chris Holly's Paranormal World and the Knightzone.

Although Chris has spent a life building different entrepreneur ventures, her one true passion has always been writing. She feels it is her destiny to relate true events of the paranormal to the world.

Chris is grateful to all her readers and reads the emails sent to her concerning the world of the paranormal. "I always read every email sent to me and try hard to respond to each and every one who takes the time to write to me." You can reach Chris at chrishollyufo@yahoo.com, or check out her Websites at http://endlessjrny.blogspot.com and http://www.fttoufo.com/chrishollysparanormalworld.htm.

Angela Thomas

Angela Thomas

Angela Thomas, also known as Oct13baby, is famous world-wide for her accurate psychic readings; her advice is widely sought by those who need honest and ethical insight into their physical, emotional, and spiritual problems. In addition to being a world-renowned psychic reader, Angela is the co-host of "P.O.R.T.A.L. Paranormal Talk Radio," a weekly paranormal radio show devoted to bringing its audience the most fascinating information in the paranormal world. Email her at oct13baby@aol.com.

Paul Dale Roberts

Paul Dale Roberts is the general manager and ghostwriter of Haunted and Paranormal Investigations International. He is a prolific writer who has investigated ghosts, werewolves, witches, vampires, and demons. Paul is also the "ghostwriter" for Shannon McCabe's Haunted and Paranormal Investigations International (www.HPIparanormal.net); Paul's Lair/HPI is now found at www.shannonmccabe.com, and you can email him at Pauld5606@comcast.net.

G. Cope Schellhorn

G. Cope Schellhorn is the author of eight books, including *Extraterrestrials in Biblical Prophecy, When Men Are Gods, Discovering Ruins and Rock Art in Brazil and Peru,* and *Man's Quest for Immortality: From Ancient Times to the Present.* He spent several decades investigating extraordinary phenomena and now lives with his wife, writes, and photographs in southwestern Wisconsin.

Paul Dale Roberts

Timothy Green Beckley

Tim Beckley began researching UFOs at the age of ten in 1967. There always remains an audience eager to know about the mysteries about UFOs, alien life forms, and the Hollow Earth, and Beckley's Global Communications has saved some old and rare books from obscurity; the company also publishes up-to-date compendiums written by more recent researchers. In addition, Beckley is the publisher of *The Conspiracy Journal* (www.conspiracyjournal.com).

Special Acknowledgments

Scott Corrales
Inexplicata: The Journal of Hispanic Ufology
www.inexplicata.blogspot.com

George A. Filer
Filer's Files
National UFO Center and Research Institute
www.nationalufocenter.com

Dirk Vander Ploeg, Publisher
Robert D. Morningstar, Editor
UFO Digest
www.ufodigest.com

Dr. Alfred Lambremont Weber
Dr. Michael Salla
EXOPOLITICS
www.exopolitics.com

G. Cope Schellhorn

Timothy Green Beckley

INTRODUCTION

As established authors and lecturers in the field of the paranormal and UFO research, each week we receive email that brings eyewitness accounts of individuals who claim that they have had encounters with extraterrestrials. While such claims have become commonplace to us during the decades that we have been seriously investigating the UFO phenomenon, it is a bit more startling when we receive alleged eyewitness accounts of aliens working side by side with human scientists in a co-operative effort to advance our space program and our civilization. Some individuals have told us that our scientists have been able to incorporate alien technology into some of our most cutting-edge aircraft and space vehicles under the guidance of the extraterrestrial visitors who oversee the technical wizardry. Many of our informants provide what appear to be authentic credentials and resumés and claim to be personally familiar with ETs working at the National Aeronautics and Space Administration (NASA) and at secret underground facilities.

Such interstellar cooperation is said to have been going on since soon after the UFO crash at Roswell, New Mexico, in July 1947. Some say that humans would never have been able to get to the moon by 1969 if it hadn't been for the technological assistance of the extraterrestrials who were working among them at NASA. Informants claim many other benefits of alien technology have trickled down to hundreds of civilian applications, from transistors to computers.

Some of the aliens (we are told by those who claim to have had face-to-face encounters) are tall, blond, very human in appearance, and are nicknamed "the Nordics." Others that are small in stature with big bug eyes, oversized skulls, and grayish skin are referred to as "the Grays." And then there are those who appear as though they are basically reptilian, a species of highly intelligent serpents. Some experiencers speak of encounters with robot-like beings or grotesque monsters.

On the less benevolent side, there are unpleasant accusations of alien abductions, cattle and human mutilations, and missing time experienced by UFO abductees. Frightening accounts of being taken on board an extraterrestrial vehicle and being subjected to painful physical examinations, including forced sexual relations, have been reported by abductees. Late night talk shows fill the airways with reports of hybrid and mutant children and stories of adult men and women being left with mysterious scars after being kidnapped by UFOnauts. Some researchers assert that the aliens have instituted an extensive program to produce alien-human hybrids to populate a new Earth controlled by extraterrestrials.

The late Dr. J. Allen Hynek, formerly the head of the department of astronomy at Northwestern University, served in the official capacity of scientific advisor to the U.S. Air Force on its Project Blue Book study of UFOs for more than twenty years. During the course of his investigations, Dr. Hynek devised a "UFO Classification System" that continues to be widely used: Close Encounters of the First Kind indicates a UFO observed at close range; Close Encounters of the Second Kind refers to a UFO leaving behind physical evidence; and Close Encounters of the Third Kind means there is interaction between a human and an occupant of a UFO.

When Project Blue Book was discontinued by the Air Force in 1969, Dr. Hynek established the nonprofit Center for UFO Studies (CUFOS) in Evanston, Illinois, in 1973. In 1985 Dr. Hynek founded the Center for UFO Research in Scottsdale, Arizona. It was there that Sherry served as Dr. Hynek's publicist and assisted him in researching and interviewing UFO contactees. Together, they were in the process of developing a motion picture and a television series based on his investigations of the UFO enigma. Sherry states that by the time of Dr. Hynek's death in 1986 he had received over 80,000 UFO reports from over 161 countries.

A December 1996 poll conducted by a magazine of politics and contemporary issues published by John F. Kennedy, Jr. found that fifty-five percent of Americans believe that life exists on other planets. Seventy-nine percent stated their contention that extraterrestrials have visited Earth in the last 100 years; seventy percent were convinced that the government is covering up the truth about UFOs.

In July 1997, the fiftieth anniversary of the UFO crash at Roswell, CNN and *Time* magazine took a poll that indicated that eighty percent of Americans think the government keeps the wraps on extraterrestrial visitation. The same poll revealed that thirty-five percent expect aliens to appear "somewhat human"; sixty-four percent believe that aliens have made contact with humans; thirty-seven percent accept the testimony of those who claim to have been abducted.

In a November 2005 Gallup Poll survey, twenty-four of Americans believe that ETs have visited Earth in our prehistory; fifty-one percent of men believe that UFOs are here now; and forty percent of women accept the reality of extraterrestrial visitors.

In 2010, the internationally respected and acclaimed scientist Stephen Hawking suggested that extraterrestrials are almost certain to exist—but we should avoid any contact. Hawking suggests: "Alien life is almost certain to exist in many other parts of the universe: not just in planets, or even floating in interplanetary space."

The universe, Hawking points out, has 100 billion galaxies, each containing hundreds of millions of stars. Earth is unlikely to be the only planet where life has evolved.

"To my mathematical brain, the numbers alone makes thinking about aliens perfectly rational," Hawking said.

He issues a note of warning that aliens might simply raid Earth for its resources and then move on: "We only have to look at ourselves to see how intelligent life might develop into something we wouldn't want to meet. I imagine they might exist in massive ships, having used up all the resources from their home planet. Such advanced aliens would perhaps become nomads, looking to conquer and colonize whatever planets they can reach."

Hawking concludes that trying to make contact with alien races is "a little too risky," adding: "If aliens ever visit us, I think the outcome would be much as when Christopher Columbus first landed in America, which didn't turn out very well for the Native Americans."

A Reuters worldwide poll conducted in April 2010 discovered the astonishing figure that twenty percent of Earth's population believes that aliens are here now, "already in our midst." This survey included India, China, Europe, the United States, England, and Canada.

Today, in 2011, some UFO research groups claim the numbers have risen to the hundreds of thousands—others claim millions.

There are several theories about the UFOnauts' actual place of origin and their true identity. Every investigator, regardless of how open-minded he or she may hope to be, has a favorite location, whether physical or ethereal, for the agents of the apparently universal and timeless UFO phenomenon. Generally, these arguments are distilled to the central issue of whether the UFO intelligences are essentially nonphysical entities from an invisible realm in another dimension, or physical beings who have the advanced technology to travel over what we consider impossible distances in a method of transport at the present time completely unknown to our science and technology.

Perhaps both theories are correct. We may be confronted by both kinds of intelligence in our spiritual, intellectual, biological, and evolutionary processes.

Or we may be dealing with an intelligence that has a physical structure so totally unlike ours that it presents itself in a variety of guises, and employs invisibility, materialization, and dematerialization at different times in order to accomplish its goal of communication with our species.

Little Green Men

Accounts of alien contact are varied. There are stories of people who are taken on thrilling flights in spaceships like a modern-day Gulliver escorted by an extraterrestrial guide to strange other worlds. And there are tales of frightening encounters in which a terrified man or woman comes unexpectedly upon "bug-eyed monsters" or "little green men."

If you accused someone of seeing a "little green man" before the summer of 1947, you probably would have been suggesting that he or she had been drinking too much and was seeing elves or leprechauns. But all that changed one summer night in 1947 (many said it was July 2) when a flying saucer crashed on a ranch located about sixty miles north of Roswell, New Mexico. After that, the accusation of seeing a "little green man" would refer to the small extraterrestrial aliens that some witnesses swore that they saw near flying saucers.

A Crashed Flying Saucer and Small Alien Bodies at Roswell

According to most accounts, on or about the nights of July 2 to July 5, 1947, a "flying saucer," as alien spaceships were called back then, developed mechanical problems and fell to Earth on a ranch located about sixty miles north of Roswell.

Barney Barnett claimed he was one of the first civilians to arrive on the scene following the crash. Barnett, a civil engineer employed by the federal government who lived in Socorro, New Mexico, said he saw alien bodies on the ground and inside the spaceship. He described them as small, hairless beings with large heads and round, oddly spaced eyes.

Barnett reported that a military unit arrived on the scene, and an officer ordered him off the site with the stern admonition that it was his patriotic duty to remain silent about what he had seen.

According to many UFO researchers, the Alien Invasion began in the summer of 1947. Sometime between July 2 and 5, an alien spaceship was said to have crashed outside of Roswell, New Mexico, and the U.S. military supposedly recovered a number of small bodies of the extraterrestrial crew. Because of the sometimes imaginative reportage of the day, people began to refer to the aliens popularly as "little green men." (*Art by Ricardo Pustanio*)

A rancher named Mac Brazel discovered the debris on his land and alerted the local sheriff. Following this, Major Jesse Marcel, intelligence officer for the 509th Bombardment Group stationed at Roswell, was ordered to go to the ranch and salvage the remains of the unknown aircraft.

Thirty-three years later, in 1980, retired Major Marcel, winner of five air combat medals in World War II, told journalists that he and his men found wreckage from an unidentified vehicle scattered throughout the area of the crash site. He readily admitted that he had no idea what it was—and nearly four decades later, was still unable to explain what they found. The strange, weightless material discovered by the 509th Bombardment Group was difficult to describe. The pieces varied in length from four or five inches to three or four feet. Some fragments had markings that resembled hieroglyphics.

Although the material seemed to be extremely strong, the military investigators thought that it looked more like balsa wood than metal. Marcel put his cigarette lighter to one of the rectangular fragments, but it would not burn. Major Marcel and his crew gathered as many pieces as they could and brought them back to Roswell Army Air Field Base.

In their book *UFO Crash at Roswell*, Don Schmitt and Kevin Randle include an interview with Brigadier General Arthur Exon. In the interview, the general states that, in addition to debris from the wreckage, four tiny alien cadavers were flown to Wright Field: "They [the alien bodies] were all found, apparently, outside the craft itself…. The metal and material from the spaceship was unknown to anyone I talked to…. Roswell was the recovery of a craft from space."

The UFO-Alien Cover-up Begins

Randle, a decorated combat veteran and a retired Lieutenant Colonel, believes that he and Schmitt have found new evidence indicating that the crash occurred on July 4, 1947, rather than July 2. It was on July 5, according to Schmitt and Randle, that Mac Brazel visited Sheriff George Wilcox and informed him of the peculiar discovery he had made near his ranch the day before.

The military unit under the command of Major Jesse Marcel retrieved the crash debris and alien bodies on July 5. On July 8 Walter Haut, the public affairs officer at Roswell, issued the press release that the Army had captured a flying saucer. But almost immediately, the military heavily promoted an official cover story of a collapsed weather balloon falling to Earth in the desert.

"If all this fuss was simply about a bunch of ranchers and townspeople finding the debris from a balloon, why did the military seek out those witnesses and threaten to silence them?" Randle asks pointedly. "There is no question that members of the Army were ordered never to talk about what they had seen. And there seems to be substantial evidence to support the claims that military representatives visited the homes of civilian witnesses and silenced them as well. At the same time there were rumors that one or more of the alien occupants had survived impact. Only recently has there been some confirmation that this allegation may have some validity."

Tom Carey and Don Schmitt, authors of *Witness to Roswell: Unmasking the Government's Biggest Cover-up* (2009), indicated that they frequently received reports from men and women who had been young children living in Roswell in 1947 who swore that they saw uniformed servicemen chasing strange little men down alleyways and across backgrounds.

UFO researcher Stanton Friedman has said that he and author-researcher William Moore interviewed at least 130 individuals who have firsthand knowledge of the UFO crash at Roswell. Both Friedman and Moore—who is also coauthor with Charles Berlitz of a book on the crash, *The Roswell Incident*—believe that an extraterrestrial flying saucer exploded in the area and that the retrieved bits and pieces were shipped off to Wright Field (now Wright-Patterson Air Force Base) in Dayton, Ohio.

Friedman, a nuclear physicist and author of numerous books about UFOs, strongly denies the official story that the military had discovered a downed weather balloon or the debris of a Japanese bomb balloon (known as a "Fugo") at the crash site. It is his contention that Walter Haut, the public affairs officer at Roswell, received direct orders from the base commander, Col. William Blanchard, to prepare an official press release. This press release from the Roswell Army Air Force Base initiated the military conspiracy to keep the truth of a crashed UFO from the public.

Friedman states that Major Jesse Marcel was very familiar with all kinds of weather or military balloons and would not have mistaken such ordinary debris for that of a downed alien spaceship. It is also highly unlikely that any of the military personnel would have mistaken alien bodies for those of diminutive human remains.

After the wreckage was properly identified as extraterrestrial in nature, Friedman contends, the official cover-up was instigated at both the Roswell base and at the headquarters of the Eighth Air Force in Fort Worth, Texas. He believes this was carried out by Eighth Air Force Commander Roger Ramey on direct orders from General Clements McMullen at Strategic Air Command (SAC) headquarters in Washington, D.C.

Kevin Randle has spent many hours attempting to sift through the claims surrounding the Roswell UFO case. Most accounts speak of five alien bodies found at the impact site north of Roswell and state that four corpses were transported to Wright Field and the fifth to Lowry Field to the USAF mortuary service.

However, numerous secondary accounts of the incident assert that one of the aliens had survived the crash and was still alive when the military arrived on the scene. Some UFO researchers maintain that the alien being is still alive and well-treated as a guest of the Air Force at Wright-Patterson.

"Better Keep Your Mouths Shut" Witnesses Are Warned

During an interview with a granddaughter of Sheriff George Wilcox in March 1991, Schmitt and Randle were told that not only did the sheriff see the debris of a UFO, he also saw "little space beings."

According to the woman, her grandfather had described the entities as having gray complexions and large heads. They were dressed in suits of a silk-like material.

Later, military men "who were not kidding" visited the sheriff and his wife and warned them that they would be killed if they ever told anyone what Wilcox saw at the crash site. And not only would they be killed, but their children and grandchildren would also be eliminated.

Randle and Schmitt also located Ms. Frankie Rowe, who had been twelve years old at the time of the mysterious occurrences outside of Roswell. Her father, a lieutenant with the fire department, had been called to extinguish an early morning fire burning north of town. He told his family at dinner that night that he had seen the remains of what he had at first believed to be an airplane, but soon saw was "some kind of ship."

According to Ms. Rowe, her father said he also saw two bodies in body bags and a third alien entity walking around in a daze. He described the beings as about the size of a ten-year-old child.

A few days later Frankie happened to be at the fire station visiting her father when a New Mexico State Police officer came in with a strange piece of metal that he claimed he had picked up from the UFO crash site when no one was looking.

To the astonishment of the firemen, the trooper tossed the object onto a table where it "unfolded itself in a fluid motion," looking not unlike flowing water or liquid mercury. Each of the firefighters took a turn examining the alien metal. Even Frankie had an opportunity to touch the material, and she remembers being able to crumple it into a ball.

Then, according to Frankie, two or three days after the strange demonstration in the firehouse, a group of military men arrived at their house and made it clear that they knew all about the fragment of the UFO that the state police officer had stolen from the crash site and displayed to the firemen and to the twelve-year-old girl.

The leader of the men told her that if she ever talked about the incident again, her entire family would be taken out in the desert and "no one would ever find us again."

Randle and Schmitt tell of their interview with Glenn Dennis, who had been the Roswell mortician in 1947. Dennis told them that he had "blundered" into the Roswell Army Air Field hospital on

As sightings of alleged aliens grew, the reports became even more colorful. Some witnesses claimed they saw little green men with antennas and multiple limbs, heads, and eyes. (*Art by Ricardo Pustanio*)

the evening that the alien bodies had been recovered. Earlier Dennis had seen some of the debris and had been told about the corpses of smallish beings by a friend.

According to Dennis, a "nasty red-haired officer" confronted him and warned him that if he ever told anyone about the crash or the alien bodies, "they will be picking your bones from the sand."

In Randle's opinion the results of their research prove beyond the shadow of a doubt that aliens exist and that something crashed near Roswell and that it held a crew. And Randle insists that "there is no doubt that the crew was not human."

A Friendly French Farmer
Is Immobilized by Curious Crop Inspectors

Elves, fairies, genies, and wee people, it would seem, have been popular in all cultures throughout history, and humans have always been baffled by the mystery of their origin. And now, when some witnesses claim that their "wee person" came from outer space, the mystery becomes even more perplexing.

On July 1, 1965, while working his field near Valensole, France, Maurice Masse was startled to see an object that looked like a giant rugby ball standing among his plants.

As Masse approached the object, which he described as being "about the size of a Dauphin car," he saw two small "men" investigating one of his lavender plants. Aside from their shortness ("about the size of eight-year-old children"), their large heads (three times the size of a normal adult's head), and their lipless mouths, Masse contended that the beings appeared human-like.

The farmer continued to approach the little men, intent on conversing with them. When they suddenly noticed him, however, one of the aliens pointed a tube at Masse and immobilized him completely.

Freed of further distractions, the two little creatures continued to chatter among themselves in a strange language and to examine the plants.

Although they sent an occasional glance toward the immobilized Frenchman, at no time did he feel that these strange little men wished to do him any harm. Nor did he feel any pain or discomfort in his paralyzed condition. He continued to observe the bizarre intruders without any impairment in his mental faculties.

It was not until about a quarter of an hour after the spacecraft left his field that Masse was able to move again. A cafe owner and the local police substantiated the farmer's tale by telling journalists that they had seen the strange tracks the little men had left and the holes made by their vehicle's six-legged landing gear. Masse enjoyed a solid reputation in the mountain village, and a *gendarme* informed news personnel that the police would not regard the incident as a hoax, joke, or lie.

Tiny Visitors in Space Capsules Emerge from a Cloud in Russia

The following case is said to have occurred in the summer of 1966 on a sunny afternoon near the city of Petrozavodsk, Karelia region, Russia.

Several children, including Margaret Borisova were playing in a field near a local pond when they noticed a strange cloud hovering in the clear sky. It rapidly descended and then hovered above a nearby vegetable garden. As the group of children—and Borisova's grandmother, who had accompanied them—stared curiously at the cloud, several small transparent capsule-like vehicles suddenly ejected out of it and flew in the direction of the witnesses. Incredibly, each small vehicle appeared to be occupied by one or two small figures. The objects moved slowly as they noiselessly floated around the astonished witnesses. In some of the capsules there appeared to be three figures.

The figures were very tiny, barely a foot tall; however, they were proportioned just like humans, with a head, two legs and two arms. They were dark in color, with eyes like blue pits, and seemed to move inside the capsules using diving or swimming movements. After a certain time the entities within the capsules began to dissolve into thin air and then the capsules also disappeared.

According to Margaret, her grandmother explained the incident away as a "mirage."

The Little Blue Man Who Appeared after a Lightning Strike

R. H. B. Winder tells of the "little blue man" who appeared to seven English schoolboys on January 28, 1967 after a single stroke of lightning (*Flying Saucer Review,* July 1-August, 1967). Rain was falling; the atmosphere was heavy. After an isolated stroke of lightning and its attendant thunder, the little blue man appeared.

When the boys ran toward the stranger who had materialized about twenty yards away, he rewarded their curiosity by promptly "disappearing in a puff of smoke." Baffled, the lads were about to continue on their way to school when they saw him again, this time to their left and a bit farther along the top of a bank. When they attempted to approach him a second time, he disappeared once more.

He appeared a third time close to the point of original manifestation. On this occasion the boys heard a deep-toned, incomprehensible, "foreign-sounding" babble issuing from the bushes down the slope and to the right of their line of vision. An understandable sense of caution prevented the children from rushing the stranger again, and when their teacher's whistle summoned the boys to school, the little blue man was still firmly standing his ground.

Upon hearing her pupils' remarkable tale, Miss Newcomb wisely separated the boys and had each of them write his own account of the adventure. Winder, who later examined the essays, describes them as "fascinating and convincing reading." The three-foot man, surrounded by a bluish glow and sporting what appeared to be a hat two-feet high, sounds for all the world like the classic description of an elf. Winder is convinced, however, that "this is no ordinary fairy tale."

The disappearances of the blue man, at first as puzzling to Winder as to the seven young witnesses, became "more understandable" after Winder and two other investigators had spoken with each of the boys.

"The 'puff of smoke' was apparently a whirling cloud of yellowish-blue mist shot toward the pursuers) possibly from a box on the belt," Winder writes…. "The glow and the mist could have been the products of ionizing radiation. Indeed, similar emanations, not necessarily from the same source, could have triggered off the lightning in an atmosphere already charged by natural processes."

Small Helmeted Aliens Appear
in a Forest Clearing on Reunion Island

The island of Reunion is located in the Indian Ocean, between Mauritius and Madagascar. It was there, on July 31, 1968, that a sighting of a UFO was made at nine o'clock in the morning. UFOs are sighted all over the world, at all hours of the day, and during all seasons of the year, but this report included something extra.

The sterotypical cartoonish image of little green men with antennas spread around the world. For many UFO investigators, the description was demeaning to the serious research of the growing number of reports of alien sightings. (**Art by Ricardo Pustanio**)

A thirty-one-year-old farmer named M. Luce Fontaine—a husband and father who is considered hard-working and honest—testified that he was in the middle of a small clearing in an acacia-tree forest, where he had been picking grass for his rabbits. Suddenly he noticed an oval object in the clearing, about eighty feet from him. It appeared to be suspended in the air at about twelve to fifteen feet above the ground. The outer edge of what he described as a "cabin" was dark blue, while the center part appeared to be lighter and more transparent, like a screen. Above and below, the object had two shiny metal feet.

Fontaine testified that in the center of the cabin he saw two individuals with their backs turned to him. The one on the right then turned around to face him. Fontaine estimated his height as about ninety centimeters (roughly three feet). He was dressed in a one-piece, overall-type uniform and a helmet. "Then both turned their backs to me, and there was a flash, as strong as the electric arc of a welding machine," Fontaine added. "Everything went white around me. A powerful heat was given off, and then as if there were a blast of wind, a few seconds later there was nothing there anymore."

After the object disappeared, Fontaine went to the area where it had been, but he was not able to find any marks or indentations in the ground. An absence of physical evidence is not too surprising, however, since he had noticed the UFO hovering at about twelve to fifteen feet above the ground.

Fontaine next told his wife what had happened, then the police. "And everyone at once believed me," he commented to the reporter from a French journal who interviewed him.

The next day the formal inquiry began—conducted by Captain Maljean of the Saint-Pierre constabulary and Captain Legros of the Service de la Protection Civile, who went directly to the site. When devices to detect radioactivity were employed, their findings showed a reasonable amount of radioactivity in the area, including some on the clothing that was worn by Fontaine the day of the sighting. According to Legros, there were eight radioactive spots on pebbles and tufts of grass, with readings up to sixty thousandths of a roentgen—quite low, but possibly indicating that "something" had been there. One explanation that was given for the low roentgen count was the fact that the readings were not taken until about ten days after the alleged landings, and there had been heavy rains during that period. Otherwise, it is believed, the readings might have been considerably higher.

There were other sightings of UFOs in the area, including one over the neighboring island of Mauritius on August 11. That craft was described as cigar-shaped, and it was also seen from Reunion.

The Authors' Thirty Years of
Investigating Contactees and Abductees

Beginning in 1968 and continuing for nearly thirty years, we participated in or conducted the hypnotic regressions of hundreds of men and women who claimed to have had a close encounter with alien visitors. Some said that they had been abducted for brief periods of time by crew members of UFOs. In some cases these contactees/abductees were left with feelings of awe, illumination, or enlightenment. Others claimed to have been traumatized by the event. In a number of instances, those selected by the aliens to be taken on board their craft were given some kind of medical examination. In some cases, they were left with peculiar markings and puncture marks in their flesh as physical testimony the reality of their experience.

Early in 1968, during a hypnotic session with Herbert Schirmer, a city patrolman from Ashland, Nebraska, we heard him describe his captors:

"They were from four and a half to five and a half feet tall.… Their uniforms were silver-gray, very shiny.… On the right side of their helmets they had a small antenna, just above where the ear would be. I never did see any of their ears.… Their eyes are the one thing that I will never forget. The pupil went up and down, like a slit. When they looked at me, they stared straight into my eyes. They didn't blink. It was real uncomfortable.… Their noses were flat. Their mouths looked more like a slit than a regular mouth."

After a detailed description of the interior of the craft and the feathered serpent emblems and medallions featured throughout the UFO, Schirmer stated that a spokesperson for the aliens told him that they had been observing humankind for a long time: "There is some kind of program of breeding analysis," he said. "Some people have been picked up and changed so they have agents in our world. They are very smart about the brain and how to change it."

From 1968 to 1985, our office was flooded by dozens of contactees who claimed that they had been left with an "implant" somewhere in their skulls, usually just behind the left ear. These contactees/abductees came from a wide variety of occupations, cultural backgrounds, and age groups.

We never found any implants detectable by X rays, but our exhaustive hypnosis sessions produced fascinating, albeit bizarre, information about underground UFO bases, hybrid aliens walking among us, and thousands of humans slowly turning into automatons because of readjusted brain wave patterns.

Strangely enough, in all these hundreds of cases, we rarely heard a contactee/abductee refer to an encounter with a little "green man." Oh, certainly, some of the smallish visitors behaved as if they were Puck-like elves, but the accusation of meeting a "green man" soon became more likely a pejorative analysis uttered by a mean-spirited skeptic.

Only a very few occupants of UFOs sighted over the past sixty-three years have been cited as having greenish complexions, though some may have been reported wearing tight-fitting green jumpsuits. However one describes these diminutive extra-terrestrial visitors, the trail that tracks them begins at Roswell.

A Curious Swede Gets a Little Too Close to a Mysterious Dome

Anders Liljegren, writing in the *UFO-Sweden Newsletter,* in September, 1970 (reprinted in *Flying Saucer Review,* November-December, 1970), reported the claim of Gideon Johansson, an electrical fitter of Mariannelund, Smaland. His UFO contact occurred in 1959 at about 6:55 P.M. one day toward the end of October, throughout the Western world, the traditional time for ghosts and goblins to appear.

As his report goes, when his electricity failed, Johansson ran out of his house to investigate.

His twenty-five-year-old son, Rolf, pointed out a blinding white light that hovered over a three-story building. At first the two men thought that they were observing a helicopter about to crash. The glowing object, however, stopped in the sky and then slowly descended and crashed into the top of a maple tree. The Johanssons heard a crackling sound, and then watched the UFO move through the branches of the tree and hover half a meter above the street.

The vehicle appeared to have a transparent dome, which offered a clear view of its interior. It seemed to be manned by two "pilots."

"Their heads were very high-crowned, and they had big, very beautiful eyes," Johansson said later. "They seemed to be friendly. Their noses were long and thin with small nostrils; they had small mouths and pointed chins, with small lower jaws."

> "They seemed to be friendly. Their noses were long and thin with small nostrils; they had small mouths and pointed chins, with small lower jaws."

"They wore neat white uniforms with broad, black belts crossed over their shoulders and chests. They were small men, about the size of a fourteen-year-old."

As Gideon Johansson watched from a distance of about three meters, one of the pilots quickly unloosened his belt and began to work on something below the level of the window, which Johansson assumed to be the instrument panel.

"His work was soon finished," Johansson recalled. "I waved at them, smiled, and tried to give the impression that I was glad to see them and that they were welcome visitors."

But Johansson noted that the craft's occupants did not return his friendly gestures. One of them stared at him for a few seconds, but neither of the entities gave any visual indication that they were in any way impressed by the hospitable Swede.

The craft began to float away, and Johansson followed it up the pavement toward his gate, a distance of about thirty feet. Then the UFO stopped, its interior illumination blinked out, and it "disappeared in a flash."

Johansson stated that no one saw where the craft went, but he was able to feel the air pressure of the vacuum left by the object.

According to writer Liljegren, certain facts tend to support the speculation that the power cut in the area had been caused by the same object closely observed by Johansson. For example, the detection of the UFO and the failure of the electrical system occurred nearly simultaneously. No apparent cause for the breakdown was found, but about one kilometer south of town, a glassy deposit was discovered on the power lines. The mysterious substance extended for about ten feet on all three lines. A grayish-white substance had been sprinkled on top of the glassy deposit.

"It is reasonable to suppose that damage may have been caused to the [UFO] if it had too nearly approached the power lines, or even collided with them, at the place where the glassy deposit was found," comments Liljegren.

Gideon Johansson later experienced some ill effects, which may have been due to his close approach to the UFO. He reported "terrible pricking pains" from his waist downward, which ceased after a few hours. He could not sleep; his glands became sore and swollen, as did his testicles; and he had difficulty urinating. His body felt swollen, and his skin began to emit a foul odor. He lost his appetite. It is interesting to note that those exposed to powerful electromagnetic energy sources, and some witnesses of psychic phenomena, may report the same physiological symptoms.

The Seventy-Two-Year-Old New Jersey Store Owner Thought that He Had Seen Everything—Until the Night He Saw Aliens Taking Soil Samples

It was a rather warm night for January 1975 as George O'Barski, 72, drove home from the small liquor store that he owned and managed.

It was about two o'clock in the morning when he moved through North Hudson Park on the New Jersey side of the Hudson River. Then, strangely, his car radio suddenly developed a lot of static.

"I began to notice my radio," O'Barski told Ted Bloecher, an investigator for Mutual UFO Network, "it got scratching in it, and a tinny sound.... I turned up the volume and got more scratching, you know? The radio stops!"

O'Barski's car window was down partway, due to unseasonably warm weather. He reported that he heard a droning sound, a bit like the noise a refrigerator makes. Then he saw something coming down from the skies: "It was a floating thing."

He described the object as round, about thirty feet in diameter, and six to eight feet high, with a dome on top. The object itself was dark, with several lighted vertical windows around the main part of the body of the craft. Each window was about a foot wide and four feet long; they were spaced about one foot apart. O'Barski said he saw nothing in any of the windows other than illumination, about the intensity of household lighting. He also noticed a lighted strip around the object at the base of the dome.

The object then reportedly moved into the nearby park, parallel to O'Barski's car, and came to rest about one hundred feet from him. At first the object seemed to hover approximately ten feet above the ground; then it settled to about four feet over the grassy area. He was not able to determine whether the object rested on legs or any kind of platform.

A square-lighted opening suddenly appeared, and nine to eleven humanoids scrambled down the steps, "like kids coming down a fire escape. "The occupants were all about three to four feet tall, according to O'Barski, and seemed to be wearing some type of coveralls, "like little kids with snowsuits on." They also wore a helmet that was round and dark, like the coveralls and seemed to be wearing gloves.

As the occupants descended the steps, each carried a small, dark bag and a small shovel. Each bag seemed to have a string or handle attached to it.

The small humanoids apparently had a clear mission, for as soon as they reached the ground, they began digging. They dug rapidly in various locations near the UFO and put the soil samples in their bags.

The whole digging episode lasted less than two minutes, then the small occupants climbed the steps once again, and the craft took off, totally disappearing within twenty seconds.

O'Barski said the occupants did not act like robots, but moved about very much like humans. Although they did not seem to notice him as he watched them, he gradually became frightened.

After the UFO and its occupants left, O'Barski's car radio once again worked normally.

In summing up the report, O'Barski commented, "I've been held up in the [liquor] store lots of times in thirty years by men with pistols and knives. I've been plenty scared, but nothing like this, ever. I was petrified!"

A Polish Farmer Was Led to a Spaceship by Little Green Men

A Polish farmer named Jan Wolsky stated that he actually was led into a spaceship by "little green men," given some kind of examination, and then released unharmed. According to a number of Polish medical doctors and psychiatrists, Wolsky, seventy-one at the time, believed what he was telling them and was not trying to be deceitful.

The farmer said his encounter occurred on May 10, 1978, as he was driving a horse-drawn cart near a forest close to his village of Emilein, about ninety miles southeast of Warsaw. Wolsky remembers seeing two little men up ahead by the side of the road. When he got closer, he could see that they were not ordinary men. Their faces were a gray-green color. They had large, slanted eyes, and their hands appeared to be webbed and of a greenish color. Each of the entities wore a little one-piece jumpsuit.

The beings leapt into his cart and motioned for him to continue driving and then to turn off the road. In a clearing Wolsky saw something as big as a bus, only "it was hovering in midair, moving gently up and down like a boat at sea, and humming gently."

Wolsky was led to the craft by the two small entities. A platform dropped down from the ship, the three of them stepped onto it, and were taken up into the spacecraft.

Wolsky remembers the interior of the craft as dark and empty. He noticed a large number of birds that had been gathered from the forest. They appeared to be paralyzed.

Two more aliens joined the couple who had led Wolsky into the craft and motioned for him to take off his clothes. The farmer complied, and then one of the little men came toward him with some sort of device that emitted a clicking sound. The entities moved around him with this instrument, indicating that he should raise his arms and stand sideways, as if they were taking photographs.

Wolsky put his clothes back on when it was signaled that he could do so. He stepped to the door, turned around, took his cap off, and said good-bye. The four entities bowed back and smiled at him.

Three witnesses from the nearby village corroborated Wolsky's story of a strange craft that had hovered in the area. They testified that they had seen "a flying ship" rise out of the forest and soar away. Upon investigating the site, the villagers said that they had found bird feathers scattered around the area.

Some researchers of the UFO phenomenon have seen parallels between the smallish alien visitors and the old legends of fairies, elves, and other wee people. (*Art by Bill Oliver*)

Additional investigations by authorities revealed that "little green men" had been sighted in other parts of the region in subsequent months.

Little Olive-Green, Red-Eyed Aliens Surrounded His Vehicle

Alberto Dieppa, a young man from the island of Gran Canaria, discussed his 1993 encounter with alien beings during an interview with journalist Carmen Machado. According to the story, Dieppa and his friends drove to the remote Finca del Duque simply to enjoy the ride. The group remained within the car with the dome light on, chatting late into the evening, when they suddenly became aware of six or seven presences outside their vehicle, staring at them intently. Dieppa turned on the headlights and was in for the surprise of his life.

"They were like little children with adult faces," he explained. "They appeared to be naked, at least from the waist up. What I did notice was their dark, olive green skin color and their intense red eyes."

The occupants of the car remained in stunned, paralyzed silence until one of them began screaming hysterically, causing the driver to set the car in motion and abandon the area as quickly as possible. Dieppa added that at no point did the "diablillos" try to block their way—in fact, they seemed to vanish as soon as he touched the ignition key (http://inexplicata.blogspot.com/6/5/2008).

Is There a Commonality in the Speech Patterns of Little Aliens?

It is interesting that a number of those who have confronted occupants of UFOs have commented on the fact that the entities spoke in a language that sounded like Chinese. Many other percipients have said that although the entities spoke in the native tongue of the place where they appeared, they used a singsong speech pattern. Others have maintained that the occupants actually seemed to be singing to them.

On July 17, 1967, a group of young French children left the village of Arc-sous-Cicon shortly after 3:00 P.M. to go for a walk through fields dotted with bushes. They had been walking upward along a gentle slope leading to a pine forest when one of the little girls who had been in the lead began to sob, and ran back toward her home as quickly as her legs would carry her. She told her mother that she had surprised several "little Chinamen" who had been sitting behind a bramble bush and that one of them had gotten to his feet with the apparent intention of grabbing her.

A few moments later, two teenage girls claimed to have seen a strange little entity with a protuberant belly running from bush to bush. The creature wore a short jacket and appeared to move distinctly faster than a human being. The girls also heard the entities speaking in a "strange singsong fashion."

The Strange Encounter of Rosa Lotti—a Classic Case

Forty-year-old Rosa Lotti lived on a farm in a wooded area near Cennina, a village near Bucine in the Italian province of Arezzo. On November 1, 1954, the mother of four had a solitary encounter with two tiny entities who emerged from a small craft.

It was 6:30 A.M., and Rosa carried a bunch of carnations to present at the altar of Madonna Pellegrina. As she entered a clearing, she saw a barrel-shaped object that immediately aroused her curiosity. It looked to her like a "spindle," barely more than six feet in length. It looked like two bells joined together, and it was covered by a metallic material that appeared more like leather.

Two beings suddenly emerged from behind the craft.

They were "almost like men, but the size of children," she reported. They wore friendly expressions on their faces and were dressed in one-piece gray coveralls that covered their entire bodies, including their feet. Their outfits also included short cloaks and doublets, which were fastened to their collars with little star-shaped buttons. Helmets crowned their small but "normal" faces.

The little men were vigorous and animated, and they spoke rapidly in a tongue that sounded to Rosa very much like Chinese. There were words that sounded like "Jiu," "lai," "loi," and "lau." They had "magnificent eyes" full of intelligence. Their features were, in Rosa's testimony, "normal," but in a later appraisal, she said that their upper lips seemed slightly curled in the center, so that they appeared always to be smiling. Their teeth, although big and broad, seemed to have been filed down and were somewhat protuberant. To a countrywoman such as Rosa, their mouths appeared "rabbit-like."

The older-looking of the two beings continually laughed like one of Santa's merry elves, and seemed concerned about making contact with her. He startled her, however, when he snatched away her carnations and one of the black stockings she was carrying. The surprised Rosa remonstrated with him as best she could despite her timidity, and the being returned two flowers before he wrapped the others in the stocking and threw the bundle into the spindle.

As if in exchange for the stocking and the carnations, the little men stepped away from Rosa to fetch two packages from inside the vehicle. Before they could return with their exchange gifts, Rosa took advantage of the moment to escape. The frightened woman ran through the woods for several seconds. It was reported that when she at last turned to look back, the entities and their strange craft had disappeared.

> Such a pattern of fear-tranquility-fear has led to the conjecture that the UFO entities are able to transmit a state of peacefulness to the percipient only when in close range.

Rosa told her story to the village *carabinieri*, her priest, and others who knew the woman to be "absolutely free of any sort of foolish fancifulness or empty reveries."

Eighteen years later, an Italian UFO study group revisited Rosa Lotti and secured a number of fresh details in what has become a classic UFO Encounter of the Third Kind.

Writing in *Flying Saucer Review*, Sergio Conti stated that Rosa wanted to emphasize that she had not felt fear when confronted by the entities. Alarm had come later, after she had fled the scene. She had begun to run when the older of the two beings produced a package that she felt was a camera. For some reason, she did not want her picture taken by them.

Conti comments that the presence of the humanoids seemed to create a state of tranquility in Rosa, a manifestation consistent with other contact reports. It appears as though atavistic fears manifest themselves only after the percipient has begun to consider the unknown phenomenon from a distance. Psychological disturbances are seldom felt by the percipients while they remain with the "visitors."

Many reports of confrontations with entities from UFOs seem to follow the pattern mentioned by Conti. When a craft lands and beings emerge, the viewer generally becomes panic-stricken and may even enter a state of shock. But when the being comes close to the percipient, the witness often experiences a state of tranquility, especially while communicating either telepathically or verbally with the UFOnaut. When the being returns to its craft, the percipient lapses back into his or her former state of fear.

As serious research of human–alien interaction began to grow, a number of investigators believed that they could find evidence of an alien influence in humankind's ancient times and even in prehistory. (*Art by Bill Oliver*)

Such a pattern of fear-tranquility-fear has led to the conjecture that the UFO entities are able to transmit a state of peacefulness to the percipient only when in close range. Perhaps it is a feeling that exudes from the entity's aural body, rather than a telepathically transmitted message. Many a contactee has fled the scene on seeing a craft land—even though hearing his name being called by the UFOnauts—without ever having experienced the peace that might have come.

Rosa Lotti described the vehicle in a flurry of minute details that show how significant she deemed the experience nearly two decades later:

"In the thickened part of the spindle, it had two portholes, on opposite sides to each other, and in the center, between them, there was a little door, enabling me to see inside. I saw two little kiddie chairs set back to back, each of them facing toward one of the portholes."

Rosa now denies that the entities' lips were curled back. She feels that the clean-shaven beings had mouths that were perfectly "normal." Nor did the craft spookily disappear after she had run about a hundred meters. Rosa insists that it was the press who claimed that the craft and the entities had vanished so mysteriously. She maintains that the little men and their spindle were still there when she at last paused to look back.

Conti writes that there is now a "vast network of collateral eyewitness accounts" available from percipients ranging from stonemasons to students, from workmen to court employees, to provide validation of the Cennina phenomenon that is "well nigh irrefutable." All of these accounts confirm that the "spindle" came down over the thicket at Cennina at about 6:30 A.M.

Matt Won't Be Taken to Other Worlds without His Girl Friend

When he emailed us in 2005, Matt confessed to us that this was the first time he had ever talked about meeting two little green men when he was sixteen or seventeen years of age.

"I can't really remember exactly how old I was, because after the event happened my memory doesn't remember times and dates in a linear fashion. I have a photographic memory and it's non-linear. People, places, times, where I worked and when is all but a jumbled mass—or it is nonexistent in my memory bank.

"My encounter went something like this:

"I was sleeping on the couch in my mother's house in Binghamton, NY, and I was lying on my back. I fell asleep and woke up to see two little green men come through the window (not breaking it; they kinda morphed through it). From the first sight of them I was terrified, paralyzed. I tried to yell for help, but I had no vocal strength.

"One of them slowly approached and with its long right hand with bulbous finger tips reached down and put his hand over my face. They were about three feet to three-and-a-half feet tall, and I can remember very vividly what they looked like. The little green men took control of my mind—almost like how it feels when I'm around my Zen teacher. It was not really 'control' but kind of like an empty/full, not knowing but completely aware kind of mental state. Words can't describe it. I don't know why they terrified me as they did, but I guess it was because I felt that they had the power to freeze me—and they used it.

"I would like to think it was just some crazy dream, but it was not. They have been trying to meet with me again, but I'm too nervous to go outside and encounter them. I don't want to go to another planet and not be with my girlfriend."

Two Argentinian Police Officers on Patrol
Encounter Four Humanoid Aliens

Two police officers, Luis Bracamonte and Osvaldo Orellano, were patrolling a rural area near Irene, Buenos Aires, Argentina, on November 7, 2007. As they approached the Felipe Fernandez ranch about 1:30 A.M., the officers stopped their patrol truck. Officer Orellano exited the vehicle and walked around the area. Officer Bracamonte remained inside the vehicle, recharging his telephone card with his mobile phone.

While looking at his phone, Bracamonte noticed a small light, which was approaching their location at fairly high speed. Suddenly the light became much larger and brighter, until it resembled a large gray truck. At the same time Bracamonte saw a small figure that he thought was a dog. As he looked more carefully, he realized that it was a small humanoid figure about four feet in height with a large head, large gray prominent eyes, and skin of a greenish color. He then tried to dial the cell number of Officer Orellano, who was patrolling nearby, but all he could get in the receiver was static.

Bracamonte then saw three more humanoid beings exiting the large grayish luminous "vehicle." Two of the creatures were similar to the first one that he had seen, but the third strange visitor was larger and more robust. At the same time he heard Orellano, who was apparently watching the same incredible event, yelling in panic.

Immediately the four humanoids ran back into the vehicle, which took off and quickly headed toward the north, dispersing a white glow, which dissipated and left a green glowing mist and a strong sulfur-like odor. As the craft vanished from sight, it emitted a sound like a thunderclap.

Two other police officers, Santiago and Carbajal, who were patrolling that same night near the village of Nicolas Descalzi, watched a large white light suddenly approach and engulf their vehicle. Although they were not harmed in any way, the engine stopped and their cell phones would not work (http://www.ufoinfo.com/humanoid/humanoid2007.shtml).

Before the Aliens Left Him, Their Eyes Glowed Softly with a Pale Blue Light

On the evening of August 29, 2007, Hal Watkins (not his real name) of Stafford, Virginia, had just let his dogs out in the backyard when they starting going wild. As the older female dog left the house, she immediately ran down the hill as if to attack someone or something. As Watkins walked out behind the dogs, he searched the area with his handheld spotlight. He then saw what looked to him to be two small beings, about four feet tall, that were glowing with a faint light around the head and hand areas. Watkins later said it was as if their bodies were being cloaked by some kind of an illuminated suit.

The figures then moved quickly about ten feet down the hill and seemed to lean or crawl up into an unseen opening or portal. It was as if they were going into a craft that had no shape or color. Watkins could only describe it as a portal or window-like opening, which didn't emanate any light.

Before the small figures entered their craft, they looked back at Watkins, and their eyes glowed softly with a pale blue light. In his report, Watkins said that he could not see any other facial features.

Watkins said that he could see that the beings had entered some sort of craft, because when it started to move away from the place where it had been resting, he could see that it hovered about two feet off the ground. As it began to leave the landing site, it moved the trees with air turbulence. Watkins said that it was almost like a moving shadow. He tried to shine his spotlight on it, but it seemed to absorb the light.

As it began to rise up into the sky, Watkins could finally make out a shape. The dog stopped barking when the object left. Watkins described the object as shaped like a spearhead about twenty feet long, pointed and narrow, but wider at the rear.

The Blond Nordics

At the beginning of the Flying Saucer Age in modern times (circa 1947), early contacts with aliens led to descriptions of smallish beings with pointed ears, large eyes, and a somewhat playful temperament. Often, there were comparisons with elves and the "wee people."

But in a short time, after contactees had become somewhat accustomed to the "little green men," much more imposing images of statuesque aliens began to appear.

A Classic Meeting with a Space Brother

In a recent issue of *Inexplicata*, Scott Corrales, "venturing into the dark vaults of South American UFO lore," recalled the "incomparable" 1968 Argentinean UFO wave. According to Corrales, editor Guillermo Gimenez remembered the story of a major Close Encounter of the Third Kind. Eighteen years after the original siting, he had sent Daniel J. Lopez and Luis Burgos to investigate the account of a very strange "Night Visitor." (http://www.ciencia-ovni.com.ar/elvisitantenocturnosolitario.htm)

The strange encounter had occurred in the mountain ranges of Córdoba where a young woman named Maria Elodia P. met a tall entity. Nearly twenty years following her experience, the eyewitness interview still presented fundamental evidence suggesting that "something indeed happened at the time." Now thirty-seven years old, Maria Elodia carefully repeated the details of that night in June 1968.

After undergoing surgery, the seventeen-year-old Maria Elodia had returned home to recuperate and to help her father manage the family motel. Her father had gone into town on business, and she was very busy with the necessary elements in keeping the hotel running efficiently.

At around 1:00 A.M. on June 14, her father, Pedro P. was driving back home along Route 20 when he saw "two large red lights over the road, too far apart to be the tail lights of another car" some fifty meters from his motel. When he approached the front door of the motel, he was startled to find it open. His daughter was too conscientious to be so careless about such things. As soon as he entered the house, he headed for her bedroom, only to find the young woman spread out on the bed, unconscious.

After she had regained consciousness, Maria Elodia recalled what she had experienced. After she had bade two guests farewell, she went to the kitchen and found that there was a rather bright light was inexplicably pouring into the hallway.

Thinking that someone had left the living room lights on, she walked into that room and found herself face-to-face with a strange and extraordinary visitor. He was a large figure, standing in excess of two meters (about six feet, five inches). He had blonde hair, which he combed backward.

He wore a friendly expression and approached her to stand a short distance away. He was clad in some sort of jumpsuit, light blue in color, that covered his body from his neck down to his feet. Small luminous rays poured from his fingertips. In his left hand he carried a crystal orb that emitted bright beams of light. In his right hand he bore a ring and a large glove that was almost a gauntlet. According to the young woman, every time the being raised the gauntlet, it was as though he himself rose into the air and remained suspended.

At that time, Maria Elodia felt herself weaken and fall down, but when the entity lowered the gauntlet, she felt her strength returning. The being advanced toward her in a kindly, calm manner, moving his lips slowly, speaking a strange, melodic language that reminded her of Japanese. He said something like "cling-gling-crish."

Maria Elodia experienced a sensation of "bubbles in her head," and she recalled breaking into heavy perspiration—but when she touched her neck, she was perfectly dry. She was able to dash to the counter, even as the entity moved the orb constantly and tried to get near her. She claimed that she could hear, in the recesses of her mind, a message that repeated: "Don't be afraid...." Suddenly, the bright orb vanished. The stranger stopped, spun around, and moved toward the outside door. As he approached the door, it opened by itself and closed as he departed. From that moment on, Maria Elodia, remembered nothing more and a few moments later, her father arrived.

Dr. Hugo V. Vaggione, the family's physician, diagnosed her as being in a "pronounced state of nerves" after the ordeal, due to the emotional impact. However, he also stated that she was far from a breakdown. She was perfectly coordinated in her statements, and her blood pressure was normal. Finding her mentally and physically sound, the doctor could find no reason to assume this was deception or hallucination.

Editor Guillermo Gimenez observed that the tall, blond type of humanoid, "so prevalent in the 1960s and which is rarely seen nowadays, has yielded its place to the ubiquitous Grays, which appear to have co-opted most of the entity case histories."

The Space Brothers and Sisters Appeared as Benevolent Beings

Interestingly, with the exception of those contemporary prophets in the Flying Saucer Movement who regularly and actively channel the space brothers and sisters, the type of entity popularly known as the "Nordic," seems to have lessened the extent of its interaction with humans to some degree. From the late 1940s to the mid-1980s, the Nordics conducted an ambitious campaign to contact Earthlings. These humanoids were nearly always described as tall, blond, light-complexioned, handsome, idealized Nordic types. Their reported place of origin was most often said to be Venus or the Pleiades.

They appeared to their contactees as benevolent, concerned entities, whose principal goal in coming to Earth was to direct the misguided *Homo sapiens* species along a more spiritual path. Their obvious historical antecedents were angels. They seemed uninterested in aiding our technological sophistication—rather, they warned us about our misuse of the tools of potential death and destruction that we already possessed. Obviously considering us unenlightened as a species, the message of the Nordics (also known as the space brothers) was heavily laden with esoteric preaching rather than practical teaching.

The philosophical, religious, and moral space brothers reminds one of the prophetic imagery that was so often presented to the revelators in the Old Testament. Perhaps, some have argued, these entities demonstrate that there may be a basic transmission of spiritual knowledge that has bombarded this planet for centuries. In each new generation, the cosmic sermons seem to adapt themselves to contemporary technology and the eccentricities of the current culture.

There are, of course, space sisters, the female version of the space brothers. They, too, are generally blond and of a classic Nordic appearance, though striking brunettes and redheads also manifest among their number. The space sisters are often reported as being transported on a beam of light. Some researchers suggest that they have often been mistaken as the Divine Mother and other sainted figures in such places as Fatima and Garabandal. Many female contactees credit the arrival of the space sisters to be coincident with the raising of feminine consciousness throughout the world.

Large segments of our species seemed to be more receptive to the possibility of otherworldly visitations beginning in 1945. But it is not clear whether the year of 1945 precipitated accelerated interplanetary concern with Earth's initial displays of atomic power, or whether some as yet unperceived evolutionary mechanism was activated according to a timing device set in humankind's prehistory.

The concept of benign human entities from other worlds visiting Earth did not really become an extensive part of contemporary flying saucer lore until George Adamski claimed to have contacted a Venusian pilot near Desert Center, California, on November 20, 1952. Adamski communicated with the handsome Venusian through telepathic transfer, with such great success that the contactee was able to produce two bestsellers (*Flying Saucers Have Landed* and *Inside the Space Ships*) and become

In the 1950s, George Adamski became the first of the Flying Saucer Missionaries to achieve international attention. Adamski claimed to be in contact with Orthon from Venus. The Space Brother allowed Adamski to photograph many of the alien spacecraft. (**Art by Bill Oliver**)

an even more controversial figure after his death than he was during his peak years as a missionary of the space brothers' gospel. To those who have made a cult of the UFO, Adamski is revered as the first ambassador to outer space.

The Coming of the New Age UFO Prophets

Just as the prophets of old had retreated into the desert wilderness to receive their inspiration, so had Adamski, the first of the New Age UFO prophets, gone to meet his space brother in the desert by prearranged cosmic signal.

After 1952, there were several other men and women who declared contact with these concerned outer space beings. There was George Van Tassel, George Hunt Williamson, George King, Truman Bethurum, Daniel Fry, Cedric Alling-

ham, Orfeo Angelucci, Robert Short, Franklin Thomas, Carl Anderson, Buck Nelson, John McCoy, Howard Menger, and Gloria Lee.

Van Tassel Introduces the World to Ashtar, Space Commandant

George Van Tassel published his first booklet in 1952 and introduced the world to "Ashtar, commandant of station Schare." Schare is said to be one of several saucer stations in Blaau, the fourth sector of Bela, into which our solar system is moving. "Shan" was the name that Van Tassel's contact gave for planet Earth. Van Tassel's Ashtar also decreed the universe to be ruled by the Council of Seven Lights, which had divided the Cosmos into sector systems and sectors.

Van Tassel founded the Ministry of Universal Wisdom based on the revelations of the space brothers. This ministry teaches the universal law, which operates on humankind in seven states: gender (male and female); the creator as cause; polarity of negative and positive; vibration; rhythm; relativity; and mentality.

Short's Korton Helps to Establish the Blue Rose Ministry

Robert Short's work also began in 1952 when he was led by the space brother Korton, principal among his extraterrestrial sources, to Giant Rock and to the home of George Van Tassel. Together Short and Van Tassel, Adamski, and Dan Fry began flying saucer conferences at Giant Rock, where the space brother faithful and members of the curious public met regularly from the early 1950s through the 1970s.

Short still maintains his Blue Rose Ministry in Cornville, Arizona and publishes a quarterly UFO newsletter entitled "Solar Space Letter."

Fry Flies to Space, Returns to Spread the Teachings of A-Lan

An employee of the White Sands Proving Grounds, Daniel Fry was invited by a space brother to travel in a flying saucer. Fry established his Understanding Incorporated in 1955 as a means of spreading the teachings of A-Lan, whom Fry claimed to have met on his first trip in a UFO. Fry remained active as a lecturer until his death in 1992, and directed one of the largest of the Flying Saucer Movement groups, containing over sixty units.

King Becomes Primary Terrestrial Mental Channel by Venusian

In 1955, George King was named the "Primary Terrestrial Mental Channel" by Master Aetherius of Venus. King has since been declared an agent of the Great White Brotherhood and a channel for both Aetherius and Master Jesus. Members of the Aetherius Society are earnestly engaged in the war being waged by the Brotherhood against the Black Magicians, a group they feel seeks to enslave the human race.

Williamson Forms Brotherhood of the Seven Rays

George Hunt Williamson (also known as Michael d'Obrenovic and Brother Philip) was the author of a number of books concerning archaeological evidence for early extraterrestrial visitation. Williamson (who died in January 1986) formed the Brotherhood of the Seven Rays under the tutelage of an entity who revealed himself as Ascended Master Araru-Muru. The Outer Retreat was established by Williamson, who then called himself Brother Philip, at an abbey near Lake Titicaca, Peru.

Bob Short has been channeling Korton of Jupiter since the 1950s. Korton has declared himself the representative for the Honorable President of the Solar Presidium, Solar Tribunal, Solar Council. Short still maintains the Blue Rose Ministry in Cornville, Arizona.

As the name Brotherhood of the Seven Rays implies, the group hoped to encompass all the Theosophical virtues symbolized as rays of light. Through its Ancient Amethystine Order, it focused on the violet rays, symbol of the present movement of the Earth.

Kro of Neptune Channels to Wallace

In 1956, a space brother group began to function near Detroit centered on the channeling of Baird Wallace, who began communicating with "Kro" of Neptune in 1956. Wallace's material was published in 1972 as *The Space Story and the Inner Light*.

A UFO Sighting at the age of Eight
Convinces Child that They Are Angels

Noel, a musician from California, has said that he has endeavored as a child, a teenager, and an adult to live as Christ would have him live. In spite of Christian beliefs that are very orthodox and conventional, Noel believes in the reality of UFOs, other intelligences in the cosmos, and the strong possibility that Christ will return in a space vehicle.

Noel was eight years old and riding with his parents near a Nike missile base when they sighted six UFOs. From that point forward, his family agreed that Earth was being visited by beings from another planet.

During the mid-1950s and 1960s, Noel visited Giant Rock, a mecca for UFO enthusiasts in Landers, California and there he met the colorful figure George Van Tassel. Van Tassel related stories of traveling with the benevolent space brothers in their beamships; and Van Tassel claimed that although the benign visitors from outer space looked just like us, in fact, a number of the Brothers had been living among humankind for quite some time.

Over the years, Noel, now in his early fifties, has had numerous dreams in which he envisions himself aboard the beamships with the space beings. Always, he says, the Brothers and Sisters are warm and friendly, truly "angels in starships."

Those contactees who claim communication with Space Brothers and Sisters most often describe their celestial teachers as idealized blond Nordic types. Some have seen similarites between them and Jesus and other avatars, who they believe were extraterrestrials. (*Art by Ricardo Pustanio*)

The Death and Resurrection of George Adamski

The death of George Adamski on April 12, 1965, by no means cooled the heated controversy, which had never stopped swirling around the prolific and articulate contactee. Adamski was quickly resurrected by his followers. In the book *Scoriton Mystery* by Eileen Buckle, a contactee named Ernest Bryant claims to have met three spacemen on April 24, 1965, one of whom was a youth named Yamski, whose body already housed the reincarnated spirit of George Adamski.

Throughout Adamski's career as a contactee, his followers steadfastly declared him to be a most saintly man, completely devoted to the teachings of universal laws. It appears that after his death certain followers wanted to provide their master of intergalactic peace with a kind of instant resurrection.

According to Desmond Leslie, George Adamski had an audience with Pope John XXIII just a few days before the Pope passed away. Leslie says that he met Adamski at the airport in London just after the controversial contactee had flown in from Rome. He drove Adamski straight to his little river cruiser at Staines where several people interested in Ufology had been spending the weekend.

Sometime during the first few days after his arrival at Staines, Adamski showed Leslie a memento that he said no one would ever take from him, an exquisite gold medal with Pope John's effigy on it. Later Leslie checked and found it was a medal that had not yet been released to anyone. When Adamski was questioned about how he had received the medal, he answered that Pope John had given it to him the day before.

Adamski went on to say how he had arrived at the Vatican according to the space people's instructions and had been taken straight in, given a cassock, and led to the Pope's bedside. It was here that Adamski had handed Pope John a sealed package from the space brothers. It was said that Pope John's face had beamed when he received the package, and he said, "This is what I have been waiting for." The Pope then presented Adamski with a very special medal, and the papal audience ended.

Leslie said that he later checked with Lou Zinstag, who had supposedly taken Adamski to the Vatican. Ms. Zinstag reported that when they had approached the Vatican and neared the private entrance, a man with "purple at his throat" (apparently a monsignor or a bishop) appeared. Adamski had cried out, "That's my man," greeted the papal official, and was led in for an audience with the Pope. Ms. Zinstag said that when he reappeared about twenty minutes later, Adamski appeared to be in a state of excitement and rapture, just as witnesses had described his demeanor after his desert contact with the space brothers in 1952.

When Leslie later asked an abbot he knew about the medal, the clergyman was amazed and said that such a medal would only have been given to someone in the most exceptional circumstances, and that no one, so far as he knew, had yet received this particular medal. Although Leslie admitted that he had initially doubted Adamski's claims of an audience with the Pope, this confirmation from the abbot dissolved his disbelief.

When Leslie asked Adamski what the space brothers' package contained, the contactee said that he did not know. He said that it had been given to him by the space brothers before he had left for Europe and that he had been given instructions to give it to the Pope. He was also told that all arrangements had been made inside the Vatican for such an audience to take place. This led Leslie to believe that the space brothers have a "fifth column" in St. Peter's seat, as well as everywhere else.

Adamski told Leslie that he thought the package had contained instructions and advice for the second ecumenical council. It is possible that the package also contained a message to the John XXIII's successors, chiding them about certain lax measures and encouraging them to get on with the serious work required on Earth.

On November 24, 1986, John Thavis of the *Catholic News Service* asked Monsignor Corrado Balducci, Vatican theologian, what his position was on the possibility of extraterrestrial life. Monsignor Balducci replied: "It is probable that there are other beings, that is not very strange, because among the human and angelic nature, of which we have the theological certainty, there is … much discrepancy."

On May 13, 2006, John Thavis brought the same question to Jesuit Father Jose Funes, director of the Vatican Observatory. Father Funes said Christians should consider alien life as an "extraterrestrial brother" and a part of God's creation.

Father Funes, an Argentine named to his position by Pope Benedict XVI in 2006, made the remarks in an interview published May 13 by the Vatican newspaper,

L'Osservatore Romano. Father Funes said it was difficult to exclude the possibility that other intelligent life exists in the universe, and he noted that one field of astronomy is now actively seeking "biomarkers" in spectrum analysis of other stars and planets. "This is not in contrast with faith, because we cannot place limits on the creative freedom of God," he said. "To use St. Francis's words, if we consider earthly creatures as 'brothers' and 'sisters,' why can't we also speak of an 'extraterrestrial brother'?"

Are the Space Brothers and Sisters Cosmic Messiahs?

There are many individuals throughout the world who claim to have touched souls—and, in some cases, bodies—with the Nordic space beings. Their accounts are circulated most often in privately printed books, which become scrolls of wisdom for thousands of questing seekers.

There seems little question that for many people the space beings function as angels. They are concerned about Earth. They seem to be actively trying to protect it and the people in it. They are powerful. They avoid, or have control, over the physical limitations of time and space, yet they are benevolent and kindly disposed toward fumbling, bumbling, ineffectual humankind.

It seems that space beings have placed themselves in the role of messengers of God, or that we, in our desperation for cosmic messiahs who can remove us from the foul situation we have made on this planet, hope that there *are* such messengers who can extricate us from the plight we are in.

The Flying Saucer Movement Continues to Grow

Regular messages from the space beings are presented to dozens of groups that have formed as part of the Flying Saucer Movement. Many of these groups have grown directly out of the old Theosophical I AM frame of reference. Others have grown up around individual contactees who channel certain space beings and spread their teachings for them.

The Solar Light Center originated in 1965 in the Solar Cross Fellowship headed by Rudolph Pestalozzi, a channel for a space entity named Baloran. The Solar Light Center was founded by Marianne Francis and Kenneth Keller, who worked together until the Light Center absorbed the Solar Cross Fellowship.

Miss Francis has been renamed Aleuti Francesca, and she usually channels for Sut-ko, the entity who originally revealed his messages to the Solar Cross organization. The Solar Light Center, through the lectures and works of Ms. Francesca, has also received contacts from Devas and other nature entities, such as those involved with Findhorn Community in Scotland.

The attractive appearance of blond extraterrestrial teachers of peace, love, and universal oneness would seem to indicate a common heritage between aliens and humans—or, as some have suggested, it might just be a clever way to mask the aliens' true appearance. (*Art by Ricardo Pustanio*)

Mark-Age MetaCenter of Miami was chartered by the state of Florida on March 27, 1967. Founders of the Center were Mark, Astrid, Wains, Zan-thu, and the major channel, Yolanda.

Sananda has become a popular name for Jesus in the Flying Saucer Movement, and, according to Mark-Age, Jesus has been in orbit around the planet since 1885 and will take on material form as those on Earth transition into a higher consciousness. Mark-Age acquired several acres of land in California and expanded its publishing program, which had already turned out a number of books in the Flying Saucer Movement.

The Space Beings' Main Mission Is to Make Humans Four-Dimensional

According to the doctrines of the space beings, the most essential element in the overall hierarchal program is to lift humankind into the fourth dimension. The UFO contactees have been informed that the race of humans on Earth has been the laggard among the solar system. Due to the efforts of the space beings and their increased emphasis upon a mass educational program designed to help humankind evolve, the citizens of Earth will soon be able to rejoin the Federation of Planets. Once this has taken place, Earthlings will coordinate and cooperate with the brothers and sisters of other planes and planets.

The Light Affiliates of British Columbia were headed by the late Mrs. Aileen Steil. She received her initial contact experience during the first week of April, 1969, when she saw a pink light in the sky over Burnaby, British Columbia, while walking her dog. She ran to the house to get her daughter Robin to come out and verify the mysterious aerial object. It was Robin who began to channel material, which led to the book *Aquarian Revelations* (1971) by Brad Steiger.

In the early 1970s Robin channeled a direct invitation to the Fourth Dimension from the space entity OX-HO:

"There is a whole new world waiting for you people of Earth. The fourth dimension is one of subtleness, of lighter shades of beauty. With your increased vibrations you will be able to see this subtleness with an intensity beyond your imagination ... the very earth on which you stand will be stepped up in frequency to match this dimensional vibration and each form of life will take on new shades of being.

"There are seven dimensions of being. Each planet understands one dimension at a time, but as we aid your evolution, your Earth will be stepped up in frequency and vibration to the next level....

"Life is interdimensional, and so is man.... Learn to flow with these dimensional frequencies and learn to become flexible. Do not allow yourself to become crystallized, for each man has a shattering point if he continues to resist the flow of dimensional evolution....

"People of Earth, you are becoming fourth dimensional whether you are ready or not. Leave the old to those who cling to the old. Don't let the New Age leave you behind."

An Analysis of the Space Brothers Channeled Messages

An analysis of the space brothers' principal messages in their channeled communications seems to be the following:

The space beings have been patient, for they have been coming to Earth for many thousands of years, ever since they were rejected by humankind during the final days of Atlantis. Many of the space beings have even incarnated on Earth and have lived as Earthmen.

The space beings are doing all that they can to help humankind, but they cannot force themselves on us or take control of the conditions here, however bad things might be. It is a dictum of the Federation that visitors from other planets cannot interfere with our free will.

Contactees have been told that the space brothers hope to guide Earth to a period of great unification, when all races will shun discriminatory separations and all of humankind will recognize its responsibility to every other life form existing on the planet. The space beings also seek to bring about a single, solidified government, which will conduct itself on spiritual principles and permit all of its citizens to grow constructively in love.

The Program of the Interplanetary Hierarchical Board

According to numerous contactees:

Some researchers have pointed out that the names given by some of the Space Brothers and Sisters are those associated with ancient gods and goddesses. **(Art by Ricardo Pustanio)**

The Interplanetary Hierarchical Board has established a program to help raise all men and women on Earth to higher consciousness. The teachings and the guidance of the Hierarchy is being beamed to Earthlings even as they lie in the sleep state.

Although the goal seems at times to be difficult to attain, the contactees have been informed that the Christ-self of each person on Earth is in full accord with the Hierarchical Board's program of increased awareness preparatory to the Second Coming of Christ Consciousness.

One of the major messages delivered by the space beings is that they come as representatives of a spiritual government: a hierarchy of intelligences seeking to elevate humankind's position in the universe and increase their awareness that they are an integral part of the Cosmos.

Certain space beings have told contactees that they have come to Earth to give us the benefit of knowledge derived from their own suffering through eons of time. They have evolved to the state beyond that which we have been able to achieve on Earth. They are well aware of the struggle of birth into this consciousness, but they promise that once it has been achieved, it is but the beginning. It is the start of life. They define life as the creative force flowing through all manifestations of God.

They declare that today we are in the dark womb of Nativity called Earth. As we emerge from this womb to cry out into the new light of day, which the space brothers define as Christ consciousness, we will see that we have just begun to live, to grow, to understand, and to be in the Father-Mother Creator's home.

Not All Space Brothers Keep Their Promises

Gloria Lee, a former airline stewardess and wife of aircraft designer William H. Byrd, saw a UFO in the early 1950s. In 1953, she began to receive telepathic communications from a space brother from Jupiter who revealed himself only as "J. W."

As Gloria Lee came to place more confidence in her space brother, she became a well-known figure among UFO cultist groups as a lecturer and a channel. J. W. revealed that on Jupiter vocal cords had gone out of use, so he began to write a book through Gloria Lee. He also led her to found The Cosmon Research Foundation, dedicated to spreading his teachings and bringing about man's spiritual development in preparation for the New Age. Through his direction and the persistence of Gloria Lee on the lecture circuit, the Foundation became a thriving organization and a second book appeared.

Then, tragically, following the instructions of her mentor from Jupiter, Gloria Lee starved herself to death after a sixty-six-day fast carried out in the name of peace. Ms. Lee had hoped to make the U.S. government officially investigate and study plans for a spacecraft she had brought with her to Washington. Gloria Lee had secured herself in a hotel room on September 23, 1962. On December 2, with still no word from the government officials—or from her space brother—the thirty-seven-year-old contactee died.

Shortly after her passing, the Mark-Age Metacenter in Miami, Florida, announced that they were receiving communications from Gloria Lee in the spirit world. The etheric form of Ms. Lee told the group that she was now able to find out how the method of interdimensional communication, which she had used to write her two books, actually worked.

As the Metacenter took notes for a booklet Gloria Lee's publisher would later issue to the faithful and the curious, Gloria's spirit spoke through the channel, Yolanda; it explained how her conscious intelligence had been transferred to another frequency, another body, of higher vibrational rate.

The Silent Contactees

It is impossible to estimate how many men and women are receiving messages from space beings. Groups continue to rise from dynamic contactees with their own variations of previous revelations and an occasional individual input.

There is also the category of revelators that UFOlogists term the "silent contactees"—men and women who have not gathered groups about them, who are not at all interested in doing so, but who have established contact with what they feel to be entities from other worlds and who have directed their lives according to the dictates of those space brothers. Many of these men and women continue to work in conventional jobs, confiding their experiences only to close associates and, in some instances, developing psychic abilities that they utilize for the benefit of their families and close friends only.

Michael Has Found It Always Pays
to Listen to His Space Guardian

Michael was five years old, alone in the wooded area near the family home in Seattle, when he heard someone call him by his first name.

He turned around to see a tall, slender, silver-haired, pale-skinned man with light blue eyes. At his waist was a belt buckle shaped like a "glittery pyramid." The strange man opened his arms to the boy, and inside his head Michael heard the being say, "I am pleased with you, my son."

Michael recalled that such a salutation puzzled him.

"You are not my father," he told the stranger. "Who are you?"

The silver-haired entity laughed and told him: "In time you will come to know me. I am all you are, have been, and will become."

At that moment, Michael remembered, he was distracted by the voice of his actual father calling to him. When he looked back to the stranger, he was astonished to see him fading from sight. "Don't forget me," the entity said. "Always remember me."

Michael stated firmly that he never has forgotten the being: "From that day forward, he has come to me in my dreams or by voice only. He tells me things that are about to happen to myself, family, or friends. He sometimes warns me of things before they occur. It always pays to listen to him."

The Grays

At about 1:45 on the morning of May 11, 1969, twenty-year-old Mike Luczkowich, a student at Manakin, Virginia, was returning home after a date with his girlfriend, who lived in Rockville, Virginia.

Just as he passed the Rockville General Store, Mike noticed something about fifty yards ahead of his car. At first he thought it might be a couple of deer, but he soon realized that he was observing two figures about three-and-a-half to four feet tall. The creatures were wearing spherical helmets that looked as large as basketballs. Circling each helmet was a pale green band that reflected the headlights of the car. The beings were motionless at first, but they soon scurried off and ran up an embankment to the left of the witness. The first two creatures had barely disappeared when a third small creature appeared from the right side of the road and quickly joined the others by climbing over the embankment.

Luczkowich reported that the men were dressed in light-brown coveralls that were somewhat baggy in the legs but were tight-fitting at the ankles. He did not see any arms, and he could not detect features behind the oversized helmets.

The student was shaken by the experience, and he did not tell anyone of the encounter until Sunday.

On Monday, Luczkowich and three other men returned to the site. They were able to locate a definite trail through the poison ivy and honeysuckle on the embankment where the three beings had climbed.

Beyond the embankment they found a barley field with a path through it, such as the three humanoids might have made. After a few feet they noticed two flattened areas. The crushed barley at one of the impressions, according to Luczkowich, showed the imprint of two small bodies, while another impression outlined one small body, as if the small entities had thrown themselves down in the grain field.

Investigators from the National Investigative Committee on Aerial Phenomena (NICAP), a civilian group, arrived the next week, but by that time the barley had been mowed, and with it the evidence that might have answered a few more questions. Unfortunately, no one in Luczkowich's party had taken photographs of the imprints in the barley field.

But on the same evening Luczkowich had sighted the curious beings, about a half mile west of the area, and about two hours earlier, eighteen-year-old Debbie Payne had reported seeing an oval-shaped, luminous object over her house as she arrived home from a date. The object appeared rather bright, then dimmed, and became bright twice more before she and her date reached the house. The proximity of the two sightings may indicate a relationship between the three small humanoids and the UFO over the Payne home.

He Declined a Three-Year Vacation on Another World

William Puckett, Director of *UFOs Northwest* (http://www.ufosnw.com) received a report of an attempted abduction, which occurred in Pittsburg, Kansas, in September of 2009.

It was around three in the morning after a late night watching TV, when the individual who was selected for an abduction locked his doors and shut off all of his lights. After he drifted off to sleep, he said he experienced what seemed like a very unusual, but vivid, dream of getting out of bed. He felt fully aware of what he was doing and did not question any of his actions.

He felt a compulsion to walk to the front door and walk across the small bit of grass in front of the house. A vehicle was parked about two feet away from his house. It was thirty feet long and maybe fifteen feet wide. It was very sleek and streamlined, dark red, and had something that resembled a spoiler on the back end. (A "spoiler" on an automobile, especially one used for racing, is an aerodynamic accessory that has been designed to improve the airflow over a vehicle for better traction and faster speed.)

The vehicle appeared to have a windshield and some windows that were solid black. The hull was composed of completely opaque windows, making it appear as if it were one, solid piece. The witness was seized by a strong compulsion to walk toward the ship. He felt as if the strange vehicle was welcoming him, smiling, with arms outstretched, like an old friend.

He continued to walk toward the craft, enjoying the sensations of a peaceful, warm breeze with cool grass under his feet. The side opened like curtains on a small stage, allowing him to enter. The witness climbed inside and took a seat in what appeared to be a fifteen-passenger van. Most of the seats were occupied by strange creatures. There were two seats in the "cockpit," with lights and a row of lights on the ceiling going from front to back.

The creatures were a little shorter than the witness, who was six feet one inch, and they were wearing silver gray uniforms. They were very slender, with large heads

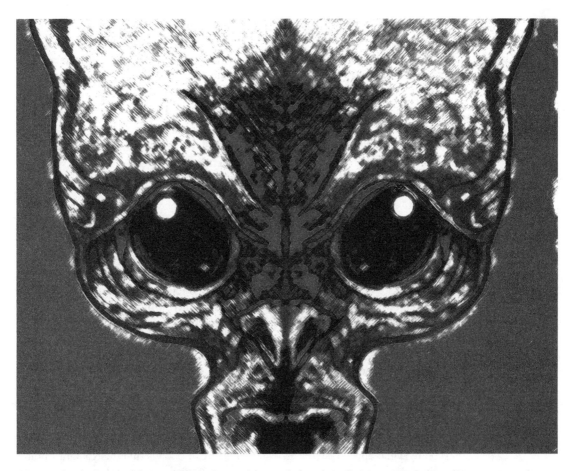

Many individuals report being awakened out of a sound sleep by a Gray staring at them. Fear, panic, and even abduction are often experienced after such visitations. (*Art by Ricardo Pustanio*)

that bulged backwards. They had tiny nostrils, a protruding, tube-like mouth, and two antennae or horns coming out of their upper foreheads. Their skin was a rough, textured darker green. They had red bulging, almond-shaped eyes, but the witness found their eyes beautiful.

When they spoke to him, they gestured a great deal with the fingers on their hands. Although they had four fingers and a thumb on each hand, their vocalization was supplemented by a great amount of gesturing with two large main fingers and their thumb. The words themselves sounded very soft and melodious, almost as if they were cooing. They did not form words as we do, but in his head he understood what they were saying.

They were very interested in him and asked many questions. They asked him if he would like to come with them for three years. He told them that was too long for him to just up and leave. They seemed sad that he wouldn't come, but told him they would be back.

It was getting light outside, and the witness noticed that they were flying two hundred yards above the trees, and moving faster than any plane. The next thing he remembered is waking up in his bed at 7:00 A.M., exhausted. He got up and noticed that his front door was wide open—and remembered his "dream."

The Controversial Stan Romanek and "Boo," an Alien Window Peeper

Stan Romanek, a computer technician, who lives near Denver, Colorado, says that his UFO experiences began in December 2000 when he sighted a spacecraft hovering over some power lines while he was taking photographs of the scenery. And it was in 2001 that Romanek claims he was first abducted after his van was followed by a UFO across Ohio, Indiana, and Illinois. Ten days later, he and his van were "beamed" aboard a spacecraft and an implant was placed in his leg by his abductors.

Romanek's claims are highly controversial, especially his video, which shows a friendly alien whom he calls "Boo" peeking in the family's window. While some do not hesitate to label Romanek a fake, others who view the video state that it would require the photo enhancements of experts and the expense of thousands of dollars to produce the movements of Boo, as he approaches the window of the Romanek home. After Romanek's appearance on *Larry King Live* in 2008, a press conference was held in Denver for the purpose of raising money to establish a commission for the investigation of extraterrestrial visitation.

Soon after the great national publicity that Romanek received following his media appearances, area skeptics showed their version of the alien peeping Tom. They had created what appeared to be an exact duplicate of Boo visiting the Romanek home with a rented alien costume, home editing software, five hours of work, and a total cost of $90.00.

In May 2010, our colleague Paul Dale Roberts, HPI General Manager/Ghostwriter/Paranormal Investigator (www.hpiparanormal.net) conducted an interview with the controversial Stan Romanek:

Paul Dale Roberts: Stan, tell us a little about yourself. Where were you born and raised, and so forth.

Stan Romanek: I was born in 1962 at a military hospital in Denver, Colorado. I am the youngest of two brothers and one sister born into an Air Force family migrating to and from various military bases throughout the Midwest and Western United States through 1972. I am now happily married. I have a daughter, and I live with my wife, two stepdaughters and stepson in a peaceful mid-sized community in Colorado. I grew up dealing with severe dyslexia, making school a challenge. Because of concern about my learning disability, my IQ was tested, and it was found to be well above average. What I struggled with in scholastic abilities I made up for in arts and sports.

Roberts: What was your first UFO experience?

Romanek: Although I remember having some minor experiences when I was a child, my true experiences didn't start until December of 2000. I was planning to film some scenery in the Red Rocks area in Colorado to entice my then girlfriend, now wife, Lisa, to come to Colorado for a visit, but I was sidetracked when I saw a lot of people pulled over looking to the sky. That is when I filmed my first UFO that December of 2000.

Roberts: Why do you think you have been the focus of your alien captors?

Romanek: After many years, I still do not know the answer to that question. However, it has been said that abduction experiences tend to run in families.

Roberts: Why are aliens abducting humans? For what purpose?

Romanek: I believe there are many alien races involved in the abduction process, all of which have their own agenda; some for their own personal gain. Perhaps it is because they find we have strengths they do not and want to strengthen their own race. Perhaps it is to help strengthen our own race. Perhaps we are an experiment.

Roberts: Where are these aliens from?

Romanek: In my case, I believe that they are from a planet six-and-a-half light years behind the star Alnitak, which is the lower left star in Orion's belt.

Although crop circles have been reported in farmers' fields around the world since at least medieval times, credit for such disturbances were given to elves or devils. In the contemporary scene of mysterious and elaborate designs found in fields, it has been theorized that aliens are attempting to communicate with us through complex mathematical formulas and symbols. (*Art by Ricardo Pustanio*)

Roberts: What is their agenda?

Romanek: I believe that there are some that want to help the human race become enlightened, but just as there are good and bad people on earth, there is also good and bad out there; and agendas will vary.

Roberts: Are they responsible for cattle mutilations?

Romanek: This topic has never been a part of any of my experiences. Although it is a good possibility, I do not know. But in most cattle mutilations, it has been found they have been drained completely of blood, and I find it interesting that an element of cows' blood, called bovine serum is used for in vitro-fertilization.

Roberts: Are they responsible for crop circles?

Romanek: A large percent have been found to be manmade, but I do believe that some are made by the extraterrestrials.

Roberts: Are the aliens working with our military?

Romanek: It is my belief that there have been some agreements in the past between governments on earth and off-world entities.

Roberts: Has the video footage been analyzed by experts and do they think the "alien in the window" footage is real?

Romanek: Absolutely, yes! Credible video analysts have analyzed the tapes, and determined that it is shot "in-camera" with no delays or special effects.

Roberts: Do the aliens have a message? If so, what is the message?

Romanek: Yes, definitely. It is my understanding that the message is that it is time for the human race to grow up and take responsibility for their actions.

Roberts: Do the aliens say anything about 2012?

Romanek: Yes. Although it is unclear exactly what will happen, they have hinted about a big event. I believe it will be first contact, and not the global annihilation that many people worry about.

Roberts: When will there be full disclosure?

Romanek: The U.S. is one of the only countries that have not yet disclosed what they know about UFOs and extraterrestrials. I believe full disclosure from the U.S. will happen within the next few years, because of pressure from other countries and from the Vatican.

Roberts: Tell us about other experiences you have had with your alien captors?

Romanek: There is a wide range of things that have happened throughout my experiences. Everything from ghostly activity to flashes of light, balls of light floating through my house, not to mention implants and ETs captured on video and digital cameras.

Roberts: How many times have you been abducted?

Romanek: To my knowledge, I have been taken at least seven times.

Roberts: Thank you for the interview. Is there anything else you may want to mention, that I may have missed?

Romanek: My case is somewhat different than other abduction cases in that most things seem to happen when there are multiple witnesses, not one individual witness like me. In addition, many cases are documented by trace evidence, but I have also acquired impressive amounts of video and photographic evidence. My case is also unique because I have drawn multiple advanced physics equations under regression and in my sleep. These equations have been analyzed by physicists throughout the world, and they are baffled as to how a person with severe dyslexia, with a fourth grade math level is able to come up with concepts and equations that have not yet been explored fully in physics.

Alien "Pediatricians" Checked Out the Health of Her Baby

UFO investigator Richard Siefried relates the tale of Pam Owens, a woman who shared her story of being taken aboard a UFO on November 25, 1978, while she was expecting her second child. She was nineteen at the time and five months pregnant, and she had no memory of the abduction until she was hypnotically regressed. Then she was able to give full and fascinating details of her encounter.

Mrs. Owens told Siefried that she was paralyzed, only able to move her eyes. She lay helpless on a table and stared up in terror at two weird-looking creatures. According to Mrs. Owens, their heads were hairless, oversize domes, their eyes big and sunk back in their skulls. The greenish skin covering their bodies was coarse. Each hand had four fingers that she described as being twice as long as a human's digits. And to her terror, one of those strange hands was holding a long silver needle, preparing to plunge it into her stomach.

Pam Owens pieced the story together after a series of hypnotic regressions. She had been standing with her husband Chris and their twenty-month-old son Brian, gazing in absolute amazement at an object that they understood to be an approaching spaceship. Then suddenly she was inside of it, alone and terrified.

At that time, Chris had been stationed with the U.S. Army in West Germany. They had been visiting friends near Trier, and it was on their way home that they saw the UFO. It was shiny, metal, oval, and perhaps one hundred feet long. Pam has a vivid memory of a red blinking light under the craft.

She told her husband to get out of there, to drive away fast, to get away from the UFO. But when they got home, they discovered that it had taken them two hours to drive what should have been a half-hour journey.

Later, when they returned to the United States, Pam contacted a UFO research organization, and the investigators there suggested that she undergo hypnotic regression with a psychologist. Under hypnosis the young mother's mind revealed what had really happened that night.

When the UFO first appeared, they had driven off the main road and stopped in a clearing. She and Chris got out of the car and held Brian while they stood there waiting, unafraid. The next thing she knew, she was lying on a table. She could move only her eyes. She was in a small room filled with yellowish-white light. The ceiling blended into the walls, so there were no corners.

The frightened young mother asked for the whereabouts of her little boy. She recalls a flat voice answering, "We are taking care of him." Then she asked about her husband and begged the entities not to hurt him. The voice kept repeating that everyone was safe.

After she had calmed down, two of the entities moved into her line of vision. She remembered that they looked almost like mummies. They had very tiny noses and straight lines for mouths. One began to speak to her, reassuring her that everything would be all right, but his mouth didn't move, and it seemed to Pam as if he were somehow talking through his eyes.

Suddenly the entities pulled up her shirt, exposing her distended abdomen. Their hands touched her, and she began feeling dizzy and sick. She began to cry for the safety of her unborn child, but the entities continued to examine her, as if they were checking on the baby's size and the way it was lying in her womb.

Then she saw the needle, and she became truly frightened, crying out, "No, no, don't hurt my baby!" But one of them stuck the needle right below Pam's navel—where she later found a puzzling pimple. She remembers that the needle hurt a great deal, and she felt as though she were going to vomit.

The next thing she knew she was standing by their car again, holding Brian in her arms as before. The family was watching as the spaceship rose into the air.

Pam feels that the ninety minutes missing from their lives have not been explained. In her opinion, the creatures, wherever they came from, were basically friendly and were examining a human body to see what it was like. "Four months after my experience, my daughter Kelli was born—perfectly normal," Pam Owens said. "Brian, who couldn't talk when it all happened doesn't seem to know what occurred that night."

Are the Grays Conducting Genetic Experiments?
Or Altering Our Evolutionary Time Table?

Many alien experiencers claim that the black, staring eyes of a Gray intruder placed them in a state of paralysis and caused a loss of memory. (*Art by Ricardo Pustanio*)

Accusations have been raised by many UFO investigators that the aliens in general—and the Grays in particular—are conducting genetic experiments to alter human evolution. On this topic, we must speculate, based on our own extensive research, whether the extraterrestrial geneticists might not be completing a centuries-old project, rather than initiating a new one.

Rather than focusing on whether or not the UFO abductors are conducting genetic experiments on unwilling men and women in 2011, the more powerful query is whether humankind might have been structured by the UFO intelligences from the very beginning of our evolutionary trek.

Our own science has made much progress in genetic engineering and we now possess the ability to transfer certain traits from one creature to another. We are able to create genetically new animals or to transfer a particularly desirable trait within the same species. If we Earthlings are steadily acquiring mastery of such genetic science, what can be expected of UFO intelligences, who clearly appear to be eons ahead of us technologically?

To look at the troubling matter of UFO abductions from the perspective of the aliens, the process of human evolutionary trial and error might not yet be completed. They may still be monitoring the development of our species through the programmed process of UFO-based examinations.

A Mass Invasion of Earth by Grays Began in 1954

According to numerous UFO researchers, the reptilian/amphibian/large-eyed alien species currently best known as the "Grays" conducted a mass invasion of Earth in 1954. The reason the great majority of our planet's citizenry were not aware of any "war of the worlds" extraterrestrial military threat was because the Aliens had already made their secret pact with the governments of the world.

Some researchers believe that there are at least seventy-five underground bases that shelter the Grays. Startling as it seems to many, these bases also include our own scientists and military personnel. Officially, these bases are designated as "emergency shelters" for our president in the event of nuclear war.

Physicist Al Bielek insists that the Central Intelligence Agency (CIA) was formed in 1947 to keep an eye on the emerging alien situation. After the UFO crash near Roswell, New Mexico, in July 1947, and subsequent crashes, the situation became tense. Shortly thereafter, a special "watchdog" group was formed, designated as MJ-12 (Majority 12). Initially chaired by the late Admiral Roscoe Hillenkoetter, the secret group assumed increasing authority as time passed.

Two additional crashes in 1948 and 1949 added "urgency" to their authority—especially when another live alien was recovered in 1949. On the heels of this startling development came the formation of the National Security Agency (NSA) and a plethora of intelligence agencies, many of which were kept highly secret.

"In the beginning, according to scientists who worked with the Grays, the aliens were very generous with their gifts of technical knowledge, and it is a matter of historical record how our sciences accelerated in their progress and expanded their accomplishments after 1954," Bielek pointed out. "Great strides in medicine were achieved, and many of these long-sought goals can be directly attributed to information provided by the aliens."

While some Grays acted benevolently toward us, others were contemptuous and regarded us as nothing more than hairless apes.

The actual truth behind the Gray "invasion," according to many who have had encounters with the bulbous-headed Aliens and scientists who have worked at their side, was that the Grays needed a new home. They had lived underground on their own world for more than 1,500 years after their civilization had been devastated by an unrestrained science that had been generated by their uncontrolled military-industrial-scientific complex.

Some researchers believe that there may be as many as six varieties of the Gray species due to the holocaust that brought about the death of their planet and scattered the inhabitants. Those who went underground became the Grays, smallish, gray-complexioned beings with digestive and reproductive problems. Others of their kind are taller, more human-like in appearance, and more distinctly male and female.

Since the favors granted them by a secret U.S. government group known as Majestic 12 included underground bases and the opportunity to study developing humankind via the agency of abductions, the Grays seemed to become increasingly aggressive toward Earthlings.

The Grays Stray from Their Agreement
with the Secret Government

Some researchers insist that the CIA was created primarily to see that the aliens followed their end of the agreement. Their agents soon noted that the Grays were abducting more humans than had been predetermined and agreed upon. Perhaps even worse, humans whose names were not on the official list of potential abductees were being taken aboard craft for study and examination. And some of those abducted humans never returned.

In addition, the CIA learned that large numbers of abductees had received "implants" that were designed to monitor them, much in the manner that terrestrial conservation officers keep tabs on bears, wolves, and deer.

Certain highly advanced technological devices designed by the Grays can literally "beam" an abductee aboard one of their spaceships while the victim sleeps in his or her own bed. The Grays have the ability to rearrange a human's cellular structure so that a selected abductee can be dematerialized and brought through solid surfaces such as walls or roofs, and reassembled on board a spacecraft. Once the examination is completed and the process is reversed, the victim may awaken in the morning with only pieces of a fleeting memory of a bizarre dream.

Incredibly, many human scientists who claim to have worked in secret underground laboratories with the Grays state that these particular Aliens have no effective military weapons. Some suggest that the more powerful reptilian species from Orion had already confiscated their weaponry before the Grays came to Earth.

The Incredible Power of the Grays' Group Mind

Scientists, such as Al Bielek state firmly that it doesn't really matter whether or not the Grays have material tools of war. "Their greatest weapon is their intelligence and their group mind," he said.

Rumors have long circulated that an entire raiding party of Delta Force commandos was annihilated by the Grays in the underground base at Dulce. How could a crack fighting unit like Delta Force be defeated by mind power alone? "I have no data on how they managed it," Bielek admitted, "but I have reports that I trust that attest to the fact that it did happen. How the Grays did it, though, I can but theorize.

"Because the Grays operate with a group mind—and because they are exceedingly intelligent—they can harness unknown mental energies and create awesome

The Grays have often been credited with amazing powers of mind control. Some have suggested that the alien beings have the ability to walk the streets of large cities and exert mental energy, rendering them invisible to unsuspecting crowds of humans. (*Art by Ricardo Pustanio*)

powers. They can focus on a human mind and cause a person to do things that he or she would not dream of doing in his normal mind state. That is how they operate so often with the human abductees and contactees: They broadcast commands and orders that the unsuspecting follow unerringly—without knowing why. And usually without even remembering the action occurred.

"The Grays with their group mind could have caused the Delta Force to fire upon itself, to destroy itself. Few human minds could resist the concentrated focus of a group mind, especially one of such practiced power as the Grays possess." As some researchers theorize, the group mind of the Grays is at once their strength and their weakness.

The Grays seem intrigued by the human ability to function alone and as individuals. They are fascinated by our creativity, our ability to improvise. Compared to the human species, the Grays are really quite drab, emotionless entities. Bielek said that his recollection of reports of the physical examination of certain Gray corpses revealed that their brain development appeared quite different from ours.

Word has leaked out that some highly classified autopsies of the Gray aliens have been conducted on bodies of the aliens who have died after such crashes as the ones at Roswell and other locations less well known. According to these "leaks," the brain capacity of the Grays is larger and has more convolutions. There is more brain matter devoted to vision. They have adapted to lower level light functioning, and they may not be able to tolerate bright sunlight. They are primarily creatures who appear to function in the dark or dim light.

Are Aliens Really Time Travelers from Our Future?

A theory about our Visitors that has become increasingly popular suggests that many of the various types of aliens are really our future earthly descendants visiting us in our present, their long ago past. Even the Grays with their seemingly overlarge heads, small bodies, and spindly limbs may provide us with a preview of the appearance of our own species as it may evolve in the future.

In his *Visitors from Time: The Secret of the UFOs,* Marc Davenport writes that many of the UFOs are not spaceships "in the common sense of the word, but vehicles designed to travel through time…. Many are not from other planets, but from a future Earth…:

> These time machines are peopled by a complex mixture of human beings, evolved forms of human beings, genetically engineered life forms, androids, robots and/or alien life-forms. These occupants make use of advanced technology based on principles that will be discovered at some point in our near future to produce fields around their craft that warp space-time. By manipulating those fields, they are able to traverse what we think of as space and time almost at will.

Author-researcher John A. Keel, author of *Strange Creatures from Time and Space, The Mothman Prophecies,* and numerous other books and articles on the Alien Mystery, theorized that there have been indications in some cases that certain UFOs could be time travelers. But he thought it was more likely that the same object could intrude into our reality in different time periods. The same UFO could move in and out of our time dimension—appearing, perhaps, in the days of the Roman Empire—slip out again, then move into our reality again in 2011. And that could be why so many UFOnauts ask contactees and abductees "what time it is." They might be referring to the year, rather than the hour.

"According to those who have held dialogues with the UFO entities, the beings don't really seem to know who or what they are, but they know that they have turned up in other periods of time, that they have been reconstructed generation after generation," Keel said. "They seem to be timeless in that sense."

Our Descendants May Have Conquered the Paradoxes of Time Travel

While Dr. Bruce Goldberg, author of *Time Travelers from the Future, Egypt: An Extraterrestrial and Time Traveler Experiment* and many other books, does not deny the possibility that some abductions of humans have been conducted by extraterrestrials, he believes the great majority of abductions are the work of time travelers. In the guise of aliens from outer space, they may accomplish healings of a wide variety of diseases and physical problems. Some of the "chrononauts," as Dr. Goldberg calls them, referring to their mastery of time, could even function as guardian angels to certain humans with particular missions to accomplish.

In his research, Dr. Goldberg has isolated four groups of time travelers: (1) the Grays, the ubiquitous insect-like aliens with the large black eyes; (2) the Hybrids, a genetic mixture of humans and beings from other planets; (3) the Pure Humans, between six and seven feet tall, blond, blue-eyed, dressed in white robes; and (4) the Reptilians, extraterrestrials who have little interest in promoting the general welfare of humans.

Among the abilities that Dr. Goldberg credits to the time traveling visitors are the following:

- They can show us our past and future by way of holograms.
- Telepathy is their basic means of communication, although they can speak when they wish.
- They can instantly induce a state of suspended animation in anyone they choose.
- They have mastered hyperspace travel between dimensions and can move through solid walls and objects.
- By existing in the fifth dimension, they can observe us and remain invisible.
- Genetic manipulation of our chromosomes is a routine procedure for them. They have participated in a great acceleration of our species' rate of evolution.
- The less advanced groups make many errors with experiments, but the more advanced are able to manipulate time and space with proficiency.

Time Travelers May Sometimes Appear Angel-Like

Dr. Goldberg has based his conclusions on thousands of future life progressions that he has conducted with subjects under hypnosis. Among the many illustrations that he selects from his files is one about a former gang member who, at the age of eighteen, was involved in a fight between rival gangs and was facing a gun in the hand of a punk who was about to pull the trigger. Before the gun could go off, however, a blue and

In the 1970s, the "little green men" had evolved in the popular mind to become the "Grays." While most reports describe the Grays as sinister and menacing, some of the entities are said to be benign, curious, and devoid of emotion. (*Art by Ricardo Pustanio*)

lavender swirling cloud surrounded the young hoodlum with the gun in his hand.

"A luminous figure of a human time traveler in a white robe stood between the gunman and my young patient," Dr. Goldberg says. "The gun went off, but the bullets seemed to enter the chrononaut's body and disappear from sight. While all this was going on, everyone else was placed in a state of suspended animation. When the swirling cloud evaporated, the time traveler was gone and every gang member regained consciousness. They just dispersed.

"The following day," Dr. Goldberg continued, "my patient resigned from the gang and his whole life changed. He began working to help support his poor family, and he became far more spiritual than he ever demonstrated before."

Time Travelers May Have the Ability to Manipulate History

Out of the nearly hundreds of abductees on whom Dr. Goldberg has conducted hypnotic regressions over three decades, he has determined that the great majority of them interacted with time travelers from between one thousand and three thousand years in our future. He is now of the opinion that our history has been manipulated by these chrononauts and that they have been responsible for the quantum leaps in our technology during this century.

His clinical experience since 1974 in working with UFO abductees has suggested such data as the following:

- Abductions begin at ages four to seven and persist to around the age of forty.
- Although reproductive experiments are conducted (human eggs and sperm samples are taken) the main purpose of these abductions is to monitor the spiritual growth of humanity.
- The time travelers function as our "guardian angels" by placing attackers in states of suspended animation to allow our escape and so on. They can manipulate our physical laws to assist us in time of need.
- These chrononauts follow us from lifetime to lifetime. They trace our souls back to our previous lives and monitor our spiritual growth.
- There are possible parallel universes in the future with many wars, emotional problems, pollution, and severe global warming that can be greatly averted if the time travelers assist us now in our spiritual progress.

In Dr. Goldberg's opinion, the basic message of the time travelers throughout history is that "each of us is unique and possesses infinite potential for spiritual, as well as technological, growth. We are each, as individuals, responsible for this growth. By establishing and maintaining a connection with our Higher Self, we can be more in harmony with a larger, whole, infinity."

The
Praying Mantises

Today, people who are familiar with Janet Russell regard her as one of the best-known and most accurate psychic sensitives in the United States. She has her own television program in New York and has appeared on hundreds of radio and television programs in both the United States and the United Kingdom. We have known Janet as a dear friend for ten years, and we have gratefully used her paranormal abilities in certain research projects. We were quite surprised when we received a response from Janet to one of our emails about abduction experiences. In her response, Janet told us that she attributes her psychic sensitivity to an abduction in which she interacted with a praying mantis-like alien.

On March 27, 1962, Janet was a twenty-two-year-old mother, pregnant with her fourth child. According to her:

I had left my home in Medford (where I still reside) at 6:00 P.M. to get to a doctor's appointment at 6:15 P.M. I arrived at 7:30. Today Route 112 is a large four-lane highway. At that time it was a small main road. I was headed for Roe Blvd. in Patchogue where my doctor's office was located.

As I was driving down Route 112, I looked up and saw in the sky the most magnificent sight. It looked like the Moon, but a Moon that kept changing colors, from purple (my favorite color) to silver, blue, red, green, and the colors sparkled as if they were sequins. I remembered pulling my car over to the side of the road and getting out to look at it closer, as it was so magnetic to the eye.

When I arrived at the doctor's office I was well over an hour late. When I walked into the office, the nurses said that my face was peeling like I had been to Florida and gotten a bad sunburn. The doctor also commented that my face was peeling. Remember, at the time I was a shy twenty-two year old, going for a visit to see how my pregnancy was progressing. Not yet realizing that I was so late, I thought it strange that when I arrived I could actually mentally hear the doctor saying, "Why is she so late?" I was stunned to realize that I could hear his thoughts.

Later, I would come to understand that what had made me late for the doctor's appointment was the missing time experience that opened up my psychic awareness.

It took me thirty-three years later at the age of fifty-five to attempt to find out what had happened to me on that March evening. I went to an astrologer to see if I could find any clues to what major incident happened to me. According to the astrologer, my astrological chart showed that a strange occurrence, possibly one from out of space may have taken place on that exact date.

Since at that time I was unfamiliar with the wide range of UFO activity, I began to peruse all the books on the Unknown and UFO that I could get my hands on. Suddenly, I could never get enough on that subject. I still have all the books, probably about five or six hundred.

> Next, I saw what appeared to me to look like two small white or gray beings with large black eyes. The strange thing was I could see what looked like their hearts beating.

At the age of fifty-five, I was regressed by Dr. Jean Mundy in her home in Southampton. Dr. Mundy had worked with Dr. John Mack, a Harvard psychologist who became interested in UFO abduction cases, and UFO abduction researcher Budd Hopkins. At the time I had worked for Dr. Edward Beller, a chiropractor, in Patchogue, who accompanied me to the regression. He actually paid to have it done, since he was so interested in what had happened to me, even though I had no idea what my regression would open up to me.

Dr. Jean Mundy regressed me back to that fateful day in my life. During the regression, I was completely surprised to discover that I had been transported up into a magnificent alien spaceship. Even now as I am telling this to you, I can see and feel the experience in my mind's eye.

In my regression I was entering the craft via a blue energy, then being lifted into a white light. Next I was taken into a small white room where I was examined by what looked like a praying mantis. The mantis held what looked like a pointer with a white energy or light at its end. I was gently told to stand before what looked like a silver screen or metallic slab, and I was poked by this large praying mantis from the top of my head to my stomach. Remember, I was pregnant about four months or so with my fourth child. When I was poked in the side of my stomach, it hurt.

Next, I saw what appeared to me to look like two small white or gray beings with large black eyes. The strange thing was I could see what looked like their hearts beating. Mentally they told me that they would not harm me in any way.

All of a sudden a creature appeared that looked like a Ninja Turtle. Somehow, he reminded me of a theater usher. I know, it sounds strange to me even when I say it now so many years later.

I was directed into different rooms in this spacious ship after I was examined by the praying mantis, which I never saw again. I was led through these various rooms. First there was a dark room—that I was told I could not enter. A quick peek while passing by revealed what seemed to look like the Universe with stars shining. The next room appeared to be a gold room, but I was told mentally that it was not my time to go there as of yet.

Then I was led by this Ninja Turtle-looking being and two little "snow men" with large black eyes who were on each side of me, constantly telling me mentally that they would not hurt me.

I remember as I was being regressed that my mind was very still, taking in the sights and events that had happened to me so many years ago. My body was shaking like a leaf. The mind was working but the body was scared.

The next room I was led into looked like a nursery. It was a very pale pink room, with approximately twenty of what looked like incubators. Each one had what I would say looked like petri dishes with embryos at different stages—each one seemed more progressed than the next.

By the time I got to the twentieth incubator, I saw what looked like a little girl baby with the most magnificent eyes. Her eyes didn't look like ours. They looked more like alien eyes, but they were sparkling and magnetic. I remember her body was so small and thin, and her skin was very white like she really needed the sun, but had never seen the sun. She had a large head, and she smiled at me as if she was my own child. I remember wanting to have her come back with me, and I was told that I would see her again one day soon. I was hoping to hold her in my arms, but I was taken to another room.

This room was a pale blue room, which also held approximately twenty incubators, but these housed what I called the Ninja Turtle-beings. They

Although some experiencers are at first terrified by the appearance of the Praying Mantis-type entities, others claim that they have been healed by or received communications from these bizarre beings. In a great number of cases, when other aliens have appeared in the company of the mantids, the huge insect-like creatures appear to be in command. (*Art by Ricardo Pustanio*)

as well were in petrie dishes, and each one seemed to be progressing in different stages of development. The twentieth one supported what looked like a small being. I was then informed both the little girl baby with the large eyes and the Ninja Turtle baby were both conceived at the same exact moment.

The next place I visited with the two little beings on each side of me and the Ninja Turtle usher leading us was a light yellow room with a misty type of energy in it. To me, it reminded me of a court room.

I was led to the front of the room where in front of me stood three small beings. As I can best describe them, two appeared to be human, one a hybrid. Then the most magnificent being I have ever seen appeared. He was tall with beautiful eyes, long light brown hair, and appeared to be very gentle. He was wearing a brown cloak.

I was led up to the front of this strange group of entities or beings, and I was still being told that I was not going to be harmed. It was then that this tall, beautiful being in the brown cloak began to press a small wire into my right arm. (This is where the scoop mark in my arm is to this day, with the implant still in it.)

As this was being implanted into my arm, I was informed that I had been tested and I passed. I was told that the information that I had been given would be known at the right time. I still remember that as this implant was being somehow inserted into my arm, there seemed to be different sounds all around me. One of the sounds seemed somewhat like our language, but at a very fast rate of speed. Others sounded like a grunting noise, not human-like at all. The strangest part of it all was when I looked at this glorious being in the cloak, he looked as human as you and I. Yet I noticed when I looked at him at an angle, he looked as if he were a hologram.

Well, that was on March 27, 1962. Since that time, I have met some wonderful people in the field, and I have had some major experiences as well.

Praying Mantis Encounters from the Files of UFOBC

The following accounts of praying mantis aliens come to us from our friend and associate Bill Oliver and the files of UFOBC (British Columbia). We have edited them for use in this present book.

Jim lives in a small town on the outskirts of London, Ontario. Here is his account sent to the UFOBC on August 23, 2003 of an encounter with a praying mantis alien that occurred to him in April 2001:

I woke up at about 2:30 in the morning to find a tall praying mantis being and a cloaked entity by the side of my bed.

The cloaked being looked at me from beneath its hood, revealing its black skin, which appeared leathery and reflected light much like a beetle's skin. I shut my eyes, thinking this must be a realistic dream! But when I reopened my eyes, the figures were unfortunately still there.

The cloaked figure looked up at the tall praying mantis type, as if it was confused as to what actions it should take next. The praying mantis turned its head towards the hooded one and made a series of high-pitched clicking sounds. I sensed the hooded entity was the one in command. Possibly the other was some kind of security guard. It was at this point that I realized, I'm definitely not dreaming. I can hear them. I couldn't move, but my brain went into a deep panic. "Oh my God, what is going on?" "What are they?"

All I recall was that the praying mantis was tall. At least seven feet, it had to bend its neck because of the height of the ceiling. Its head was pointed with large eyes. Its forearms were extremely long, and it moved in a jerky fashion.

The cloaked figure was closer, crouching by my bed, so I couldn't tell how tall it was, but I could clearly see that it was wearing some kind of overlapping ridged armor, including a metallic looking breastplate that had a series of circles on it. Its head was dome-like with emotionless facial features. Its eyes were large and surrounded again by detailed ridges. It acted in a way that reminded me of a robot or insect.

I remember thinking to myself, nobody's going to believe this! A bloody giant-sized mantis and medieval-style dressed alien—what the hell is this?

Before this incident, although I hadn't seen one, I was familiar with the gray-type aliens, but I had never heard of the praying-mantis types. At this point, the mantis bent its upper body over my bed and directly above me. In its hand it was holding a long metal object that looked like a needle. A green light shot directly from the needle and into my right eye. Maybe it was a laser of some kind; I am not sure, but I do know that it felt very painful. I could see all the veins from my eye, the same effect you get when an optician checks your eyes.

I screamed but no noise came out. I then felt something stick into my skull! I'm not sure what because by that time I had my eyes closed. I went into deep panic! My mind was racing at a million miles per hour. I heard a great whooshing sound and when I next reopened my eyes, thankfully they had gone. I lay shaking and confused for what seemed like hours and just couldn't return back to sleep.

At no time did I feel like they cared about my health or me! They seem to have an insect-cold type mentality. I really thought I was going to die.

The next day I spent the whole day in bed and felt as if I had been through a major operation. It's very painful to recall, and since this incident, I sometimes hear clicking sounds inside my head. I was in shock for a long while afterwards; I can say that this definitely happened, this definitely was real. I have no answers or conclusions but I think it's important to get real life accounts out there.

An Update from Jim Regarding Additional Encounters

The UFOBC sent Jim a response thanking him for sharing his account. On September 2, 2003 they received another e-mail from him that included two drawings and a computer generated graphic of the cloaked entity, as well as a very interesting sound file.

I don't feel any pain at this moment, but I can tell when I've been "taken" because the next day I'm completely wasted. Like I've been in a medical operation, I just cannot move or do anything much at all. Dealing with this and being self-employed as you can imagine is no fun at all.

I can't remember anything else from the main encounter other than when I first woke up they were doing something to my legs and that there must have been a light source for me to see so much detail, but where it was emitting from I can't say, possibly the cloaked figure was holding a staff.

Although I do have some very good friends whom I've told, they were initially skeptical, but now they do believe me, knowing me not to be a liar or fantasy prone.

An astonishing number of alien experiencers have claimed to have had close encounters with extraterrestrial beings that closely resemble Earth's Praying Mantises. (*Art by Bill Oliver*)

The day after the incident in 2001, I did do a word search on "mantis-type aliens" and got nothing. So at first, although I knew it did happen, I really just put it down to a very realistic dream and denied it to myself. Six months ago while surfing the Net, I came across a drawing of a praying mantis alien holding a needle device. It was exactly what I had seen. I had a panic attack just looking at it. After a little research I realized that these were well-defined aliens within Ufology. If other people were seeing what I'd seen, then either it's a coincidence or it's really happening!

Why do I think they chose me? Well, I've had many of what a lot of people would describe as strange experiences while I was a kid, (seeing UFOs, the walls talking to me every birthday), but I think a lot of kids have these things happen? I prefer to concentrate on the things that I can say really happened.

I was 18 years old in the summer of '92, and while working in London, I sneezed and a metal ball fell out of my left nostril! I told my friends "Wow London's so polluted; I must have breathed in some lead, 'cause a metal ball fell out of my nose!" I now suspect it was possibly an alien implant.

And in the summer of '96, it was a really hot night, so I thought I would climb out of my bedroom window and on to the roof of my house. I got the strangest feeling of being watched. I looked into the star-filled night sky and had the crazy thought of trying to communicate with aliens telepathically. I just sent out feelings of love and that if anyone can pick this up, I'd like to communicate.

To my utter amazement, way up high, a ball of light appeared. I assumed it to be a satellite until it turned, dived and hovered two hundred feet above me. I could clearly see it was a ball of light. It made no sound whatsoever. I stared in utter amazement. I felt calm and euphoric, completely at one with the world. The ball then just disappeared. I climbed back into my bedroom and fell into a deep sleep.

Since then, I started to have really strange experiences. I'd wake up in the middle of night floating above my bed! One time I even floated outside my house, and in the distance I could see the ball of light and that I was getting pulled towards it. I imagined myself surrounded by white light, and I flew back to my bed with a thud. I don't think I was astral projecting, this felt real.

These experiences completely stopped. And then the praying mantis encounter happened.

I'm really not sure why they choose me, maybe they sensed a spiritual awakening within me—or more likely it was just mere opportunity. They just spotted some young fool on a roof of a house and thought, "He'll be easy pickings." One thing's for sure; I really felt no spiritual vibes or energy (if you like) from these beings at all. I just felt like a lab rat.

Praying Mantis Account from Chicago

Below is an account posted on February 12, 2006 from a different witness in a different country. This occurrence was prior to Jim's encounter. The similarities (including the purple cloak) appear to be more than coincidental.

Humanoid report 1999
Case# 103.
Location. Chicago, Illinois
Date: August 1999
Time: late night

A man visiting a friend's house and sleeping on the sofa in the bedroom suddenly woke up feeling very panicky and totally unable to move. Looking towards the front door he saw a huge humanoid figure over seven feet tall standing by the door. The figure resembled a large "praying mantis" and was wearing something resembling a black and purple cloak. Its skin was dark gray in color. It slowly approached the witness and reached out to him with a large hand with long thin fingers and grabbed his shoulder. At this point the witness lost consciousness and does not recall anything else of the incident. He remembered also feeling very cold during the encounter.

Compiled by Albert R.

Her Friend Was Visited in the Hospital
by Praying Mantis Aliens

Another similar account was received in May of 2008 and signed with the letter A. This account follows:

I first want to say I have never followed any UFO stories, and I'm not even a sci-fi fan. I had an experience last year, and when I wanted to research it further, I was pretty shocked to find any info at all about praying mantis aliens online. Here is my story:

My best friend was viciously attacked and left to die in 2008. She barely survived the horrible attack where she was knocked unconscious after being hit in the head over and over with an object. When I saw her at the hospital she was unrecognizable. Her beautiful face was swollen to the size of a basketball. I almost felt like this was not her, like I was looking at a stranger. I've known her for forty years, she was my closest friend. We grew up together.

> I saw freshly sliced raw flesh, and these aliens/ praying mantises were busily removing pieces of bone, rock or whatever from her brain.

She was in a drug-induced coma after they removed part of her skull, so I was afraid to even touch her. I wanted to lie down and just hug her, hold her, but wasn't permitted with all her head injuries.

The night after I saw her at the hospital, I felt helpless but began to meditate on my friend. I stood there over her body in my meditation, afraid to touch her head, afraid to send any energy, not knowing where to start. I began to cry. I stood there helpless for the longest time, not knowing what to do but feeling a real sense of panic. Something had to be done quickly.

All of a sudden there were two beings that appeared next to my friend. They seemed to push me right aside and silently went right to work on her, like skilled surgeons. They stood to her left, standing together and working furiously on my friend. I had no idea who they were, what they were doing, but the first thing I thought of was "are they aliens"?

I stood there and watched them more than what they were doing. I thought they looked like praying mantises. Alien praying mantises. Never in a million years could I make this up. I did not see everything they were doing, because I was pretty much amazed at what I was seeing.

Then I focused on my friend and saw that her head was split wide open. These aliens sliced it perfectly open. I saw freshly sliced raw flesh, and these aliens/praying mantises were busily removing pieces of bone, rock or whatever from her brain. This did not look anything like what I would imagine the inside of a brain to look, but it was just such a clean cut. These two aliens/praying mantises worked quickly, without speaking one word. I seemed to black out and don't remember any more of it.

I've heard of spirit guides helping with healing, but where in the world did these creatures come from? I have friends that I can openly talk to about these things, and I told them about my alien/praying mantis experience. I told them that I was too afraid to touch my friend because of all the damage to her head and these beings stepped right in to save her. Someone mentioned hearing of praying mantis healing before and told me to look it up on the Internet.

I did some research and found your praying mantis accounts. I was surprised to find anything at all about praying mantis. I do see things in my healings and meditations that I don't understand, but this was the weirdest of them all.

I'm sad to say that even with the alien healing, my friend only survived another two weeks before she died. It's just remarkable that she survived at all after her injuries. I don't know why I experienced this, but it's something I will never forget.

Sincerely, and oh, yes, this is one hundred percent truth, the whole story.

A Skeptical Scientist Reports His Own Praying Mantis Encounter

The following account comes from M.J.:

I have long been suspect regarding alien claims. In addition, I'm a scientist, so, you know, a bit Cartesian.

On January, 2007, my life changed at around 2:00 A.M. Briefly, I heard a two-tone very loud digital sound, awoke, thinking there were children outside being loud. I awoke and found a large creature next to my bedroom window and bed. It looked to me like a cricket, of course, like a praying mantis, by your description. I had an odd calm feeling of recognition. I told it, oddly, "It's about time you're here." I then "saw" some sort of craft, two discs rotating around each other, it gave a clear impression of orange, yellow and red, radiation and glowing, rotating around a common axis. Over an hour and a half passed by the time I looked at my clock again.

Under Surveillance by Praying Mantises Since He Was Eight

The account was received February 17, 2009:

I was talking to my fiancé about an incident that happened to me in 1977 when I was around eight years old. I was brought to a large place where there were many people and many small gray aliens. I even remember facing a small blonde-haired girl about my age, and I told her telepathically "as I was pushed along" not to be afraid.

I was transported or astral projected to some kind of game being played between two small grays. They were using telekinesis to push a fireball back and forth in the air in an indoor tennis-type court that had what looked like lava or fire at its edges. Eventually, one of them lost the link and was thrown by the fireball into the fire, and he perished in the flames. I felt the telepathic cheer in my mind as if someone scored a touchdown in football—and no remorse.

My praying mantis figure was very kind to me. He urged me to stay calm and telepathically reassured me everything would be all right. My right eye was removed by a device that came down from the white ceiling. I started to really panic but the "mantis" kept me from really freaking out. Then it was replaced.

The "mantis" also told me telepathically that I was a special person who would really make a difference here on earth. I am now forty-four years old and have made no real significant differences to the human race. I think he may have just wanted to reassure a child at the time.

When the "mantis" first appeared he was at the foot of the hospital bed I was strapped to. I could only at first see an outline, but as I watched, it blended from the white wall into a brown cloaked figure.

I have retained one thing from my encounter. I still have the power to see major global disasters before they happen. I only report them to either my fiancé or my close family members, because I know anyone else would just call me crazy. But now they believe me for the most part. Because when I see something clearly and tell them, it always happens.

I also had a small round device placed into my right thumb. I was told by the "mantis" if it ever came out I would die. Well, I ripped it out of my thumb two years or so after feeling I had been visited again and again, just not remembering anything those further times. I knew—that's all I can say. I don't believe they can find me now, and I have led a productive life since the age of eleven without them "finding" me and not feeling "watched " anymore.

Reptilians and Serpent People

Since witnesses began openly reporting sightings of aliens in the late 1940s, there have always been those who describe the beings as somewhat reptilian in appearance. Actually, since the earliest reported encounters in ancient times, humans have claimed frightening meetings with reptilian creatures that have most often been described as demons.

Nearly every culture has its legend of a handsome seducer, who, once he has selected his human female victim, reveals himself to be a grotesque reptilian or amphibian entity. Such legends are by no means relegated to ancient times or the Middle Ages. Even today, whether stories involve creatures from other worlds or local lakes and rivers, reptilian monsters have never left our folklore.

Impregnated by the Bufeo Colorado

Scott Corrales' online *Inexplicita: The Journal of Hispanic Ufology* (February 22, 2010) carried the account of a woman from Peru who claimed to have been inseminated by the "Bufeo Colorado," a legendary elemental who inhabits the Amazon River. Scott mused that accounts, such as this one, which originated in Mazan, Peru, are frequently found in the Latin American tabloid press, "but in an age when we freely admit the possibility of insemination by 'space aliens,' who can deny the likelihood that river elementals are up to no good?"

It is said that when the Bufeo Colorado falls in love with a girl, it adopts the appearance of a very handsome man and appears at a party where he can find his beloved and woo her. Once the girl has been ensnared, he lavishes attention upon her, visits her every night, gives her presents, and leaves before daybreak. Within a short period of time, the girl longs to be by the riverside all the time. Eventually, she throws

In recent years, there have been increasing numbers of reported interaction with reptilian aliens. (**Art by Ricardo Pustanio**)

herself into the water to be with the Bufeo Colorado forever.

In this case, Reyna Yumbato Huamán, 28, traveled from the region of San Jose in the district of Mazán to the Loreto Regional Hospital, where she was admitted due to complications with her pregnancy. She said that she had three children. Those pregnancies caused her no problems but the current one had brought intense pain, accompanied by dreams in which she allegedly saw the "Bufeo" impregnating her.

The staff gynecologist, Beder Camacho, said that this case was a "threatened abortion" and that "Bufeo legend" was clinically impossible. The woman, he said, received treatment and no longer had any problems. (Translation © 2010, S. Corrales, IHU. Special thanks to *Planeta UFO*)

Meeting the Lizard Man Face-to-Face

In June 2005, a thirteen-year-old boy was out hunting with his grandfather near Big Springs, Texas. While he was following a flock of quail, he became separated from his grandfather. The teenager, carrying his shotgun and a bag of shells, injured his leg when he scraped it on a rock. As he paused to tend to the wound, he heard ducks nearby and knew that there had to be a pond to wash his cut. After arriving at the pond he began to apply water to wash off the blood from the scratch on his leg, when he suddenly heard a splashing sound.

He looked up and saw a man opposite him on the shore, leaning over to drink from the pond. It only took him a few seconds to realize that this was no ordinary man. This man had scales and a lizard's head.

The teenager was petrified. He stood there frozen, watching the strange creature drink, when all of the sudden the lizard man jerked its head up and turned to look at him. It eyed the witness for what seemed like hours, then jumped in the water and began swimming toward the boy. The boy managed to shoot three shells at the lizard creature, then ran from the area as fast as he could (http://naturalplane.blogspot.com /2009/12/humanoid-cryptid-enc. 12/18/2009).

Encountering a Reptilian in an Old Basement

Chris Holly related the following incident to the authors.

REAL ALIENS, SPACE BEINGS, AND CREATURES FROM OTHER WORLDS

Years ago my good friend told me her brother had a terrible experience while working in New York City. He lived on Long Island and often worked in the city. He was a construction worker who specialized on renovation projects of old city buildings. But he was so traumatized, he refused to return to the job or go back to the city for any reason.

The event occurred while he was working on a very old building that still had the original freight elevator. The construction crew was using it to carry material to and from the basement of the building to the different floors they were working on. The basement was deep and old. It bottomed out many floors below street level into the bowels of New York City's underworld.

None of the work crew on this project liked this old iron-gated ancient elevator or the old deep basement so many levels below the modern-day street level. It was creepy and dank, but it seemed to be the only place to store tools and materials needed for the renovation. A few times each day someone from the work crew would need to go into the desolate basement area.

This one fateful day it was my friend's brother who needed to take the old iron-gate elevator to the basement in order to gather a few tools he needed. He rode the slow elevator to the last level in the building and pulled open the old iron gate. As he stepped out into the open space of the basement, he quickly caught some movement out of the corner of his eye over in the corner of the room. He moved a few feet closer to see what it was and stood frozen in horror at what stood looking back at him from the corner of the room.

There stood a creature about six feet tall with legs and arms in a human form but a head like a lizard or reptile. It had a snout and large mouth with fang-like teeth and red eyes that were long, thin slits. The thing was greenish-gray in color and did not wear any type of protection or clothing. It had a slight odor, like that of a musky animal. It stood there simply looking as shocked as my friend's brother.

The man quickly backed into the elevator and, with heart beating hard against his chest, fought to get the iron gate closed while punching buttons until the old freight elevator started its climb back up to the top floors of the building. By the time he made his way back to the work crew he was hysterical and so terrified that the other men in the work crew thought that he was having a heart attack. When he was able to calm down enough to tell them what he had seen, the men did not know what to make of his claims—however, not one of the men would volunteer to go see if the thing was still there.

Those who have encountered reptilian entities have reported the gamut of alien types, ranging from lizard-like beings to creatures more humanoid in appearance. (Art by Ricardo Pustanio)

I do not know the particulars of how the event ended that day. I do know that a search was made of the basement and nothing was found, except for the old tunnels and large water pipes that connected the building to the old city infrastructure. That maze exists under the city to this day.

My friend's brother went home early that day and to my knowledge has not returned to New York City since. I dare say I do not blame him.

The Horrible Reptilian Thing That Lay in Wait—in My House

By Chris Holly

When I was sixteen years old, I lived through an awful event. Someone or something broke into the house my family and I lived in on the south shore of Long Island. The thing laid waiting inside my house for me or one of my family members to return home.

I was first home that day, and thankfully had friends with me. The thing inside my home began turning the inside lights on and off, which we noticed before entering the house. We were frightened and called for help, waiting outside in my car, watching as whatever was in the house tried to bait us inside by flickering lights on and off. As we sat locked inside my car in the front of my house we could hear the thing howling and growling in rage at not being able to get us to enter the house.

When help did arrive, we found this creature had placed rope and knives around the house. It had also clawed the walls and ripped some of my clothing to shreds, spreading the pieces all over the house. And it left a pungent odor of sulfur and rot that lingered for days after.

This thing came back later and tried to enter my neighbor's house as their seventeen-year-old daughter sat watching television in their family room. It tried to get to her by ripping a large window out of the house, frame and all. The mother was at home and did get a look at the arm of the thing as it frantically tried to reach into the home. She described it as having snakelike skin on what looked like a semi-human arm. Its hand had long claws instead of nails. This family also reported a horrible odor coming from the creature.

No one ever was able to explain who or what this intruder was.

Generally, an encounter with a reptilian entity inspires terror. (Art by Ricardo Pustanio)

I received an e-mail from a reader asking me if I had any information on a strange incident he recalled seeing on television years ago. It was such an odd happening that he could not understand why he could not find any reference to it anywhere when he clearly recalled what he had seen.

My reader recalled the event being reported on the news that the emergency services in the city were receiving frantic calls in the middle of the night about strange lights in the sky around New York City. Enough calls came in for patrol cars to be sent out to investigate. Someone who had called in the incident brought a camera and was able to film part of this incident.

The film shows an area that appeared to be on the side of a brick apartment building, maybe fifteen stories tall. If I can remember correctly, there was a bridge nearby. Anyway, the person behind the camera caught something moving on the side of the building, and I think they even heard it growling or making some sort of noise. It lurked back in the shadows. As they zoomed in, you could see a not very human-like creature literally scaling or clawing up the side of the wall.

Whatever it was, it was not any animal that I had ever seen before.

Just like the reader who sent me the inquiring e-mail, I remembered this TV report from the very late '80s or early '90s and always thought it odd that nothing else was ever reported about it.

Chris Holly Wonders What They Are Making on Plum Island

Plum Island has been a top secret lab of extreme experiments located right off the main body of Long Island. Only those with top-secret clearance are allowed near the place. The only method of getting to it is by boat. It has been an ongoing shop of horrors that needs to be taken seriously and considered highly dangerous.

Recently a report was released that a strange body was found on the coastal shore of Plum Island. The body was reported to be a male about six feet tall with extremely long fingers! The report was quickly pushed under that infamous rug with all the other odd things heard about once and then never again. Plum Island is, and has always been, a very secretive place. When I hear of events like the ones above I realize they seem simply too incredible to believe. If I had not lived through an event that involved an unknown creature, I would have a far more difficult time digesting them. I did, however, deal with a very strange creature and do believe something very odd is going on out there.

The question to ask is who or what are these creatures that some of us encounter? What is it that walks with us on planet Earth? Alien visitors? Beings from another dimension that slip into our time and space? Experiments that have gone wrong at dangerous locations like Plum Island? What in the world are these creatures?

For now reports of strange beings will continue to be looked at with skeptical eyes, leaving traumatized witnesses all over our planet. All we can do is pay attention to our surroundings and try to live our days in a safe and healthy way. What else can we do? It is impossible to say who will be the next to find they are looking into the eyes of one of these mysterious creatures of the unknown!

An Enigma: Are Reptilians the Overlords of Earth?

Perhaps the reason why the most frequently reported UFOnauts resemble reptilian humanoids is that this is exactly what they are: highly evolved members of a serpentine species. Perhaps what some researchers term "the overlords" are themselves reptilian or amphibian humanoids.

Some theorists feel that there is strong evidence to indicate that millions of years ago, extraterrestrial super-scientists first attempted to accelerate our reptilian predecessors on this planet.

An archaeological enigma with which we dealt extensively in an earlier work—*Worlds before Our Own*, by Brad Steiger (Putnam, 1978; Anomalist Books, 2007)—has to do with what appear to be humanoid footprints that have been found widely scattered around the planet—but especially in the southwestern United States—in geologic strata that seem to date from a *quarter of a billion* years ago.

This bipedal creature with a human-like stride left footprints, shoe prints, and sandal prints on sands of time that have long since hardened into rock. This bipedal being apparently vanished and left a baffling riddle that has had scientists scratching their heads for decades—for only four-legged, belly-sliding, tail-dragging amphibians were supposed to be around at that time.

In the majority of alien encounters, the contactee characterizes the aliens' skin as hairless and gray or grayish-green in color. Their heads are described as large and round, with faces dominated by extremely large eyes, very often with snakelike, slit pupils. They are said to have no discernible lips, just "straight lines" for mouths and nostrils nearly flush against their smooth, hairless faces. On most occasions, the witnesses comment on the absence of a nose or noticeable ears.

Two Theories of Reptilian-Amphibian Humanoids Walking the Earth Millions of Years Ago

There are two popular theories regarding the interaction of the reptilian or amphibian species that walked the Earth millions of years ago:

1. Terrestrial amphibians evolved into a humanoid species that eventually developed a culture that ran its course—or was destroyed in an Atlantis-type catastrophe just after it began to explore extraterrestrial frontiers. Today's aliens, then, may not be extraterrestrials, but, rather, the descendants of the survivors of that terrestrial amphibian culture returning from their space colony on some other world to monitor the present dominant species on the home planet.

2. The UFOnauts reported by many contactees, abductees, and other witnesses may, in fact, be a highly advanced amphibian or reptilian culture from an extraterrestrial world, who evolved into the dominant species on their planet millions of years ago—and who have interaction in Earth's evolution as explorers, observers, caretakers, and even as genetic engineers.

As early as 250 million years ago, these reptilian star gods may have visited our planet and began efforts to accelerate the evolution of certain terrestrial amphibians and reptiles in an attempt to replicate their own culture on Earth. As many theorists have noted, there has been more than enough time to have had two or more evolutions on this planet. There could have been an evolution of reptiles, followed by one of mammalians.

Two Scientists Create a Humanoid Dinosaur

In the early 1980s, Dale Russell and Ron Seguin of Canada's National Museum of Natural Sciences at Ottawa created an imaginative model of a humanoid dinosaur while fashioning a life-sized reconstruction of *Stenonychosaurus*, a small, meat-eating dinosaur that had lived near the close of the Age of Dinosaurs.

As more researchers have become intrigued with reports of alien entities, some have suggested that these beings have been visiting our world and have interacted with our species for thousands of years. (**Art by Ricardo Pustanio**)

The February 1982 issue of *Discover* magazine relates the process used by Russell and Seguin. Using *Stenonychosaurus* as the model, they fashioned a creature that might have evolved—rather than dying out with the rest of the dinosaurs—sixty-five million years ago.

The result is a strikingly human-like four-and-a-half foot creature that Russell called a "dinosauroid." It has a large brain, green skin, and yellow, reptilian eyes. In other words, from our perspective, it looked very much like the reptilian aliens described by contactees and abductees.

Nature has a way of filling unoccupied ecological niches with whatever evolutionary lines are available, and Russell reasoned that if the mammals had not been around to evolve into intelligent beings through the primate line, the reptiles might have done it instead.

"There is a trend in evolution toward increasing brain size," Russell said, and the trend includes dinosaurs as well as mammals."

Some witnesses to alien activity have described interaction with reptilian humanoids that, with minor cosmetic surgery, could pass for humans. (*Art by Ricardo Pustanio*)

In the May 1982 issue of *Omni* magazine, paleontologist Russell made a few additional speculations that caught the attention of those who researched alien UFOnauts.

Russell stated that they could have given their dinosauroid some ears, since they are proven useful for directionality. They did not do so, he admitted, because it made the creature look too human. Regarding the question of a possible language, Russell theorized that the sounds the dinosaur man would make would be "avian rather than mammalian. Their voices would be more birdlike than grunting."

Interestingly, so many men and women who have claimed to have encountered reptilian aliens have said that the entities made sounds that were suggestive of whistles, hummings, chirps, or musical notes—all uttered in a birdlike, singsong manner.

Russell remained very cautious in his suppositions about Dinosaur Man and emphasized that he was largely playing "let's pretend" when it came to speculations about the imaginary creature's familial and societal evolution. About the only time that Russell became dogmatic was when he declared that intelligent mammals and intelligent reptiles could *not* both have developed on the same planet. Mammals, he stated in the *Omni* article, would have remained at the level of insect-eating rodents. Humankind would never have existed, because the dinosaurs would have preempted the niche that has been occupied by mammals. Russell, of course, speculates as a cautious scientist.

It would seem that our planet is old enough to have witnessed the evolution of intelligent amphibians or reptilians, followed by intelligent mammalians as a successive dominant species, especially if both species had help from the star gods, intelligent members of a species of reptilians that created a technology that made them master creators of the universe.

Our Reptilian Brain

Dr. Paul MacLean, one of the world's most eminent brain researchers, theorizes that during the course of evolution humans have acquired three very different brains:

1. A primal mind from reptiles
2. An emotional mind from early mammals
3. A rational mind from more recent mammals

The very center of our brain is composed of the primitive reptilian brain, largely responsible for our self-preservation.

The late Dr. Carl Sagan made extensive use of Dr. MacLean's theories in his bestselling book, *The Dragons of Eden*, and the triune brain hypothesis has stimulated numerous scholars in the social sciences. Is it really too much to theorize that there may be an even more dramatic, more *direct*, reason for our reptilian heritage?

As we have mentioned, in our more than fifty years of investigation into the UFO mystery, we have often heard those human participants of close encounters with alleged UFOnauts describe the aliens as reptilian-appearing humanoid beings with disproportionately large heads. The serpent people may have an extremely large brain capacity, perhaps 3,000, or even 4,000 cubic centimeters compared with humankind's average of 1,300 to 1,500 cubic centimeters.

Did the Star Gods Take Part in Creating Humans?

British author Brinsley LePoer Trench was intrigued by the fact that the Hebrew version of the Old Testament employs the word "Elohim" instead of "God" in Genesis. Elohim means many gods, rather than a single deity. "Let us make man in our image," the Elohim say in 1:26, "after our likeness."

Although conventional biblical scholars hold that the word Elohim is used to represent the many facets of God in his relationship to Earth as its Creator, Trench insists that one has missed the entire point if one considers the various names of Jehovah as simply representative of different aspects of the same deity. He points out that the Hebrew language is carefully and efficiently constructed to denote gradations in meaning by the structure and form of the words employed.

In Trench's view, the Jehovah are members of a family, or even a race of godlike beings, much as the Olympians in ancient Greek myth. Or, as we might further define the concept, an extraterrestrial race of beings thought by primitive humankind to be gods from the stars:

> Jehovah, then, is a name adopted quite recently, as such things go, to designate the People from Somewhere Else in space who deliberately created, by means of their genetic science, a race of hu-man beings peculiarly adapted to perform certain definite and predetermined functions," Trench tells us.

> In addition to their adapting human life-forms to their own ideas they probably also make special adaptations of plant and animal forms.

Trench is quick to assure his readers that the existence of many deities (or extraterrestrial beings) need in no way alter one's belief in a single Universal Spirit, who set the cosmos into motion and who will continue to nourish life through eternity. He is merely postulating that there may well be many godlike beings in an ever-expanding scale of grandeur.

Throughout history, these godlike beings have been referred to as the "serpent people"; for example, Quetzalcoatl, the "feathered serpent," the culture-bearer of the

Aztecs, was said to have descended from heaven in a silver egg. The awesome respect that our ancestors had for these wise serpent-like humanoids could surely have been retained in our collective unconscious today.

According to some star god theorists, whether the extraterrestrial super-scientists were reptilian, mammalian, or other-dimensional intelligences beyond our present awareness, when they came to this blue-green oasis in space they viewed it as a great biological laboratory. And they must also have computed that it would take the slow process of evolution a hundred million years to alter a species or to develop a new one.

For whatever reason, they seem to have made a decision to accelerate the normal process of evolution on Earth and to fashion a rational creature before its time.

The Americas—A Genetic Laboratory

The puzzle of humankind's origins becomes even more difficult to solve because the genetic engineering efforts of the reptilian overlords apparently did not always achieve the exact results that they wanted.

Archaeological digs in the United States have discovered skeletal remains of primitive men and women more than seven feet tall, hominids with horns, giants with double rows of teeth, prehistoric people with sharply slanting foreheads and fanged jaws, pygmy cultures far smaller in height than any known groups that exist today.

In the vast majority of encounters, reptilian humanoids inspire an intensification of the universal fear and loathing that most humans experience when seeing earthly reptiles. (*Art by Mike Mott*)

As more and more such anomalous discoveries are unearthed in the geologic strata of our continent, it begins to seem as though the Americas in particular might have served as some vast living laboratory in genetic engineering. Perhaps all of these apparent stops and starts and dead-end spurts of the *Homo* family tree might really have been the failures and near successes of ancient extraterrestrial scientists. Even the monster-humans of mythology might have been abortive genetic experiments that were rejected by the serpent people as they sought to achieve *Homo sapiens* in the field laboratory of Terrestrial Biology 101.

Robert Morning Sky's Story of Bek'Ti, Survivor of the Roswell Crash

As we carry on our research, we always find it of great interest when we find contactees from other cultures who tell of their interaction with the serpent people and other aliens.

Robert Morning Sky says that his grandfather was one of six young Native Americans who witnessed the now-famous Roswell flying saucer crash in 1947. When the young men reached the site, they found one being who was still alive. Gently, they took the star visitor back to their camp and nursed him back to health. They kept him carefully hidden, for they were well aware that the military men they saw searching the crash area were anxious to capture the survivor.

Morning Sky's grandfather said that they called the stranger from the stars "Star Elder" out of respect. As time passed, the alien revealed his name in their language. He was called Bek'Ti, and through many nights of talk around the campfire, he revealed the history of humankind and the planet Earth.

In the late 1960s when Morning Sky started college, he found himself doubting some of the things Bek'Ti had told them. He enrolled in Religious Studies, an independent study program that would allow him the opportunity to research ancient records, thinking this way he could prove or disprove the many stories of Star Elder.

Morning Sky submitted a thesis entitled "Terra, a Hidden History of Planet Earth" that summed up his three years of research. Within days, his professor had labeled the thesis "a work of blasphemy and outrage!"

Having had no success in the academic field, Robert Morning Sky decided to try his luck with a number of UFO organizations and researchers. The general response was to label the work "the stuff of myth and legend of Native Americans, not suitable to the serious study of scientific phenomena."

Such total rejection made him angry. For nearly thirty years, he refused to pick up a book on UFOs or the paranormal.

Circumstances changed right before Robert's grandfather died. He made Robert promise to try once more to tell the history of humankind and Earth as revealed by Bek'Ti. This would be a great challenge, for while the story tells of the creation of humankind and clarifies its place in the universe, the story is both exciting and frightening. Morning Sky knew that the human species' nobility and pride would be injured. In Bek'Ti's stories the abduction phenomena and the attending gray beings are integral parts of humanity's history, explained against a framework of the star beings' purposes for humankind.

"In our galaxy are billions of star beings," Morning Sky said. "Many races are descended from many life forms: reptiles, insects, dinosaurs, birds, and other life forms humankind cannot begin to imagine."

Bek'Ti had said that one of the oldest star races in this sector of the universe is the reptilian Ari-An, which descended from dinosaur ancestors in the star system of Orion. "Ruled by Queens," Bek'Ti said, "they created the most powerful empire in this galaxy. Ari-An warriors were unmatched for ferocity and bravery, and the Ari-An Empire was unmatched in power and size. Enemies became obedient servants of the reptilian queens' throne. In this way, the Ari-Ans eliminated resistance."

Robert Morning Star believes that millions of years of countless battles between various extraterrestrial races continue to this day. He details the evolution of humankind and Bek'Ti's history of Earth on a number of websites, including http://www.canadastreetnews.com/terrapapers.htm.

Robots
and Androids

In response to modern society's desire for increased leisure time and labor-saving mechanisms, science is going to great lengths to create robots capable of performing distasteful and tedious tasks. Many technologists dream of fashioning economical robots to relieve the housemaker of the depressing drudgery of housework, to aid in mowing the lawn and pruning fruit trees, or to take over tedious production- line tasks so that factory workers can be given more challenging work. There is no reason, these futuristically-oriented technical wizards argue, that robots cannot serve humankind in performing mundane chores as well as sampling Martian soil and probing Jupiter's atmosphere.

We might look with caution on entrusting high-level positions of responsibility to robots, which might turn traitor, recalling "Hal" in Arthur C. Clarke and Stanley Kubrick's film, *2001: A Space Odyssey* (1968). On the other hand, films have taught us through the years to have complete confidence in such loyal friends as Gort from *The Day the Earth Stood Still* (1951, 2008) and R2-D2 and C-3PO from the *Star Wars* films (1977–2005). Currently, moviegoers must learn to distinguish the good *Transformers* (2007) from the bad ones. From the exploratory perspective of 2011, it does not really require a far-forward leap of the imagination to conceive of an advanced alien culture that might find it far easier and more desirable to send their robots to explore and evaluate environments on other worlds than go themselves. Some researchers have theorized that the grays might actually be remarkably advanced robots, rather than living creatures.

At any rate, it seems that not all UFO occupants are humanoid, for many reports have indicated that the crew of these mysterious vehicles have appeared, in form and demeanor, to be robots rather, than men.

In certain close encounters, the extraterrestrial appears to be a very efficient robot, far beyond Earth's present scientific accomplishments. (*Art by Ricardo Pustanio*)

An Encounter with Giant Robots in France

One such sighting took place in France at St.-Jean-en-Royans on January 9, 1976.

Jean Dolecki was driving his pickup truck on a side road about seven o'clock that evening when he suddenly saw a brilliant ball in the dark night sky. It was Friday night, and Dolecki was hurrying home after a tiring week at work. He paid little attention to the ball in the sky—at first.

Suddenly the object began to lose altitude, and it appeared to be coming toward him. He slowed his truck down and watched it closely. He studied the object with great care, drawing upon the skills of observation his years as a Baltic seaman had taught him.

"I had the impression that it was a big globe," he told investigators. "It shone as if it were covered with silver paper. I certainly thought it was going to crash onto my truck or right in the middle of the road." He hit the brakes on his truck and pulled over to the right side of the road. He was fascinated by the light of this strange globe. He turned off the ignition, but as he left the truck he decided to leave the lights on to get a better look.

The brilliant globe landed in a field about 340 feet away. He estimated the craft to be forty to fifty feet in diameter, with the upper part slightly larger than the bottom. "I don't believe the machine rested on the ground," he commented, "because the bottom emitted a bizarre light which did not diffuse around."

Dolecki admitted that he was afraid, and he said that he retreated several feet. He did not get back into his truck, however. Apparently his fascination was stronger than his fear.

Next he saw a door open at the upper part of the sphere; he estimated that it was about six and a half feet high. Three forms, dressed in silvery suits, appeared at the doorway. "They were not men! I can assure you of that," he emphasized. Rather, according to Dolecki, "They were robots! Giant robots! Of the same height as the door." Their motions were stiff, with no suppleness, as they rapidly descended from the UFO. "I saw then that they had small legs, and, for arms, telescopic poles that made me think of fishing rods." He portrayed their heads as "square," but found it difficult to come up with a more detailed description.

The three robots moved away from the craft, but only a short distance. They walked like mechanical toys, in jerks and jumps, wagging their arms—or poles—up and down as they moved along. "I did not move—I could barely breathe! I could only think that the headlights on my truck, which I left on, would surely attract them. But, no, they didn't even notice me," Dolecki said.

About ten minutes passed, and the robots reentered the craft. The door closed and, with the exception of those on the very top of the sphere, the lights went out. The craft then took off at a fantastic speed.

"I got back in my truck. Once in the cab, I made the sign of the cross. I was trembling so, I couldn't get started. But there was only one thing I wanted to do—to get home," Dolecki admitted. When Dolecki finally arrived home, he found that his wife and daughter had started dinner without him. They could tell by his manner that something was wrong. Dolecki told them the entire story. In spite of their skepticism and their efforts to calm him down, he telephoned the local police to make a report of the evening's events.

The police investigator was far less skeptical than Dolecki's family. The officer no longer made jokes about UFOs. The possibility of visitors from other worlds had been serious business to him since a day in 1974 when two of his men witnessed a mysterious object over St. Nazaire-en-Royans. In addition, the investigator, brigade commander for that region, had a longtime acquaintance with Dolecki and knew the seaman was a sensible man, not prone to hallucinations or likely to perpetrate a hoax.

Further investigation of the incident revealed that the reported sighting took place just a short distance from the Alphonse Carrus farm. On that evening, January 9, the Carrus family had been watching television. On several occasions during the evening, numbers and letters had flashed across the screen; periodically, the picture disappeared. The time of the sighting reported by Dolecki and the time of these strange interruptions coincided. However, another farm family near the site of the incident noticed nothing unusual on their TV screen during that same period of time on January 9.

The investigation of the Dolecki case seems to end here, but there were other similar reports in that region of France—so many, in fact, that local authorities say that they became overwhelmed with the calls and that there were too many to record accurately.

A Giant Dressed in a Suit of Brilliant Color

One such case, involving ten-year-old Jean-Claude Silvente, who lived near Domène, had

Creatures that appear to be a remarkable blend of a machine and biological entity have been reported. (**Art by Ricardo Pustanio**)

taken place a few days earlier, on the nights of January 5 and 6. The lad told of a "giant" dressed in a one-piece suit of brilliant color that came out of a mysterious flying machine on January 5th. The boy was terrified. Twice the giant had walked toward the boy, who ran away as fast as he could.

On January 6, the flying saucer came a second time, and landed in the same spot. This time Jean-Claude had brought others to witness the spacecraft and its giant occupant. Those with Jean-Claude for the encore performance included his mother; his seventeen-year-old sister, Elaine; and a friend of Elaine's, Marcel Solvini, twenty years old.

The machine, a sphere that looked like "a big red headlight," came down from the sky as though it were going to land on the four of them. The witnesses fled the scene and reported the object and the occupant to the authorities.

Strangers with Metallic Voices

Sporadic sightings occurred in Argentina and Chile through the remainder of July and August 1968. Then, on September 2, after numerous citizens witnessed a UFO over Mendoza and two employees of a casino claimed to have confronted UFO occupants, Jose Paulino Nunez, an employee of a distillery, allowed his contactee story to be released.

Enrique Serdoch, chemical technician of the company laboratory, served as spokesman for his friend, who had kept silent for over a month. Fellow employees Alberto Gonzalez, Roberto Micelatti, Carlos Wengurra, Hugo Torres, Enrique Aporta, and Ricardo Schmid testified to their companion's sobriety and responsible nature. They, too, had been aware of Nunez's encounter with the UFOnauts, but they had respected his decision not to report the incident. At the time Serdoch received permission to release Nunez's story to the press, the contactee was in the hospital undergoing surgery, but this was unrelated to his UFO encounter.

Here is Nunez's story as related by Serdoch:

At 1:15 in the morning on the last Sunday in June, Jose found himself on the beach allotted to the analysts. The section is very dark, and the only people who are found there are guards. As Jose came down from a fuel-oil tank, he encountered two people who he thought were guards. He was soon set straight in this regard when the strangers showed him a spherical object some thirty centimeters in diameter, in which colorful figures moved.

"As Jose watched, he saw people who walked about as if they had been filmed by a hidden camera. The depth of the images was clear. The dress and activity of the animated figures within the sphere did not offer anything special to catch his attention.

"Then, enigmatically, one of the strangers asked Jose: 'Do you know these people? They were like you. Many more will be like them. Many people in the world will see the same thing that you have seen. We will talk to you about this again. If you should mention this to anyone, be certain that it is only with responsible people.'"

And, Serdoch told the assembled journalists, Nunez could not explain how he suddenly found himself back at the laboratory.

"What's wrong with you?" Alberto Gonzalez, Nunez's partner, asked.

"Why?" Nunez wondered. "What *seems* to be wrong with me?"

"You are white as a sheet of paper!" Gonzalez told him.

Nunez began to weep, and it was nearly an hour before he could compose himself enough to return with Gonzalez to the oil tanks on the beach where he had encountered the two beings. Nunez said that the strangers' voices had been metallic, as if they had been emitted from the interior of a telephone receiver. Their suits had been one-piece, similar to the kind worn by frogmen.

Authorities in Argentina were kept busy early in September. First two casino employees, Villegas and Piccinelli, claimed contact with UFOnauts. Then Nunez authorized a friend to tell his contact story. As if this were not enough, several employees of the Belgrano Railroad reported that the lights of the station house had been mysteriously turned off at 3:30 A.M. on September 1. At the same time, the owner of a Renault automobile experienced a loss of power to his vehicle as he drove in that vicinity.

Some believe that cyborgs would be the perfect solution to survey other worlds in advance of biological explorers. (**Art by W. Michael Mott**)

A Most Unusual Visit by a Humanoid Gardener

UFO sightings have been taking place worldwide constantly since 1947, but for some reason humanoid sightings have been rare in Belgium. But a visitation is said to have been witnessed by a twenty-eight-year-old Belgian, who is identified simply as V. M., and who is said to live in the industrial city of Vilvorde, just a few miles northeast of Brussels.

A very strong wind blew over the area on that particular night in December 1973. V. M. awoke at about 2:00 A.M. to go to the toilet, which is located in a small courtyard next to the kitchen of his duplex. He tried to be quiet so as to not wake his wife, and he took a flashlight so he would not have to turn on the bedroom light. Just as he got to the kitchen he heard a noise outside the house that sounded like a shovel falling. He then noticed a greenish light filtering into the kitchen. As he looked out the window he saw what he described as a glow that reminded him of the diffused illumination of an aquarium. His garden was usually in complete darkness at that hour.

He continued to watch the garden area, and soon saw a small being dressed in a glowing uniform that was the source of the light. The humanoid seemed to have normal arms and legs and was of about average build. The uniform looked as though it had been coated with a metallic paint, and the creature's head was covered by a bowl-shaped transparent helmet with a hose leading down to a rectangular backpack that covered his back from shoulders to waist. The clothing, so far as V. M. could see, had no buttons, zippers, or seams. Around the alien's waist was a belt that emitted a red light from a square box where a buckle would normally be. The humanoid was in the garden, and he was operating a device that looked like a vacuum cleaner or a mine detector. He moved the object back and forth over a pile of leaves V.M. had left in the garden. The little being seemed to have difficulty walking. He swayed from side to side, and he bent his knees slightly as he walked.

Suddenly V.M. turned his flashlight on the garden area, and the humanoid turned around. Apparently he was not able to turn his head, because he moved his entire body. It was then that V. M. could see that the strange little visitor had a dark complexion. V. M. could make out neither a nose nor a mouth, but he clearly saw small pointed ears and yellow, oval-shaped eyes. The humanoid's eyes were huge and shiny and circled at their edges in green. The pupils were also oval and black.

The strange little visitor looked at V.M. straight in the face.

Then, with the detector in one hand, he raised his other palm and made a "V" by spreading the index and middle fingers. With that sign, the little humanoid walked over to the garden wall and proceeded to walk right up one side, like a housefly, and down the opposite side.

In a few moments an aura of white light appeared on the other side of the garden wall. A sound was heard above the breeze as a circular object climbed a short distance into the air. The object hovered for several minutes, making a noise like a cricket.

V. M. described the upper portion of the UFO as phosphorescent orange, topped by a transparent dome, which emitted a greenish light. The lower half of the craft was claret red, and three lights could be seen in the lower portion, one blue, one red, and one yellow. An insignia was visible on the platform that ringed the UFO, and V.M. described it as a black circle crossed diagonally by a yellow slash that resembled a lightning bolt. In a short time the UFO rose vertically into the air, then shot skyward, leaving a glowing trail behind it. Soon it was nothing more than a speck in the wintry sky.

V. M. did not receive any verbal or telepathic messages from the humanoid, nor did he experience fear. He also told investigators that he did not feel the least bit upset by the whole event. In fact, he soon went back to bed and slept soundly for the rest of the night.

The Highway Was Suddenly Blocked by Cylinder-Shaped Beings

James Townsend, a nineteen-year-old radio announcer for station KEYL of Long Prairie, Minnesota, was driving west along Highway 27 about four miles east of

Long Prairie on October 23, 1965. The time was approximately 7:15 P.M. As the young man rounded a curve at a good speed, he was confronted by a tall object standing in the middle of the road.

Townsend slammed on the brakes, and his 1956 model car skidded to a halt, twenty feet before what he described as a rocket ship. Immediately, the motor, lights, and radio of his car stopped functioning, although the scene in front of him remained illuminated.

The rocket ship was shaped like a cylinder with a blunt taper on one end, and although it was only about ten feet in diameter, Townsend estimated that it was over thirty feet in height. Realizing the consequences of such a find, the announcer's immediate thought was to knock the thing over and retain the ultimate evidence of his sighting. But the engine of his car would not turn over when he turned the key in the ignition.

The tall, narrow craft looked unstable, sitting on protruding fins in the middle of the highway. Townsend thought that he might be able to tip the craft by hand. Jumping out of the car, he moved closer to the apparently deserted rocket. The young announcer was astonished when three incredible objects moved out to meet him: small cylinders moving on spindly legs no thicker than pencils.

Several UFO investigators have maintained that some kind of extraterrestrial intelligence has sent thousands of robot probes to test the environment of Earth. (*Art by Ricardo Pustanio*)

Although they had no distinguishing features, Townsend described their movements to be more like those of creatures than of robots.

Townsend had no idea how long he and the objects confronted each other, but he said it "seemed like forever." Then he retreated to his car, and the little cylinder-like beings moved toward their craft. They disappeared in a brilliant beam of light that glared from under the main section of the rocket. While the radio announcer watched through the windshield of his car, the light became even more intense, as a humming sound increased in volume until it hurt Townsend's eardrums. Then the rocket lifted off, reminding the radio announcer of a glowing flashlight, and the landscape around Townsend was lit "as bright as day." Once the thing was airborne, the light in the bottom went out.

As Townsend watched the vehicle ascend into the sky, the lights and the radio of his car came back on. The car, which he had been unable to start only minutes before, began running by itself. Townsend later said he was sure he had not touched the starter, even though the car had been left in "Park" and the ignition remained on. Unnerved, Townsend turned his car around and sped back to Long Prairie. Without hesitation, he went directly to the sheriff's office to report what he had seen. With considerable effort, Sheriff James Bain and police officer Luvern Lubitz were able to calm the agitated young man. Both of these men later confirmed that Townsend had obviously been badly frightened. Sheriff Bain described him as "excited, nervous, and shaky," while Lubitz observed that he was "not his natural color."

The first thing Townsend said to these men was: "I am not crazy nor am I drunk; neither am I ignorant." Bain and Lubitz agreed with the statement. Everyone who knew James Townsend testified that he was a levelheaded, hard-working young man, not known to drink. Furthermore, he was a man of strong religious convictions, and had spent the summer as a counselor at a Bible camp.

Both men at the sheriff's office listened to Townsend's story and acted immediately. Although Townsend was reluctant to return, Bain and Lubitz convinced him that he should take them to the spot where he had seen the strange craft. When they arrived at the spot, all three of the men observed a peculiar orange light moving in the northern sky. Lubitz thought it was "more yellow-white than orange, flickering off and on and leaving a sort of yellow trail."

A close inspection of the spot where the rocket ship had been standing showed that three strips of an oil-like substance had been left on the pavement. They were three feet long and four inches wide, running parallel to the highway. Lubitz said that he had never seen anything like those marks left on any kind of surface. After puzzling over it for some time, the men returned to Long Prairie. Sheriff Bain could not determine any reason for the marks that had been left on the pavement. They had to be related to the fantastic tale that Townsend had told him.

Shiny Metal Robots Bathed His Truck in Light

Eugenio Douglas, a truck driver, told correspondents of the Monte Maix, Argentina, *El Diario* that on the evening of October 18, 1963, on the highway approaching Monte Maix, his entire truck was enveloped by a brilliant white light. Douglas had only a few moments to speculate about the source of the light before his entire body began to tingle like "the peculiar sensation one gets when his foot goes to sleep." Douglas lost control of his truck and drove it into a ditch. The beam seemed to "shut itself off," and, as his head cleared, the truck driver saw that the brilliant light had come from a glowing disc, about twenty-five feet in diameter, which blocked the highway. As he sat in disbelief, he was approached by "three indescribable beings," which he could compare only to "shiny metal robots."

The terrified truck driver vaulted from the cab of his vehicle, fired four revolver shots at the approaching creatures, and began to run wildly across the open fields. When at last he stopped to catch his breath and look over his shoulder, he saw that the "indescribable beings" had boarded the disc. He was soon to learn that the "robots" had not taken kindly to being fired on. After the disc became airborne, the luminous flying object made several passes over the head of the truck driver, now desperately running for his life. "Each time the disc swooped down on me," Douglas told newsmen, "I felt a wave of terrible," suffocating heat and that prickling sensation."

Eugenio Douglas ran the entire distance to Monte Maix. When he arrived at police" headquarters, he was in a near-hysterical state. As painful evidence of his incredible encounter, his body bore several weltlike burns, which the medical examiner had to admit were "strange and unlike any that I have ever seen." *Accion* reporters from Agrega, Argentina, published an interview with the doctor, in which the physician conceded that he could "offer no explanation for the burns."

That Metallic Creature Could Really Run Fast!

Jeff Greenhaw, police chief of Falkville, Alabama, responded to a call about a spacecraft with blinking lights. Greenhaw reported that while he did not find a spaceship, he did see a metallic creature in the middle of the road! "I got out of my patrol car and said, 'Howdy, stranger,' but he didn't say a word. I reached back, got my camera, and started taking pictures of him," Greenhaw said.

The creature ran when Greenhaw turned on the blue light atop his cruiser. "I jumped into my car and took off after him, but I couldn't even catch him with my patrol car. He was running faster than any human I ever saw."

Greenhaw described the creature as robotlike, silent, and without features on its face, but with a pointed head.

Greenhaw was plagued by a series of personal misfortunes after his celebrated encounter, including the destruction of his home by fire. To him, it was becoming obvious that "someone" wanted him to leave Falkville, but he refused to do so. He reiterated his belief that the picture he took was that of a being from another planet.

Against Her Will, She Stopped for a Metallic Hitchhiker

Mrs. Robinson was driving from Huntsville, Alabama, to Tifton, Georgia, on the afternoon of October 19, 1973. She stopped at a service station for gas and the customary service check, then drove on at high speed.

As she came within twenty minutes of Tifton on I-75, the systems in her car all mysteriously ceased functioning. It was about 3:30 in the afternoon, she recalls, when she glided off the interstate highway without power steering or brakes.

As the car came to a stop on the shoulder of the highway, Mrs. Robinson began to experience what she described as a "strange" feeling. She sensed something weird, and when she turned toward the window next to her, she beheld it: a four-foot-tall metallic "man" with a suit that resembled pewter. There was a "bubble" on his head that contained no features except two rectangular slits for eyes. Although she could not bring herself to look directly at the creature, Mrs. Robinson stated that if the window had been down she could have touched the being.

The bizarre entity walked in front of the car and around to the back, then disappeared. Mrs. Robinson estimated that this took about five or six minutes. She felt that the creature was more robot than human, because of its mechanical motions.

Given our own rapid advances in robotics and artificial intelligence, it might not be so difficult to envision that our first onslaught from outer space could be in the form of highly efficient robots. (*Art by Bill Oliver*)

When she was certain that the creature was gone, Mrs. Robinson got out of her car, fearful that it might blow up. She raised the hood to attract passing motorists, and smoke came billowing out. When a wrecker towed her car to a garage, about one and a half hours later, it was noted that the heat under the hood had been so intense that the engine had almost melted. The metal was so hot "it looked like you could poke your thumb through it." It was another hour and a half before the engine had cooled enough for the mechanic to work on it.

Investigators noted that Mrs. Robinson had not been drinking and was not taking tranquilizers or drugs of any type.

Abducted from His Home by Robotic Beings

On February 12, 2001, Raymond L., 33, left his work as a cook at an all-night truck stop in southeastern Georgia at 3:30 A.M. When he returned to his apartment, he decided to watch a little news and have a beer to unwind. It had been a very busy night, and he knew that he was "past exhausted" and wouldn't be able to fall asleep right away.

He was flipping channels, trying to catch the scores of various basketball games when he suddenly became uneasy. It felt to him as though someone had entered the room and was standing directly behind his easy chair.

The next thing Raymond knew is that he was lying in his bed on top of the spread and blankets. He glanced at the bedside alarm clock and saw that it was nearly time for him to be getting ready to go to work. Raymond swung his feet over the edge of the bed. He had no memory of walking from the chair in the other room to his bedroom. He still heard the television set, and he became even more puzzled. He never left the set on or the lights burning in his small living room. But then he had no idea of now he had gotten into bed. Or how he had slept for so many hours without awakening.

When he went into the bathroom to relieve himself, he noticed that his shorts were on backward. And, even though he was still wearing his shoes, his stockings had disappeared. While he was puzzling over his vanishing socks and his backward underwear, Raymond became aware of painful burning sensation on his back. Turning so he could view his back in the mirror, he saw strange red lumps between his shoulder blades. And, when he stripped to take a shower, he saw three red spots in the shape of a triangle on the back of his left leg.

It was while he was taking a shower that Raymond had flashes of memory of someone ushering him into another kind of shower that sprayed him with an acrid-smelling liquid. And then he remembered the four smallish gray beings that had appeared beside his easy chair and shone a light in his eyes. He had awakened on a transparent, free-floating tabletop with the aliens bending over him with shiny instruments in their hands. Two much taller beings came toward Raymond from some other room and seemed to give him a quick examination. He remembered the tall aliens looked much more human-like than the smaller beings.

"There was something about the small gray creatures' movements that made me think that they were some kind of robots," Raymond said. "Their large black eyes seemed almost metallic or like some solid crystalline substance. Even the manner in which they handed the instruments to one another seemed mechanical. They seemed to have no feelings, emotions, or even a normal kind of awareness of me or even each other. It was as if they had been programmed, somewhat in the manner of a computer, to perform their assignment. Thankfully, they put me to sleep before they made those cuts or burns or whatever those markings were on my body."

Raymond said that he has not shared his experience with any of the staff at the truck stop where he is still employed. He expressed strongly how his fellow cooks and the waiters and waitresses would assess his mental faculties. "They would never stop teasing me," he said, so he resolved that he would never tell them of his UFO abduction.

Raymond approached us after one of our lectures. "I don't know what happened to me or why," he said, and he asked us if we had ever heard such a wild story. We told him that the scenario was quite familiar to us.

"Every night when I drive home after my shift, I keep looking up at the sky," Raymond said. "I know they marked me for some reason that I surely cannot understand—and I hope they never return to check me out again. I don't care if they never return my stockings to me. They can keep them."

Hairy Dwarves and Bigfoot Types

On July 31, 1966, a number of Erie, Pennsylvania, residents felt certain that "something" from another world had landed on the beach at Presque Isle Peninsula Park. Pastor Robin Swope, the "Paranormal Pastor," has always been fascinated by this strange case and the claims of young people who attest to encountering a monster at the scene of a UFO landing. He has shared his research for this book.

Close Encounter at Presque Isle

Presque Isle State Park is Pennsylvania's most frequented State Park. With over seven miles of beaches on Lake Erie, it is usually jam-packed through the warm summer months. It was on the hot and humid night of Sunday July 31, 1966 that six people had come from nearby Jamestown, New York, to enjoy a refreshing visit to popular Beach 6 along the northern edge of the park. Present that night were: Betty Jean Klem (16); Douglas J. Tibbets (18), who had come with Gerald LaBelle (26); and Mrs. Anita Haifley (20) who brought her children, Sandra (2) and Sara (6 months). Somehow during the evening their car became stuck in the sand in the east end of the beach parking lot. Try as they might, the men could not dislodge it. Others who were leaving the park offered to take Mr. LaBelle to find someone to tow his car.

Within a few minutes after Mr. LaBelle left, park policemen Ralph E. Clark and Robert Loeb Jr. drove by the beach and noticed the trapped car. Stopping at the car they promised that they would return to render assistance if Mr. LaBelle could not find anyone to help by the time they returned.

It was around 9:30 P.M. when something strange happened. Mrs. Klem recounts the events, which were recorded in the August 1, 1966 *Erie Times News*:

We were sitting in the car waiting for help. We saw a star move. It got brighter. It would move fast, then dim. It came straight down. The car vibrated. I know we saw it; we had taken a walk in that area earlier. There was nothing between those trees then. All of a sudden it was just there.

According to the witnesses, the object was mushroom-shaped with an oval structure rising out of a narrow base. There were also lights on the back of the object. The UFO approached from the north and briefly hovered over the area before landing. Ms. Klem said a beam of light came from the craft and moved along the sand in a straight line as the craft disappeared behind the tree line: "It lit up the whole woods in the path. It wasn't like a searchlight. There was light along the ground, along the whole path." She said the light did not waver but continued to extend into the woods.

About this time the patrol car with officers Clark and Loeb returned as promised to offer assistance. Immediately, the light from the object was extinguished. The officers approached the car. The occupants told the patrolmen about the craft that landed in the woods, and Mr. Tibbets offered to show them the general area where he thought it had touched down. With Douglas Tibbets leading the way, the officers walked off, leaving the two young women and the children alone in the car.

Moments later, as Betty Klem sat behind the steering wheel of the car, she saw something emerge from the woods where the three men had just entered. She thought at first that it was an animal, but then she saw the shape and size of it. It was a dark, featureless gorilla-shaped humanoid about six feet tall. Although not in the initial 1966 report, Mr. LaBelle stated in an interview on June 12, 2008 that the girls told him that it circled the car from a distance and then came close and clawed at the car. Screaming in utter terror Ms. Klem immediately sounded the car horn frantically. The creature then sluggishly moved back into the brush, and the UFO rose and took off with incredible speed to the north just minutes before Mr. Tibbets and officers Clark and Loeb came running to aid the women.

The men felt such a sense of urgency, that one of the officers lost his service pistol in the sand but decided to forgo the seconds it would take to recover it because he felt they should reach the distressed women as soon as possible.

Both girls were in a state of panic, and it took them a while to calm down. Mrs. Haifley was in such shock that she refused to talk about the incident. Ms. Klem initially refused to talk about it also, but after she left the location, she began to relax and told the tale. The officers noticed scratches on the car where the being had made contact, and the four adults in the party insisted that the marks were not there before the visit to Presque Isle. The four adults and two children were taken by patrol car to the Park Ranger station where they detailed the story. According to Mr. LaBelle, more heavily armed patrolmen came in to assist with the situation and they refused to let the young people go back to their car to retrieve their belongings until morning.

By 7:00 A.M. the following morning, the State Police and United States Air Force were involved. Officers Paul Wilson and Robert Canfield investigated the area and found unusual impressions in the sand. About 350 to 400 yards away from the car two diamond-shaped imprints about eighteen inches wide and six to eight inches deep were discovered ten to twelve feet apart. In another place, three impressions were

Many researchers have posited that there is a connection between Bigfoot and UFOs. Some "Bigfoot hunters" have observed the giant forest creatures surrounded by beams from extraterrestrial vehicles and have witnessed Bigfoot being deposited in the woods by beings from alien spacecraft. (*Art by Bill Oliver*)

found in a triangular pattern about eleven feet apart from each other. Finally, Officer Wilson found tracks that led in a straight line to the car. They were conical shaped, about eight inches wide, five to seven inches deep, and five to eight feet apart. Officer Wilson reported that he did not believe that they were footprints, but they seemed to have been made by some kind of heavy object or objects.

Sometime during the morning, Air Force investigators took a statement from Ms. Klem. Soon after the incident she was also interviewed by a psychiatrist who affirmed that the testimony she gave about the incident seemed to be true and not due to illness or delusion.

In the days following the sighting, Beach 6 was filled with UFO enthusiasts waiting to catch a glimpse of what those young people had seen that Sunday night, but no one else had a sighting.

This report has been told many times over the years. Various versions add or subtract some details. The memory of this incident lingers on in the small port town of Erie, Pennsylvania and every once in a while it is discussed by the local media.

This was the case with a report from Brian Sheridan, a local ABC news reporter, who did a piece on the incident in 2005. Right after this report Mr. Sheridan received a phone call from a local truck driver, Mr. Kim Faulkner. He claims that this incident was nothing more than a hoax. Mr. Sheridan interviewed him and found his story to be legitimate. He did a follow up report "UFO at Presque Isle, Part 2—Solved!"

Mr. Faulkner allegedly confessed to having unintentionally caused the event by letting loose an eight-foot tall hobby balloon that August night in 1966. The videos can be viewed on Mr. Sheridan's YouTube page, http://www.youtube.com/user/brian sheridan.

After seeing these videos, I contacted Brian Sheridan and asked if he thought Kim Faulkner's story was just a way to get his fifteen minutes of fame. He wrote me back saying,

> … His brother confirmed the story Faulkner told. He was also the only one who contacted us after the first story ran who did not claim they did it as a hoax or prank. It made the most sense of anyone we talked with at the time. Other people just wanted to brag. Faulkner didn't even want to go on camera. He just called to fill me in on the story after his brother told him about the first piece we aired.

The balloon that Mr. Faulkner launched as a child on that July night was purchased through an ad in *Boy's Life* and can still be purchased today. It is a red and white striped tissue balloon that is very fragile. Somehow this child's balloon had made the journey northwest from the Faulkner home to land on Presque Isle and caused all the commotion. The teenager's overactive imagination turned an eight-foot striped children's balloon into a large flying saucer. In Mr. Sheridan's video, a park policeman who was at the scene seemed to doubt the veracity of the teenagers as well, chalking up the encounter to youthful naïvete.

So it seems the case is closed. We have a cause and a park policeman from the original report who seems to doubts the veracity of the sighting.

Or is it really closed?

Something just didn't sit right with me about the report. According to the report, the wind carried the balloon northwest from Mr. Faulkner's boyhood home on 1817 West 22nd street (almost at the corner of 22nd and Greengarden Avenue), a distance of almost three miles.

I have spent many hours in the outdoors of Erie County and frequently observed weather patterns. I could be mistaken, but it seemed that during the summer months the winds primarily came from the southwest, which would have driven the balloon to the northeast—not the northwest.

So I went back to the newspapers of July 30th to August 1st of 1966 and found that the indeed the winds off lake Erie at the time were coming from the southwest, varying from nine to twenty-two knots. I contacted local meteorologists to make sure I was not mistaken, and I was told that unless there was some strange pattern that was not recorded then, the balloon would definitely have traveled to the northeast. That means that the path of Mr. Faulkner's balloon would be in the opposite direction from the location of the encounter.

Now I am by no means calling into question either the reporting of Mr. Sheridan or the veracity of Mr. Faulkner's statement. But it just doesn't seem possible that the Faulkner balloon was the source of the encounter on July 31, 1966. Leaving out the wind trajectory alone, the report does not jibe with the details of the report. Even given gullibility or mass hysteria, it would seem to be a far stretch that the sighting of a nine-foot children's hot air balloon would cause the frenzy that ensued on Beach 6 that hot July night.

There is also the physical evidence that verified some of the details of the witnesses' account—classified as evidence by professional policemen and the United States Air Force, and not just park police, who usually have far less experience in such investigations. Many articles I have read about the case cast a shadow on the young people of the story, making them out to be naive teenagers out for a late-night romantic interlude at a secluded location who, when caught, make up a fanciful story. Mr. LaBelle even told me he was accused of fabricating the incident by using a flashlight and playing tricks on the passengers in the car for a practical joke. But the facts show nothing of the sort. And Mr. LaBelle, thirty-two years after the fact, holds to the story.

Also, it is a little-reported fact that the UFO was observed by more than these five individuals at Beach 6. In the August 1, 1966 *Erie Times News* a side story is included with the initial report of the UFO at Presque Isle. It is titled "Eight Others See 'UFO' in Erie Area." These eight individuals saw a UFO the same evening between the hours of 8:00 P.M. and midnight.

Steve Lupe was on Beach 2 with a group of friends that evening and he, along with three others, spotted an object hovering near the Peninsula around 8:30 P.M. French exchange students Helena Roche and Alain Orcel, who lived at 412 Frontier Drive, about a mile away from the beaches of Presque Isle, saw a lighted silvery object flying low that evening. Stephanie Mango of 4704 Homeland Ave. also saw it, saying it flew silently at treetop level. She has stated that it was round and of an undistinguishable color. She saw the object move toward the beach and then change course and move toward Erie's bay area where it disappeared from sight.

Sue Karie, Linda Henderson, and Janice Dickey were sleeping out in the yard of the Karie household at 1012 Shenley Drive when, around 11:00 P.M., they spotted the silvery object flying from south to north. Ms. Karie reports that "I heard a whistling sound and looked up and saw an object moving north as high as The Boston Store (about 138 feet). It was very low, and we all ran and got into the station wagon and locked the doors when we saw it." She said at first that it looked like a star, but it kept fading in and out. It was round and saucer-shaped, and they saw it for a minute before it disappeared.

So it appears we do not have to rely solely upon the testimony of those who encountered the UFO close-up at Beach 6 that July evening in 1966. I think the evidence is irrefutable that something landed on Presque Isle that night. And it seems to have had an occupant that looked very much like a Bigfoot-type hominid. What it was is as much a mystery today as it was back in the summer of 1966.

Do UFOs Bring Bigfoot Creatures to Earth?

Reports that combine UFO landings and alien Bigfoot-type monsters are not new, and UFO researchers and cryptozoologists have been arguing about the possibility that the giant hairy humanoids are in some way connected with flying saucers. The question boils down to a few basic theories. Some say the monsters are the missing link between man and ape, while others insist that they are pets or laboratory animals from UFOs used to test the environment of the Earth, preparatory to landings by the actual aliens. Still others speculate that the monsters themselves are the aliens.

Bigfoot from a UFO Attacks Couple in Turkey

A bizarre incident occurred in Turkey on the night of May 14, 1964. Ismir Bey and his wife were driving along a road that ran adjacent to a railroad track when they spotted a spinning disc in the sky, described by them as "the size of a house." Suddenly, it seemed to plummet out of the sky, and as the two watched, the object crashed to the ground in a burst of flames. This is unusual—one of the few reports of a UFO crashing. And, to add a bizarre twist, the Beys reported that a huge, hairy monster scrambled out of the wreckage and headed for safety by walking toward the Beys! In an effort to protect his wife, Bey flung himself at the beast, and was rewarded for his valor by being pounded into unconsciousness. Mrs. Bey reported that the monster did not try to harm her, but flung her husband in the direction of the railroad tracks and ran off into the nearby woods.

> In an effort to protect his wife, Bey flung himself at the beast, and was rewarded for his valor by being pounded into unconsciousness.

Ten-Foot Ape-Like Monster Outside of Portland

In late May 1971, Joe Mederios, the maintenance man for a trailer court near Portland, Oregon, was watering flowers in front of his office. As Joe looked across the road to a cleft in the bluff, he saw what he later described to a sheriff's deputy as "a ten-foot tall, gray-colored monster with arms that hung quite low." He further described the creature as looking like an ape, and stated that it definitely was not a bear.

The next day, while Joe and three Portland businessmen were speaking, they spotted something in the field below the hundred-foot rock bluff. They told authorities that the monster came down from the rocks and walked through the open field across from the trailer court. The creature stopped by an eight-foot tree, which gave the foursome an accurate way of estimating the monster's height at about ten feet. It is interesting to note that Joe Mederios claimed in the report that he had purposely not mentioned the event of the previous day to the other men, "in fear that I'd be called a nut."

More reports were filed in the same part of town, and two nights later Richard Brown, a music teacher at the junior high school, was returning home to the trailer court with his wife when the headlights of their car caught the outline of a figure standing near an oak tree in the field. It was about 9:30. Brown raced to their trailer and returned with his hunting rifle, which was equipped with a four-power scope.

The creature remained in the area and did not move for about five minutes, giving Brown a good opportunity to study it through the scope. His description seemed to substantiate the report made by Joe Mederios, but, like so many of the elusive Bigfoot-type monsters, it disappeared from the area, and no conclusions were ever made about the creature.

UFO Sighting Brings Bigfoot Visitor

Mr. and Mrs. Philip Arlotta had just stepped into their car, preparing to return home after visiting relatives in Greensburg, Pennsylvania. It was ten o'clock on the evening of May 18,1975. Mrs. Arlotta had started the car's engine when she noticed a strange object just ahead of them in the sky. She mentioned it to her husband, who suggested that if she turned off the engine, perhaps they could hear something.

The object was moving from east to west, and they described it as being about as big as holding a cantaloupe at arm's length. It was oval and bright yellow near the bottom, but darker near the top. In the darker section were six square windows, which showed a red light behind them.

The Arlottas heard no sound, but they continued to watch the object for about a minute before calling their relatives to join them. Five people witnessed the strange craft as it appeared to move toward them at what they estimated was an altitude of less than one thousand feet. The craft suddenly made an abrupt right-angle turn to the left, and at the same time it changed color from yellow to orange before it began gaining altitude. The witnesses followed the object in the car. As they continued down a back road, they noticed that the object appeared smaller and brighter orange in color. As they turned onto Route 130, they lost sight of the UFO, but they estimated that they had watched it for about four minutes.

The next evening at about dusk, a lone motorist was heading to his home in Jeanette, Pennsylvania. When he entered that same area on Route 130, something caught his attention just to his left. He stopped his car and backed up. At a distance of a few hundred yards he noticed what he thought was a German shepherd—although it was running with movement that was more like that of an ape than a dog. After a few seconds, the creature stood up on its hind legs and ran like a man into the woods. The being was described as seven- or eight-feet tall and covered with thick, black

Could Bigfoot be an animal domesticated by aliens on other worlds that is then sent to Earth as a kind of laboratory rat to test the environment? (Art by Ricardo Pustanio)

hair. The witness, who had been a Bigfoot skeptic in the past, suddenly found himself an instant convert.

The UFO sighting on the first night and the creature sighting on the second night took place within one quarter mile of each other. This was the first creature sighting in this area in more than a year.

The Dwarves of Lovers Lane Earn the Title Los Diablillos

Scott Corrales, editor-publisher of *Inexplicata—The Journal of Hispanic Ufology* states that the ominous name of La Matanza ("the slaying") has been given to diminutive, dark olive green-colored beings that appear after dark at a beautiful country retreat known as Finca del Duque. The beings have been reported on many occasions by visitors to the area.

Locals and visitors alike agree that the dwarves known as "los diablillos" (the imps) are also very real. At first it was believed that the short-statured creatures were attracted by the activities of couples using this remote area as a lovers' lane. Further cases have shown that any human presence after sundown produces the appearance of the "diablillos."

"In November 1992," reports *Inexplicata*, "an anonymous resident of Tenerife drove to the lovers' lane one evening with his girlfriend. From within the car they were able to hear the sound of branches rustling as if being parted by someone. The driver looked out the window and allegedly saw a creature some three feet tall and covered in grayish or black fur all over. The entity carried a staff or rod of some sort in its hand, and was described as having 'cat-like eyes.' The couple left the area in a hurry, refusing to return ever." (http://inexplicata.blogspot.com.)

Strange Creatures in Brazil

Dr. Rafael A. Lara is the co-founder of the Institute of Hispanic Ufology. He has authored numerous articles about "high strangeness" events in Brazil. Recently, Scott Corrales summarized the result of certain aspects of Lara's research.

It should be noted that Brazil is one of the largest countries in the world, spreading over an expanse of 8,511,965 square kilometers. It is the fifth largest nation after Russia, Canada, China and the USA. Perhaps what makes Brazil such rich hunting grounds for UFO reports and sightings of alien creatures and humanoids is that most of the country is made up of unexplored jungles. Great savannas and a number of mountain ranges remain enveloped in dense vegetation. And then there is the vast swampland of the Amazon, which harbors what seems like a separate universe of creatures and beings—some of them known to science and others known only through tradition and sporadic sightings made by explorers and aborigines.

Dr. Lara's research shows that two groups of entities should be taken into consideration:

1. Strange beings linked to the apparition of UFOs (bearing in mind that Brazil has the greatest number of sightings, landings, contacts, abductions, etc., in the world)

2. Giant cats, winged creatures, hairy humanoids, dwarves, sea monsters, gigantic serpents, etc., which steer the investigator toward a cryptozoological or paranormal explanation

Dr. Rafael Lara has amassed thousands of reports in which one can find a direct relationship between UFOs and strange creatures. However, in the report for *Inexplicata*, Lara limits the scope to only the most relevant cases and those that present the most varied morphology. We have selected only a handful from Dr. Lara's files—those that principally illustrate the range of dwarflike beings and other aliens that seem to enjoy frequenting the skies and landscapes of Brazil.

Strange Creatures Associated with UFOs That Have Visited Brazil

Pontal, November 4, 1954— Jose Alves was out fishing when he met three diminutive creatures wearing white outfits and tight-fitting helmets. The entities had emerged from a discoidal vehicle some three to four and a half meters in diameter.

Porto Alegre, state of Rio Grande do Sul, November 10, 1954—An agronomer from Porto Alegre allegedly saw two strange-looking men emerge from a discoidal structure some five meters in diameter. The figures were human-like, with long hair, and wearing coveralls.

Quebracoco, October 10, 1957—Spanish naval officer Miguel E. and a companion witnessed a giant UFO whose portholes offered a glimpse of seven small humanoid beings, no larger than children, with long hair and clad in luminous outfits.

Cruzeiros, state of São Paulo, August 14, 1965—A railroad worker in Rio de Janeiro, Joao do Rio, had a close encounter with a creature measuring approximately seventy centimeters in height, with large luminous eyes recessed in a large bald head. The singular creature had emerged from a flying saucer.

São Joao, state of Pernambuco, September 10, 1965—Antonio Ferreira, a forty-five-year-old farmer, was startled to behold two disc-shaped objects no larger than one and a half meters wide and sixty centimeters thick, which disgorged two small beings of a generally human-like appearance, beardless, with reddish-brown skin and waxen complexions. They wore form-fitting outfits.

Alto Dos Cruzeiros, Canhotinho Municipality, Pernambuco, October 26, 1965— Jose Camilo Filho, a fifty-six-year-old mechanic, witnessed a UFO flying over his neighborhood. Minutes later, driving along a highway, he noticed two small beings, less than a meter tall, with brown skin, wrinkled and furrowed faces "like those of old men," white hair on enormous heads, and slanted eyes. One of these dwarves wore a pointed cap made of dark material, and had a patchy beard. Both creatures wore silvery outfits and luminous belts.

The hairy dwarves reported in the proximity of UFO activity could be the aliens themselves or mysterious multidimensional beings drawn to the area by the event. (*Art by Ricardo Pustanio*)

Agua Branca, Quipapa, state of Pernambuco, February 25, 1966—Maria Marluce and Maria Marilucy de Silva had an encounter with a disc-shaped object about three to four meters wide. Standing beside the object was a humanoid being about two meters tall surrounded by six small, large-headed creatures in coveralls. The creatures appeared to be talking among themselves.

Alexania, Brasilia, December 27, 1967—Wilson Placido Gusmao, a resident of Brasilia, ran into five humanoid entities shortly after having witnessed a UFO. The creatures belonged to the oft-described category of long-haired blondes, with porcelain-like complexions and shimmering, form-fitting outfits. One of the humanoids, presumably the leader, had a light in front of him.

São Paulo, August 25, 1968—Maria Jose, a worker at Serafin Ferreira Hospital, was startled to encounter a strange woman with fair skin, wearing a light blue cloak over a silvery coverall with tight cuffs. The entity floated into a pear-shaped object, which hovered less than a meter off the ground.

Preitetura de Lins, state at Sao Paulo, October 2, 1968—Turibio Pereira witnessed five identical beings, which appeared to be repairing a luminous object that rested on the ground. The witness described the creatures as being about one and a half meters tall, wearing radiant blue tunics, which covered their head, arms and torso. Two other individuals wore brilliant red tunics.

Bairro Pinheiro, Pirassununga, February 6, 1969—Several residents of this community reported seeing the descent of a large luminous object around 7:30 A.M. Two small men emerged from the object. Witnesses described them as having slender lips, flattened noses, dark eyes with neither pupils nor whites, wearing aluminized outfits that covered their bodies.

Colegio Batista, March 22, 1969—Two girls observed a small man wearing a helmet, which projected a greenish glow through bulbs shaped like "cat's eyes." Two hours earlier, the girls had seen a strange luminous object, which appeared to be following them.

Itaperuna, December 20, 1971—Manuel da Silva Souza witnessed a strange discoidal object on the ground. Standing beside it were four diminutive humanoids with bare round heads, with no apparent mouths, but thin noses and slanted eyes. They were wearing emerald-colored clothing.

Baldim, Minas Gerais, July 12, 1972—Joao Alves Sobrinho saw two small beings along the roadside, wearing light-colored, long-sleeved clothing, standing beside a dark object with seven luminous sources outside it.

Londrina, January 5, 1973—Joao Marques reported seeing an airplane-sized object, which released a humanoid occupant, dressed all in white, wearing a helmet. The creature made a friendly gesture at the witness.

1973 (precise date and location unknown)—Bernadette Gomez, adopted daughter of General Moacyr Ulloa, was taken to some location in the Amazon where she witnessed an extraordinary blue light that produced a normal-sized entity wearing a tight-fitting outfit. The creature cured the young woman of a disease known as Mal de Chagas—a fact corroborated by Santa Lucia Hospital in Rio de Janeiro.

Paciencia, Rio de Janeiro, September 15, 1977—Antonio La Rubia allegedly encountered an unknown object resting in the middle of a football field. Upon turning away from it, he was faced by three robot-like figures measuring about 1.20 meters. Each robot had antennae, which extended over its head like a football, in the center of which was a band of tiny transparent mirrors in shades of blue. The robots had thick bodies and appendixes resembling arms that narrowed at the tips. (La Rubia compared them to an elephant's trunk.) The witness claims he was abducted by these creatures. (http://inexplicata.blogspot.com/4/15/2008).

Frightening Encounters and Acts of Hostility

On June 29, 1964, a Wellford, South Carolina, businessman was returning home from Atlanta, Georgia, when he claimed that a UFO swooped down over his automobile, burned his arm, and blistered the paint on his car roof.

"I saw the object so clearly, I believe that I could build one of the things," B.E. Parham said. "It came hissing down and stopped in the air right over my car [as he was traveling on the highway]." Parham said that he had been driving about sixty-five to seventy miles per hour, but when the UFO approached, the car's engine began to slow down.

Parham, the district manager for a Spartanburg, South Carolina, firm, said the object made three passes over his vehicle. It had come from high altitude, then swooshed over the top of the car, leaving behind an odor something like embalming fluid. Parham said the UFO gave off "terrific" heat and had a number of holes and openings in its sides.

When an Air Force analysis of the incident stated that Parham had been "frightened by ball lightning," the indignant businessman fumed that there was not a cloud in the sky when the object swooped down on him. In addition, he said, "Lightning wouldn't rotate at the top and the bottom, as this object did. Lightning would not stand still."

Parham also felt that he had more than adequate physical evidence to substantiate his claims: His arm was badly burned. Secondly, the paint on the roof of his automobile was blistered and coated with an oily substance. And, thirdly, the radiator and other parts of his late-model car began to deteriorate as a result of the close approach of the UFO.

While Camping in the Everglades
a Beam of Light from a UFO Blinded Him

On April 12, 1965, James Flynn, a rancher of East Fort Myers, Florida, claimed that a beam of light shot out from the bottom of a UFO and struck him in the forehead while he was on a camping trip in the Everglades. Flynn said that he had instantly lost consciousness.

When he awakened, he was blind in his right eye and left with only partial vision in his left eye. Dimly, the rancher could see a symmetrical circle of scorched ground where the cone-shaped UFO had been hovering and the top branches of a number of cypress trees had been burned.

Not until Flynn walked into the office of Dr. Paul Brown did he realize that he had been unconscious for twenty-four hours.

Dr. Brown was very concerned about his patient's loss of vision. Due to hemorrhaging in the anterior chamber of the eye, Flynn's right eye looked like a bright red marble. His forehead and the area around his eyes were inflamed and swollen. He was almost completely blind.

Because of the rancher's solid reputation, his story of being struck down by a ray from the interior of a UFO made the national wire services. Skeptics might not consider the physical evidence of the scorched cypress and the burned circle of grass as proof of the UFO's hostile intent, but the fact remains that James Flynn was left with cloudy vision in his right eye and a depressed spot of about one centimeter in his skull above the same eye.

Shocked, but No Burns

On April 24, 1966, Mrs. Viola Swartwood was admitted to Memorial Hospital in Auburn, New York, for treatment of electrical shock after a UFO swooped down over the automobile in which she had been riding. Physicians at the hospital said that Mrs. Swartwood's right side looked as if it had been subjected to an electrical shock, but she had no burns on her body.

Nearly Blinded by a Flashing Light

Mrs. Charles F. Jones was nearly blinded by a brilliant light that flashed from a UFO as she was driving her grandson to a doctor's office in Merrill, Michigan, on April 25, 1966.

Describing the object as triangular, with no wings and a "stubby nose," Mrs. Jones said the UFO "seemed to be gliding southeast, but then it stopped over the trees and dropped straight down."

Object Left Them with Strange Blisters on Their Car

On June 17, 1966, at 12:30 A.M. on the outskirts of Georgetown, a UFO splattered a late-model car with some unknown chemical substance when a Brampton, Ontario, housewife was traveling along Highway 7. She reported that a bright, round, silver object suddenly flew in front of her car and crossed from right to left.

"I watched it for about three seconds," said the woman [who wished to remain anonymous]. "The object itself looked huge. I stopped my car, and another car in front of me stopped as well. The experience frightened me dreadfully."

The next morning when she and her husband examined the car in the sunlight, they were shocked to find the entire front part of the roof blemished by tiny, hard, transparent chemical blisters. The unknown substance had set rock hard in thousands of bubbles over the fenders, grill, and hood.

Globes of Light Transformed into Five Alien Beings Surrounding Them

It was about 10:45 EST on March 20, 1967, when a man—pseudonymously dubbed "Mr. Rible" by Robert A. Schmidt, then secretary of the Pittsburgh UFO Research Institute—asked his daughter Jean to accompany him in the family Volkswagen. They drove to the outskirts of Butler, Pennsylvania, in the hope of glimpsing some unusual aerial light phenomena that Rible had been observing. Since they lived only a mile from a private airfield, Rible felt rather strongly about his ability to recognize lights from conventional aircraft.

Although the majority of the sightings of the Grays describe beings with mere slits for noses, other witnesses report them as having extremely large noses. (*Art by W. Michael Mott*)

They parked the Volkswagen on a back road, and after a few minutes they spotted two globes of light. The illuminated objects appeared at first to be two airplanes flying parallel to the highway, toying with the notion of landing on the road.

A short time later they gave the appearance of having done just that. Then, from a distance of about a quarter of a mile away, the vehicles came up the slope toward the Ribles at a speed of about eighty miles per hour. The Ribles, who had stepped out of their automobile for a better look at the globes of light, now prepared themselves for what seemed to be an inevitable collision with the two berserk aircraft.

The crash they expected never came, but instead the Ribles faced a challenging impact to their construct of reality.

The lights seemed to transmogrify into a semicircle of five figures, who stood just a few yards from the hood of the Ribles' Volkswagen. Both Ribles jumped back into the car, but while her father worried over starting the vehicle, Jean got a good look at the humanoids. Schmidt quotes her as describing them in the following manner:

"They looked like human beings, but their faces were totally devoid of expression.… Their eyes, if you could call them such, were horizontal slits.… I could not see any irises or pupils—just slits. Their noses were narrow and pointed, not unlike a human nose, and their mouths were slits like the eyes."

Jean said that four of the figures were about five feet seven inches in height, while the fifth was about five feet tall. They all wore a kind of flat-topped cap, and had ear-length blond hair except for the shorter humanoids, whose hair was shoulder length, causing Jean to suspect this being might be a woman.

All five of the beings were dressed alike, in gray-green shirts and trousers. The skin on their faces and hands was rough-looking, resembling "scar tissue or skin which has been severely burned."

Jean admitted that the semicircle of staring entities gave them "the creeps."

"We heard no noise in connection with either the lights or the figures," she told investigators. When their car engine started, the Ribles had to "reverse and then go forward and 'round the figures to miss them."

Under persistent questioning designed to ferret out details of the experience that might have been forgotten under stress, Jean remembered what may have been a most significant factor. As the lights swiftly approached their car, she heard a "chorus of voices" in her head, not with her ears. She seemed somehow to have sensed them with her brain.

"The voices said: 'Don't move … don't move … don't move….' They kept repeating 'Don't move … don't move,' but they dragged it out—'Dooooooonnnn't Mooooove.' When the lights vanished, the voices stopped at once," Jean said.

The UFOs' "Rainbow Lights" Became a Hot Blast Directed at His Chest

On May 20, 1967, Steve Michalak was out looking at land just north of Falcon Lake, Manitoba, when he noticed a number of geese were cackling. Glancing up, he saw two objects coming from a south-southwesterly direction. The objects were "glaring red," and Michalak stated later that he couldn't estimate how fast they were traveling. His main concern at that moment was that one of the objects was "cruising about ten feet above the ground"—and then it landed.

Michalak was hesitant to rush forward with his hands raised in the traditional salute of peace and welcome the alien crew to Earth. He watched the grounded UFO for at least half an hour before he approached it.

Michalak described the UFO as being about thirty-five feet long, eight feet high, with a three-foot protrusion on top. It appeared to be constructed of stainless steel, and the Canadian said he was awed by the most perfect seamless joints that he had ever seen. He couldn't understand how anyone from anywhere could have done such perfect work. There was no welding, no rivets, no bolting—and, although he found out later than there was a door, when it was closed he could see no sign of it. He recalled that the ship gave off rainbow reflections. When, at last, the door opened, all Michalak could see was a brilliant violet color. The ship seemed to be making a sort of whistling noise, like it was sucking in air.

As Michalak approached the object, he could hear voices coming from within the shiny shell. Being multilingual, he tried addressing the UFO in English, Russian, German, Italian, and Polish.

At the sound of his voice, the door in the side closed, and the object began moving counterclockwise. Before the UFO blasted off, jets of heat came from a pattern of holes in its side, seared Michalak's chest, and burned his clothing.

Michalak's wife told the press at that time that her husband had not been able to retain food since his frightening experience—and she also complained of the strange odor emanating from his body.

Shadowy Figures in the UFO Directed a Bright Beam of Light that Scorched a Teenager's Legs

On February 7,1969, hundreds of people in the area of Pirassununga, Brazil, watched a strange, circular aerial vehicle swoop low over the town, then settle in a nearby valley on tripod legs. Nineteen-year-old Tiago Machado was nearest to the mysterious craft when it landed, and he began cautiously walking toward the object.

As he later explained his terrifying experience to the Brazilian press, Tiago said that the craft seemed to be made of a material similar to aluminum, but it was luminous. The teenager described the rim of the UFO as "spinning around the center." According to him, "It never stopped whirling."

Tiago said that the center section of the vehicle was stationary and appeared to be constructed of a transparent substance. He could see what seemed to be shadowy figures in the cabin, gathering around what appeared to be an instrument panel.

> The next thing Tiago knew, a bright beam of light shot out from the disc and struck him in the legs. He toppled over, partially stunned and paralyzed....

The teenager said that he crept to within thirty feet of the UFO. He was aware that dozens of people had gathered on the distant hills to watch him approach the craft.

The next thing Tiago knew, a bright beam of light shot out from the disc and struck him in the legs. He toppled over, partially stunned and paralyzed, as the UFO suddenly rose into the air and soared into the sky at an incredible rate of speed. Within moments, the craft had disappeared from the view of the gathered crowd.

Tiago Machado's legs turned bright red, and it was obvious to all the witnesses that his legs were painfully swollen.

Although many thought that Tiago's injuries resembled an electrical burn, Dr. Henrique Reis, who attended to Tiago at a local hospital, found no visible wounds or marks to account for the bright red swelling.

Within a Matter of Hours after Encountering a UFO the Body of a Robust Man Becomes a Skeleton

In the December 1971 issue of the French journal *Phénomènes Satiaux* (later reprinted in the March-April 1973 issue of *British Flying Saucer Review*), Professor Felipe Machado Carrion reported on a grisly incident involving a healthy, robust farmer in Sao Paulo, Brazil.

According to Professor Carrion, forty-year-old Joao Prestes Filho was stunned and knocked to the ground by a mysterious beam of light from the sky. He managed to make his way to the home of his sister, where numerous friends and neighbors came to his aid.

Eyewitnesses later told authorities that Prestes showed no trace whatever of burns, but within a matter of hours, the once vigorous farmer began to deteriorate before the eyes of his startled friends and family.

Although at no time did Prestes appear to feel any pain, his internal organs began to show, and his flesh started to look as though it had been cooked for many hours in boiling water. The flesh began to come away from the bones, falling in lumps from his jaws, his chest, his arms, his hands, his fingers. Soon every part of Prestes' body had reached a state of deterioration beyond imagination. His teeth and his bones were exposed, utterly bare of flesh. His nose and ears fell off. His decline was so rapid, he had not even been able to reach a hospital before he was nothing more than a grotesque skeleton.

Six hours after Prestes had been struck by the terrible beam of light, he was dead. And the cause of his demise remains a mystery. During his final hours, he attempted, unsuccessfully, to communicate the details of his awful experience.

A Grim Massacre by Aliens in Vietnam

When Bill English, the son of an Arizona state legislator, was serving as a Green Beret captain in Laos from 1969 to 1971, his ten-man team was sent to investigate a B-52 bomber that had gone down in a thick jungle. According to the information that Captain English received, communications had been received from the bomber before it went down. The essence of the message was that the B-52 was being attacked by a large light, a UFO.

English and His Men Found the Plane Intact in the Jungle

There was no crushed swath of vegetation to indicate a crash landing. Only the bottom of the fuselage showed any damage. "Although the plane was intact," Captain English said, "the crew was dead. We found them sitting in their safety harnesses. They were all mutilated. Their anuses had been cored out to their colons. Corkscrew patches of skin had been sliced from their necks and jaws. Their eyes and genitalia had been removed by extremely precise surgery, yet no blood had been spilled anywhere."

Two Louisville Police Officers on Helicopter Patrol Find Themselves in an Aerial Dogfight with an Alien Craft

Two police officers on a helicopter patrol over Louisville, Kentucky, were attacked by fireballs from a UFO on a late spring night in 1993.

Officers Kerry Graham and Kerry Downs were already airborne when they received a call around midnight about a break-in. On their way to check out a possible theft, they spotted what they at first believed to be a large bonfire on the ground. But when Downs directed the powerful chopper spotlight down toward the bonfire, it looked more like some kind of balloon. Perhaps activated in some way by the brilliant spotlight, the object now began drifting back and forth as it ascended. The glowing object slowly rose until it hovered at an altitude of five hundred feet, the same height as the police helicopter. As it hovered near them for a few seconds, the officers could see that they had engaged a strange, glowing, pear-shaped object.

Then the UFO took off at a speed that Officer Downs said he had never seen before. The object circled the police helicopter twice, then began to move up on it from behind. Officer Graham was afraid that the thing was going to ram his tail rotor, so he pushed the chopper to one hundred miles per hour in an attempt to evade the mysterious pursuer. To Graham's complete astonishment, the UFO easily moved past them at an even faster speed, then shot hundreds of feet up into the air. At first, the officers were baffled by the object's maneuvers and uncertain of its intent,—and then horrified when the UFO blasted three fireballs at them.

Officer Graham expertly banked the chopper to avoid being struck by the fireballs, but by the time they circled and returned, the UFO had disappeared.

According to journalist Louise Milton, the extraordinary encounter of Officers Graham and Downs was confirmed by two other police officers who witnessed the aerial dogfight from the ground.

Officer Mike Smith said that he watched the UFO for about a minute and saw it shoot three fireballs at the police helicopter. Smith's partner, Joe Smolenski, said that the bizarre encounter over Louisville constituted the closest that he had ever come to something he couldn't explain.

There are numerous reports of balls of glowing light transforming themselves into grotesque creatures. (Art by Ricardo Pustanio)

The Mysterious Bright Neon Green Clicking Light
Terrified and Chased Two Little Girls Home from the Park

This firsthand account of a sighting is related by Chris Holly:

During my childhood I lived on Long Island, New York along the shores of a river that connected to the Great South Bay. It was a wonderful place to grow up. It was also a place of strange encounters and sightings.

A vast, beautiful park covered a huge portion of the river area where we lived. The river ran out to the Great South Bay, which went directly into the Atlantic Ocean. Because we were small community in a direct line with the ocean and sandwiched between the large park on the river side and a state-owned beach park along the land side, we were a perfect stopping off place for any air traveler. After all, we were locked between the two parks and the ocean. The only people around were the small community where I lived. We were a perfect spot to drop by for a fast abduction or an encounter with the isolated population of a small community.

The children in the area used the parks as their private play lands. We would picnic, play, and run wild along the paths and wooded areas of the park along the river. Rarely did you see adults, or many people at all—just a few kids from the neighborhood playing games. I would often set up my Barbie dolls and play for hours under a huge willow tree in the park that was the coastline of the river.

My favorite willow tree was close to a small outlet branch of the river. A swan family had made a home there, and built a huge nest on a small sand bar in the outlet. I would play for hours; the swans would float about or sit in the nest. The world seemed to be a happy place.

One hot summer day I packed up my dolls, my lunch, and some comics and, with my friend Melinda, headed out for a long lazy afternoon under that willow tree in the park. We arrived about noon, had our picnic, read a few comics and then got into some serious Barbie doll play. Everything seemed fine until it happened.

Melinda noticed it first. She stood up and looked toward the river outlet and asked: "What's that?" She was pointing toward the swans. I looked over toward her outstretched finger to see a ray of light. I stood up. The moment I did, the swans started to squeal in a strange frantic manner. I never saw or heard them do anything so frenzied before. They were flapping and trying to fly away, but were so disoriented that all they did was fly into one another.

The light was odd. It was a color I had never seen before or since. It was neon green. It was so bright it hurt to look at it. I immediately felt fear. I noticed that the rays seemed to be coming up from the river instead of down from the sky.

I became terrified and dropped my doll to the ground and whispered to Melinda, "We have to get out of here!" She backed toward me and started to reach down for our belongings. I took her hand and said, "Leave them, we'll get them later."

I held her hand, and we both started to move toward the path. We barely breathed. We moved very slowly, trying to escape the notice of that mysterious light.

We were on the path and moving away from the tree and the light when we heard a low, crisp, clicking sound. It was a sound I have heard more than once in my lifetime, but this was the first time I encountered it. It sounded like a combination of a water sprinkler that clicks across the lawn and the sound of bugs on a hot summer night. That is the best I can explain it. Click … click … click … swoosh with a hidden low chirping behind it.

The sound was coming closer and closer, the ray of light fanning out larger and larger. We were heading carefully away down the path toward the main path, which exits the park.

As we retreated, the sound of that clicking moved closer toward us through the woods, along the path adjacent to the water. We picked up our speed until we were both at a full run.

The faster we ran, the louder the clicking sound became. The ray of light was expanding, and I could now see it over the treetops. We ran as fast as we could. I can remember thinking my heart might explode, it was pounding so fast. I was terrified. Melinda was right beside me; she was sobbing in fear as we ran.

I knew we could not make it back to the main exit, and I pulled Melinda toward the fenced part of the park, which lined up along a main road back into our community. We hit the fence at a full run and scaled it with the clicking right behind our every step. We flew over the fence and tumbled onto the main road.

A neighbor lady nearly ran us over as we fell into the road right in front of her car. She slammed on her brakes, avoiding hitting us by only a few feet. She started to yell at us, but soon realized we were crying and frightened half to death. We told her something was following us in the park. She loaded us into her car and drove us to my house.

Our parents called the police and told them of something or someone chasing us in the park. My father returned to the willow tree to look around and collect our dolls and items we left behind.

When he came home, he had some of our things, but told us most of the doll items were missing or burned. By the time he arrived at the willow tree, my father saw that a large area of the ground was covered with burn marks. My Dad told us it looked as if someone had a large charcoal fire right where we were playing. A few doll dresses and items were burned and the rest were simply missing. The swans were gone, nest and all.

My parents called the police and the park many time, inquiring about what happened that day. But everyone brushed it off and tried to make it somehow our fault. They felt we were just silly kids trying to cause an uproar. They even accused us of starting the fire. Thank goodness our parents never believed that for a moment. After that day, we not allowed near the park.

What happened that day in that park is anyone's guess. I know it was an encounter with the unknown. I also know I did the right thing and ran for my life. I feel fear every time I think of that day. I feel sick to my stomach when I think about the experience as I know I came very close to dealing with the unknown and doubt I would have ever been seen again. The experience taught me to pay attention to my surroundings and heed my intuition and always outrun the clicking!

One day I may go back and look at that old willow tree one more time. Up until now I have not had the courage.

A Luminous Entity Panics Bus Passengers in Chile

On March 1, 2010, the sighting of a luminous being on the shore of the region of Tarapacá caused panic among passengers of an intercity bus from Iquique to Santiago de Chile. The encounter occurred at 5:00 A.M. when the passenger bus made a stop along Route A-1, linking Iquique to Tocopila near the Vicente Mena Beach, between Punta Gruesa and Chucumata.

Strangely, one of the female passengers who had fallen asleep during the trip began mumbling as if in a waking dream: "They're there, outside, they're here." One of her traveling companions awakened her, and once awake, the woman began screaming as she looked outside the bus. When the other passengers looked out of the bus windows, they saw a fluorescent cylindrical structure in the sea.

> Collective panic gripped the passengers, who "claimed to see a top-shaped spacecraft emerging from the sea."

Collective panic gripped the passengers, who "claimed to see a top-shaped spacecraft emerging from the sea," according to researcher Raul Rivera.

Just after everyone inside the bus calmed down enough to realize they should try to photograph the luminous structure with their cell phones, a being standing approximately three meters tall, thin, and surrounded by impressive flashes of light, began walking toward the highway, and everyone began screaming once again.

When they arrived in Santiago, the passengers of the bus went their separate ways, making it difficult for researchers Raul Rivera and Enrique Silva to undertake an investigation. They were able to locate only eight of the many eye-witnesses who saw the mysterious craft and the glowing alien.

A bizarre aspect of the investigation is that neither the bus driver nor his assistant can be found. Some witnesses claim that the driver's assistant took photos and videos of the encounter. "There are key witnesses to the case. We cannot say who they are, nor the company to which the bus belongs. I can only say that something happened, as the eyewitness accounts are in agreement. I can say that a strange phenomenon occurred at that site," Silva stated explicitly. (Source: *La Estrella de Iquique*, translated by Scott Corrales for his publication INEXPLICATA, http://www.estrellaiquique.cl/prontus4_nots/site/artic/20100325/pags/20100325001020.html?s=www.estrellaiquique.cl.)

A Very Strange Job Interview:
They Told Me It Was Time to Come Home with Them

This personal account is given by Angela Thomas:

I'm going to tell you this because it is true. It's up to you whether you choose to believe me or not. Call me crazy if you'd like, but nothing will change the truth about what happened to me in Texas. I'm talking Texas here, not some studio back lot where movies are made, but Texas.

It was dusk when I entered my apartment to find it in shambles. I thought I had been robbed. Every drawer in the house was open. My belongings and papers were scattered all over the place. I was sick with fear and anger.

I did what most people would do: I called the police to report a robbery. They told me on the phone they would send out two officers to investigate. It was almost dark, so I stepped outside into the parking lot to look for the police car. Instead, a long black car with odd looking headlights pulled up beside me and the driver rolled his window down partway.

"Are you the woman that reported a robbery?" the man asked. A strange glow appeared from within the car. Another man sat in the passenger seat.

"Yes. I'm so glad you are here," I said.

"Anyone there in your apartment with you?" he asked.

"No. My children live with me, but they are visiting friends tonight," I answered.

"I'll park the car and take a look," he said.

I stood there waiting for both men to exit the car, but they didn't get out immediately.

I glanced at the long, black car and thought how it looked out of place with other modern vehicles. It reminded me of those heavy metal cars that weighed a ton and got a few miles to the gallon. Come to think of it, it resembled a luxury car from the late 1930s or 1940s. But, what did I know? I never paid too much attention to the make and model of a vehicle, but I knew it wasn't the regular type of car that police drove. From what I could make out, the windows were tinted and the license plate had three letters on it. Both men got out of the car and started to approach me.

"We'll follow you," he said. His voice was rather flat.

"I was just admiring your car. Is that something new detectives drive these days?" I asked. No response. I headed for my apartment.

I walked into the apartment and felt sickened again from the sight. My privacy was invaded. I no longer felt secure. To make matters worse, it was going to take me a long time to get it back in shape.

I wondered what was taken, especially since the television and stereo were still there. With two detectives following me into the apartment, I felt safe enough to enter my bedroom to see if my jewelry had been stolen. The jewelry was tossed on the bed, but from what I could tell, the more valuable pieces were still there.

"I'm back here," I said thinking they would come to my room to check things out. Instead, there was nothing but silence. I could hear them moving about the apartment. Maybe they didn't hear me.

I decided to go into the living room where I heard them rummaging through the debris. When I stepped into the room, the men had their backs to me and were talking quietly between themselves. They turned around, and I was startled at the sight them. They were all dressed in black: black pants; a black turtleneck; a long, black jacket and black hats. They wore sunglasses, which appeared very dark against their pasty, pale skin.

"You'll have to come with us," one said in a monotone. "We have some questions we'd like to ask."

My heart began to race. I sensed trouble, but nothing made sense at all. I didn't know whether to stay or run.

"I'm not going anywhere. You can ask me here," I said defiantly. "I'm the victim. You can take the report from here."

Something told me these were not police officers, nor detectives. After what happened to me the day before the apartment incident, I had a feeling they were sent.

I realize I'm jumping ahead of myself. You see, there was an strange incident even before these strange men appeared. But to comprehend it, you'd have to understand Dallas and how it used to be back then.

Dallas, Texas, was as big as its reputation, and in the early 1980s, it was a sight to see. Tall buildings with tinted windows reflected the prosperity of Texas, acquired from oil, real estate, and investments. It was, as most people thought, the place to be if one had a dream and a bit of ambition.

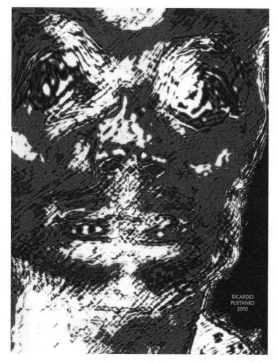

My family felt full of hope and ambition when we arrived in our new home. Just twenty miles north of Dallas, in a town called Lewisville, we settled into our new house that resembled every other house in a sprawling subdivision filled with Yuppies. With its manicured lawns, high-fences and great location, the neighborhood looked like a picture in a magazine. We were happy to be there and eager to fulfill our dreams.

Those dreams did not last though. Within a year, the real estate market bottomed out, investors were going broke, and the oil boom had come to a halt.

My marriage came to a halt as well. I took an apartment close by so my children could finish out their school year. What I would do after that, I had no idea. I needed another income, so I went in search of a job.

Finding a job was not an easy task. After filling out a ton of applications, mailing off resumes and making what seemed to be enough calls to fill a telephone directory, I finally began to get feedback from my search. A pile of rejection letters began to arrive, dashing my hopes of employment. Then, sev-

Far too many who experience UFO phenomena find themselves facing a terrifying entity and becoming victims of deliberate acts of hostility. (**Art by Ricardo Pustanio**)

eral weeks later, I was happy to receive a letter requesting an interview. It read something like this: "After reviewing your application, the management of DB&J Enterprises is very interested in interviewing you for a position in Sales. The interview has been scheduled for 2:00 P.M., Friday, April 18."

It was very dry and factual. Nothing remotely piqued my interest about the interview request other than landing a job—any job. A hand-drawn map along with hand-written directions were enclosed with the initials D. D. prominently stamped on the top of the page.

I had never heard of the street before, nor could I find it on a local map. I found it odd that a company would set an appointment date without giving one the benefit of selecting from a range of dates and times. Funny, too, that I could not recall ever applying for that position.

When I arrived for the interview, a young blond woman escorted me down a long hallway far away from the company's lobby. She signaled that we were almost there. "Here we are," she said. "Someone will be with you momentarily."

When she opened the door, the office looked empty and devoid of any color. It was starkly furnished with a cheap desk and two chairs, unlike the company's lobby, which was filled with fresh flowers, lush furniture, and expensive art. The woman motioned me inside, and I obliged, despite my hesitancy. "He's on his way. Good luck," she whispered and quickly darted out of sight.

A large-framed man filled the doorway. He was remarkably tall, and he hunched over to avoid hitting his head on the door frame. "My name is Don. Don Dearing. It's nice to meet you," he said as he extended his hand.

As we shook hands, he stopped and held my hand. I began to feel faint. Just when I thought I was going to collapse, he touched me on the shoulder and asked if I was all right. The dizziness stopped as quickly as it had started.

It took me a moment before I could answer back, "Yes, I'm all right." It did not take long before I realized that I wanted no part of the company, nor the man that sat across the desk from me. He was vague about the job opportunity and there was something about him I did not trust. He kept looking at his watch and pacing the room while asking questions that did not pertain to the interview. I felt he was stalling for some reason.

"Ever read *Illusions: Adventures of a Reluctant Messiah?*" he asked.

I hadn't read it.

His face took on a more serious look when he asked, "How about *Jonathan Livingston Seagull?*"

I decided to end the interview. I stood up and began to head for the door. "Thank you, Mr. Dearing for the opportunity to interview with you, but I really must be going."

His demeanor changed. "Patience never was one of your virtues," he said as his face turned red. I thought I misunderstood what he said.

"Excuse me?" I asked. "What did you say?"

He stood there, red faced, and did not reply.

There was a knock on the door, and a man came rushing in. He was out of breath as though he had been running. "Sorry to disturb you. I'm running late. Don, may I see you outside?" the man asked. "It will only take a minute."

Don signaled for me to stay. I decided I would give it a few more minutes and that was all. Not only was the interview a waste of my time, but I felt agitated. I could hear both men talking outside the door. It sounded like mumbling, but then I heard them clearly.

"Don, don't do this. Just leave her alone. We'll find another way," the man insisted.

Don shouted, "You'd better remember who you are talking to, Jimmy."

A few minutes passed before the door opened. Don stumbled into the room. "Before you leave, I'd like to talk to you a little more. Sit, sit. I suppose you were wondering about our earlier conversation. Not much of an interview, was it?" he said with a smile. "Jimmy will be joining us in a few minutes and he'll explain more about the position. In the meantime, why don't we get to know each other more?"

Don opened the desk's drawer and pulled out a deck of playing cards. "I used to play a lot of cards in Vegas," he said as he began to shuffle them. "Want to guess which card is in my pocket?"

His attitude had softened and his manner changed. He seemed more relaxed.

"Sorry. I'm not good at that sort of thing," I replied. "I'll wait for Jimmy."

"Come on! Lighten up. Focus a little. Let me see if you can do this," he laughed.

I saw an image in my mind of a royal card. "It's the queen of hearts," I said.

Don pulled the queen of hearts out of his shirt pocket and held it up. That was luck, I thought.

"How about another one?" Don asked expectedly. "I'll bet you're good at this."

A picture of a two of clubs enters my mind. "Two of clubs," I stated. Don slowly turned over the two of clubs. I was surprised.

Jimmy walked in bringing a chair.

"Jimmy, she's very good at this," Don said. He turned to me and asked, "How about one more?"

"Are we ever going to get to the interview?" I asked. Don looked at Jimmy.

"Thank you, but no, Don." I wanted to end this foolishness. "I'm eager to talk to Jimmy about the job." Don sat encouraging me and said, "One more time."

"Last one," I responded. I could not get the images of two cards out of my mind. "I'm sorry, I can't do this. I guess I'm mentally played out."

"What do you see?" Don asked. He kept his eyes fixed on me.

"I'm undecided. I see two cards, not one," I explained. I closed my eyes trying to focus more, but still I saw two cards. "It's the five of diamonds and the four of clubs."

Surely, I would miss and Don would stop playing games and get down to business. Don pulled two cards from his pocket. It was the five of diamonds and the four of clubs. It was unbelievable, to say the least.

"You and I would do great in Las Vegas. Wanna go tonight?" he asked jokingly.

"I need to grab some information about the company," Jimmy said. "I'll be back in a few minutes."

Jimmy sped out of the door before I had the chance to tell him I couldn't wait.

Don stood up and sat on the corner of the desk. He leaned in closer to me and whispered, "How do you think you did that?"

Don was a little too close for comfort and I had the feeling he was doing this deliberately. He leaned back and closed his eyes. When he opened them, his eyes looked as if they had changed. He looked different. His very being seemed as if he was somehow changing.

"Tell me, what do you fear the most?" he asked, almost demanding an answer.

I immediately felt fear. Fear that the man in front of me was insane and I was in danger. The fact that I was a long way from the lobby and sitting in an isolated room with a madman didn't help matters. Who in their right mind would ask me such a question? I didn't even know this man. I decided to take control of the situation as best as I could and try to talk my way out of the situation.

Attempting to throw him off, I leaned toward him and whispered, "Why would I tell you that? You'd use it against me." I giggled to make it appear as if I was joking with him.

It was then that everything changed. A current of energy began to soar through the room and a high-pitched sound filled the air. I was disoriented. I wanted to leave, but I could not move.

Glancing to my left, I noticed that the wall seemed to move and disappear. What replaced it was astonishing. An elaborate garden with pools of running water was in plain view where there once was a wall. I could hear the water flowing.

> It was then that everything changed. A current of energy began to soar through the room and a high-pitched sound filled the air. I was disoriented. I wanted to leave, but I could not move.

This is not really happening, I thought. I blinked my eyes several times, thinking I was hallucinating. But the garden was still there.

Don began to pace the room. "You never answer my questions. Why do you refuse me?" Don shouted. "Every time I come to you, you refuse me!"

"I don't know you," I said, barely able to speak.

"You know me! How many times have I come to you before? You know who I am!" he screamed. "I need you this time. I'm not taking 'no' for an answer."

I tried hard to place him. Nothing came to my mind. He did not look familiar, but the energy that was soaring in the room felt like I had experienced it before. I got another glance at the garden and then it vanished. The wall was once again intact.

This is crazy. He's crazy. Maybe—I'm crazy, I thought.

I kept my eye on Don fearing what his next move would be. He had changed quite a bit in the small time I'd been around him.

"Crazy? Isn't that what you people call out of your mind?" he asked. He had heard my thoughts. "Don't you think I know you?"

I didn't know what to think. My mind was spinning and I could no longer function.

"What do you want?" I asked. I never expected to hear the answer I received.

"I want you to come home," he said. "I need you to stop this and come home. Don't refuse me anymore. It's time."

"Home?" I asked.

Either I had lost my mind or my entire life up until now had been a dream. I could not understand how this was happening. I was there only for an interview.

Don pointed up. "Home ... where you and I are from," he said seriously. "Don't you remember? This is not your home! Earth is not your home!" he shouted.

He ranted on and on about home and named a place I had never heard of.

"I brought you here today with that letter. I knew you would come. That's what it took to get you here today. A job! Come on, Angela. Don't tell me you don't know who I am now," he said while looking at me with disbelief.

"I want to leave," I said.

The door was only a few feet away. I still felt something keeping me from it. Don's appearance seemed to change more and more.

"Who are you?" I asked. Then a horrible feeling came over me. I no longer felt the man before me was human. Demon or alien, it had to be one or the other.

"Who are you?" I demanded. "No! *What* are you?"

"You know who I am. You know what I am," he said shaking his head. "Don't refuse me again! You and your damn abilities. It means nothing unless you use them like you did before."

Suddenly, Jimmy opened the door and grabbed my hand. He started leading me to the door.

"She stays," Don said.

I didn't know what to expect at that point. I was confused.

"Leave her alone," Jimmy said. "Give her time to digest it all. She'll remember. She'll come around."

Don seemed resigned to my leaving. Jimmy led me down the hallway and back through the lobby. "Get in your car and don't look back," he said. "I'll do what I can to protect you. Now go!" Jimmy shouted.

I hurried to my car, opened the door and pushed the key in the ignition. My hands were shaking uncontrollably. I was stunned by what had happened. I prayed the entire way home and thanked God for my safety.

The next day the strange, scary-looking men came to my apartment. I no longer knew what to expect anymore. I thought Don had sent these men to kill me.

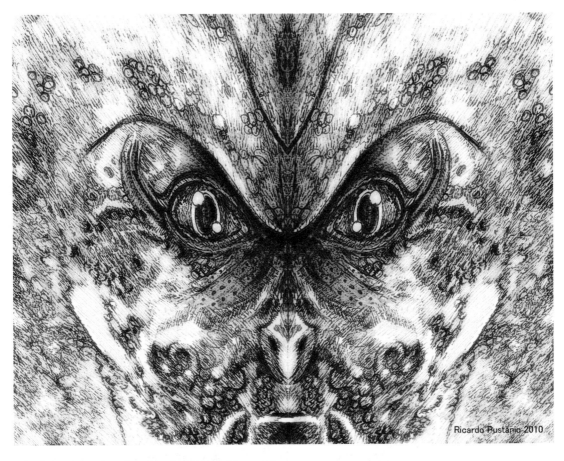

The face of alien hostility. (*Art by Ricardo Pustanio*)

I call them men. I'm not sure if that's what they really were. I think it's more likely they were aliens. I described them as pale, but their skin was actually more like a shade of gray, come to think of it. I was scared when I told them I wasn't going anywhere. One stepped toward me.

"This is not a choice," he said in a monotone voice. "You are leaving."

The next thing I recall, I was sitting in a chair. The room I was in was dimly lit. There was a feeling that I was in a basement or a lower room of some kind. I had no idea how I got there. There were several people in the room with me dressed in military attire. I could hear a door open.

"I'm Air Force Colonel Boyd, this is Lieutenant General Perry and Special Agent Reese. We'd like to ask you a few questions. What you say is between us, but it is of interest to the military, our intelligence and national security."

"Do I need an attorney?" I asked. I could not fathom why I would be stuck in a room full of military personnel.

"No, no. An attorney is not needed. We have a few questions for you, and we would appreciate your cooperation," the colonel said. "We understand that you were near Love Field yesterday."(Love Field is a small airport that serves the Dallas area.)

"How would you know that?" I asked. "There are literally thousands of people in that area at any given time. Why would you know about me being there?"

"Special Agent Reese was in the area and happened to see you leaving a nearby hangar. In a hurry, I might add," the colonel said. "He checked you out."

"I wasn't in a hangar. I had an interview in a normal office building," I said. "What's this all about?"

"On Siowan Street?" the colonel inquired. That was the street named on the map I had received. "We'd be interested in how you found out about Siowan. It's another name for the hangar you were in."

"I repeat, I wasn't in a hangar. The address was on a piece of paper I received from a company."

The colonel held up the hand-drawn map and shoved it in front of me. "Is this the paper you are referring to?" he asked.

It was then that I realized that my apartment was in shambles because of them. They had found the paper.

"Sir, I was born on an Air Force base. I'd know if I was inside of a hangar," I retorted.

"Yes, we know all about you. You've seen quite a few bases in your lifetime including Ft. Meade. NSA ring a bell? We also know you spent some time at the Pentagon. Care to share that with us?" he asked.

"That has nothing to do with this," I said. "I was just visiting."

"Visiting? No. No one just visits the NSA and the Pentagon without a reason," he said smugly. "Never mind. Let's go back to yesterday."

Special Agent Perry stepped forward and said, "We have reason to believe that you encountered an operative working against the United States. D.D. to be specific."

Don Dearing, I thought to myself. "Operative? No, you have it wrong. There was a man by the name of Don Dearing I came across yesterday," I said. "I don't know about operative, but I can say he was high-strung and crazy."

I hesitated to tell them the story, but was anxious to try to explain the unexplainable. They would certainly think I was lying, or at the very least, making things up to avoid answering their questions.

About that time, Lieutenant Colonel Perry lit a cigarette and handed it to me. "You seem a bit nervous. Calm down. You are here to help us shed some light on some things," Perry said. "We are trying to understand why you were in the hangar yesterday. That's off limits to civilians. Was this Dearing guy with you there?"

"I wasn't in a hangar. Maybe Special Agent Reese thought I was in this hangar you speak of when he spotted my car. You have the wrong person," I said.

"We have the right person," the colonel said. "Why were you with Dearing?"

I found myself in a dilemma and began to share my story. I started at the beginning: the end of the marriage, the job search, the interview and the crazy thing that happened while I was there with Don Dearing. They all looked at one another, but didn't respond right away. Special Agent Perry shuffled through a file folder, which I assumed was on me.

"Would you say that your experience yesterday was some sort of phenomena? I mean, how would you know what cards he was holding? You say the wall disappeared and a garden stood in its place?" Lieutenant Perry asked. "That sounds like a quantum physics sort of thing."

The questions concerned me. How could I explain what I knew without sounding like a complete nut. I didn't want to tell him that I had experienced psychic phenomenon before, nor that I was capable of using what would later be known as remote viewing. "Phenomena, yes. That's one way to explain it," I said cautiously.

Another door opened and a four-star general entered the room. I saw his uniform long before I saw his face. When he appeared, I recognized him. He was an old friend of my father's. It was Patterson, a man that had often visited with my family when I was a child.

"Mister Patterson. Sorry, I mean General Patterson," I said relieved to see a familiar face. He stood there looking at me as if he was trying to place me. Then a glimmer of recognition came to his face.

"Angela. It's been a long time. I would like to say we should've met again under better circumstances, but this is not it. This is serious," Patterson said.

No matter how serious it was, I was more comfortable with him there. He walked over to Perry and opened the file. He began writing something in it. "She's a sensitive. That explains it," Patterson said to Perry. "You know what to do from here."

I was there for hours and hours. They questioned me again on Don Dearing, the entire incident and even my own beliefs about psi matters. When they were confident that I didn't know who Dearing was, they stopped questioning me. Everyone left the room except Patterson.

"You know me, Angela. I would never lie to you, so when I say this, you must know that I mean business," he said seriously. "You were never here. This did not happen. What you saw yesterday did not happen. Understand?" he said firmly. "They will be keeping an eye on you for awhile. Our investigation will continue. As for Dearing, I'm afraid he'll try contacting you again. Those types of encounters rarely stop with one visit."

Encounters? Surely he wasn't saying what I thought he was saying. "I don't understand. This guy spoke to me about going home, not sabotaging the United States of America. Besides, something tells me that he was not from this world," I said carefully. I wanted to avoid the word "alien."

"He's not a normal operative, and he is not one of us," Patterson said. He pulled out a card and handed it to me. "Call me if he shows up again."

At that point the general stood up and pointed to the door. "This way," he said. We left the room and stepped out into a long corridor. Two armed men were standing on each side of the door we had walked through.

"Remember, this did not happen," Patterson said with a warning. "I'll deny it." The general walked quietly down the corridor with me, and when we arrived at the door, he looked at his watch and said, "It's 1600 hours," and motioned to a guard that was nearby. "See that she gets home," the general said to the guard. He then turned around and walked away.

The guard escorted me up some stairs and opened the door that lead to a large air hangar. He was joined by another man in uniform. I sat down inside a truck and felt enormous relief that it was all over. We were definitely on some sort of base; I would learn later that it was Carswell Air Force base in Fort Worth, Texas. I was driven home and accompanied to the door. When I opened the door, my apartment was completely in order.

"Everything all right, ma'am?" the man asked. "You look a little pale."

"Yes, I'm fine," I said. What else could I say?

I was unsettled at the thought of staying at the apartment that night, but my children came home and I felt a little more normal. The following day, I picked them up from school and headed to Garland to visit a friend.

As I was nearing the intersection of Interstate 35 and 635, the traffic came to a halt. I was stuck in five o'clock traffic. As I went under the overpass, I could see people getting out of their cars and pointing to the sky.

> When I inched up further, I could see a huge, metallic craft sitting over the interstates where they intersected. It was unlike anything I'd seen before.

When I inched up further, I could see a huge, metallic craft sitting over the interstates where they intersected. It was unlike anything I'd seen before. It was a UFO, several stories high and resembling a crown with layers that varied in appearance. The craft did not move or hover. It was perfectly still. There were no sounds coming from it, no fumes to indicate it ran on fuel.

I wanted to leave, but was stuck among thousands of cars. I turned on the radio and every station was covering the sighting. One station urged people to stop calling as their PBX system was being flooded. I remained calm, for the sake of my children. I kept reassuring them that we were going to be okay.

It was well over thirty minutes before the traffic began moving. As I drove forward, I looked in my rearview mirror and still saw the image of the UFO.

It would be awhile before the whole incident sunk in. I wondered why a UFO would expose itself in broad daylight. It certainly was not trying to avoid being detected. It was then that I began to question its intent.

My thoughts quickly turned to Don Dearing. He wanted to go home. Was it there for me? Were there more aliens among us than previously known? I'll never know the answer.

Later that night, a news story aired about the sighting. No pictures were shown, but they did quote a report from Carswell Air Force base that said it was "a possible weather balloon." I spent many years on air bases. I was familiar with weather balloons, and what I saw in Dallas was not a weather balloon. It was a UFO.

It would be a few years later before I came across a book titled *The Gulf Breeze Sightings*, a book that was filled with pictures of the same type of UFO I saw in Dallas.

Nothing since then has occurred: no contact from Dearing, no visits from strange beings dressed in black, no sightings of UFOs. I still keep everything in the back of my mind, though, and wait for something more to take place.

Contactees

Ever since 1967 we have been conducting a serious study of UFO contactees, whom we call "flying-saucer missionaries." We have found that some of the information dispensed in their cosmic sermonettes has contained accurate information and that a number of their predictions have come true.

Although several of the contactees seem to parrot each other, delivering the same basic "message," it is possible to discover important clues hidden in their fanciful dissertations, but it requires working a bit harder to separate the cosmic wheat from the celestial chaff.

Many of the flying-saucer contactees are convinced that they are in direct communication with "space intelligences" through telepathic thought transference. In other cases, the contactee also claims a personal and physical meeting with a beneficient "Space Being," who originated the contact.

After the initial contact experience, there does seem to be a heightening of what one would consider extrasensory perception. In one instance, for example, we had a contactee describe our home in exceptionally minute detail while we sat in a room several hundred miles away. Along with such demonstrable clairvoyant abilities, the contactee is often left with a timetable of certain predictions of future events.

In spite of some setbacks (unfulfilled prophecies, etc.), a good many of the contactees continue to have an almost religious fervor to spread the message that has been given to them by the space beings. The zeal with which these flying-saucer missionaries desire to preach the cosmic gospel must surely remind one of the early Christian apostles, who were given the divine mission to "go quickly and tell."

One should be cautious when seeking wisdom from entities who claim to be from other worlds. (**Art by Ricardo Pustanio**)

Teachings of the Space Beings

The Outer Space Apocrypha can be summarized in this way:

- Humankind is not alone in the solar system. Space brothers and sisters have come to Earth to reach out to and teach responsive humans.

- The space beings have advanced technical information that they wish to share with those on Earth in the hopes of creating an intergalactic spiritual federation.

- The space beings are here to teach, to help the human spirit rise to higher levels of vibration so the people of Earth may be ready to enter new dimensions. According to the Outer Space Apocrypha, this was what Jesus (Sananda), Confucius, Krishna, and other leaders or prophets of the great religions have tried to teach humanity.

- Humankind stands now in a transitional period leading up to the dawn of a new age. With peace, love, and understanding, the people of Earth will see the dawning of a great new era.

- If the Earthlings fail to raise their vibratory rate within a set period of time, severe earth changes and major cataclysms will take place. Such disasters will not end the world, but will serve to wake up unreceptive humans. Those who die in such necessary purging will be allowed to reincarnate. At this greater level of development, they will be saved through more advanced teachings on a higher vibratory level.

How the Contactees Receive Their Initial Contact

How do the flying-saucer missionaries, our apostles of intergalactic peace and harmony, receive their initial contact and summons from the space beings? Here a definite pattern has emerged in both our own research and in the investigations of others. So far, contactees have had these experiences:

- The prospective contactees saw the UFO on the ground, hovering low overhead, or heard a slight humming sound above them, which drew their attention to a mysterious craft.

- A warm ray of "light" emanated from the craft and touched the contactees on the neck, the crown of the head, or the middle of the forehead. Usually, the contactee experiences a slight "tingling" sensation before the contact proper. In certain instances, the contactees may have lost consciousness at this point and, upon awakening, may have discovered that they could not account for anywhere from a minute or two to an hour or two of their time. Some contactees, however, have no recollection of any period of unconsciousness, but maintain that they "heard" a voice speaking to them from inside their head.

- The contactees who retained consciousness and communicated with either an attractive space brother or sister were told that they were selected because they were, in reality, someone very special. Many contactees were told that they were reincarnations of notable world figures of the past. A good number were informed that they are aliens who were planted on Earth as very small children.

- A great percentage of contactees seem to have suffered through several days of restlessness, irritability, sleeplessness, and unusual dreams or nightmares immediately following the initial contact. Many reported noticing a terrible thirst after the departure of the entity. After a period of a week to several months, the contactee who has received a command to spread the cosmic message feels prepared to go forth and preach the word.

- A few of the flying-saucer missionaries seem to fear their solar brothers and sisters. But most of them look forward to a return visit from the space beings, and the majority of them have been promised repeated contacts.

- Family and friends find the contactees radically changed, a different person after their experience.

Are the Space Beings Really from Outer Space?

Can it really be true that aliens from other worlds seek to program these flying-saucer missionaries in an effort to encourage humankind's propensity to believe, and our capacity to love and understand?

Is a yet-to-be-determined *someone* systematically selecting certain individuals for some worldwide program of psychological conditioning?

Has some yet-to-be-identified agency set in motion an extensive propaganda campaign that has been designed to prepare humankind for a dramatic confrontation with an alien race or culture?

As a result of our own investigations and the research of others, we can no longer doubt that such "contacts" are taking place on a global scale, but we must challenge certain beliefs about the UFO occupants, especially in regard to their place of origin—that is, outer space.

We do not dogmatically rule out the extraterrestrial hypothesis, but we do lean toward the theory that UFOs may be our neighbors right around the corner in another space-time continuum. What we have thus far been labeling "spaceships" may be, in reality, multidimensional mechanisms or psychic constructs of our paraphysical companions.

We have even come to suspect that, in some instances, what we have been terming "spaceships" may actually be a form of higher intelligence, rather than vehicles transporting occupants.

We feel, too, that these intelligences have the ability to influence the human mind telepathically in order to project what may appear to be three-dimensional images to the witnesses of UFO activity. The image seen may depend in large part upon the preconceptions that the witnesses have about alien life forms; thus, our reported accounts of occupants run the gamut from bug-eyed monster types to little green men to metaphysical space brothers.

> Could it be that the UFO entities have been fibbing to us about their true identity and their true place of origin since antiquity?

The mechanism employed by the UFO entities is always relevant to the witness' time context. At the same time, the form in which the UFO construct appears—and the symbology it employs—are always timeless, archetypal, and instantly recognizable at one level of consciousness. Elves, fairies, and angelic beings, it would seem, have been popular in all cultures since the beginning of recorded time. The complete experience of any witness of UFO activity is quite probably part of a process with a purpose too complex for our present level of comprehension.

Could it be that the UFO entities have been fibbing to us about their true identity and their true place of origin since antiquity? On the other hand, perhaps, little by little, we are being provided with the bits and pieces of some supercosmic jigsaw puzzle, which one day, when properly assembled, will give us the complete picture of the entire UFO enigma.

A Multi-Faceted Contactee-Abductee Case History

In February 1976, UFO researcher Timothy Green Beckley conducted an extensive series of interviews with the contactee/abductee Brian Scott. At that time Scott was a thirty-two-year-old draftsman for a Mission Bejo firm and the father of two. He had stated that on several occasions he was taken aboard a strange craft piloted by beings from an alien planet.

Scott's first abduction reportedly occurred in the Arizona desert near Phoenix in 1971, and he claimed that another had just occurred on December 22, 1975, in Garden Grove, California. In between, Scott said, there were three other terrifying sessions with the aliens and he had been visited at home repeatedly by balls of light and a transparent being that called itself "the host."

Scott believed that his involvement with the alien beings began on his sixteenth birthday, October 12, 1959. He was coming home from celebrating when he observed a ball of light hovering over his dog. The ball was oval shaped and semisolid, with more solidity toward the center. It was six to eight inches in diameter and reddish-orange.

The ball of light came right at his head until it was just a few inches from his face—then it shot straight up. Scott believed that at that time he had received some sort of communication from the ball through thoughts and pictures that were apparently transmitted directly into his mind.

It was more than twelve years later, on the evening of March 14, 1971, that Scott was transported aboard a hovering craft with a purple light emanating from its underside.

Scott found himself, for no reason he was aware of, driving into the desert near the Superstition Mountains outside Phoenix. He remembers standing alone, seeing a strange craft fly overhead. Then he felt a "pulsating, pulling feeling" that lifted him upward, into the vehicle.

Incredibly, Scott found that a friend of his was already inside the craft. The two of them were taken into a small room that started to fill with a fog or a mist. Then they were confronted by four or five "very horrifying" creatures. Scott described them as having gray skin like that of a crocodile or a rhino, with a thicker patch of hide over the front torso.

Scott and his friend were disrobed and then led off in different directions. Scott recalls that he was either carried or made to travel without bodily movement. The beings were seven feet tall, according to Scott, and looked like a combination of Earth animals. They had three fingers and a thumb on one side.

After undergoing a physical examination, Scott felt his mind transported to an alien world, where he observed more of the strange creatures walking about a planet of jagged peaks in a misty atmosphere. After the mind trip, he was rejoined with his friend and returned to the ground. The last memory he had of the strange craft was a terrible odor, like "rotten socks, as if someone hadn't taken their shoes off for twenty years."

Scott's next experience also occurred in the desert near Phoenix on March 22, 1973. At that time he began to receive the distinct impression that, in addition to being under observation by the beings, he was being slowly educated by them.

Because resultant poltergeistic phenomena in the home is very often associated with UFO contactee or abductee experiences, Tim began asking Scott about the kind of manifestations that had been occurring in his household.

Scott replied, "There are streaks of light. A white light just streaks its way through the house, filters, and then just goes very quickly. Then there is the ball of light itself in the house and outside the house. There have been pure flashes, as if you put a flash cube right up to your eyeball. The light blinds you. You see it for just a few seconds, and then it dis-

Thousands of contactees throughout the world have listened to the voices of alien teachers. (Art by Ricardo Pustanio)

appears. There is another object, a rather odd, brown-shaped thing that has from time to time shown up. It dashes around the room in crazy directions, and every time that it does, it creates some damage to the home. All the electricity and all the circuits in the house have melted, frozen, and burned up."

Beckley Quizzes Brian Scott for Details of His Strange Encounters

Tim Beckley: What happened on the day your wife was sent to the hospital?

Scott: She had been to work, pretty much handling everything that was going on around her. Then I got a call that she wasn't feeling very well. I brought her home, and after about fifteen minutes of sitting there talking with her, she was saying several things, none of which made any sense to me or to her. She said that she had been in the bathroom and suddenly felt hands all over her body. It was as if someone had broken into the house and molested her. When she calmed down and started making explanations to me about what the hell was wrong with her, it was as if, from her description, the aliens I had seen aboard the craft in 1971 had visited her. This is odd, because she has never even seen any sketches that I made of those entities.

Beckley: So this was an actual materialization of the entities in the house?

Scott: I don't know what it was.

Beckley: But she was so upset that you decided to take her to the hospital?

Scott: Later that evening, it seemed as if she was okay. I was on the phone, and the baby was getting into everything so I couldn't carry on the conversation. I got up and went looking for my wife. I heard a bumping sound and a moan coming from the bathroom. My wife was on the floor, hyperventilating. I got her up and onto a chair in the living room. I was on my way to call her mother when she just fell flat on her face. I called the paramedics, and while they were on the way, she got up and fell down again. Then she began to become hysterical. It took four paramedics to hold her down. She was throwing people around as if they were tissue paper. Men were thrown backward against the furniture. Finally they loaded her up in the ambulance. I came back in the house, and the baby was not in the playpen. I panicked, because I couldn't find our one-year-old child. I ran back in the house. The dog was yipping at the back door. We finally found the baby sitting over in a corner of the patio. A one-year-old baby who got out of a playpen!

Tim Beckley Asks Scott about the Host

"There is one entity that comes through that calls itself 'the host,' whatever that means," Scott attempted to explain. "It speaks in what sounds like some kind of computerized language. The voice seems to come out of me, an inner voice that is not mine. The entity says that I am one with it. It says, 'I am; I am' or 'You are one with me.' When asked if it has a name, it will just come back and say, 'I am; I am.'

"The other night we heard some strange sounds coming from the bedroom. I began to speak in a foreign language that we later found out was Greek. Where that came from, I don't know. I wrote in Greek backward. On top of that, I was writing with my left hand, and I am right-handed.

"This voice was talking. We asked who it was, and the name Ashtar came out.

"Then it began to use the name Ashtar and speak to my wife. It told her things about her past that only she could know. This went on for a while, then it went on to say it would give her all the money in the world. It only wanted one thing in return—her soul."

Beckley pointed out that it sounded as though diabolical entities might have materialized, attracted by the extreme vibrations. He also observed that Ashtar sounded very much like Ishtar, an ancient Babylonian goddess.

The host told Brian Scott that it would return on December 24 in the year 2011. He would descend on the spider figure in the Nazca lines. From there he would go to other ancient city sites where Scott and concerned parties were to construct pyramids.

An Extensive Evaluation of Scott's "Alien" Voice Prints

Beckley also interviewed J. D., an investigator associated with a civilian UFO investigation group. J. D. said that when he was first contacted by Brian Scott he thought the man was totally out of his mind, but as he began to investigate he became more curious and intrigued. He was especially impressed when the voice tapes that he had taken of various entities—which either spoke through Scott or from other areas around the house—appeared to produce prints different from the abductee's normal voice.

Beckley pursued this matter, learning that the mechanical voice of the host "lacked all harmonics and seemed to be nothing but a series of small ripples."

Beckley knew that even if a person tried to disguise his voice or attempt to imitate another person's voice, the voiceprints would reveal the sound as the voice of the deceiver. There are individual characteristics in each voiceprint that designate a particular speaker, much as fingerprints are unique to each person. So, the investigators were fascinated to learn that the voiceprint analyses of the various entities' voices were allegedly different.

Beckley asked J. D. how he would differentiate between what may have originally been an abduction case and the various types of poltergeistic phenomena that now seemed to prompt Scott's resultant trance state. Were they one and the same? Were they closely related mysteries? Or were they entirely different aspects of a more general phenomenon?

Beckley found out that J. D. was aware of other cases such as Scott's. The manifestations of balls of light streaking through the homes of contactees and abductees apparently are more frequent than many investigators realize.

J. D. also mentioned that one voice, a horrible voice, came through and claimed to be Beelzebub, the Devil. But J. D. was convinced that the entity was simply trying to frighten away the investigators.

Beckley commented that the contents of the messages that Scott had relayed to him all seemed to be very sophomoric in content. Although a great deal of material was coming through from the alleged aliens, in Beckley's opinion, the content of what was said did not appear to have any substantial value.

Beckley spoke further with a technician who claimed he analyzed the various voices associated with the Scott case. He, too, indicated that they were quite different from one another. This technician worked for a company that wired Scott for twenty-four hours a day for one week. They used a four-channel recorder, recording different frequency spectrums on each channel. They recorded the vibrations of the house on the low-frequency channels, and the static electricity was recorded on the high-frequency channels.

They concluded that Scott was not producing the various voices of his own will. Although the technician did not claim to be the final authority, he commented that some of the frequencies that they recorded were, in his opinion, so low that, generally speaking, a human voice could not produce them.

> J. D. also mentioned that one voice, a horrible voice, came through and claimed to be Beelzebub, the Devil. But J. D. was convinced that the entity was simply trying to frighten away the investigators.

"Here again," he added, "we are going on the knowledge of standard speech, not necessarily something that is unusual in nature. But for all practical purposes, I am convinced that Scott was not doing this of his own will."

Beckley and other investigators formed a kind of consensus of the Brian Scott story. The entities that were contacting Brian Scott seemed to be of two basic groups.

The primary group appeared to be multidimensional in nature, indicating only that they were from a time beyond all time. Those people were tall and appeared human, but they often wore a bulky mass of loose gray skin as their "cloak of sorrow."

The secondary group was composed of beings who were small, with frail bodies, milky white skin, large bald heads, thin lips, and enormous eyes. It was stated that these beings had a common rapport with Earth beings and in fact were responsible for the genetic evolution of human life on this planet through sexual implantations over 4,500 years ago. Supposedly this group, perhaps from the sixth of seven planets around the star Epsilon Bootes, placed a satellite in orbit around our moon twelve thousand years ago. These beings may be considered antagonistic by some, but in reality they are working hand in hand with a cosmic intent of elevating humankind's consciousness. It appears to be their mission to adjust the genetic structure of *Homo sapiens*. This adjustment will move humankind higher along the evolutionary scale.

The multidimensional beings, the taller, more human-like entities from "time beyond all time," have the power to veto actions planned by those beings of the secondary world, but they will not interfere unless humankind presents a greater threat to the universe.

Scott was told that his channeling would bring ten specific gifts to humankind. Some of these gifts would be spiritual in nature, but most would bring new technologies to Earth. His individual mission, however, was to begin to design a pyramid in Tiahuanaco, Bolivia, which was to be built before 2011 on the site of an existing inverted pyramid. He was also instructed to tell civilization about the relationship between the world of humankind and the multidimensional world surrounding it. In addition, Scott was to design a transportation technology that would move matter through space. He was to master quantum displacement physics and begin to develop a mind transference machine that would unite all humans. Such a machine would help to develop a philosophy of cosmic brotherhood.

The above tasks, of course, seem impossible, even for a person who was a combination of Einstein and Superman, but they are typical of the type of grandiose mission assigned to many contactees and abductees. Although the assignments may be impossible to complete, as the contactees attempt to fulfill a mission, they may inspire ideas that others may eventually be able to develop into workable technologies.

Scott was understandably confused as to why he was selected for such a mission. He theorized that he may have simply been in the wrong place at the wrong time. Or he may have been a reincarnated pyramid designer, a reborn spaceman.

Some alien teachers claim to have been confidantes of the contactees in past lives on other worlds. Some maintain that they have been masters of esoteric arts in ancient times on Earth. (*Art by Ricardo Pustanio*)

Each group of investigators had a different set of theories to explain Scott's phenomenal experiences, but they agree that he was "touched" by the host at age sixteen, and the host seemed to be a spiritual guide to those who originated in the "time beyond all time."

As with so many contactees/abductees, Scott appears to have been changed by his experiences. His wife commented that his intelligence "skyrocketed" after his December 22, 1975, UFO contact. Allegedly, second-and third-degree burn scars were removed from his abdomen.

And, after that time, their relationship became strained because of Scott's increase in scientific knowledge. According to his wife, his mood became serious and determined, whereas before the experiences, he had been "just an average guy, a lot of fun."

The Master Ashtar

The Master Ashtar appears in much of UFO contactee literature. One cannot help noting the ancient origin of the name: Ishtar, Ashtar, Asta—described always as a god or goddess of evil or negativity in the Bible. The original Ashtar may have been an extraterrestrial commander whose motives were misunderstood by primitive earthlings. Or perhaps he or she was more indifferent to the needs of humankind than some of the other aliens allegedly walking around Earth in ancient times. This can only be the subject for a great deal of speculation. Ashtar seems to belong more to the contactees than the abductees, but there are instances where those who claim to have been forcefully taken aboard UFOs describe an interaction with beings who represent themselves as emissaries of "Ashtar's Grand Plan."

George Van Tassel was told by Ashtar that the space beings' purpose was to save humankind from itself. Once that great obstacle has been met, then the minor problem of how to deal with nuclear fission will right itself through the profound harmony that will then exist on the planet Earth.

The space beings seem very concerned with the spreading of what has come to be known as "New Age" concepts—fresh methods of looking at metaphysics, universal laws, brotherhood, and even health and hygiene. And the space beings appear definitely concerned with seeing that all humankind is "united as one" on this planet.

The contactees seem to assume that the space beings have enormous scientific knowledge. After all, if they have traveled to Earth from other worlds, then they must be extremely and sublimely intelligent.

Hard-nosed Earth scientists, however, remain singularly unimpressed with the specific technical information that has been relayed by the contactees.

One might argue that either the UFOnauts deem their science to be incomprehensible to humankind at this point, or they are not at all concerned with relaying technical data, which might make humankind even more baffled and beset by machines and technology than it already seems to be.

Most contactees, however, seem to agree that although the Space Beings have technology that is dazzling, their prominent characteristic is wisdom.

Other theorists might state that the contactees are not contacting alien entities at all, but, rather, a higher aspect of their own psyches, perhaps the pure essence that is free of the mundane limitations of time and space and is able to tap a kind of universal, cosmic reservoir of wisdom.

The UFO Movement

Dr. J. Gordon Melton, Director of the Institute of the Study of American Religion, has commented that the UFO contactees are best understood as "an emerging religious movement with an impetus and a life of their own."

The UFO contactees may be evolving prototypes of a future evangelism. They may be the heralds of a New Age religion, a blending of technology and traditional religious concepts.

UFO contactees often speak of an impending New Age wherein humankind will attain a new consciousness, a new awareness, and a higher state—or frequency—of vibration. They speak of each physical body as existing in a state of vibration and of all things vibrating at their individual frequencies.

The UFO intelligences, they say, come from higher dimensions all around us, which function on different vibratory levels, just as there are various radio frequencies operating simultaneously in our environment. We can attune ourselves to these higher dimensions in much the same manner as a radio receiver tunes into the frequencies of broadcasting stations. Different entities travel on different frequencies, according to their vibratory rate.

Then the question arises whether such information comes from the contactee's own higher self or from a separate and distinct outside intelligence. Certain investigators, whose search for the truth about UFO contact will simply not permit them to accept the validity of channelled messages, could consider the possibility that such entities as spirit guides, angels, or space beings might be but externalized projections of the contactee's own personality.

> Angels and space beings could be the externalization of religious feelings that have been progressively denied expression in an increasingly secular world.

Parapsychologists have generally agreed that the poltergeist, the "noisy ghost" that levitates objects and generally raises havoc in a household, is not an autonomous being at all, but the externalized aggression of someone undergoing the emotional stress of a severe adjustment problem. Psychology maintains the axiom that whatever the conscious mind represses, the unconscious embodies in allegorical form, either in dreams or in conscious creative imagery. Demons, for example, often serve as personifications of undesirable emotions, such as lust and hatred.

Angels and space beings could be the externalization of religious feelings that have been progressively denied expression in an increasingly secular world. The fact that contact with the space beings seems to be accelerating all over the world could be an affirmation of man's need to fashion a new religious structure that will satisfy the basic spiritual requirements of the psyche while, at the same time, be representative of space-age society.

In *2001: A Space Odyssey* Arthur C. Clarke postulated mental beings from Jupiter who assumed more than an academic interest in the cultural development of Earth's man-apes. In the same way, perhaps we might conjecture soul beings from other dimensions who assume an interest in humankind's spiritual development. When the Old Testament speaks of the *Elohim* creating people in their image, we might speculate that these higher intelligences were actually more concerned with presenting humanity with a spiritual, rather than a physical, pattern for development. Clarke imagined his interplanetary tutors planting monoliths to probe the man-apes' minds, map their bodies, study their reactions, and evaluate their potentials so that they might one day evolve to explore the stars. We might imagine cosmic missionaries implanting spiritual truths in "human monoliths" so that humans might one day evolve to a new age, spiritually equipped to explore new dimensions, new frequencies of being.

It does seem as though *someone* has been broadcasting certain essential universal truths ever since man became man. At this point in our research, it is impossible to offer a universally acceptable answer to the question of the true identity of the space beings who are allegedly communicating with the UFO mystics.

They may be God's angels speaking to the UFO prophets in order to guide humankind through the difficult period of adjustment as the old, corrupt Piscean Age enters a transitional time of cleansing and purification before we embark upon the Age of Aquarius.

They may be our cosmic cousins, aliens from another world or dimension who, over the ages, have interacted with us in a very complex kind of symbiotic relationship, and who do not wish us to destroy the biosphere, which is somehow very important to them, as well as to us.

Or maybe the contactees are only employing puppet-like projections of their own fantasies to voice the protest of humankind's collective unconscious over the hideous, scalding specter of nuclear-annihilation, the unfathomable ecological truth of what may be the death of our biosphere by the poisonous fouling of our own nest, and the trauma of an old world dying and a new world being born.

Whoever or whatever the space beings may be—whether cosmic missionaries or projections of the higher self—the channelled material of the contactees may very well be the scriptures and theological teachings of a new age.

Cautions for Those Who Wish to Contact Space Beings

Aleuti Francesca, "Telethought Channeler" for the Solar Light Center in Central Point, Oregon, has communicated with space beings since 1954.

In Aleuti's opinion, one must use the utmost caution in dealing with the mystery of contact.

"One should never inform the press, radio or TV people of his or her contact and nothing at all should be publicized until, or unless, at least one major prophecy has come true for a specific date and has thus established the accuracy of the source. A great deal of harm can come from several neophyte channelers running about the country crying 'wolf' in regard to the sinking of lands, and so forth. So many of these prophecies with nonfulfilled dates have plagued the space and psychic field of late, and they cause intelligent people to turn away in disgust."

Aleuti also warns of the danger of "astral entities" masquerading as space beings.

"This is not uncommon lately in the psychic field," she said, "but it is rarely that I have known space people to make contacts through Ouija boards or some other such device. So many young people know nothing of astral impersonators or unconscious fraud and they cannot see that what they are doing is not what it seems."

The following is Aleuti's advice to those who wish to attempt telepathic or physical contact with the space brothers:

"I will no longer suggest or recommend interested people attempting such contacts unless they are willing to put themselves through a specific kind of program of *self-discipline* and *self-knowledge*. Over the last few years I have observed such juvenile antics and ego-inflation taking place in untrained and unprepared mentalities as to be downright dangerous, both to the cause and to the individuals themselves.

"If the Space intelligences want to contact you, they will do so; they do the choosing."

Then for those who might desire to make themselves fit candidates for contact, she presented the following questions and comments:

1. Have you dedication of a spiritual nature?

2. Have you courage to stay with your convictions without bravado—quietly, reasonably, *peacefully*?

3. Do you really know yourself inside and out, through hell and high water? If not, start a self-knowledge program.

4. Have you an inferiority complex or a secret desire for power? If so, forget about space people and go to work to balance your ego and attain inner poise. When you truly know yourself, you will find that knowledge of others will follow.

The space brothers need highly *stable* individuals. Are you one?

Astral interlopers, masquerading as space intelligences, clutter up the space field. They flourish in the purely psychic realm. They feed on vanity and ego. Organizations have even been formed around power-mad individuals claiming space contacts from such sources. Be alert! Be aware!

> Space men and women from the solar and galactic confederations are concerned with the good of all peoples, of every nationality on Earth that they can reach.

Space men and women from the solar and galactic confederations are concerned with the good of all peoples, of every nationality on Earth that they can reach. They preach no dogmas or creeds, neither do they feed "ego food" to their channels. All true channels are part of a plan to assist the Earth and its peoples through the great change or initiation. Some play a greater part, some a lesser, but all are part of the plan, cosmic and spiritual in nature. The desire to serve, to love, and to understand, is the real mark of a true light server. "By their deeds shall ye know them."

Abductees

On September 16, 1962, Telemaco Xavier is said to have been kidnapped by three aliens from a UFO. According to witnesses, Xavier was last seen walking home along a dark jungle trail after attending a soccer match in Vila Conceicao in northern Brazil.

A workman at a nearby rubber plantation told authorities that he saw a round, glowing object fall from the sky and land in a clearing. Three occupants emerged from the UFO and grabbed a man who was walking along the jungle trail. According to the workman, the victim put up a brief struggle before he was dragged off to the fiery vehicle.

Rio de Janeiro newspapers quoted authorities who had discovered signs of a struggle where the worker said the fight had taken place. To the Brazilian newspapers it seemed evident that Mr. Telemaco Xavier was kidnapped by the occupants of a flying disc.

Argentine Farmers Fight Off Group Abductions by Aliens

In the small farming community of Torren, Santo Time, Argentina, UFO occupants attempted to kidnap residents on several successive evenings in February 1965.

The first attack came on a dark night, when a UFO landed in full view of a small group of terrified farmers. Two strange entities, about six feet tall, emerged from the craft and walked directly to a farmhouse, where they attempted to drag off the farmer who lived there. Rallying to their friend's defense, the other farmers managed to thwart the aliens' kidnap attempt and drive off the invaders.

On the next night, when the persistent aliens landed again to carry out their mass abduction, the angry farmers met them with gunfire. Although the aliens' space suits appeared to protect them from serious injury from the farmers' bullets, the attack seemed to weaken them physically—and the farmers had little difficulty in discouraging the aliens from preying on their village.

No one on either side of the eerie interplanetary brawl appeared to have received any serious injuries; however, reports said the farmer who had the longest physical contact with the cosmic kidnappers came down with a strange skin disease.

The Interrupted Journey of Betty and Barney Hill

Since the mid-1980s, more and more individuals have reported abduction experiences with aliens. These reports accelerated with the publication of Whitley Strieber's book *Communion* (1987), in which the author details his own abduction, and the abduction research of artist Budd Hopkins in his books *The Intruders* (1987) and *Missing Time* (1981).

At a conference on the alien-abduction phenomenon at the Massachusetts Institute of Technology in June 1992, it was estimated that the number of adult abductees in the United States alone stands between several hundred thousand and more than three million. While such a figure seems mind-boggling, some UFO researchers say that an accurate figure would be much higher. In 2010, according to Dr. David Jacobs, who has studied the phenomenon for decades, an estimated 2 percent of the population of the United States—or roughly six million people—claim to have undergone an alien abduction experience.

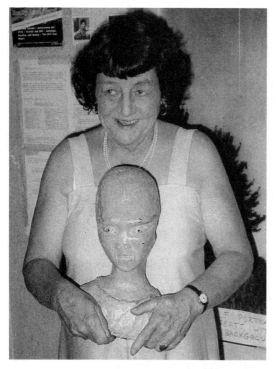

Betty Hill poses with a bust of her alien captor.

With such attention being directed to the *new* claims of alien abduction, few people seem to realize that there have been a number of dramatic cosmic kidnappings many years before those currently gaining so much attention. Many people fearful of the thought of aliens carrying them away are not even familiar with the prototypical UFO abduction that occurred to Betty and Barney Hill on September 19, 1961.

The Hills, a couple in their forties, were returning from a brief Canadian vacation to their home in New Hampshire when they noticed a bright object in the night sky. Barney stopped the car and used a pair of binoculars to get a better look at the light, which soon showed the well-defined shape of a disclike object moving in an irregular pattern across the moonlit sky.

Intrigued by what he saw, Barney walked into a field to get a better look at the object. Through the binoculars, he was able to observe the UFO and to distinguish what appeared to be windows. And from the windows, the occupants of the ship looked back at him.

Barney suddenly became terrified at what he was seeing. He got back in the car and raced away from the place where he and his wife had pulled over. Then, for some inexplicable reason, he drove down a side road where—as if it had all been somehow prearranged—five humanoid beings stood blocking the path of the car. Once in sight of the beings, the Hills could no longer control their movements. It was as if they had been placed in some kind of trance, and they permitted the aliens to lead them into the spacecraft.

Details of the Hills' remarkable encounter were retrieved under hypnosis, for the couple had been programmed by the aliens to forget everything about the nearly two hours that had passed between the time when they initially sighted the light and their return to their car. The abduction would probably never have been brought to light, but the Hills were troubled by the fact that they could not account for the two-hour gap in their trip home from Canada. And then there were the weird dreams they both started experiencing.

The Hills were sensible, down-to-earth people. Barney was a mail carrier and Betty was a social worker. They both wanted to know what could be causing their troubling dreams.

Betty sought the help of a psychiatrist friend, who suggested that the memory of their missing two hours would quite likely return within a few months. But in spite of such assurances, the details of their abduction remained lost until the Hills were hypnotized by Boston psychiatrist, Dr. Benjamin Simon.

During separate hypnotic sessions, the couple freed the memories of what had actually occurred to them on that remarkable evening in September. Although neither of them knew what the other had revealed until later, Betty's and Barney's accounts agreed in most respects.

Both told of being shepherded aboard a UFO by small humanoids who appeared to be wearing uniforms and helmets. When the aliens began to examine him, Barney feared that he was going to be tortured. Betty experienced no such terror. Later, both of them said that they said they felt were treated like laboratory animals.

The nearly two hours aboard the craft consisted primarily of various physical examinations. The Hills were each given a hypnotic suggestion that they would not remember anything that occurred while they were aboard the UFO. Apparently, their induced amnesia was broken when they were hypnotized by Dr. Simon.

When Betty was placed under hypnosis again in 1964, she recalled a detail of their strange adventure, which seemed to add a great deal of credibility to their experience. Betty's request to take some artifact with her to prove the reality of their experience was nearly granted. Although she was not allowed to take an object with her, she was shown a star map and she was given to understand that the chart depicted the aliens' place of extraterrestrial origin.

Researchers later discovered the map Betty had seen showed the location of two stars, Zeta 1 and Zeta 2 Reticuli, and they speculated that this was the home base of the space travelers. The existence of the two stars was not confirmed by astronomers until 1969—eight years after Betty saw the star map aboard an extraterrestrial spaceship. And Betty could only know of their existence because of the star map; Zeta 1 and Zeta 2 Reticuli, two fifth-magnitude stars, cannot be seen by observers north of Mexico City's latitude. The stars would be invisible to anyone viewing the night sky in New Hampshire.

Despite this fact, Betty's famous star map has both its defenders and detractors, and it remains an object of much controversy.

A Series of Abductions Seemed to Begin with an Ethereal Visitor

In *UFO*, Volume 2, Number 3 (1987), Jozaa Buist gave the details of her first experience with UFOs, which began on August 23, 1975. That was the evening that she and a friend noticed eight objects moving across the South Pacific night sky, coming in from the northwest.

A few days later, a peculiar stranger, a woman named Valerie, who had pure white hair and a baby-soft complexion, approached Jozaa and claimed to know her very well. A series of very peculiar occurrences followed, somehow all connected with the ethereal Valerie.

Jozaa's first abduction experience occurred in July of 1980 at about 11:00 P.M. She and her husband—who was in the military—were in Hawaii. They had decided to retire for the evening, and Jozaa had gone upstairs to take a shower.

Afterward, she was cooling off by the bedroom window, which faced west. She looked out and noticed a dark, orange object heading east. After about three minutes had passed, she began to feel very faint. She called to her husband, and he came running in, asking what was wrong. Jozaa remembers that sweat was pouring from her face.

Her husband took her to the Navy Regional Medical Center. The doctor reported that all her vital signs were normal and that he could see no reason for her faintness. He asked Jozaa if she were in pain, and she answered that she had experienced no pain or discomfort whatsoever.

Many abductees state that they were snatched from their bedrooms—or even from their automobiles—and taken aboard a spacecraft to be probed by alien doctors who gave them extremely invasive and painful examinations. (*Art by Ricardo Pustanio*)

About a week later, Jozaa was sitting on the edge of her bed, planning to read a magazine and take a nap. The next thing she recalled was lying on a metallic table and looking up at three aliens staring down at her. They were dressed in doctor's uniforms with operating masks over their mouths. Their eyes were slits.

Jozaa became aware of three metallic discs hovering over her body, making whirring sounds. Jozaa told the alien doctors that the whirring noise bothered her, and they said they would give her something so the sound wouldn't disturb her.

She was given a shot in the crevice of her right arm. "I seemed to calm down, but I was nervous about what was in store for me. Then I saw them take a rather large hypodermic needle. I asked them what they were going to do and if it would hurt. They said it would, but only for a little while."

The next thing Jozaa knew, she was back in her bed.

It was about 5:30 A.M. She got out of bed, and as she began to stand up, she screamed out in pain. She was unable to stand.

The excruciating pain lasted throughout the course of the day, becoming progressively worse. Finally she decided she could endure the pain no longer, so she went to the Army Medical Center. The doctor, who had treated her before for minor problems, was concerned about her frantic crying, and questioned why she was so upset.

Jozaa feared the doctor would send her to see a psychologist, but against her better judgment, she told the doctor the details of her memory of the bizarre operation the night before. She told him that she had never had any kind of surgery in her life.

The doctor looked at her stomach and asked her about the scar that was clearly visible. He also noticed a mark on her arm. To her utter amazement, the physician said that he had examined another patient earlier that week who had told him a similar story.

Jozaa went to the lab and had blood work and other tests done. The results camee back normal, as she had known they would. For three weeks straight, she had a burning sensation in her navel, which she was convinced had come from the needle that the aliens had inserted.

The next visit from the aliens was a lot more pleasant. Jozaa was offered a drink of dark green "coffee." The entities asked her why there was so much pollution on our planet. Didn't we understand that we were destroying ourselves?

Then Jozaa asked a question of her own: What was their purpose in coming to our world?

They replied that they were simply observing humankind.

Jozaa and her husband were transferred from Hawaii to San Diego in 1982. She felt that she had left her agony behind in Hawaii, but that was not to be the case.

One night as she lay down on the couch to fall asleep, she was awakened about 7:30 P.M. by a severe pain in her arm. Jozaa called her mother, who was living across the highway, and told her about the pain.

When Jozaa arrived at her parents' home, her mother asked her to remove her blouse. She turned Jozaa's left arm around and asked, "My God, what is that on your arm?" and got a mirror so that Jozaa could see for herself.

"I stopped dead in my tracks," Jozaa stated. "I am dark complexioned, and the mark on my arm was pure white. It was the shape of a triangle. I measured it, and it was two and one-half inches on all three sides. A line stretched from the top of the triangle, and there was a white dot in the middle.

"My arm hurt badly. It went on for three weeks before I went to the Navy Regional Medical Center. The doctor said he could not X ray it because it was so swollen, and he asked me about another lump or a bump that he felt. He gave me some medication."

Jozaa came back a month later, and the doctor who had treated her had been transferred. The new doctor seemed very understanding, and she had an X ray taken.

Later, the doctor looked at the X ray and told Jozaa that he could not understand what he was seeing. He decided to send it back to the hospital.

When Jozaa returned, the doctor's attitude seemed to change and he was indifferent and evasive.

Jozaa inquired about the location of her X ray and asked about the official medical interpretation of it.

The doctor replied that he had no definite answer for her, but it looked as though there were a disc in her arm. He refused to discuss the matter any further. For the time being, at least, Jozaa was unable to get any answers.

At a later date, Jozaa had to undergo a physical examination with another doctor to adopt two daughters, and when the doctor looked at her arm, she asked about the strange marking. Once again, Jozaa was sent for X rays. And, once again, the results were baffling. Two days later, the technician who took the X ray said that he wouldn't touch her arm with a ten-foot pole.

When Jozaa, understandably disturbed, asked him what he had meant, he replied that he couldn't explain it to her.

After six months, the pain began to subside. She had finally given up on going to doctors because she had received no tangible results. She had come to the conclusion that they didn't really understand what had happened to her.

In September of 1986, her husband was transferred to Nevada, so Jozaa thought she would see what could be done there. Once again, she went to the Navy Regional Medical Center where they took more X rays.

According to Jozaa, she never received a sensible answer. She wishes that she could ask the alien doctors for an answer to the mystery of the unexplained markings on her arm. After all, the Navy doctors have told her they could not help her and civilian doctors have shunned her. The marking is still visible to the naked eye. She has told her story over and over again, knowing that the aliens were real. She knows she did not imagine them.

In some cases, couples reported being abducted from their home and then scanned and examined by reptilian aliens. (*Art by Ricardo Pustanio*)

Abducted by a Seven-Foot Alien with Eerie Catlike Eyes

In 1981, Barbara Warmoth, of Franklin, Ohio, was abducted twice.

According to this mother of six, she was studied by eerie seven-foot aliens with yellow, catlike eyes and pointed chins.

Her first experience, on February 15, occurred when she saw an incredibly brilliant light filling her bedroom at 2:00 A.M. She got out of bed, looked through her window, and saw a saucer-shaped craft hovering nearby. That was the last thing she remembered.

Under hypnosis, she later learned that she had been aboard the UFO for one hour and fifteen minutes. The entities who examined her tried to reassure her. They told her that they had come from a planet called Antares and that they intended her no harm.

Her second abduction occurred on August 19, 1981, as she was driving along an interstate highway near her home. This time her experience occurred in broad daylight, and she lost two hours after the blinding glare of a silvery UFO forced her to pull off the road.

The being that examined her was dressed as before, but on this occasion, its face was uncovered. Mrs. Warmoth was now able to see more than just slanted yellow eyes. She could perceive that the being had no ears; a long, thin nose; pointed chin; and thin, almost colorless, lips.

She was placed in a large chair in a room that seemed to her very much like a laboratory. She saw what appeared to be electronic equipment everywhere. The being gave her a glass of greenish liquid, and then she lost all consciousness. She awakened back in her car, apparently unharmed.

The Ohio housewife is convinced that the aliens will abduct her again, but she emphasizes that she has no fear of the beings. They never mistreated her, and they told her repeatedly that would not harm her.

Two Fishermen Found Themselves "Caught" at Pascagoula

In October 1973 Charles Hickson, forty-five, and his fishing companion, nineteen-year-old Calvin Parker, were fishing from an old pier in the Pascagoula River, near the city of the same name in Mississippi. The men reported seeing a fish-shaped object, emitting a bluish haze, approaching from the sky. The craft landed, and the men allegedly were taken aboard by three weird creatures with wrinkled skin, crab-claw hands, and pointed ears. The men claimed they were examined, then released.

Sheriff Fred Diamond of Pascagoula told investigators that the two men were so frightened when they filed a report with him, that he feared they might be on the verge of heart attacks.

Their story was interesting enough to draw the attention of Dr. J. Allen Hynek of Northwestern University in Chicago, who had served as scientific consultant to the Air Force's Project Bluebook, and Dr. James Harder of the University of California. Plans were made to have the two fishermen hypnotized. Hynek concluded that although the men could be hypnotized, their experience was so traumatic that it was necessary to progress slowly with them.

Under hypnosis, Hickson and Parker revealed their traumatic experiences aboard the strange craft.

Harder commented, "These are not imbalanced people; they're not crackpots. There was definitely something here that was not terrestrial, not of the Earth."

This is the story the two men told.

They were fishing for hardhead and croakers from an old pier near the Schaupeter Shipyard, a sun-bleached skeleton of a barge dry dock. At about eight o'clock on the evening of October 11, a UFO suddenly hovered just above them.

"There was me, with just a spinning reel," said Hickson, "and Calvin went hysterical on me. You can't imagine how it was."

According to the report of the sheriff's office at Pascagoula, Hickson said that the luminous, oblong craft landed near them. Three creatures paralyzed him, floated him to their craft, placed him in front of an instrument that resembled a big eye, then put him back on the pier.

Calvin Parker was not able to add much to the report.

He apparently fainted when the creatures approached them, and he said he did not know what had happened inside the strange craft. After a couple of days, the two men refused further interviews with the press.

Beyond Pascagoula

Alyne A. Pustanio related this tale to the authors:

The aftermath of the Pascagoula abduction is well known: Parker and Hickson were repeatedly interviewed by local law enforcement agencies and eventually subjected to testing by armed services medical staff at Keesler. Although the Sheriff had issued a gag-order, the media somehow got hold of the story and it became a free-for-all; ultimately only Hickson survived unscathed, later writing a book about his experience. Parker, however, was eventually committed to a mental health facility suffering from "emotional breakdown."

Much skepticism still surrounds the Pascagoula abduction incident and opinions vary about what actually happened to Parker and Hickson. In recent years, however, reports have surfaced from a variety of individuals about other strange sightings occurring within days of the Pascagoula incident.

In 2001, retired Navy Chief Petty Officer Michael Cataldo revealed for the first time that he had observed a strange, tambourine-shaped object with flashing lights hovering over US Highway 90 near Pascagoula on the same night Parker and Hickson had their encounter. And on the night of October 10, 1973, the night before the Pascagoula incident, fifteen different witnesses, including two police officers, reported seeing several unidentified objects flying over a subdivision in the city of Slidell, Louisiana. And there are others.

The night was October 12, 1973. Teenager Darla Timbach (not her real name) finished clearing the dinner dishes and headed out the front door of her home in the mid-city area of New Orleans. It was a Friday evening and Darla had her mom's permission to visit a school friend who lived across the street. But as she stepped off her porch, Darla's attention was drawn to a strange object hovering over her friend's house.

According to Darla the object looked like "a bowl turned upside down. It had flashing lights along the sides and the top was smooth and white, like an eggshell."

Darla heard a "humming" sound and watched as the craft that was hovering over her neighbor's house suddenly shot away, straight up into the air; with a jerk to the side, it halted over another house nearby. Then, in a flash, it zipped back and came to rest once again over her neighbor's house, the lights pulsating to the humming sound.

"That's when I turned around and headed back inside!" Darla laughed.

Darla Timbach never shared her story with anyone. But across town, in eastern New Orleans, another teen girl was writing a diary entry about her own strange experience.

> According to Darla the object looked like "a bowl turned upside down. It had flashing lights along the sides and the top was smooth and white, like an eggshell."

That same Friday night, Aileen Artillo (name changed) invited a friend to come along with her and her parents to see the double-feature at a local drive-in theatre. Aileen's mom always made every outing a party and this night was no exception. She laid a quilt out on the ground next to the car and stretched the speaker as far as it could reach, and the girls spread out with tubs of popcorn, sodas, and candy.

During the intermission between the two features, Aileen lay back on the blanket and looked up at the stars, something she had always loved to do. The night was clear and the air crisp, but not cold. As she scanned the skies, Aileen's eyes became fixed on a group of lights that looked like stars but were moving swiftly from west to east across the sky.

At first Aileen thought she was looking at airplanes, but the lights—spots really—were moving too fast and close together. Then, before her eyes, the formation of the lights instantaneously changed, from a square shape, to a triangular shape, to an oval, and finally taking on a diamond shape which, to her amazement, seemed to stretch out and then shoot off into the night. Aileen wrote about the experience in her diary later that night.

Neither Darla Tambach nor Aileen Artillo were aware of the events that had unfolded in Pascagoula just two days before.

Then there was the case of Gary and Jennifer Nivers (names changed). Early in the morning of October 13, 1973, the couple had picked up their friend Karen Barnett (name changed) from the late shift at work and were heading home through the darkened New Orleans streets. They were making their way toward the Seabrook Bridge, crossing the New Orleans Industrial Canal at Lake Pontchartrain. As they reached the top of the bridge, all three cried out suddenly as something approached them from the night sky. Coming toward them, flying soundlessly, was a strange vessel.

"It was shaped like two giant pyramids end-to-end, overlaid on top of each other," Gary Nivers said later. "The ends were rounded and this made it look like a large football that was a deeper shadow against the dark night sky."

"It was the size of a football field," said Karen Barnett.

A series of pulsating amber lights glowed on the underside of the vessel as it flew directly over them, traveling end over end in a tumbling, rolling motion. Gary remembered looking over at his wife's face.

"It was glowing with this vivid amber-colored light," he said, "the brightest I've ever seen." The three watched as the strange object flew toward the New Orleans Lakefront Airport, a small, regional field directly nearby. Then something even stranger occurred.

"Just as it got over Lakefront Airport," said Gary, "all the lights went out—the landing strip lights, lights on the airport buildings, streetlights—they all went out." The silent, tumbling object was lost in the pitch blackness of the night.

The next night, Nivers and his wife traveled the same route as the previous night. As they approached the Seabrook Bridge they noticed that a pervading darkness—the streetlights leading up to the bridge were off, and the tiny airport was indistinguishable from the darkness around it. But the sky overhead was crowded with small planes and helicopters circling the skies over the airport and Lake Pontchartrain. Judging by all the activity, Nivers assumed they had just missed another sighting of the strange, unexplained object.

But this was not Gary Nivers' last experience.

On a winter night in 1981 he was with Karen Barnett once again, driving home from a project along Interstate 59, just outside of Slidell, Louisiana. It was after midnight and, except for the occasional 18-wheeler thundering by, the road was mostly empty. Somewhere near the Pearl River exit, Nivers and Barnett became aware of several small lights moving swiftly through the woods along the roadside; they seemed to be keeping pace with Nivers' truck. Suddenly, the small lights appeared to coalesce into one large light. It moved out of the woods and came alongside, but just as quickly it jumped in front of the car. Nivers and Barnett were instantly blinded by a searing, white light.

The next thing Nivers knew he was sitting his truck on the side of the road; the truck was running and both doors were wide open. Karen Barnett was lying in the grass outside the truck, shaken and groggy, but unharmed. By Nivers' estimate they had lost nearly four hours of time. Neither has any memory of what happened in those four hours, but Barnett has experienced strange dreams and occasional time slips—though none as pronounced as the one she experienced that lonely, winter night.

Can it be that the famous Pascagoula abduction was actually only part of a larger series of encounters involving two states and several eyewitnesses? These eyewitnesses think so.

Respected Researchers Consider This Case of Abduction to Be among the Most Convincing on Record

On the night of January 6, 1976, three Kentucky women were returning home from a late supper when they were abducted by a UFO crew and put through a torturous ordeal for more than one hour.

The three women, all reportedly of the highest moral character, were Elaine Thomas, forty-eight; Louise Smith, forty-four; and thirty-five-year-old Mona Stafford. All lived in or near Liberty, Kentucky. Two of the women were grandmothers, and Mrs. Stafford was the mother of a seventeen-year-old. None of the three could recall the full details of their experiences until they were placed under hypnosis by Dr. Leo Sprinkle.

It was 11:30 P.M. as the three women drove toward their homes from Stanford, Kentucky. They were about a mile west of Stanford when they saw a large disc come into view.

"It was as big as a football field!" stated Mrs. Smith, who was driving the car that night. She further described the ship as metallic gray, with a glowing white dome, a row of red lights around the middle, and three or four yellow lights underneath.

The UFO first stopped ahead of them, then circled around behind their car, at which point the car suddenly accelerated to eighty-five miles an hour. The others screamed at Mrs. Smith to slow down, but she found that she had no control over the car. Some force began dragging the car backward.

At that point, the three women lost consciousness and remained unconscious for the next eighty minutes.

The next thing the three frightened women could remember was driving to Louise Smith's home. They should have arrived about midnight, but they noticed the time was actually 1:30 A.M.—nearly one hour and twenty minutes were missing from their lives that night.

Abductees remember being roughly handled by aliens. (**Art by Ricardo Pustanio**)

Louise complained that her neck hurt. When Mona examined it, she saw a strange red mark about three inches long and an inch wide, like a burn that had not blistered. Elaine's neck had the same type of mark on it.

The frightened women called Lowell Lee, a neighbor who lived next door to Louise. After hearing their story, he had the three women go into separate rooms and draw a picture of what the strange UFO looked like. The three drawings were very much alike.

Although the burn marks were gone in about two days, the three women still could not account for the time loss, nor could they recall anything from the time the car was pulled backward until they were driving eight miles from where they first saw the UFO.

Following a series of hypnosis sessions, they were given polygraph tests by Detective James Young of the Lexington police department. Young, in a sworn statement, said, "It is my opinion that these women actually believe they did experience an encounter."

Dr. Leo Sprinkle, University of Wyoming psychologist and UFO investigator, stated that the three women, in his opinion, had been observed and examined by strange beings. He felt it would have been impossible for them to fake their reactions, and he commented that their experience during the time loss was similar to reports provided by other UFO percipients.

Sheriff Bill Norris, of Lincoln County, Kentucky, said that there had been a number of UFO sightings in the county that January.

In an article by Bob Pratt that appeared in the *National Enquirer* on October 10, 1976, Len Stringfield (1920–1994), a director of Mutual UFO Network, who investigated the incident, commented, "This is one of the most convincing cases on record."

The Hunter Became the Hunted in Medicine Bow Forest

In 1976, a forty-one-year-old Wyoming oil field worker claimed to have been kidnapped by alien beings while he was hunting elk in a remote wilderness area.

Carl Higdon of Rawlins had taken his rifle and a borrowed company truck to the north edge of the Medicine Bow National Forest to hunt wild game. About 4:00 P.M. he walked onto a rise and spotted five elk grazing in a clearing a few hundred yards away. He picked out the largest buck, lined it up in his telescopic sights, and pulled the trigger.

He could not believe his eyes when the powerful bullet from his magnum rifle left the barrel noiselessly and, in slow motion, floated like a butterfly for about fifty feet, then fell to the ground.

Higdon heard a twig snap, and he turned to face a strange-looking man, unlike any human Hidgon had ever seen.

The entity was over six feet tall, about 180 pounds, and had yellowish skin. The being possessed a head and face that seemed to be attached directly to its shoulders, with no visible chin or neck. The humanoid had no detectable ears, small eyes with no brows, and only a slit of a mouth. Coarse, golden, strawlike hair stuck out from the being's head and two antenna-like appendages protruded from its skull.

The entity was wearing a tight-fitting, one-piece suit, similar to the outfits that scuba divers use. It also had a thick metal belt with a pointed star at the buckle. There was an unidentifiable emblem just below the star.

The alien being raised its hand in greeting and floated a package of pills in the hunter's direction. Higdon remembers that he swallowed one of the pills when the entity directed him to do so.

The next thing Higdon knew, he was inside a cube-shaped object with the being and at least one other alien, together with the five elk. Higdon was strapped to a seat with a helmet—very similar to those worn by football players—on his head.

Higdon said that he was lifted aboard a spacecraft and taken millions of miles to another planet where he saw other earthlings living with alien beings. It was Higdon's impression that the aliens had been taking people—and a sizable stock of various animals and fish—from Earth for many years. Higdon was given a physical examination, told that he was unsuitable for their needs, and would be returned to Earth.

When he looked out of the transparent sides of the spacecraft he observed five other beings who he felt were definitely humans. There were three adults and two children. The children were female, and one of the younger adults was female. In spite of his inquiries, Higdon was given no information about the other earthlings on board.

The UFO set down again in Medicine Bow National Forest. Higdon was placed back in his truck without incident. His rifle was returned. He was relieved of the pills that the being had given him.

Although he was dazed by the strange experience, Higdon managed to radio for help. Then he apparently blacked out until he was found several hours later.

Higdon spent three days in the Carbon County Memorial Hospital at Rawlins, undergoing extensive tests and rambling and shouting about four-day pills and men in black suits.

Higdon soon recovered from the experience and said that he would like to forget about the entire incident, but knew he never would.

There is physical evidence that apparently supports Higdon's story. First of all, he was able to recover the spent bullet that was crushed when it smashed into what may have been a force field

Abductees are left with terrible nightmares of being hooked up to alien probes that scanned their entire essences. In most cases, they recall fluid and tissue samples being taken from various areas of their bodies. (Art by Ricardo Pustanio)

between him and the elk that he intended to shoot. Forensic experts say that the odds against retrieving a spent bullet after it has been fired are millions to one under normal conditions.

The truck that Higdon was driving was found six miles from the location he last remembered. It was mired in a sinkhole considered inaccessible to normal two-wheel drive vehicles. Members of the search party looking for Higdon also observed strange lights and bizarre phenomena in the area.

Higdon apparently experienced a miraculous healing of a tubercular-type scar on his lung. A problem with kidney stones also disappeared after his trip to outer space. Dr. Leo Sprinkle has observed that such unexplainable recoveries from ailments often occur among people who claim to have been examined by alien beings.

Higdon told Dr. Sprinkle that he witnessed portions of what appeared to be a futuristic city of tall spires and towers and revolving multicolored lights.

The question that remained in Dr. Sprinkle's mind was whether Higdon had actually had a real physical experience—whether he was actually taken aboard a craft and flown somewhere—or whether he was mentally programmed to believe that the trip to outer space had occurred.

Whoever or whatever the intelligences may be that are confounding us, Sprinkle has commented, it appears that they are trying to teach us that the world is more complex than we have formerly believed: "I think we are being taught to perceive that science and religion are not separated in this world—to recognize that as we gain greater technological knowledge, it will enable us also to gain spiritual awareness."

Interstellar Kid Gloves: A Child Abduction Observation

Ash Hamilton, the founder and host of (www.theparafactor.com), a quality radio program dealing with the paranormal and the unknown, shared this story of his encounter with alien abductors:

Recently, I marked over two years that I have been broadcasting my weekly show on the paranormal. Having the show has afforded me the opportunity to meet many interesting and many opinionated people. It has also helped to lay a baseline of similarities in experiences that I have shared with some of my guests.

One guest that was particularly interesting was Paul Schroeder, a self-proclaimed abductee. Paul's case, like that of most abductees, starts out weird and graduates to a level of high strangeness. A lot of abductees share tales that make their experiences not only hard to categorize—even in the paranormal—but often the subject of ridicule, even in a field that usually frowns upon narrow-mindedness.

I rarely relate my own experiences, because I have tried to take the focus off of myself, and not only in interviews with my guests. I feel as though I'm on a different journey of discovery right now, but I cannot deny when someone else's experience has some of the same qualities as my own. Like many abductees, Paul Schroeder's experiences in adulthood have triggered memories reaching back into his childhood. Not unlike Paul, I have a childhood memory that has troubled me far into the current stages of my life.

I was raised in a rural part of Illinois, just far enough south of Chicago to practically feel as though we existed in an entirely different country. My father worked third shift as an electrician at a local automotive factory and, like most men his age in that part of the country, basically worked all of the time. We had a single-level ranch home at the edge of town at the end of a dead-end street. Our home was fenced in between the small rural town that served as our community on one side, and two cornfields and an old abandoned elementary school on the other.

The old school was a magnet, and drew in many of the kids living on the three or four blocks surrounding the old edifice. The building itself was off limits, but the old playground was—for the most part at least—intact and very inviting to those kids whose parents couldn't police them enough to keep them off of the property. My parents figured that I was close enough to come home with a skinned knee or an injury and let me and my sister (who was five years my senior) play there almost every day. Eventually the bond between my sister and me would wane as boys started to take interest in her, and I suddenly became the annoying little brother. Suffice it to say that playground became more of a gathering place for her and her friends to socialize. Chances are, I would have had more fun at the more often used and approved park on the other side of town. This park was close to home, however, and that meant more play time and less time to-and-from.

My bedroom was less of a sanctuary than the old playground, and I can remember the uneasiness I often felt alone in that room. In fact, I often spent more time in my parents' bedroom because I often suffered bad dreams and night terrors that would land me in the comfort of their bed—much to their chagrin, I'm sure. I had a closet that always felt particularly suspicious, ominous and sinister, and a window that felt equally malevolent to me. It is the memory of that window, more so than the closet, that serves as muse and monster to me now.

I was no more than seven when my own stranger came calling. My favorite book was an illustrated number called *Grandpa's Ghost Stories*. In retrospect, this might be one of the earliest memories of my fascination with the bizarre. I would often have my mother read this book to me, and the protagonist's journey through the spirit world somehow stimulated my curiosity the way baseball cards excited other children.

However, it would not be phantoms that would call up my fears and feed on my terror, but something else entirely.

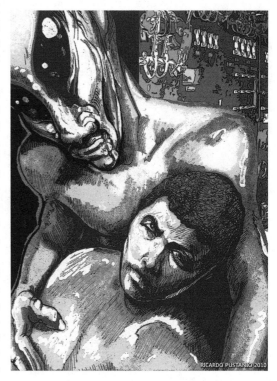

Sometimes memories of abductions resurface as terrifying nightmares. On other occasions, details of the alien examination may be revealed through hypnotic regression. (*Art by Ricardo Pustanio*)

I had no reason to wake up from my sleep and look out that window. There was no noise, no light, no reason. I just did.

What I saw wouldn't occupy even a margin note in *Grandpa's Ghost Stories*. Children typically don't scare other children unless they're the school bully or have an illness or physical or mental disability that isn't understood. Children playing by themselves rarely scare other children at all. Instead, this is often viewed as an opportunity to meet another child or claim a little stake on valuable playground property.

The child that I saw playing outside of my home when I was seven quite simply shouldn't have been there. Not alone. Not in the middle of the night. Not looking at me, looking at him. There shouldn't have been that much light around him. In fact, I couldn't remember seeing exactly where the light was coming from, it was just there, showing me what my eyes couldn't see in the blackness outside my window.

As curious as kids are, that curiosity knows little loyalty and jumps from one thing to the next like a lonely fall wind. This child appeared to be fixated on me, and when he smiled he reminded me of the animatronic Teddy Ruxpin that my family had purchased for me for Christmas. It could open its mouth and even tell me a story, but it could never quite match its inflection with its robotic maw. It was a device used to mimic a very human and very simple emotion. It was supposed to endear the child to the toy. That's easy for a stuffed teddy bear to do with children. They usually don't even have to talk to win a child's heart.

I was glad that this Teddy Ruxpin, standing spotlighted outside of my childhood home, had not tried to talk. I think the awkwardness of it might have been too much even for my *Grandpa's Ghost Stories* kid-brain to wrap itself around. As it stood, I do remember being very confused as if someone had pulled a quarter out from behind my ear. It was a feeling very much like knowing that someone had just played a trick on you that had nothing to do with magic, and you are left trying to figure out how they did it.

One thought still stays with me, despite the fog between that time so long ago and now:

I just knew this wasn't really a kid. I felt like I was somehow looking at an adult that had managed to disguise itself as a potential playmate. It had all the coverings of another seven year old, but its motives were far older.

That's where my memory ends, and I have no idea where it comes from, or if the event itself escalated at that point in time. I don't remember what, if anything, happened after I spotted the "child" in the night. I only have assumptions, and they are quite varied.

So as I was listening to Paul Schroeder tell me about his contactee experiences as a child, I felt that, as different as these experiences might be in context, there were similarities that offer little in the way of answers, but might give clues to motive, method, and process.

The abduction experience among children has some defining characteristics similar amongst experiencers. While most scenarios in the adult years are often frightening and nightmarish, aliens approach children in a different way. Children seem to be drawn more gently into the experience, and are allowed to acclimate themselves to the dreamlike quality of the event by looking out of a window or down a flight of stairs,

The Grays are often accused of participating in abductions. Many abductees recall being "beamed aboard" spacecraft after being surrounded by a number of the entities. (*Art by Bill Oliver*)

for example. Adults on the other hand, are definitely thrust into the "kid gloves are off" arena of experience.

This difference in approach raises a lot of questions.

I find it hard to believe that the differences here are based on any sensitivity on the part of the entities. I have come to suspect that although these powerful forces are capable of emotion, it is usually ill tempered. What then would be the provocation to adjust the methods that seem to be an across-the-board routine used for the adults of our species?

Maybe we've been approaching this from the wrong direction. Maybe it's not misplaced politeness on the part of our invasive little visitors, but a much-warranted apprehension.

What if the process of child abduction and the way it tends to vary from adult abduction is not so much preferential as precautionary? This certainly separates the sentiment from the sentient with our hosts, and it definitely follows in line with their cold and pragmatic behavior. Again, this might not be leading us to any new answers, but it might start us on the road to asking the right questions.

Aliens Investigate a UFO Investigator
Seeking Evidence of Chupacabras in Puerto Rico

The following testimonial is by G. Cope Schellhorn.

My wife and I visited Puerto Rico in April of 1996 at the height of the *chupacabra* phenomenon. My intention was to investigate a number of purported incidents and write an article. The trip was abundantly fruitful, but I decided in August to return to the island alone and add to the fascinating firsthand reports I had already collected.

Jorge Martin, foremost among Puerto Rican ufologists, gave me several new leads, which I set out to investigate. One of the most interesting cases was that of Maria Mojica, her husband, and her neighbors in the small *communidad* of Rio Lajas located about twenty miles outside San Jose. Maria and her neighbors were continuing to have an on-going series of contacts with *chupacabras*. Her husband had previously fired seventy-two shotgun blasts at the birdlike creatures without a discernible effect. Several of her neighbors had also fired at a group of *chupacabras* tearing up a bamboo grove, also without discernible effect except for traces of a blue fluid. As of the moment, no one was shooting at them. The locals, like Maria, had decided they meant no real harm. She had taken photos of the creatures' nests, but unfortunately heavy rains had destroyed the possibility of gathering any feces samples.

Maria seemed to attract these creatures like bears to honey. A strange rapport existed between her and them and, interestingly enough, between a certain species of little grays that were often found in the vicinity and appeared from time to time in her home. There was, however, no obvious connection between the grays and *chupacabras*, although Maria speculated that the creatures were being released by other ETs she had seen in the neighborhood.

One could go on and on about Maria Mojica, her neighbor Teophilo Cartagena, and the people of Rio Lajas. Suffice it to say that by the time I left her home I was thoroughly satiated with lemonade and new material. I returned that afternoon to San Jose and my little hotel, the Mango Inn, to try to make sense of it all.

That evening I had trouble falling asleep. The next thing I knew I was lying supine on my bed staring into the eyes of a little gray fellow with a heavily wrinkled face. I could feel a tingling sensation on my back at about shoulder level and also on my feet. Somehow I knew immediately that someone was behind me, someone was also at my feet, and I was being put into an altered state of consciousness. I looked at the little face a foot and a half from mine and said, "I'm not going to resist you." I swear he smiled. The next thing I knew I was levitated to ceiling level headed upward. I looked down and saw my bed. When I looked upward, I could see a round, extremely bright, yellowish light. I remember asking, "Will this hurt my eyes?" but I don't remember getting an answer.

The next series of events are in the order in which they occurred as well as I can remember. Keep in mind that I was in a partial state of altered consciousness—not, however, nearly as deep as it could have been. I ascribe this to my lack of resistance to the "abduction," if one can call it that. I did not, after all, resist accompanying my new companions.

I remember being given a physical. I was lying on my back and recall saying, "Could you stop the bleeding in my bladder?" I thought at the time the answer to my question was either, "We do not have the equipment," or, "We are not authorized to do that." This bleeding, caused by a series of internal capillaries or small blood vessels comprising an area no bigger than a quarter of a dollar, broke out from time to time and caused very bloody urine. A scary problem. Whether there was intervention on their part, I do not know. The condition, however, disappeared after this, and I have not been bothered since.

The next thing I knew, I was on the ground somewhere. It seemed to be a base. There were human-like ETs around me. Attractive, friendly people, all looking about thirty years old on average. A nice looking young lady approached me and we talked. About what I could not say. I could see in the background what appeared to be small hovercraft-like ATVs shuttling more wrinkled-faced, little grays about.

A "young" man approached me. We talked. I asked him what planet his friends were from. He answered with something like "Restar, Restat...." I said, "What did you say?" and he said, "You just rest well now." I caught the intended pun at the time, which surprises me now.

Another young lady with coal black hair approached me. She told me she had read my "Thoth books." I had never thought of my early books as Thoth books but, on second thought, it seemed appropriate, and flattering to boot.

The next thing I remember is being in a room with what I took to be the crew sitting around a table. The only two standing were me and a girl by a window. She was the only one who wasn't svelte and extremely fit looking, although she was, by our standards, barely overweight.

A young man sitting at the table in front of me said something disparaging about Earth and humans, and I was on the verge of saying, "Why don't you try living here for awhile. It isn't easy." I kept my mouth shut, however, although he—and the others—may have been able to read my mind.

> The next thing I knew, I was on the ground somewhere. It seemed to be a base. There were human-like ETs around me. Attractive, friendly people, all looking about thirty years old on average.

The girl near the window said, "Here comes _____." Someone else said, "He looks like he's dressed for the Middle Ages." The slightly stocky one rejoined, "I don't care how he looks. He's the best."

I don't remember being interrogated, but I am sure I was. For the life of me, I couldn't tell you who was in command or where this base of operations was located. I can't even say for sure why I was abducted. That is all I remember. I awoke in my room to a loud clapping sound. I was instantaneously fully awake.

The next day I telephoned Jorge Martin. He asked if I was sure I had been abducted. I said pretty sure. He said it sounded like it.

He wondered if I could have been dreaming. We both agreed that also was a possibility.

Then he said, "You know, they often follow up with a return visitation. Don't be surprised."

But, as far as I know, they did not visit me again.

For several days after this episode, I had a burning sensation in my eyes. I concluded this must have been caused by looking at the bright light emanating from the ship as I was being levitated upward. It was the burning in my eyes that finally convinced me that dreaming wasn't the best explanation for what I had experienced.

Several weeks later I told my story to noted ufologist Budd Hopkins. He advised me to keep it to myself unless I wanted to become known as an abductee which, he believed, would compromise the reception of my investigative reporting. I did keep quiet for some time, but primarily because, after twenty years of keen interest in UFO phenomena, I had become convinced of its legitimacy and my interests were now growing in fields outside Ufology.

The Puerto Rican experience was my first conscious contact with ET intelligences. I was fifty-six years old at the time. Since then, several other brief personal incidents have caught my attention and have left me pondering possibilities. How much happens to us, I wonder, of which we are barely conscious or totally unconscious?

The Multiple Experiences of Abductees

In the course of the numerous hypnotic regressions that he conducted with UFO abductees, Dr. James Harder said that he had found much evidence to support the theory that aliens employ a means to find and to reexamine abductees at various intervals, sometimes throughout a person's lifetime and sometimes without the person being aware of it.

"It's as if some sort of extraterrestrial group of psychologists is making a study of humans," Dr. Harder observed.

Dr. Harder and others have discovered that a high percentage of people who have been abducted have undergone multiple experiences with UFO entities. Most abductees who have had more than one experience with UFO aliens usually undergo the first encounter between the ages of five and nine. These abductees remember the alien as friendly and quite human in appearance. Upon further hypnotic regression and careful probing, however, the investigators have learned that the entity did not look human at all.

In most cases, the entity usually tells the child that he will be back to see him throughout the course of his life. He also admonishes the child not to tell his parents about the encounter. In a great number of cases, memory of the encounter is somehow blocked out of the child's mind. Harder has also discovered that during the adult abductee experience, men and women undergoing the encounter will often report having a vague memory of their abductor, and they will say things such as "I feel I've seen this entity before."

In Dr. Harder's opinion, the multiple UFO abduction is not a random occurrence. "If it were random, the possibility of it happening to the same person more than once is extremely remote."

He Awakened to Find Shadowy Figures
Deciding on the Best Procedures to Use on Him

Charles B., of Miami, Florida, is haunted by the memory of lying on a table in a small room made of a material similar to metal in some kind of vehicle. The light

The Grays are also most often blamed for cattle abductions. Some researchers claim that the Grays have developed a genetic digestive disorder and they are best able to sustain themselves on Earth by ingesting an enzyme, or hormonal secretion, most readily obtained from the tongues and throats of cattle. (*Art by Bill Oliver*)

in the room was radiant, soft. He felt sedated, calm, and trusting. Shadowy figures were moving around him, and he sensed that they were deciding on the best procedure to follow with him.

Charles is convinced that during that experience, which he believes was more than a vision or a dream, something was implanted in his brain.

"Ever since then, I feel heat, pain, and hear a crackling, popping sound in my head, like some integration process is trying to happen. My perceptions have changed dramatically. The intensities of those sensations have decreased quite a bit, almost as if the graft has taken."

Charles's girlfriend is very open to his experience, and he is able to discuss his feelings freely with her—the blackouts, the amnesia, and the urgent aching feeling that he experiences inside. "I know what's happening," Charles says. "I'm being prepared for something. I feel so impatient. I just want to get on with it."

Charles isn't certain when the initial abduction happened to him. It may have been one night when he was driving home late from work. It may have been another evening when he stopped by the side of the road because he felt sleepy as he was driving home from his girlfriend's place. But he recalls seeing—not more than ten feet above him—a circular vehicle with a square bottom and a distended portion covered with white lights.

He remembers feeling groggy and hazy as he gazed at it.

Then an invisible beam of energy shot through him, and his entire body, especially his chest, vibrated and got very warm. "Something exploded in my heart," Charles said. "I felt afraid, but I was determined to trust. The sensation, like a kind of electrocution, lasted quite a while, then stopped, and I went into a deep sleep."

But in spite of the deep sleep, certain impressions have come back to haunt him. He has begun to recall images of entities working around him in that circular craft, trying to decide what procedure to follow with him.

Charles is convinced now that seeing UFOs or extraterrestrials is not necessary for the complete evolution of his thoughts and his awareness. He sees the physical experience as a crude level of blending and communicating. He feels that the actual process of communion is on a much subtler level.

"I know them deep inside. I feel them. I sense them.

"But I can't see them. The old patterns of 'show me, then I'll believe,' need to go. I feel the need to broaden and to sharpen my deeper levels of perception."

Sex with Aliens

Although many people in the United States say they have had "close encounters of the most intimate kind," one of the earliest accounts of human-alien sexual intercourse came from Brazil.

British researcher Gordon Creighton translated the accounts of this incident, which were originally published in the Brazilian magazine *O Cruzeiro*. Shortly after the publication of Creighton's translations in *Flying Saucer Review* (1965), he received correspondence from Dr. Olavo Fontes, one of the original investigators of the alleged act of possible procreation between beings from two different worlds. Dr. Fontes included transcripts of the initial declaration made by the young man who had been abducted on February 22, 1958, and the official report on his medical examination.

Dr. Fontes stressed that although intelligent, the young man, Antonio Villas Boas, had little formal education. Such matters as UFOs and alien beings simply were of no interest to Antonio and his fellow farmers near the town of Francisco de Sales in the state of Minas Gerais.

According to his deposition, Antonio first saw the UFO through his bedroom window one night after his family had had a party on their farm. Antonio described it as appearing "like the light of a car lamp shining downward." In the darkness, Antonio and his brother Joao watched the "light penetrating through the slats of the shutters, moving toward the roof, then shining down between the tiles."

About nine days later, the strange light sought out Antonio a second time, while he was plowing a field. Once again, his brother also witnessed the light "so bright it hurt the eyes."

On the next night, October 15,1957, Antonio was plowing alone when an egg-shaped object came at him and began to hover above his tractor. The twenty-three-year-old farmer realized that escape was impossible on his slow-moving tractor, and that the soft earth turned up by his plow blades would impede escape on foot.

"I could see the shape of the machine clearly," Antonio said in his deposition. "It was like a large elongated egg with three metal spurs in front. On the upper part of the machine there was something which was revolving at great speed and also giving off a powerful fluorescent reddish light."

When the object began to land, Antonio observed three metal supports being lowered to take the weight of the craft on the soil. The young farmer admitted that he lost what little self-control he had so far preserved and decided to run. He only managed to run a few steps, however, before someone grabbed his arms.

He wrenched himself free of the grasp of his first pursuer, but he soon found himself being boxed in by three other "men" who grabbed his arms and legs and lifted him off the ground. Antonio, a well-muscled Portuguese Amerindian, said that his abductors were about his height (about five-foot-four) and strength. Later, in his deposition, he stated that he thought he could have put up a good fight if the aliens hadn't ganged up on him.

As the kidnappers carried Antonio toward the egg-shaped craft, the young farmer began to scream for help and curse the strange men. "My speech seemed to arouse their surprise or curiosity, for they stopped and peered attentively at my face every time I spoke."

Once inside the machine, Antonio stood in a brightly lit room as two of the men held his arms and others gathered around to talk about their catch.

"I say 'talked' only as a way of putting it," Antonio told Dr. Fontes and the other men who recorded his deposition. "For in truth what I was hearing bore no resemblance whatever to human speech. It was a series of barks, slightly resembling the sounds made by a dog."

After the aliens had finished "discussing" the situation, Antonio was stripped naked. The husky young farmer tried once again to resist such manhandling, but the aliens seemed to be trying to convince him that "they were a polite people."

Deciding that it would be simpler to comply with their wishes, Antonio allowed himself to be thoroughly examined. A chalice-shaped glass flask, with a nozzled tube, was applied to his chin, and some minor operation was performed that left a scar still visible to Dr. Fontes and the investigators.

Another tube was applied to the young man's side, and Antonio saw his blood "slowly entering the chalice until it was half full. Then I was bled once again on the chin, from the other side, where you gentlemen can see this other dark mark like the first one. This time the chalice was filled to the brim and then the cupping-glass was withdrawn. The skin was grazed at this place, too, burning and itching, just as on the first side."

When the aliens had finished pricking and poking Antonio, he was left alone to rest on a couch. He had not lain there long before he became aware of gray smoke that began to enter the room from some tubes protruding from the walls. The smoke had a suffocating odor "like painted cloth burning," and Antonio felt very nauseated and vomited in a corner of the room.

After a few more minutes, Antonio seemed to adjust to the nauseating odor and began to breathe easier. It was then that the startled young farmer had a most surprising visitor.

The door to the room was opened, and a well-proportioned and totally naked woman joined him on the couch. She had large blue eyes that seemed to slant outward, a straight nose, high cheekbones, a nearly lipless mouth, and a sharply pointed chin.

In spite of the bloodletting and skin sampling he had just endured, and in spite of his embarrassment at finding himself naked in the presence of a woman who might be from outer space, Antonio felt himself responding to her frank advances.

Later Antonio told Dr. Fontes that the aliens must have doused him with an aphrodisiac to have made him enter into such a rapid sexual union with the woman.

After the sexual act had been completed, one of the alien men appeared in the room and barked to the woman. Before she left the room, she turned to Antonio, pointed to her stomach and to the sky.

The man handed Antonio his clothing and indicated that he should get dressed. It was obvious that the young farmer had served the purpose for which he had been obtained, and the occupants of the UFO no longer had need of his blood or his body.

Since the mid 1950s, an increasing number of people have reported strange and frightening cases of forced sexual intercourse with alien beings. (*Art by Ricardo Pustanio*)

If the aliens left satisfied that they had gotten what they had desired from their visit, it turned out that they were not really as considerate of Antonio as they had seemed. The next day the farmer became ill. His eyes began to burn and a series of sores broke out on his arms and legs. In the middle of each of the sores was a little lump or spot that was very itchy. Two weeks later, Antonio's face became speckled with yellowish spots. Some doctors stated that such symptoms strongly suggested radiation poisoning or exposure to some type of radiation.

During the period of his abduction, Antonio had had plenty of time to study his captors while they had been busy examining him. It seems worthwhile to quote some of these observations because they bear great similarity to the descriptions of aliens given by so many who have witnessed UFO occupants. They are doubly valuable because this unsophisticated farmer from the Brazilian interior had not previously been exposed to UFO contactee or abduction stories. As Gordon Creighton translated Antonio's description:

> [The aliens] were dressed in tight-fitting overalls made of a thick but soft cloth, gray in color, with black bands here and there. This garment went right up to the neck, where it joined a sort of helmet ... of the same color,

which seemed stiffer and was reinforced at the back by strips of thin metal, one of them being triangular and on a level with the nose....

The height of their helmets must have corresponded to double the size of a normal head. It is probable that there was something else as well in the helmets ... but on the top, from the center of the head, three round silvery tubes emerged which were a little thinner than a garden-hose pipe. These tubes, one in the center and one on each side, were smooth, and they ran backward and downward, curving in toward the ribs.

The aliens wore five-fingered gloves of a thick material, but that did not hinder them from gripping Antonio tightly, nor from deftly handling the rubber tubes they used for extracting his blood.

All of the members of the crew wore, at chest level, a sort of round shield, the size of a slice of pineapple, which from time to time gave off luminous reflections.

The trousers were also tight-fitting over the seat, thighs, and legs.... There was no clear separation at the ankle between trousers and shoes; they were a continuation of each other.... The soles of their feet, however, had a detail different from ours. They were very thick, two or three inches thick, and quite turned up (or arched up) in front.... Despite this, the men's gait was quite free and easy, and they were nimble in their movements.

Gordon Creighton, a former British consulate officer in Brazil, subsequently offered a few theories of the Antonio Villas Boas incident, labeling it "The Most Amazing Case of All."

Antonio makes it clear that all of his little men were wearing helmets with pipes coming from a device located on their backs. The girl, who did not leave the UFO, wore no such helmet or device, presumably because she was 'at home' in her own atmosphere. It is of course true that Antonio had no helmet or breathing device either, and he claims to have been able to survive in there. Let us not forget, however, that he did have an attack of violent vomiting.... Does this perhaps mean that their atmosphere, although disagreeable to us, can nevertheless be tolerated by us, and is not fatal? That, by contrast with this, our atmosphere is impossible for them? In such a case, would not the obvious solution be to breed a mixed race, a new race which would have inherited some of our characteristics, including our ability to live in a mixture of eighty percent nitrogen and twenty percent oxygen? A new race, in brief, which is destined to live here, and to populate the vast uninhabited areas of Brazil?

Have the UFO crews been seeding a new race, not only in the remote areas of Brazil, but across the Earth? If such a master plan of genetic manipulation is in progress, it would be much easier to deal only with embryo-stage humans taken from earthwomen.

Or, in the case of Antonio Villas Boas, bring an alien female, whose egg is ready to be fertilized, to the earthman. The nature of human male sexual response being what it is, the aliens need only provide a woman of their species who would most nearly correspond to an earthman's ideals of feminine beauty and douse the man with a powerful aphrodisiac to help him overcome any innate shyness and fear. Presto, the whole problem of interbreeding becomes much easier to accomplish. The alien woman waits out her gestation period in comfort, tended to by her own kind, and the earthman is left with either a memory of a bizarre dream or a story that no one will believe. The aliens would gain another healthy product of crossbreeding; the inhabitants of Earth would receive only another case study to confuse their already tenuous and hesitant efforts to derive a meaning from the UFO abduction reports.

Not All Human Sperm Donors Are Abducted

Such cases as Villas Boas' one-on-one sexual encounter with an alien female are not nearly so common as those in which human males become unwilling sperm donors without being abducted.

"Don't think I'm some kind of nut," the letter began in a familiar plea. "I never did believe in UFOs, but here is my experience. I will not reveal my name, but I live in Las Vegas. I love women, and since I am married, I must be very careful.

"A girl and I were parked on a very lonely desert road. We had a blanket on the ground and were very busy in a certain act, when a very, very hot wave fell on us.

"I looked up to see two men, both about five feet, six inches tall, standing beside us in a soft light. They had on some kind of coveralls that looked like divers' suits. Their faces didn't look strange, but they had no hair on their heads. They spoke a language I couldn't understand. Behind them, hovering about twenty feet off the ground, was a craft that had a circle of small lights around its middle.

"The two men raised us up by our arms, and they felt all over our naked bodies. They pushed the backs of our knees and made us kneel. They placed some kind of vial over my penis and extracted semen. One of them cut off some of my girl's hair, put it in a container, and pointed toward the sky. Then they walked beneath the ship, stood in the circle of a spotlight, and they were gone. The UFO disappeared from sight in ten seconds."

Peggy's Daughter Says Her Father Is an Alien

Peggy of Dearborn, Michigan, has begun to question the true origin of her daughter Sara and who her child's father might really have been. A single mother, Peggy chose to keep her child when she became pregnant and decided not to marry the man she had been dating.

Because of the accelerated growth of Sara's head, Peggy had the child X-rayed when she was three. The doctor said that although Sara's head was adult-sized, there was no need to worry. Sara had excessively rapid brain development and was an exceptional child with potential genius ability.

When Sara was four or five, she began to draw pictures of spacecraft and an entity she identified as her father. She also began to speak of the lessons that "Daddy" taught her at night. According to Daddy, Sara had come on Earth to show people the way to the light—before the planet was destroyed.

Mary's Contact Began When She Was Only Five

Mary of New York began having "dreams" of UFO people when she was only five years old. She would see a large ship hovering over her parents' home and then, on a beam of light, entities would come into her room and look at her.

They always seemed to be examining her, as if they were doctors. They never spoke, but their mouths seemed to be fixed in a permanent kind of quizzical smile. She was never alarmed but, rather, fascinated by the procedure.

Shortly after she turned ten, she remembers the entities coming to her, taking her by the hand, and seemingly lifting her out of her body.

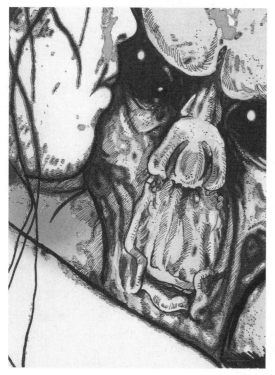

In many cases in which people report having sex with aliens abductees claim they were given a powerful aphrodisiac that rendered them helpless and subject to the will of their captors. (*Art by Ricardo Pustanio*)

She was taken to a lovely pink room where everything was soft, gentle, and loving. Pleasant music was playing. She could not recognize the music, but it relaxed her and made her comfortable. She felt as if she had been taken to a very special nursery.

Mary's most dramatic experience occurred when she was nearly fourteen years old. She was visited in her room by the entities, who stood back in the corner while a more human-appearing figure approached her. In spite of her youth and her inexperience, Mary knew that she and the man were engaging in sexual intercourse. The man caressed her, but did not speak.

Within three months Mary knew that she was pregnant. She was very frightened. She would not turn fourteen for another month. She could not work up the nerve to tell her parents. She considered going to her school counselor with her plight, but she could not bear the shame and humiliation.

In her report to us, Mary swore that she had not had any type of sexual encounter with any boy her own age or any older man. Her only sexual experience had come from the man who entered her room accompanied by the same entities who had been visiting her since she was five years old.

And then Mary told us that the strangest thing happened.

She had another dream in which the entities came to her room and once again seemed to examine her. This time she felt a bit of pain, and she remembered that she lay as if paralyzed while they performed some kind of operation on her.

When she awakened the next morning, she found a light smear of blood on her left thigh and a few drops of blood on the bedsheet.

"But I had an inner knowing that I wasn't pregnant anymore," she said. "A short time after the weird dream of surgery, my periods resumed."

Several months later Mary had the last of her "UFO dreams." The entities took her aboard their craft, to the beautiful pink nursery.

"This time I was looking at a baby—a beautiful baby boy," she said. "The entities smiled and indicated that I could pick up the baby. I did so, and I had the strongest feeling that I was holding my own child. I caressed him and held him and said, 'I love you.'

"Then everything became hazy. The pink room seemed to get smaller and smaller, and I seemed to be covered with a pink mist. I awakened back in my room, and I have never had another UFO dream of that type."

Aliens Have an Extraordinary Interest in Earth's Women

We first began receiving letters revealing the aliens' extraordinary interest in our planet's females in 1966, and such letters of alleged sexual abductions continue to this day. The letters and emails come from all sections of the country and from overseas, and they all have a desperate similarity and contain a strong sense of urgency.

One such letter began, "I am not a nut; I am on the dean's list at college, majoring in physics. This is my real name, and if you are suspicious of me, you can check me out.

"Last summer I saw a flying saucer at close range. It hovered over my car for several miles as I drove to my parents' farm home. It was definitely a metallic object.

"Shortly after that sighting, I was aware of something in my bedroom one night as I was preparing for bed. I could see nothing, but I could not shake a feeling of uneasiness.... I was not yet asleep when I felt a pressure on the bed beside me. When I sat up, I saw nothing, but I felt something touching me. I wanted to scream, to get out of bed, but I was unable to move.... I remember nothing more until I awakened the next morning, but I have reason to believe that something made love to me while I slept. I believe this incident was associated in some way with my sighting the UFO."

A series of letters from a college girl in a northwestern state detailed how an invisible *something* began to annoy her in her bedroom after her sighting of a UFO. She described fainting spells and inertia that would come over her whenever she attempted to tell anyone of her experiences.

This young woman, who planned a career in law enforcement, continued to write, describing a series of materializations and testifying that "aliens" walked among us, infiltrating our society on all levels.

"You can tell them by their eyes," she wrote. "I have come to realize that they are here to help us, and we should cooperate with them."

Her Lover Is an Alien

Psychic sensitive Ron Warmoth told us of a client of his who had also been given "marks" by which to remember her alleged alien lover.

"I just looked at this woman in amazement when she told me that she was having sexual intercourse with a spaceman," Warmoth said. "She told me how she had seen a UFO and had established mental contact with one of the crewmen on board. Later, according to her, the spaceman had begun to materialize in her bedroom at night and make love to her."

The woman told Warmoth that her otherworldly lover was well versed in sexual techniques, but that his torrid embrace often left her with round burn marks. Warmoth expressed some skepticism about the woman's story; then, before he could protest, the woman raised her skirt and displayed the evidence on her body.

"I can't say, of course, how the marks got there," Warmoth said, "but her inner thighs and her stomach were covered with small round burns. It almost looked as if someone had placed a hot metal grid work against her flesh."

> The woman told Warmoth that her otherworldly lover was well versed in sexual techniques, but that his torrid embrace often left her with round burn marks.

Are the Bedroom Invaders Aliens or Demons?

The late John A. Keel, author of *Strange Creatures from Time and Space* and many other books, wrote articles for two popular magazines on mysterious bedroom invaders and he was amazed by the amount of mail he received in response.

"Many readers wrote to tell us, sometimes in absorbing detail, of their own experiences with this uncanny phenomenon," Keel said. "In most cases these experiences were not repetitive. They happened only once and were not accompanied by any other manifestations. In several cases the witnesses experienced total paralysis of the body. The witness awoke but was unable to move a muscle while the apparition was present.... Such visions could possibly be created by some kind of hypnotic process or by waves of electromagnetic energy that beam thought and impressions directly to the brain. This would mean that the experience was not entirely subjective but was caused by some inexplicable outside influence."

Keel once told us that he had concluded that cases of UFO sexual liaisons are actually a variation on the age-old incubus phenomenon. "Induced hallucinations seem to play a major role in these cases," he said. "There may be considerable validity to the theory that Brad expounded in one of his books (*Haunted Lovers*, republished as *Otherworldly Affaires* [Anomalist Books, 2008]) ... that semen is extracted from human males in some succubi events and that this same semen is then introduced into human females in incubi incidents. The true nature and purpose of this operation is completely concealed behind a screen of deliberately deceptive induced hallucinations. Early fairy lore is filled with identical cases, as you know. And such sexual manipulations are an integral part of witchcraft lore."

Vividly sensual descriptions of intercourse with demons were wrung from witches during the terrible tortures of the Inquisition by priests trying to make the witches confess their sins. The graphic accounts of sexual molestation by alien intruders are wrung from the subconscious of abductees during hypnotic sessions by UFO researchers seeking confirmation of their theories. Even though there doesn't seem to be a correlation, fair-minded students of either, or both, phenomena would have to concede the enormous number of similarities between being impregnated for Satan's pleasure or being fertilized to produce hybrid soldiers for an alien takeover of Earth. Indeed, according to some researchers, the two violators may be one and the same demonic entity, and the complete domination of Earth may be the goal.

Let us briefly consider a parallel between contemporary accounts of UFO abductions and the legends that grew up around the old religion of witchcraft in the mid-1400s. For centuries the Christian Church had officially ignored the practitioners of the ancient ways. But at the dawn of the Age of Enlightenment, when an emerging science was beginning to study the structure of the universe, certain members of the Church hierarchy suddenly became obsessed with devils and their lustful designs upon earthwomen.

In his *Anti-Christ and the Millenium*, E.R. Chamberlin makes an excellent point that should be kept in mind while considering the ever-increasing reports of UFO abductions, alien impregnations, and sexual molestations by aliens:

"Paradoxically, it was the Christian Church which, seeking with all its powers to combat the practice of satanism, gave that same practice a form. It was necessary to define witchcraft in order to combat it, and by so defining, the Church gave shape to what had been little more than folklore. Most of the elements that eventually went to make up witchcraft had long been abroad in Europe, but for centuries the Church had been content to dismiss them as mere fantasy. The legend of the women who flew by night came in for particular scorn. 'Who is such a fool that he believes that to happen in the body which is done only in the spirit?' Such sturdy common sense was forced to give ground at last to a rising tide of fanaticism."

Donna and Sam Fear that Their Abduction Made Them Unwilling Participants in Creating a Hybrid Race

Donna and Sam C. have a farm in Nebraska about forty miles from the Missouri River. One night in September of 1981, Sam observed what he called at the time a strange bright light in the sky that seemed to hover over him while he was working late in the field.

Two days later, while he was getting the cattle home in the evening to feed, he noticed a strange, circular burn mark in the pasture. He paced the mark and found that it was roughly thirty feet in diameter and formed an almost perfect circle.

He called Donna out to observe the mark, and together they tried to determine what might have caused such a strange blight on their pasture. They investigated to see if it could be some kind of ant or burrowing insect that had eaten away the grass and made the ground appear brown and lifeless. They found no insect of any kind.

Donna suggested that if there had been any rain or thunderstorms it could have been a strike of lightning. But both of them agreed that even if there had been an electrical storm it was unlikely that a lightning strike would leave a perfectly circular mark, though they had heard of such a phenomenon occurring.

The next morning, Sam noticed two more burn marks in the pasture, again perfectly circular, roughly thirty feet in diameter. He mentioned the new circles to Donna that night as they ate dinner, and they wondered what could possibly be causing such peculiar and unprecedented marks in their pasture.

The next evening, when Donna was bringing home the cattle, she saw what she thought at first to be one of the neighbors' children watching her from the cornfield. As she looked closer, she saw that it was not a child, but a strange-looking man, roughly five feet tall with an unusually round head and very large eyes that seemed to stare at her in an eerie, expressionless way. In spite of her initial wariness, she waved to the stranger. The smallish man raised his hand in answer to her salutation. Then he walked into the cornfield.

Sam became quite upset with her report that night over dinner, because he felt that one of the neighbor boys might be spying on his wife. Donna assured him that it was not one of the children. They were on familiar and friendly terms with each of their neighbors, and she would surely have recognized one of the young boys.

Sam became even more concerned at that point and suggested that Donna might have seen a runaway or lost child, who was somehow surviving in the cornfields or in the barn and outbuildings. That morning he said he would see if he could find any sign that someone had been living on their farmland.

Although he did not spend a great deal of time in the search, he examined areas where it seemed logical to him that someone might seek shelter, and he found no trace that anyone had attempted to do so.

About three o'clock the next morning, Sam was awakened by the sound of cattle bellowing nervously in the stockyard. As he got out of bed and looked out the bedroom window, he saw a disc-shaped object hovering above the barnyard. It was glowing a kind of greenish color.

Then on the ground he saw shadowy figures, smallish men moving about. He was about to awaken Donna when he turned suddenly to see three of the entities standing in the doorway of their bedroom.

He shouted in alarm, and Donna awoke. She let out a short scream when she saw the beings.

According to both Sam and Donna, after their initial outbursts of fear, they were both overcome with a marvelous feeling of peace and tranquility. They permitted the entities to take them by the hand, lead them down the stairs, out through the front

Men have reported having their sperm removed, while women had their eggs taken or fertilized by emotionless entities operating in a laboratory-like environment aboard a spacecraft. (*Art by Bill Oliver*)

porch, across the yard, and toward the disc-shaped craft that was now hovering over the orchard near the farmhouse.

Donna remembers clearly that as they approached the craft, a stairway seemed to move down noiselessly and touch the ground. She recalls walking side by side with her husband up the stairs and into the dimly lighted interior of the hovering craft.

At that time, although she did not feel greatly fearful, the experience became less pleasant for her. She felt very apprehensive when the entities asked her telepathically to lie down on what she described as "something like a large piece of smooth white ivory." As she lay there, manacles moved out to clamp themselves around her wrists and ankles. When she found she was unable to move, she became quite alarmed.

At that point an entity, whom she somehow felt was more female than the ones she had seen previously, moved toward her and began to remove her nightgown. The nightgown was cut away so that it could be slipped over her shoulders.

The alien that seemed more feminine was, in Donna's recollection, a bit shorter than the other entities, with even larger eyes and a bit more pointed nose and fuller lips. Other entities, who stood around and watched the procedure, appeared taller, with only nostril openings rather than a pronounced nose, and with tight, expressionless lips.

The feminine entity who removed Donna's robe made a musical, humming sound as she extended her hand. One of the attending entities approached Donna with what appeared to be a large hypodermic syringe.

Donna remembers shrinking from the needle and watched it enter the flesh of her abdomen. But she felt no pain, and all the time the entities surrounding her were making soft, musical sounds that she described as almost like the cooing of doves.

Donna recalled that even though she had not yet been harmed, she still felt a natural apprehension as to what would happen to her. Would she eventually be cut open like some livestock animal being slaughtered and her body discarded? Or would she be deemed healthy and therefore eligible to be taken away from Earth to some far-away and unknown planet?

The entities around her moved swiftly. She remembers a bit of her hair being snipped, one of her fingernails being clipped, and portions of her skin being rubbed with what she said felt like her husband's after-shave—a liquid that left a kind of cool, tingling sensation. She was also aware of the odor of her own burning flesh when the entities removed a mole under her left arm.

Sam's recollection was that of being taken into a small cubicle where two entities approached him with a green vial filled with a liquid. He remembers that the entities did not form human words when they communicated with one another, but that they made a sound that reminded him of birds chirping. The words of communication seemed to enter his mind telepathically, and he understood clearly that they wished him to drink the greenish-colored liquid.

Sam felt apprehension in doing this, and when he drank the liquid, he had a terrible feeling that he might have been drugged or poisoned. He began to feel very hot all over and then chilled, as if he were getting a fever.

To his embarrassment he could feel that he was uncontrollably attaining an erection. To his further embarrassment, this seemed to be what the entities were seeking to achieve: With a pleased kind of humming noise, they moved aside the drawstrings of his pajamas and clamped some kind of mechanical device over his erect penis.

Within a few moments Sam was aware that semen was being drawn from his body and deposited into a vial.

Sam and Donna awakened in their bedroom the next morning. They were concerned at first because they had overslept and fieldwork was in full swing for harvest time. They did not remember the experience for several days.

When they began tentatively to discuss the mysterious dreams they were having, dreams of being taken aboard a craft and given a physical examination, they became very uneasy. Donna even became nauseated with the discussion, and they dropped the entire matter until around Christmastime, when Sam began to have nightmares.

What seemed to trouble Sam the most was the memory of his semen being taken from him. A religious man who was very orthodox in his beliefs, Sam began to have nightmares of his semen being used to produce alien babies on some other world.

When he at last shared this fear with his wife, Donna began to express more details of the experience and her own conviction that it had not been a dream. As they began to discuss the matter freely, they recalled the scorched marks that they had found in their pasture, and Donna remembered vividly the strange man she had seen watching her from the cornfield. Upon further discussion, Sam remembered watching the entities in the barnyard apparently collecting a wide array of specimens for some unknown purpose.

While the young couple could remember no further UFO interaction since that particular autumn, they both admit to being nervous about having another encounter. Sam, especially, feels that he was used. Donna speculates that bits of her skin and tissue might have been removed in the examination, and although she does not claim to be an expert in such matters, she wonders if enough of her body could be cloned in a way to interact with whatever embryo or fetus might have been fathered by the semen that was taken from her husband.

Not wanting to sound like victims of some science fiction thriller, the young couple have theorized that they might have been used in some strange program of creating hybrid beings. Perhaps, they suggest, Sam's semen was used to impregnate an alien female or an Earth female, who is somehow influenced by and under the control of alien beings. In either event, they are uncomfortable with the experience and with the memory of the encounter. Both of them feel as though they may have been used in ways opposed to their will and their beliefs.

Donna has gone even further in her speculations by suggesting that if bits of her body could have been used to create a clone and if Sam's semen could somehow be used at a future time to impregnate such a clone, then alien beings could be breeding their own brand of humans. She fears that this could be an organized program to create an army of human-like robots that would be totally under control of aliens in their master plan to conquer Earth.

Alien-Human Hybrids

Sometime in the summer of 1975, when her husband was out of town for a few days on business, Karen of Grand Rapids, Michigan, dreamed that she heard a voice calling her name. It seemed to be coming from the hill behind her house, so she got up, put on a robe, and walked over the hill. In the field behind the hill was a very large UFO. She saw three figures standing beside the craft, and she began to walk toward them.

"The aliens were dark-complexioned with slightly slanted eyes," she said. "They were small of build and stood about five feet tall. They wore two-piece suits with belts around the waist. On their belt buckles was some sort of symbol, like some kind of bird in flight." The three aliens informed Karen that they were there because she was one of their kind and they wanted her to bear a child. "One of the three men came up to me and slowly started slipping off my robe," Karen said. "I tried to move, but I could not. The man on my left stepped forward and started touching me. All I could do was cry. They told me that they would not hurt me, so I should not worry. As they helped me with my robe, I could hear them speaking to me. Their mouths were not moving, so I knew that they were using telepathy. The next thing I knew, I was at my patio door."

In her report to us, Karen said that within a few months she knew she was pregnant. Almost nine months to the day of her unusual "UFO dream," her daughter Casey was born.

"Casey is now five years old," Karen wrote. "She has been observed levitating by me and by some of her playmates. She speaks intimately of relatives, deceased before her birth, and she has already outlined her future as a healer in a hospital."

She Was Used by Aliens to Produce Two Hybrid Children

Christa T. said that she first became aware of her abductions in 1975 when she was used in genetic experiments, one of which resulted in a full-term pregnancy and the birth of what she believes is a hybrid child.

Hypnotic sessions enabled Christa to remember a series of abduction experiences that had actually begun at the age of ten. The last time, she was kidnapped and taken to an underground facility that was jointly run by aliens and the military.

She also recalled that a device was implanted in her left ear when she was very young. "I remember that the alien 'doctor' who implanted the 'tagging device' was more human-like and a lot nicer than many of the other aliens."

As she grew older, the gentle alien doctor told Christa that they would soon be playing a game with her called "planting a garden." At the time she was certain that he meant the aliens would plant something in the backyard—but she was wrong. A small device was implanted in her abdomen, and she was shown a three-dimensional screen with symbols on it.

In September 1981 Christa was again visited by the same beings. "This time they inserted a long needle from a long tube coming from the instrument panel. I was fairly certain that they were extracting ovum. They examined and changed something in my left ear, then they placed a transparent capsule-like device into the area of my abdomen. When they withdrew the instrument, the capsule was gone. After this examination, I became pregnant—although I had not had sex for eight months."

Her Handsome Lover Turned Out to Be a Reptilian Alien

At the time of her encounter, Lona K. was a sophomore honor student majoring in chemistry. To focus, to relax, to escape from the pressures of the classroom, Lona found great release in camping. Her father had been an avid camper and had taken her along on trips ever since she was a child of five or six.

Lona was attending a college in Colorado, and she took great delight in exploring the beautiful forest and mountain country on weekends. She found the out-of-doors the most perfect place she knew to recharge her batteries for the rigors of classroom discipline.

She remembers clearly that the incident occurred on a very lovely May evening. She was lying in her sleeping bag beside an idyllic forest stream with the sound of the waters lulling her into a restful sleep when, through, half-opened eyes, she saw a streak of light slash across the night sky and appear to come down in the forest. Her first response was that she was observing a meteor, but she knew that the light was too bright for any but the largest meteors. Then she thought that perhaps the light had been merely a trick of the eye, perhaps due to her own fatigue.

She had drifted off into a light sleep when, about 3:00 A.M., she became aware of movement in the forest and what she at first identified as the sounds of men and women singing. She assumed that since the words were indistinguishable she was hearing a group of half-drunken college students thrashing through the woods.

Lona looked up from her sleeping bag and saw lights bobbing in the forest. The musical sounds continued, but now that she was fully awake, she was able to determine that this was not a chorus, but independent solos being hummed. It was almost as if a moving opera was wending its way through the forest, she recalled, the cast members humming their lines.

Expecting at any moment to see the forms of half-stoned college students burst from the brush, she was astonished when she saw smallish figures with unusually large heads emerge. In the shadows created by their flashlights, they had grotesque, gargoyle-like appearances. They looked to Lona as if they were snakes, or amphibians, two-legged toad-like beings, moving through the forest. Their eyes were unusually large, and they appeared to have no lips, just a straight line for a mouth, again reminding her of a reptile or an amphibian. She could see no discernible nose but only slits.

Ricardo Pustanio 2010

There are thousands of women who claim that their children are alien hybrids. (**Art by Ricardo Pustanio**)

One of the individuals was carrying a boxlike object in his hands. It was emitting strange, crackling sounds, and rays of light were shooting out from it. Suddenly the entity carrying the box stopped and began to let out high-pitched squeaking noises. The other entities gathered around the one carrying the box, and they began to look around them into the darkness of the forest. A shiver moved through Lona when she received the clear impression that somehow the technology of that particular box had detected her presence, and now the toad people were looking for her.

She lay there in utter silence, afraid to breathe, feeling sweat trickle down the back of her neck. A dryness entered her throat, and she decided to leap up from her sleeping bag and run into the woods. She could count as many as six or seven of the strange entities, and her conclusion was that it was better to try to make a break for it. After all, she had been a medalist in her high school track days. She should be able to outrun the short-legged, amphibious creatures.

Just as she was about to bound from her sleeping bag and head for the woods, a gentle touch on her shoulder caused her to turn, aghast with fear. Her terror quickly subsided when she found herself looking into the face of the most handsome man that she had ever seen. He had long golden hair that touched his shoulders. His eyes seemed large and loving, and even though in the darkness she could not determine the color of his eyes, she somehow felt that they were a deep, beautiful blue.

All of her fearfulness subsided; all concern for the smallish, alien figures was removed from her thoughts. Although the stranger did not speak, he began to caress her, to put his arms around her. Lona felt herself responding in a very open way. Although she was not a virgin, her sexual activities had been very limited. She had been dating a fellow chemistry major who had taken advantage of a scholarship in Europe. She had not seen him for seven or eight months, and she had had no sexual contact with anyone else in the interim. As this stranger took her in his arms, she felt herself becoming sexually aroused with an intensity that she had never before experienced. She remembers making love beside the forest stream. She had not a concern in the world. She had no apprehensions, no misgivings, and the shock of seeing the alien beings had been completely removed from her consciousness.

The next thing she knew she was blinking against the sun of high noon. Somehow she had slept through the morning. Her mouth felt dry, and she had a slight headache when she awakened. She looked about her, hoping to see the beautiful, silent stranger of the night. She felt a flush move over her as she remembered the passion and the gentleness of their lovemaking. After a few minutes of calling out to see if her lover were somewhere near, she concluded that the whole idealistic romantic interlude had been a dream, perhaps prompted by her own sexual frustration.

Then the memory of the strange reptilian entities struck like a blow in the stomach. She jumped up immediately, prepared to run, or if need be, prepared to fight for her life against the grotesque beings. But all she could hear was the sounds of the forest birds, the sound of the stream. As she looked around her camp, there was no sign that anyone or anything had been there the night before—especially creatures so alien and strange.

After a few weeks of suffering some vivid nightmares, she began feeling extreme nausea in the mornings. She felt tired, irritable, as if she could not get enough sleep. Three months later the campus health service physician told Lona that she was pregnant.

Lona insisted that she had not had sexual intercourse with anyone for nearly a year. Suddenly her thoughts returned to the encounter beside the forest stream and the lovemaking that she had concluded long ago was just a lucid dream. Could it somehow have been real on some level of reality? And was the handsome stranger human or…. She shuddered at the thought that some hideous reptilian being had made love to her after placing her into some kind of trance.

Against the strongest arguments of her parents and her closest friends, Lona decided against aborting the child—whoever his father might have been—and she carried the child full term and swore that she would keep it. She had never told anyone of her son's heritage until she confided her story to us after a seminar.

Her son was born without any apparent physical abnormalities. Her fears that he might appear reptilian with slit-eyes proved to be unfounded. However she had been impregnated, the true sperm donor must have been human—with perhaps a few altered genomes added to the mix.

Lona named her son Kleto, for she "knew" on some level of consciousness that was his father's name. Kleto has unusually large dark eyes and a very light complexion.

His head might be considered a bit larger than that which is considered normal in size, but otherwise he does not display any overt reptilian characteristics.

Lona married two years after her graduation from college and has given birth to twin daughters. Kleto is loving and gentle with them, she reports, and the girls, now eleven, respond to him in a very beautiful way.

Kleto seems to be gifted with psychic abilities far beyond the ordinary, and he has excelled in all of his studies ever since he entered school. Kleto is also a superb athlete, although he specializes in track and field events rather than in team sports. He is a brilliant student and plans to major in chemistry when he goes to college.

Lona is convinced that the beautiful man with whom she made love was perhaps one of the reptilian entities that had the ability either to alter its own appearance or to create the illusion of being a human male. However she became pregnant, she is certain that Kleto's father was not a native of Earth. She is convinced that she has given birth to an alien child, a Star Child, whose appreciation of Earth exceeds that of most of those whose heritage is totally of this planet. Kleto, in Lona's opinion, is a citizen of the Universe, filled with love, filled with compassion, and filled with a responsibility toward all living things.

Lona admits that she used to long to see the father of Kleto once again, regardless of whether he would appear in reptilian form or in the idealized masculine human form. She says that she no longer maintains such a desire. She has gone about her life, and she feels that she has been privileged to serve as one of those individuals who may literally be the mother of a new race composed of earthlings and aliens.

Alien Light Beings Said She Was Once One of Them

Natalie, of Milpitas, California, was contacted first by a being of light who showed her the physical reality of their spacecraft. Then, on June 26, 1980, she once again encountered the same entities:

"They gave me a demonstration of their powers, which were awesome to say the least. They can make things appear and disappear at will. They also told me to start practicing telepathy, as I will need my *previous* abilities.

"I was informed that the craft that I had flown in a past life had crashed to Earth, because it had materialized at the wrong angle to counteract the planet's gravitational pull. I was being activated at

Growing numbers of women claim to remember having their fetuses taken from them at an early stage of development by aliens. Later, according to these women, they are shown their child in the care of an alien surrogate mother. **(Art by Ricardo Pustanio)**

this time in this life experience in order to help establish a direct communications link between their planet and Earth.

"The alien Light Beings took me on a tour of the interior of their ship. I felt that I should bow to them, but they told me not to. They said that I had once been as they now appeared to me. I got this overpowering feeling of love and goodness from them. Other beings on the ship sent me peace and love vibrations. The beings glowed. They are very advanced, but they still wish to assist us during our coming times of change."

Her Alien Guide Told Shelly She Was Brought to Earth to Heal

Shelly B., of Minneapolis, Minnesota, said she was born on June 15, 1950, at 1:00 A.M. to a mother who had had three previous miscarriages and who had to remain flat on her back for the first three months of her pregnancy to enable her to keep her baby.

Shelly was told by her mother that at her birth she did not cry like the other babies did, but just uttered a few little sounds. Shelly wasn't red and bloody like the other newborn children were. Her mother said that Shelly refused to take her breasts, so she had to be put on a formula immediately.

Shelly was told by her mother that during her toddler years she never spoke much, but she always seemed to make her needs known. She was late learning to speak, because she and her mother had developed telepathic communication. To this day, she and her mother "know what one another mean to say and often will say the same thing simultaneously."

When Shelly was five years old, she experienced a very bright light shining in her eyes that awed her so much that she called out to her mother in the middle of the night. Shelly asked where the light had come from, but her mother couldn't answer her. Shelly continued to see night lights of different colors. At the same time, she became preoccupied with pixies, fairies, and elves, and she began to draw pictures of them. Some of the drawings were deemed so professional by her parents that they were displayed in art showings and in galleries in the local area.

> There was something about *Close Encounters* and the scene of the great mother ship and Devil's Tower that particularly struck her.

At the age of eleven, Shelly became infatuated with a being from a parallel world. She drew a portrait of him and began letting him speak with her voice. She told no one about her fantasy, not even her mother, in whom she confided nearly everything. All through her teenage years, Shelly communicated with this being consciously, allowing him to speak with her voice, until she reached the age of twenty-four, when she met the man who is her husband. She is convinced that this other-dimensional being had been her companion even before she realized his existence at the age of eleven.

When the motion picture *Close Encounters of the Third Kind* was released in 1977, Shelly felt a very powerful chord being struck in her heart. She and her son went to science fiction films together, for both of them yearned for the stars. There was something about *Close Encounters* and the scene of the great mother ship and Devil's Tower that particularly struck her. Soon after, Shelly was visited in her sleep by the same guide who had begun appearing to her and speaking through her when she was eleven years old. She was pulled out of her body and led to an asteroid where the guide told Shelly who he was and what he was to her. He was warm and reassuring and loving.

Shelly states that she has suffered ups and downs, but through courage and determination has managed enough compassion to remain with the man she has married, a man whom she feels is not her true husband—although she loves him with an understanding type of love that she feels borders on unconditional love. She knows in her heart that the guide who appears to be a being of great wisdom is her true husband, her true "cosmic mate," as she has come to call him.

In 1986, however, she was told by him to give up her attachment to the idea that he was a physical being. When she did that, she experienced a period of spiritual growth that had been unequaled in her entire lifetime. She was introduced to new techniques in meditation, New Age thought, books on spirit guides, and channeling. And in January of 1987, Shelly found what she finally believes to be her professional calling. She decided that she was put here to heal, not just physically or psychologically, but spiritually.

She Was Abducted because
Aliens Wanted to Incarnate through Her Body

Shortly after Doriel, of Chicago, Illinois, saw a UFO in March of 1998, she suddenly found herself on board the craft. Two beings appeared to her: "One, a female, was named Leita. The other, a male, was named Garnal. They told me that they wanted to incarnate through me. I asked them, why me? They told me because I was one of them. They said that I could provide the right environment for their souls.

"I have a daughter now. I gave her Leita for a middle name. I was told six months before I was pregnant that a child would be coming to me. I practiced yoga exercises prenatally and had natural childbirth.

"After she was born, I told her what solar system she was in, which galaxy, and that I would be her guardian. Physiologically speaking, I had been told that I would be unable ever to become pregnant."

She Remembers Being Brought to Earth as a Child

When Mary P. was employed by a television station in California, things began to happen in her life that caused her to reassess who she really is and her true place of origin. She began to think seriously about where "home" is for her.

While she was reassessing some of her perplexing experiences by going deep within her inner self, the planet Venus kept coming to her attention. In her dreams, she was told to buy and study quartz crystals, which she began to do. At the same time, she began recalling that when she was five years old, she had visitors in her room at night. She had memories from that time of being taken aboard a spacecraft or arriving on Earth in a spacecraft.

When Mary was twenty-six, her life was in great danger. At that time, a beautiful white figure appeared in a shaft of blue light. The entity told Mary telepathically that she should not worry about being harmed, because she was being protected. That experience strengthened her conviction that there is no death after leaving the physical body. And it also showed her that she had friends in the spirit world.

Since that time, Mary has had other visitations. She has had precognitive dreams, and she has experienced conscious astral projection. She has felt every earthquake in California (those that measured 4.5 and above on the Richter scale) twelve to twenty-four hours before it occurred.

Frank Has Had a Life-Long Relationship with an Alien

Frank, a printer from Michigan, was three years and nine months of age when he encountered his "lady" in the apple orchard one afternoon in June.

"Much of what she said to me has been lost and forgotten due to adults ridiculing my stories or giving me explanations for what I 'thought I saw'," he told us. "The only thing I remember vividly was the loving feeling and the thought: 'You have so much to learn and so little time. You are one of us.' She repeated that statement over and over again—never actually speaking, but rather transmitting the thought while smiling."

Frank's parents couldn't keep him in the house after that encounter with the lady. He would crawl out of his window and lie on the porch roof most of the night. When they moved to a farm in Illinois, he would sleep in the trees so that he might be nearer the stars. Then, one night when he was eleven, he and a friend were standing on a small bridge when a very bright object swooped down from the east and hovered over their heads. "I tried to get my friend to look at it," Frank remembers, "but he seemed in a trance, so he did not see it."

Frank began a quest that evening that has taken him to nearly every part of the United States in search of more meaningful answers to life.

After his wife died in 1994, they continued an "exchange of wisdom" until his lady arrived and took her spirit to a "place of learning." The lady's last appearance to Frank took place on April 17, 2000. Since then his teachings, warnings, and guidance have come from a male entity.

Frank receives his transmissions "preceded by a pulsating buzz, a bright flash of light, then it's down to business and to the point."

Frank's son was born two and a half months premature, just as he himself had been. The boy walked and talked intelligently at the age of nine months. Then, when he was about four years old, he received nightly visits from the lady for three weeks in June. Because Frank was receptive to his son's discussions of his visitations, the child told him that the lady had said that he "had much to learn in so little time." Supported by Frank's interest, the child went on to relay the entity's teachings about death, the life beyond, and spiritual protection.

Is There an Alien Blood Type?

Two sisters, Bonnie and Mabel Royce, approached Brad after one of his lectures on the West Coast and asked if he was an Rh-negative blood type. When he responded that he was, they became very excited, declaring that he then could be a descendant of the ancient astronauts that visited Earth in prehistoric times.

Mabel and Bonnie have been trying to puzzle out where Rh-negative people come from. Most people familiar with blood factors, they said, admitted that people with this blood type must at least be mutations, if not descendants of a different ancestral line. If Rh-negative people are mutations, they wondered, then what caused the mutation? And why does such a mutation continue with the same characteristics? And who was the original ancestor who had the Rh-negative blood?

It has been demonstrated, they went on, that the majority of humankind—at least eighty-five percent—has a blood factor in common with the Rhesus monkey. This is called Rhesus-positive blood, usually shortened to Rh-positive. This factor is completely independent of the A, B, and 0 blood types. Mabel and Bonnie pointed out that, according to the study of genetics, we can only inherit what our ancestors possessed, except in the case of mutations. Therefore, if man and ape evolved from a common ancestor, their blood would have evolved in the same manner.

Notably, blood factors are transmitted with much more exactitude than any other characteristic. It would seem that modern man and the Rhesus monkey may have had a common ancestor sometime in the ancient past. All other earthly primates also have this Rh factor, but, Mabel and Bonnie emphasize, this leaves out people who are Rh-negative. If all members of humankind evolved from the same ancestor, their blood would be compatible. Where did the Rh-negatives come from? If the Rh-negatives are not the descendants of prehistoric humans, could they be descendants of UFO beings who came here aeons ago?

Warming to their thesis, the sisters pointed out that all animals and other living creatures known to science can breed with any other of their species. Relative size and color makes no difference. Why, they ask, does hemolytic disease occur in humans if all people belong to the same species?

Hemolytic disease is the allergic reaction that occurs when an Rh-negative mother is carrying an

Throughout history there have been legends of fairies and other supernatural creatures taking human babies from their cribs. According to many reports, today aliens are responsible for the cosmic kidnappings of human infants. (*Art by Ricardo Pustanio*)

Rh-positive child. Her blood builds up antibodies to destroy an alien substance in the same way that it would eliminate a virus. This process destroys any subsequent Rh-positive infant she may conceive. Why, Mabel and Bonnie ask, would a mother's body reject her own offspring? Nowhere else in nature does this occur naturally.

The highest percentage of Rh-negative blood occurs among the Basque people of Spain and France. About thirty percent of these have RR (Rh-negative blood) and about sixty percent carry one Æ negative gene. Only fifteen percent of the average population is Rh-negative, while in some groups the percentage is even smaller. The Asian Jews of Israel have a high percentage of Rh-negative blood types, although most other Asian people are only about one percent Rh-negative. The Samaritans and the black Cochin Jews also have a high percentage of Rh-negative blood.

Mabel and Bonnie asked the pointed question: Could Basque people be the descendants of an extraterrestrial colony? Or to go even further, could the Basque region have been the site of the space beings' original colony on Earth?

The origin of the Basque is unknown. Their language is unlike any other European language. Some theorists maintain that Basque was the original tongue of the Book of Genesis. Some believe it was the original language spoken by humankind and possibly the speech of the "gods" who came in ancient times.

Quoting Genesis 6:2: "That the sons of God saw the daughters of men that they were fair; and they took them wives of all which they chose." Who were the children of these marriages? In Genesis 6:4 it states: "God came in unto the daughters of men, and they bore children to them, the same became mighty men which were of old, men of renown."

Mabel and Bonnie found it fascinating that the word *blood* is mentioned more often than any other word in the Bible except *God*. Those two words, they said, could be found on almost every page—*blood* and *God*. The blood of the gods, as they pointed out.

Mabel Royce said that they had searched in vain for scientific proof that Rh-negative blood was a natural earthly occurrence. Instead, she said, she had found proof that the Rh-negative type had not evolved on Earth in the natural course of events.

"For many years people have been searching for the missing link," Mabel said. "Could the true missing link actually be man himself! The unknown link between Earth and the stars—hybrid man? Man may be the missing link between primate and extraterrestrial. It seems inconceivable to me that those working on the evolution theory have overlooked this possibility. How can they state that these people are lacking a factor contained in all other earthly primates including the naked ape, and not ask why? What other characteristics are common among these people that are uncommon to others? Is there a real difference other than just a different blood type? The Rh-negative blood, which appears not to have originated on Earth, may prove to be a major factor in demonstrating that humankind is a hybrid."

Mabel admits that examining Rh-negative blood may not be the entire answer, but she insists that it is a key toward unlocking the genetic puzzle of our true heritage. "My research has shown that the majority of those men and women with psychic powers and abilities also have Rh-negative blood," Mabel said. "Most psychics and faith healers have this blood type. Strangely enough, many of those doing research into the ancient astronaut theory and other phenomena also have Rh-negative blood.

"Why is there such a large percentage of Rh-negative in these unusual fields? Could these people have a vague memory of their true origin?"

Jeff Has Always Known He Came from Somewhere Else

Jeff M., of San Diego, has a distinct memory from the time when he was about five years old. He remembers standing outside, facing south, and having the sudden realization that he had come from "somewhere else."

"Associated with the place from which I had originally come were feelings of love, harmony, and longing," he said. "I longed to go back there, but I knew that I had a purpose for being here on Earth and that I would die before I could go back. I also knew, with some resignation, that I would live to attain a very great age before I would return to that beautiful place, my true home."

Jeff has known all of his life that he volunteered to come to Earth to help humanity. He has done this more or less in isolation. Lately, though, he reports that he has been feeling a strong desire to connect with others like himself. "I have intellectually known that they were out there all the time, but it did not seem right to search for them. I know that I have entered a new cycle of awareness for myself. I am now feeling a sense of renewed purpose. Both my spiritual growth and psychic abilities seem to be accelerating, and I am feeling a growing sense of urgency to find my true identity."

Jeff states that he has had multiple spiritual experiences and visions. He remembers one vivid experience in which he was driving with his girlfriend in a van near a large lake. Suddenly he sensed that there was a spaceship nearby, and it was coming to pick him up. Jeff became alarmed and thought to himself, "Not yet; don't take me yet. I haven't finished my mission."

The next thing Jeff knew, he and his girlfriend were on the ship, and beings dressed in flowing robes were ushering the two of them to a lounge-like area where other humans were sitting around chatting.

"They took me to a part of the ship that had a console with a viewing screen which at the

Individuals report encounters with beings that appear to be human-alien hybrids—citizens of two worlds. (**Art by Bill Oliver**)

moment was depicting a caravan crossing the desert in what appeared to be ancient Egypt. I got the impression that the viewing screen was used for monitoring and/or recording events that either have taken place, are taking place, or will take place on Earth. "The most interesting thing was that the being who escorted me to this console said, 'I think you already know how to use this,' and sat me down as if I were expected to immediately go to work. Amazingly, I found myself manipulating various dials and levers and producing valid images as if it were second nature to me."

The alien who brought Jeff to the screen appeared again after about an hour or so and told Jeff that it was time for them to return to the dimension on Earth in which they lived. Jeff began to protest. He wanted to stay among his own. The alien shook its head and promised that it would not be much longer and Jeff would fully understand his mission on Earth and be able to communicate with his Space brothers and sisters with greater ease.

Jeff remembers beginning to argue with his host, and the next thing he knew he was fully conscious again, sitting in the van with his girlfriend beside the lake.

Memories of Having Lived on Another Planet

Arlene from Cincinnati, Ohio, has felt since childhood that she does not belong on this planet, and she has experienced dreams of another world, as well as what would seem to be past-life memories of having lived on another planet.

"I am adopted. I do know the name of my maternal mother, though I have no idea who my natural father is. I was adopted by the registered nurse who helped deliver me. The adoption procedure was done very quickly, and I have never been able to find out anything about my father. I have an unusual blood type—it is 0 negative—and I have been told that it is very rare. For about the past ten to fifteen years, I have had recurring dreams of being involved in a great experiment, which implies to me the idea of having been seeded here on this planet.

"In many dreams I have found myself on board a spaceship. In several of these I have been able to look back and see Earth spinning in space. I have also dreamt of being on a planet with a green sky and two moons.

"I am extremely sensitive to light, and I usually sleep with my head all the way under the covers. I can function on four to six hours of sleep a night and sometimes can go one or two days with no sleep.

"Sometimes I am troubled by the fact that I was such an unwanted child. My mother was only sixteen, and my father's identity has always been kept totally secret from me.

"I dream of the great experiment and when its true purpose will be revealed to me. It seems to me that the time is coming to awaken to my true mission, my great work, my actual purpose here on Earth."

Although She Loves Her Earth Parents, She Knows Her True Family Is from the Stars

Chris, from Alberta, Canada, was born the sixth of thirteen children to "good and honorable North American Indian people." She was a difficult home birth, and her brother followed only fifteen months later. She was given to her grandparents to be raised by them until she left home when she was seventeen.

As long as Chris can remember, she has always known that her Earth parents weren't really her parents. Although she loves her parents, her grandparents, her brothers and sisters, she has never really felt close to them. She has always been aware that they weren't her real family. Knowing she was different from everyone else always left her with a feeling of isolation.

When she was about four or five she was playing on the shore of a lake near her home. Suddenly she looked up and felt a warmth and a beauty around her. There was a radiant white and gold light shining around her, filling her with overwhelming love. She got down on her knees and swore that her life would be devoted to God.

Now, as a grown woman, she has been "communicating with aliens on starships psychically." She sees three UFOs around her home quite frequently. One is a large, saucer-shaped craft, and there are two smaller, cigar-shaped ones, which appear to travel together.

One November evening, Chris was sitting quietly reading when she felt a sudden atmospheric change in her home. Standing suddenly in front of her was a small (about four and a half feet tall) clay-colored man in a dark green robe with a wide black belt worn diagonally across his chest. He didn't speak to her at that time, but she felt a tremendous love and calm emanating from him. She was overwhelmed by the feeling, and she knew that she had known the entity before and may even have been his mate. All he said to her, in thought transference, was, "Soon."

This has happened many times since. Chris reports that the entity now comes with two other beings. One night she was preparing to sleep when she felt his presence, but it was different this time. She looked up and saw that two beings were accompanying the robed entity, standing beside and behind him. They were dressed similarly, but in beige. Again he said to Chris, "Soon. I must not speak to you now. You are to fall asleep immediately, and you may come with us."

Chris was not afraid, and she remembers telling the entity that she loved him. In the morning she woke up feeling extremely excited. All she has ever felt toward the entities is a great amount of love.

The Star People

Writer-researcher Paul Dale Roberts sent us an interesting interview that he had conducted with Analee Aurora, who claimed to be "an alien shape-shifter."

"When I first met Analee Aurora," Roberts said, "I was dazzled by her brilliance. She seemed very cosmically aware of the universe around her. She gave me the impression that she had stepped from one parallel universe to another." Below in her own words she explains her life as an alien shape-shifter:

"It's been difficult being an extraterrestrial in a human body. When I was a child they took me on board the mother ship from time to time, for company and commiseration, but after they found that this made it even more difficult for me to relate on three-dimensional Earth—that, in fact, I displayed a real urge to fly away altogether—they quit doing that. In fact they grounded me for the duration: no further shape-shifting for me.

"I remember back on the home planet when our group volunteered for this assignment: 'Ah, that'll be a piece a' cake! No worries.' They warned me: "You'll be going to one of the darkest corners left in the universe. Very few of the inhabitants there even believe there are intelligent life-forms beyond their own. This whole assignment's been generated because they haven't grown up enough to clean up the mess they made: they're actually about to destroy their own planet with pollutants of all sorts! Completely immersed in illusions of duality and conflict. They still even communicate with words."

"What are words?" I asked, used to giving and receiving information in multi-sensory mental light-packages. My own ET body (presently tucked inside this one in a state of suspended plasmic manifestation) has a mouth, which doesn't even work to make words: just a little hole with which to drink liquids, which is what passes for food with us. The energy expended here around the act of eating never ceases to amaze me. I myself eat just one small meal each day in order to give this body a few calories to go along with the energy it gets from sunlight. I try to make the meal of something which doesn't kill its mother when harvested, like fruit or milk.

So, yeah, presently there's a huge ritual around food here, even beyond the truly massive amounts of energy involved in maintaining the food chain itself, not to speak of the karma involved in killing other sentient beings and devouring them on a daily basis. Oh, my goodness: the gathering of seeds, the planting, the tending, the harvesting, the cooking, the eating, the cleaning up afterward—three times every day ! Then there are the expectations of others to eat along with one, the fine restaurants with their own ritual communion between waiters and customers, the tacky depressing fast food eateries.... It all keeps me in constant amazement.

> I'll be so happy when I'm back home in a circle with one of our number generating a multi-sensory movie, enriched by the inner reactive thoughts and feelings of everyone else in the circle!

It's just difficult to function at all in this body. It's like I've been given deficient equipment. I'm always running into walls, inner and outer. It would have been easier had they programmed the memory of who I truly am into this—well, what passes for a brain—from birth, but no, they had to have the memory stream of humanity before the coming shift as closely as possible from the point of view of an actual human being, so as a result nobody got notified until they were in their thirties at least.

We all had to figure out this arcane system of social expectation by ourselves, and believe me it hasn't been an easy task. Simply having to use words to communicate makes things incredibly more difficult. Spoken language is in essence a dual system: stating a thing automatically excludes everything which that thing is not. How is one supposed to communicate whole concepts that way? The answer is: here, they don't deal in whole concepts at all, at least not yet; and not yet is when my assignment is so I'm, not to put too fine a point on it, screwed.

To make things worse, much of the time they're communicating something or other which has very little to do with the actual words they're speaking. Eighty percent of it has to be figured out from body language and tonal indicators! Then there's the ability to lie; a possibility I never even considered back home. Wouldn't work there, even if we found any sort of reason to try it.

Thank goodness they arranged to send the personalities of a couple of hundred volunteers along with me with which to attempt to make myself acceptable to various different types of humans, as I have found that the average human will reject another for practically any little difference they can detect. Man, I did not know what I was getting into when I volunteered for this mission.

Gathering information is very hard under the limitations of this mucous-cap brain they put on everyone here in order to maintain the illusions of duality—"the veil," some of their primitive psychics call it—pain, death, separation, loss, distance from the divine, and so forth. I understand some of these natives volunteered themselves to become humans in order to learn compassion—in the manner of actually doing math problems instead of just reading a text. I never imagined there could be a place in which so much compassion is needed that it appears to the inhabitants there isn't enough to go around. Of course, if each one of them just cleaned up the karma on their own ground most all the problems would simply disappear.

I'll be so happy when I'm back home in a circle with one of our number generating a multi-sensory movie, enriched by the inner reactive thoughts and feelings of everyone else in the circle! Oh, well. Only a couple of years to go. It's not forever. Just feels like it."

While Analee deems herself a shape-shifting alien, thousands of other men and women throughout the globe seem to be awakening to the memories that their essence comes from some nonterrestrial source in the cosmos. These individuals term themselves "Star People."

Her Body Has Never Seemed Solid

"I don't know exactly what kind of an 'animal' I am," muses Patricia, a writer from New York City. "From a medical standpoint, I am not supposed to be here. My mother was told that she could never have a child because of she was infertile. After nine years of trying, she somehow had me.

"But my body has never seemed solid. It is more 'plastic' and susceptible to my deliberate mind control. To a large extent I know that I 'designed' how my face and body looks.

"I am now over thirty years old, and it still seems strange to me to have a physical body. My fiancé has often chided me for bumping into things as if I had no sense of having a body. I tell him that I was an 'energy being,' a 'creature of light' who has taken physical form. Since I was seven years old I have written and spoken constantly about aliens, semi-divine beings, and elementals."

She Always Knew that She Had Chosen to Come to Earth

A. S. was born in one of the Soviet satellite nations. When she was three, she told us in an e-mail, she used to paint a creature over, and over which she called "a man from the universe."

"When my parents asked me about my paintings," A. S. said, "I told them it was a 'man' who visited me every night. In 1991-92, after the Soviet Union fell in 1989, many magazines were being published about UFOs. My dad was interested in this subject and told me that he and some friends had seen UFOs above our city. He went on to say that none of the pictures in the magazines looked like the ones that he and his companions had seen.

"During my childhood I always felt that I was different from the others, and I believed that I was like an alien here on Earth. I couldn't understand other people very well. Some well-meaning people tried to change me, telling me that I was too kind and too good to others and that I was always being teased or taken advantage of. I always felt that I was too sensitive to energies that surrounded me. I always felt that I was being watched by somebody. Sometimes I felt the presence of other energies, like ghosts, or whatever they were. Always, I knew that I had chosen to come to Earth and to help people in some way."

"Something" Fooled Everyone When She Was Born

Her birth itself was unusual, wrote C.J.T. "I was born twenty years after my parents married," she said. "My two sisters were nineteen and eighteen years older than

The Star People are men and women who do not claim to be extraterrestrial aliens, but feel that their true origins lie somewhere in the stars and that they are here to fulfill a mission of helping others achieve higher awareness. (*Art by Ricardo Pustanio*)

me. I wasn't planned. They didn't 'see' me coming. Medical pregnancy tests gave incorrect results. My mom didn't even have her normal pregnancy symptoms. It was as if something wanted to fool everyone.

"I feel like I am being watched and watched over. I've always felt that way. There are so many things in the world that remain hidden. I feel reality is so much larger than our very small perception of it."

She Can Feel the Universe Building toward a Unique Moment in Time

Another star person we'll call B.J. said that her mother's pregnancy was almost impossible. "She had cervical cancer, and everyone told her to have an abortion.

But she wanted a baby and felt I was the daughter she had always wanted. She was only able to have one baby and it was me.

"I had very low blood sugar at birth, chronic ear infections that should have left me deaf, but healed completely each time my ear drum burst. I was hit by a car as a child and only got a bruise. My family says I must have an angel watching over me.

"Oddly enough, I don't remember most of my childhood. It feels unimportant. Like my whole life is only the build up to something far more significant. The daily life stuff is sometimes hard to focus on, because it doesn't feel as important as what's coming and the part I will play. I'm not really sure what that means. It's weird. I've tried talking to people about it and they think it's strange

"Sometimes, I feel a kind of panic that I'm not doing what I'm supposed to be and that I'm looking for someone or something. People don't really understand me. I feel like they can't see what seems obvious to me. It's sometimes frustrating to try to share ideas with people who don't understand or can't. I feel like the energy in the universe has been building towards a single point in time. I'm not sure what it is but I feel very eager about it."

People Have Called Him "E.T." Since He Was a Boy

Alex, an artist from St. Paul, makes a statement that echoes so many of the others: "From my earliest memories I knew that I did not belong here. When I was seven I began asking who put me on this planet. I was never a bit like anyone else in my biological family. I have those strange, wide eyes, so that people are always calling me 'E.T.'"

Alien to Earth, He Felt More at Home after Meeting the Stranger

Daniel, a former law enforcement officer who is now an ordained religious counselor, recalls that when a Navy doctor recorded his blood pressure at 55/30, the medic was amazed that Daniel could be walking around. "I have Rh-negative, type O blood, which is present in less than seven percent of the world's population. My normal body temperature is 96.4. I learned that I have a transitional lumbar/sacral vertebrae when I injured my back in a fall in 1979." Although Daniel had the uneasy feeling that he had been misplaced on the planet, he tells of a strange encounter that helped to make him feel more comfortable with his sojourn on Earth.

"I was a small child, walking with my mother down a street in the Illinois town in which we resided. A stranger, who was somehow familiar to me, approached us, greeted my mother, then told me not to fear his kind or to fear what I was. His parting words to me were, 'Learn well, for you will teach many.' He also gave me a book that disappeared after I read it. I cannot remember either the title or the content.

"Incidentally, his words of admonition to 'learn well' echoed what my grandmother told me before she crossed over when I was two years old."

People Say Her Sons Have "Alien" Eyes

Jacquie, a thirty-three-year-old housewife from El Paso, Texas, is the mother of two boys with "those eyes." Jacquie herself says that ever since she was in grade school she has been told that she has "bedroom eyes" or "the evil eye."

"Ever since I was twelve," she said, "I have wanted to go 'home.' I always felt like an alien that was either left here by accident or by some sort of an elaborate plan. My sons have huge, tilted eyes. One has gray-blue eyes; the other has dark brown eyes. People always make a fuss over their eyes. They say that they look like aliens."

The Beginning of Star People Research

Organized Star People research began in the period from 1967 to 1972, when, during the course of his UFO investigations, Brad Steiger began to meet men and women who claimed to have memories of their "soul essences" coming to this planet from "somewhere else." The great majority of these people claimed to have had experiences with UFO beings or multidimensional intelligences since their earliest childhood. Almost without exception, they were of the conviction that they were to somehow serve as "helpers" and "guides" during the coming days of change and transition on the planet Earth.

> "My sons have huge, tilted eyes. One has gray-blue eyes; the other has dark brown eyes. People always make a fuss over their eyes. They say that they look like aliens."

Most of these sincere people were well aware of how a psychiatrist might interpret their "memories" and their mystical experiences, but in point of fact, a good number of them were psychiatrists, psychologists, and university professors. These men and women argued that they had both the wit and the wisdom to distinguish between fantasy and a personal truth that was somehow an integral element of their private cosmology.

Pursuing the subject of their unusual memories, Brad found that a great majority of these unique men and women had always had a feeling, a knowing, that their physical—or spiritual—ancestors had come to Earth from another planet or another dimension of being. At least an equal number of these individuals believed that they had experienced a prior lifetime in another world or another dimensional reality.

Philosopher Eric Hoffer echoed such sentiments when he mused that he had always felt that man was a total stranger to Earth: "I always played with the fancy: maybe a contagion from outer space is the seed of man. Hence our preoccupation with heaven, with the sky, with the stars, the gods, somewhere out there in space. It is a kind of homing impulse. We are drawn to where we come from."

American engineer, inventor, and futurist Buckminster Fuller often speculated along similar lines. "We will probably learn that Darwin was wrong and that man came to Earth from another planet," he once offered as a wry comment.

Star People "Remember" Starship Crashes and Earth Colonies

Many of those Brad interviewed in the late 1960s spoke of a "starship" that crashed and left survivors marooned on Earth. Some had painted colorful scenes from their soul memories of that fateful collision on an alien world. Others somehow remembered a star craft that had come to this planet about twenty thousand years ago on a mission to observe, study, and blend with evolving Homo sapiens. It was their goal to use their seed to enrich the developing species and accelerate the time frame when their Earth cousins could begin to reach for the stars—their true cosmic home.

Interestingly, far from fostering cosmic snobbery or aloofness such inner knowing had caused these people to recognize that they had a mission to help others to evolve and to assist the planet Earth to survive. They felt the need to share their "starborn" awareness.

A Pattern Profile of the Star People

As early as 1967, Brad had begun to take note of patterns of certain physical and psychological characteristics that form a profile of the star people.

For example, he found that nearly all the star people have eyes of an extremely compelling quality.

Although they come in a wide range of physical shapes and sizes, and from all ethnic groups, birth signs, social strata, occupations and professions, the star people have great magnetism and personal charisma. Strangers are instantly attracted to them and pour out their life stories and most intimate secrets within minutes of meeting them.

They seem to be very sensitive to electricity and to any other type of electromagnetic field. Many star people complain of vertigo when standing under neon lights. Others seem to interfere with television or radio reception if they are seated close to a receiver.

They have unusually sharp hearing. They generally avoid noisy crowds because they become "audio sponges" and soak up so much sound it becomes painful to them.

The majority of star people have a lower than normal body temperature. For them, 98.6 can be a fever.

A high percentage of the star people have extra or transitional vertebrae. An equal number suffer undetermined pain in their necks. Nearly all star people endure chronic sinusitis. An astonishing number have Rh-negative blood type.

The Activating Incidents

Although the star people shared so many physical similarities, Brad was really intrigued by the commonality of experiences that he came to term the "activating incidents":

Star People believe that the stars are the ancestral well of the universe and that humans themselves are made of star matter. (*Art by Ricardo Pustanio*)

For example, at around the age of five to seven, nearly all the star people experienced a dramatic interaction with an angel, an elf, a holy figure, or a UFO intelligence who openly revealed its identity. At around the age of six to eleven, many star people suffered some traumatic event, such as a severe accident, the divorce of their parents, or an illness that caused them to withdraw from their peers and society at large for a period of time.

Continuing Star People Research

In 1987, Brad combined elements of his investigations with that of the researcher Sherry Hansen, who had created a similar analytical questionnaire in 1970 as a counselor at the State University of New York at Stony Brook. Both Brad and Sherry found that their respondents were often the "helpers" here on Earth, for they spoke of being sought out for advice and counsel by friends and strangers alike. Brad and Sherry found such individuals in all ethnic groups, social strata, occupations and professions. Although these men and women expressed the feeling of being "strangers in a strange land," great numbers of them actively served in such helping professions. They worked in law enforcement, or as nurses, doctors, teachers, clergy, social workers, media professionals, or psychic and psychological counselors.

In 1993, Brad Steiger and Sherry Hansen Steiger fashioned the questionnaire that they have placed on their website (www.bradandsherry.com). Over 90 percent of the approximately forty-five thousand individuals who have returned the questionnaire report having experienced a sense of "oneness with the universe." A remarkable 86 percent claim some kind of contact with other-worldly or other-dimensional beings. The greatest single commonality is a desire to be of service to the planet and to all of its creatures, great and small. This driving sense of mission has caused many star people anxiety until they have found their specific task to fulfill here on Earth.

The Star People's Sense of Urgency and Mission

Marielle of Honolulu epitomizes the sense of urgency that nearly all star people report: "I am plagued with anxiety attacks and a sense of tremendous urgency to hurry and fulfill my mission before I run out of time in this life. And yet, I have no idea what that mission *is*! My burning quest is to find out what I was put here to do. Frankly, if I didn't think there was a higher and better purpose to my existence, I would have exited during one of several near-death episodes I've had during my life."

Marielle also experienced a most interesting physical anomaly: Her tailbone that had been surgically removed grew back. "My coccyx [tailbone) was broken in a fall down a steep flight of stairs at the age of twenty-six and *surgically removed*. It took three weeks for me to relearn my balance in order to walk again. There was no mistake: My coccyx was removed.

"After a similar fall off a ladder at age fifty-two, X rays revealed there to be a coccyx at the end of my spine. It showed up as a single, rudimentary bone, rather than the fusion of four vertebrae, but it is a tailbone, nonetheless."

Affecting Electrical Appliances

"I seem to affect all electrical appliances," states Brenda, a high school teacher from Vancouver, British Columbia, voicing yet another common star person problem. "My presence causes malfunctions with telephones, dishwashers, blenders, juicers, movie projectors, and lamps. All my cars soon develop electrical problems when I begin to drive them. I project so much electrical energy that a palmist couldn't even take a palm print. The ink kept running no matter what she tried. She gave up after four attempts."

He Messes Up Anything Electromagnetic

Another Canadian star person, Todd of Edmonton, Alberta, described his effect on electromagnetic force fields: "I have messed up everything electronic in nature at one point or another. I have never been able to wear watches except for quartz-crystal types; they simply quit running. I've even ruined digitals. Every car that I have owned has experienced severe electrical or charging problems. Microchip memories lose their data around me. I know that soon the time is coming for me to awaken to my true mission—my great work, my actual purpose here on Earth."

According to the National Air and Space Museum, Smithsonian Institution, Washington, D.C.: "We are the matter of the universe itself—combined in new shapes—struggling to comprehend its origins, its symmetry, its destiny.... The stars guard the answers to our mysteries; they hold the keys to both the future and the past. And among the stars, we may not be alone." (*Art by Ricardo Pustanio*)

Alien Memories of Past Lives on Other Worlds

The very notion that otherwise sensible men and women are suddenly claiming alien memories invites considerable study and speculation. Without question, the skeptical will dismiss all such accounts as the result of overactive imaginations or a peculiar kind of self-delusion. Perhaps these so-called star people, the skeptic will argue, are simply very sensitive people who may be unconsciously rejecting an association with earthlings because of the terrible inadequacies and shortcomings that they witness all around them. The belief that they have an alien heritage may enable them to deal more objectively with the multitudes of problems that confront members of contemporary society on a daily basis.

In certain cases, the skeptics no doubt have a valid argument, but the longer one explores the UFO enigma and all of its many shadings and facets, the more one discovers that there are no simple, easy answers. We have long ago accepted the reality of the UFO mystery, and we do not doubt the sincerity of those men and women who earnestly claim that they have made contact with some kind of intelligence external to themselves. Exactly what that intelligence may be and where it may originate remains a matter open to continued research. We may, after all—at least in some cases—be dealing with an illumination or a cosmic consciousness experience all dressed up in contemporary technological costuming.

Some years ago, when Brad was conducting extensive one-on-one hypnotic regression sessions with people who claimed past-life alien memories, he noted four basic categories of prior existences among the star people: the refugees, the utopians, the energy essences, and the helpers.

Those regressed subjects who fit into the refugee category told of surfacing memories of coming to Earth as survivors of great civil wars or cataclysmic occurrences on their planet of origin. In some cases, they recalled crash-landing on this planet and becoming marooned on Earth.

The utopians had memories of arriving on this planet as deliberate colonizers. Their home planet seemed idealistically perfect in their descriptions of their social and political structures.

The energy essences saw themselves as essentially disembodied entities of pure energy. In some regressions, the subjects talked about drifting rather purposelessly through space, or in other instances, approaching specific planets with the intention of inhabiting already existing physical bodies.

The helpers expressed themselves in the soul memories of men and women who recalled coming to Earth for the specific goal of raising the level of humankind's consciousness. The subjects who spoke of such past-life experiences seemed imbued with a strong sense of mission and a strong desire to work toward bringing about a higher level of awareness on Earth.

Results of the Steiger Questionnaire Updated February 2010

The number of respondents to the questionnaire now number over forty-five thousand, from nearly every part of the globe. We stress that this survey is not to be considered scientific, but is a collection of data to be used only for our research in exploring the UFO and alien mysteries. The following list shows the percentage of respondents in various categories.

Religious/Spiritual Background
- 44% are of Protestant background
- 39% are of Roman Catholic orientation
- 22% claim association with a New Age spiritual expression
- 11% are members of Judaism
- 4% are Hindu

- 2% are Muslim

- 9% belong to an "Eastern" religion

- 7% fall into the category of Other/Free Form

- 1% have no religious or spiritual affiliation

- 93% believe that their physical or spiritual ancestors came to Earth from some other world or dimension.

Marital Status and Family Support

- 23% had parents who were sympathetic to the mystical, the metaphysical, the paranormal, or to Ufology

- 46% had parents who were violently opposed

- 59% had siblings interested in UFOs/paranormal

- 16% had siblings who were strongly opposed

- 46% are married

- 31% are married to a spouse interested in UFOs or the paranormal

- 9% are married to a spouse who is strongly opposed

- 26% are divorced or separated

- 51% have children who share an interest in UFOs or the paranormal

Dream Scenarios

- 59% have had dreams or visions in which they were viewing a city or a planet made of crystal or diamonds

- 49% describe being in a doctor's examination room with smallish figures examining them [possibly an abduction experience]

- 60% state that since childhood they have "dreamed" that they were taken during sleep to receive special teachings in an unusual classroom or temple setting

- 79% experience flying dreams regularly

- 69% have had vivid dreams in which they are in a spacecraft and viewing Earth from a perspective far away from the planet

- 36% have memories of having been asked to eat a strange food during a dream

- 39% recall having to drink a peculiar liquid that was offered to them

- 53% experienced dreams in which they see Earth as it might have appeared in prehistoric times

- 54% perceive themselves in dream scenarios as a member of a UFO crew

- 43% state that they have in dreams observed themselves coming to Earth as a being of light

- 44% have dreams in which they sense themselves encircled by smallish entities (perhaps suggestive of an abduction experience)

- 49% have regular dreams or visions in which they are drawn aboard a UFO to receive counsel and instructions
- 79% have viewed themselves in "biblical" times communicating with known religious figures, such as Jesus, Moses, Elijah, or one of the disciples

Mystical Experiences

- 94% have experienced a sense of oneness with the universe
- 70% report an intense religious experience
- 86% claim an illumination experience
- 92% have experienced telepathic communication with another entity—material or nonmaterial, human or alien
- 76% have seen a ghost
- 79% have perceived the spirit of a departed loved one
- 72% accept reincarnation as reality and have experienced prior-life memories
- 85% believe that they have lived a prior existence on another planet or in another dimension
- 95% report out-of-body experiences
- 62% claim the ability to perceive auras
- 71% have experienced a white light during meditation
- 69% have been able to accomplish dramatic healings of themselves or others
- 41% practice automatic writing
- 87% believe that they have received some form of communication from a higher intelligence
- 77% have perceived spirit entities
- 75% have experienced clairvoyance
- 66% have made prophetic statements or experienced prophetic dreams or visions that have come to pass

Interaction with Light Beings, Angels, and Guides

- 79% report the visitation of an angel
- 77% have seen the manifestation of a light being
- 54% feel that they have been blessed by the appearance of a holy figure
- 93% are convinced that they have a spirit guide or a guardian angel
- 87% admit to having had an invisible playmate as a child
- 43% state that they once spotted an elf, a "wee person"
- 73% have perceived devas or nature spirits
- 87% are certain that they have encountered alien entities of an extraterrestrial or multidimensional nature

Physical Anomalies and Elements in a Pattern Profile

- 96% have chronic sinusitis

- 46% have extra or transitional vertebrae
- 58% have an unusual blood type
- 90% have a lower-than-normal body temperature
- 71% have low blood pressure
- 87% have hypersensitivity to sound, light, odors, etc.
- 88% have swollen or painful joints
- 78% have pain in the back of the neck
- 87% are adversely affected by high humidity
- 72% have difficulty in expressing or dealing with emotions
- 97% experience a persistent feeling of great urgency to accomplish their mission
- 49% have survived a life-threatening illness
- 58% have been involved in a severe accident
- 72% have had a near-death experience
- 87% are "night people"
- 89% have been told that they have unusual or compelling eyes
- 87% have experienced the "activating vision/experience of seeing an angel, elf, alien, light being, holy figure," etc. around the age of five
- 88% have experienced a life-altering event between the ages of six and eleven

Aliens and the Military

On October 9, 1955, General Douglas MacArthur told the *New York Times* that the nations of the world would have to unite. "The next war," he said, "will be an interplanetary war. The nations of Earth must make a common front against attack by people from other planets."

MacArthur returned to the theme of an invasion from outer space again and again.

In 1962, while addressing the graduating class at West Point, he stated: "We deal now not with things of this world alone. We deal now with the ultimate conflict between a united human race and the sinister forces of some other planetary galaxy."

It would appear that General MacArthur knew something about the truth behind the UFO mystery that was being kept from the general public. Perhaps he was aware that there appeared to be those alien intelligences who are genuinely concerned about our evolutionary welfare, and there are those who seem largely indifferent to our personal needs and our species' longevity. And, in some cases, there appear to be those aliens who are hostile toward our species.

In the Fall 1992 issue of *UFO Universe*, Judith Willms wrote an article entitled "Close Encounters Update" in which she quotes retired General Thomas Du Bose, who at the time of the Roswell incident was a colonel and chief of staff to Brigadier General Roger Ramey, the commander of the Eighth Air Force at Fort Worth, Texas. According to Willms, General Du Bose has freely admitted that in July 1947 the military investigators had no idea what they had found in the mysterious crash wreckage. "But the word came down from Air Force headquarters that the story was to be 'contained,' and we came up with this weather balloon story, which I thought was a hell of a good idea. Somebody got [a weather balloon], ran it up a couple of hundred feet and dropped it to make it looked like it had crashed—and that's what we used."

Lewis Rickett, eighty-two years old, was a master sergeant and counterintelligence agent stationed at Roswell Air Field. Rickett and Captain Sheridan Cavitt, another counterintelligence agent, were among the military personnel at the site. "It was no weather balloon," Rickett said. "The fragments were no more than six or seven inches long and up to eight to ten inches wide.... They were not jagged ... but curved and flexible. They couldn't be broken." Rickett and Cavitt collected a bushel basket of fragments, which were sent to Washington, classified top secret.

Oliver "Pappy" Henderson, two years before his death, swore at a reunion of his World War II bomber crew that he had flown the remains of four alien bodies out of Roswell Army Field in a C-54 cargo plane in July 1947.

Aliens Harass Military Bases in 1947

"The aliens declared a kind of war against our military bases in 1947 when mysterious green fireballs rained down at White Sands-Holloman and Los Alamos, two of the top-secret military installations in the United States," said one of our informants.

"I think the message the extraterrestrial intelligences were broadcasting to the citizens of the world was that all the combined military agencies of Earth could do nothing to stop them if they really wished to conquer the planet."

Lieutenant General Twining Declares UFOs Warrant Serious Study

In September 1947, Lieutenant General Nathan Twining of the Air Material Command (AMC) expressed his opinion that the many reports of flying saucers were substantial enough to warrant a detailed study. On December 30, 1947, a letter from the chief of staff directed the AMC to establish a project to collect, collate, evaluate, and disseminate all information concerning UFO sightings.

The project was assigned the name "Sign," and the responsibility for the task was delegated to the Air Technical Intelligence Center. Project Sign became "Project Grudge" in December 1948. In March 1952 the project was given the title "Bluebook" until its official termination in December 1969.

Secret Air Force Evaluation of Flying Discs

The following is a transcription of General Nathan Twining's letter as Commander of the Air Material Command, September 23, 1947:

SUBJECT: AMC Opinion Concerning "Flying Discs"
To: Commanding General Army Air Force
Washington 25, D.C.
ATTENTION: Brig. General George Schulgen
AC/AS-2

1. As requested by AC/AS-2 there is presented below the considered opinion of this command concerning the so-called "Flying Discs." This opinion is based on interrogation report data furnished by AC/AS-2 and preliminary studies by personnel of T-2 and Aircraft Laboratory, Engineering Division T-3. This opinion was arrived at in a conference between personnel from the Air Institute of Technology, Intelligence T-2, Office, Chief of Engineering Division,

and the Aircraft, Power Plant and Propeller Laboratories of Engineering Division T-3.

2. It is the opinion that:

a. The phenomenon is something real and not visionary or fictitious.

b. There are objects probably approximating the shape of a disc, of such appreciable size as to appear to be as large as man-made aircraft.

c. There is a possibility that some of the incidents may be caused by natural phenomena, such as meteors.

d. The reported operating characteristics such as extreme rates of climb, maneuverability (particularly in roll), and motion which must be considered <u>evasive</u> when sighted or contacted by friendly aircraft and radar, lend belief to the possibility that some of the objects are controlled either manually, automatically or remotely.

e. The apparent common description is as follows—

- Metallic or light reflecting surface.
- Absence of trail, except in a few instances where the object apparently was operating under high performance conditions.
- Circular or elliptical in shape, flat on bottom and domed on top.
- Several reports of well-kept formation flights varying from three to nine objects.
- Normally no associated sound, except in three instances a substantial rumbling roar was noted.
- Level flight speeds normally above 300 knots are estimated.

f. It is possible within the present U.S. knowledge—provided extensive detailed development is undertaken—to construct a piloted aircraft which has the general description of the object in sub-paragraph (e) above which would be capable of an approximate range of 7000 miles at subsonic speeds.

g. Any development in this country along the lines indicated would be extremely expensive, time consuming and at the considerable expense of current projects and therefore, if directed, should be set up independently of existing projects.

h. Due consideration must be given the following:

- The possibility that these objects are of domestic origin—the product of some high security project not known to AC/AS-2 or this Command.
- The lack of physical evidence in the shape of crash recovered exhibits which would undeniably prove the existence of these subjects.
- The possibility that some foreign nation has a form of propulsion possibly nuclear, which is outside of our domestic knowledge.

3. It is recommended that: Headquarters, Army Air Forces issue a directive assigning a priority, security classification and Code name for a detailed study of this

Although it is said that the flying saucer invasion began in 1947, Army Air Force Corps pilots were reporting encounters with mysterious unidentified flying objects as early as 1943. (*Art by Ricardo Pustanio*)

matter to include the preparation of complete sets of all available and pertinent data, which will then be made available to the Army, Navy, Atomic Energy Commission, JRDB, the Air Force Scientific Advisory Group, NACA, and the RAND and NEPA projects for comments and recommendations, with a preliminary report to be forwarded within 15 days of receipt of the data and a detailed report thereafter every 30 days as the investigation develops. A complete interchange of data should be affected.

Majestic 12: UFOs-Top Secret! What Every President since Truman May Know

The disclosure of secret documents known as Majestic-12, or "MJ-12," has revealed a conspiracy of U.S. military leaders to enforce a lid of security on UFOs. Majestic-12 was established on September 24, 1947 by special classified executive order of President Harry S. Truman.

Admiral Roscoe Hillenkoetter prepared MJ-12 on November 18, 1952 to brief President-elect Dwight D. Eisenhower on the details of a UFO that had crashed on July 7, 1947, in a remote region of New Mexico, approximately seventy-five miles northwest of Roswell Army Air Base. The "official" report also described the recovery of the bodies of four "human-like beings" that had been found near the wreckage of the downed extraterrestrial spacecraft. According to these documents all four of the entities were dead, and their corpses had been mutilated by desert scavengers and were badly decomposed due to exposure to the elements.

"Although these creatures are human-like in appearance," the secret report stated, "the biological and evolutionary processes responsible for their development has apparently been quite different from those observed or postulated in *Homo sapiens*." MJ-12 went on to describe how all military and civilian eyewitnesses to the downed UFO and its alien crew had been "debriefed" and a cover-up story of an errant weather balloon had been issued to the press. A strenuous program would be established to discredit any individual who might later attempt to say the crashed "flying saucer" and its strange occupants were real. The program was so carefully guarded that its existence was not made known to the public until 1987.

We were lecturing at the Twenty-fourth Annual National UFO Conference in Burbank, California, on June 14, 1987, when we were introduced to UFO researcher and documentary filmmaker Jamie Shandera. Shandera, with the help of two prominent UFO researchers named Stanton Friedman and William Moore (both of whom we had known for many years), had tested the truth of the MJ-12 documents. At the conference, they were going to reveal what purported to be documentary proof of a government cover-up of UFOs that began in 1947. Moore, in fact, had invited us to be seated at the front table while they made the formal announcement of their startling research, promising us that we would be excited by the implications of what was about to be revealed to the gathered audience of UFO enthusiasts.

According to Jamie Shandera, in December 1984 he received an anonymous packet in the mail containing two rolls of undeveloped 35 mm 172 / film. The film, once developed, revealed what appeared to be a briefing report to President-elect Dwight D. Eisenhower, which described details of the recovery, analysis, and official cover-up of the 1947 UFO crash outside of Roswell, New Mexico. The documents that had somehow found their way to Shandera had allegedly been prepared by a group of twelve prestigious and top-secret investigators who worked under the code name of "Operation Majestic-12." Some unknown source had mailed the documents to the film-maker within weeks of the death of the last member of the original MJ-12 operatives.

According to the documents leaked to Shandera, the Majestic-12 consisted of the following very influential individuals:

Lloyd V. Berkner, known for scientific achievements in the fields of physics and electronics, numbered among his many posts and positions that of special assistant to the secretary of state in charge of the Military Assistance Program. He was also executive secretary of what is now known as the Research and Development Board of the National Military Establishment.

Detley W. Bronk, a physiologist and biophysicist of international repute, chairman of the National Research Council, and a member of the Medical Advisory Board of the Atomic Energy Commission. Bronk's main field of research lay in measuring changes in nerve cells during the passage of stimuli to the brain.

Vannevar Bush, a brilliant scientist with an almost endless list of credentials, awards, medals, and academic posts held at nearly every major U.S. college. From 1947 to 1948, Bush was chairman of Research and Development for the National Military Establishment.

Gordon Gray, three times elected to the North Carolina Senate, succeeded Kenneth Royall as secretary of the Army in June 1949. Gray first came to the Pentagon in September 1947 as assistant secretary of the Army.

Dr. Jerome C. Hunsaker, an innovative aeronautical scientist and design engineer, developed the Shenandoah, the first large airship constructed in the United States. Among numerous academic positions, Dr. Hunsaker served as chairman of the National Advisory Committee for Aeronautics.

Robert M. Montague was the Sandia base commander, Albuquerque, New Mexico, from July 1947 to February 1951.

> Some unknown source had mailed the documents to the filmmaker within weeks of the death of the last member of the original MJ-12 operatives.

General Nathan F. Twining was in command of the 8-29 super-fortresses that dropped the atomic bombs on Hiroshima and Nagasaki. In December 1945 he was named commanding general of the Air Material Command headquartered at Wright Field. In October 1947 he was appointed commander in chief of the Alaskan Command, remaining in that position until May 1950, when he became acting deputy chief of staff for personnel at Air Force headquarters in Washington, D.C.

Dr. Donald H. Menzel, director of the Harvard Observatory at Cambridge, Massachusetts, was long acknowledged as a leading authority on the solar chromosphere. In 1941, together with Dr. Winfield W. Salisbury, Menzel formulated the initial calculations that led to the first radio contact with the Moon in 1946.

James V. Forrestal served first as undersecretary, then secretary, of the Navy for seven years. In September 1947 he became secretary of defense, responsible for coordinating the activities of all U.S. Armed Forces.

Sidney W. Souers, a Naval reservist who rose to the rank of rear admiral, became deputy chief of Naval Intelligence before organizing the Central Intelligence Office in January 1946.

Hoyt S. Vandenberg, a much-decorated Air Force officer who rose to the rank of commanding general of the Ninth U.S. Air Force in France in 1944, then named assistant chief of staff of G-2 (Intelligence) in 1946. In June 1946 he was appointed the director of Central Intelligence.

Rear Admiral Roscoe H. Hillenkoetter was summoned from the post of naval attaché at the American Embassy in Paris to become the first director of the Central Intelligence Agency (CIA), serving from May 1947 to September 1950. (The CIA was the permanent intelligence agency that evolved from the office organized by Souers.)

Barry Greenwood, editor of *Just Cause*, mused that his first thoughts upon seeing the list of MJ-12's alleged personnel was that if a UFO *had* crashed and was recovered, this would be the kind of panel that he would want to put together. "All of these individuals were at the top in their respective areas of expertise during the late 1940s and had the added benefit of government experience behind them."

In October 1987 we appeared on a UFO panel at the Whole Life EXPO in Los Angeles, which included Stanton Friedman and William Moore. Although they admitted they were still in the process of validating the MJ-12 documents, they stated they were "reasonably convinced" of their authenticity.

Friedman told the large audience in attendance that one of the principal purposes for the official government cover-up of UFOs—as disclosed by the MJ-12 debriefing document—was that there had been "almost a public panic in response to the sightings in 1947."

As of this writing in 2011, the validity of the MJ-12 documents remains highly controversial. UFO researchers are divided in their analyses of the investigation of Shandera, Moore, and Friedman.

Although military personnel must consider UFO overflights over bases and interference with their activities as classified information, a number of dramatic sightings have been revealed through the Freedom of Information Act as well as former military officers speaking out in their later years. (*Art by Bill Oliver*)

Project Bluebook

The late Dr. J. Allen Hynek, who was teaching astronomy at Ohio State University at Columbus in 1948, was selected to serve as astronomical consultant to Project Sign and Project Bluebook. Dr. Hynek was chosen both for his professional acumen and for the fact that he was teaching not far from Wright-Patterson Air Force Base, where the office of UFO research was established.

When Dr. Hynek came on board, he initially felt that UFOs were a symptom of postwar nerves, a bizarre kind of fad that somehow kept people's minds occupied. "The government was trying like mad to determine whether [the UFO phenomenon], the Martians or the Russians were responsible for the elusive discs being tracked in our atmosphere," Dr. Hynek told UFO researcher Timothy Green Beckley. "To put it bluntly, they needed a competent astronomer to tell them which cases arose out of the misidentification of planets, stars, meteors, and so forth."

At the beginning Dr. Hynek said that he would have taken bets that the "whole mess" would be forgotten by 1952, "at the very latest." He admitted that nobody enjoyed "busting holes in a wild story" and showing off more than he did. "It was a game, and a heck of a lot of fun.... Never in my wildest dreams did I suspect that [UFOs] would turn out to be a global phenomenon."

Project Bluebook's staff was assigned to carry out three main functions:

1. To try to find an explanation for all reported sightings of UFOs

2. To determine whether or not the UFOs pose a security threat to the United States

3. To determine if UFOs exhibit any advanced technology that the United States could utilize

A Bluebook officer was to be stationed at every Air Force base in the nation. It would be his responsibility to investigate all reported sightings and to get the reports sent to Bluebook headquarters at Wright-Patterson Air Force Base at Dayton, Ohio.

The Flying Saucer Enigma Turns Deadly

The chaos and confusion of those early days of saucer activity took a sinister turn with Captain Thomas Mantell's tragic encounter with a UFO over Godman Field Air Base in Kentucky.

The morning of January 7, 1948, offices of the Kentucky State Highway Patrol received a number of calls inquiring about any unusual aircraft that the Air Force might be testing in the area. Residents at Marysville, Kentucky, had sighted unfamiliar aircraft flying over their city. At 1:15 P.M. the Kentucky highway patrol called the control towers at Godman and asked if they had any craft that might be flying over Marysville and troubling the city's residents. Godman Field checked with Flight Service at Wright-Patterson and received a negative response to their query of test craft in the area.

Within about twenty minutes, however, the highway patrol informed the tower operators at Godman Field that they were now receiving reports of strange aircraft—"circular, about 250 to 300 feet in diameter"—over Owensboro and Irvington. In another ten minutes the tower operators at Godman were sighting the object for themselves. Once they were satisfied that they were not seeing an airplane or a weather balloon, they put in calls to the base operations officer, the base intelligence officer, and several other high-ranking personnel.

At 2:30 P.M., forty-five minutes later, base personnel were still discussing among themselves what course of action would be best to direct against the UFO. At that time four F-51s were sighted approaching Godman Field from the south. The tower radioed flight leader Captain Thomas Mantell and requested that he take a closer look at the flying saucer and attempt to identify it or provide a more complete description of the object. Mantell was still climbing at ten thousand feet when he made his last radio contact with the tower at Godman Field: "It looks metallic and it's tremendous in size. It's above me, and I'm gaining on it. I'm going to twenty thousand feet."

Those were Mantell's final words. His wingmen saw him disappear into the stratospheric clouds. A few minutes later Mantell crashed to the earth in his F-51 and was killed. The Air Force issued an official explanation that Captain Mantell, experienced though he was as a pilot, had "unfortunately been killed while trying to reach the planet Venus."

Such an explanation of Captain Mantell's tragic demise remains as controversial today as it was in 1948. If Mantell, an experienced pilot, misidentified the planet Venus for an unidentified flying object, then in addition to Captain Mantell's fatal misidentification, the crew in the control towers, the base operations officer, the base intelligence officer, and several high-ranking personnel had all been deceived by the planet Venus. The official explanation would have us believe that even when Mantell found himself below the object and described it as "metallic and tremendous in size," he was actually aiming his F-51 at a planet that was millions of miles distant in outer space.

Another Attack over Fargo, North Dakota

On October 1, 1948, George F. Gorman, a twenty-five-year-old second lieutenant in the North Dakota Air National Guard, was waiting his turn to land at Fargo when he was startled by the sudden appearance of a bright light that made a pass at him. When he called the tower to complain about the irresponsible pilot who had nearly collided with him, he was informed that the only aircraft in the vicinity was a Piper Cub that was just touching down on the landing field and his own F-51.

Baffled, Gorman scanned the skies and found that he could still see the mysterious light off to one side. More than a little irritated by the careless pilot's near-fatal misjudgment, he decided to investigate and determine the undeclared aircraft's identity.

Within moments he found himself under attack when the strange light put itself into a collision course with his F-51. Gorman had to take his craft into a dive to escape the unswerving globe of light. Then, to his terror, the UFO repeated its charge, and once again he just managed to escape collision.

When the UFO at last disappeared and ceased its passes at his F-51, Gorman was left shaken and convinced that "its maneuvers were controlled by thought or reason."

Memories of World War II and Fears of the Cold War Added to Concern over Flying Saucers

"The late 1940s were the early days of the Cold War, and for a time the possibility that the 'flying discs' might be Russian in origin, the product of kidnapped German scientists, seemed very real to the Air Force," said Hayden C. Hewes, a longtime UFO researcher. "By the summer of 1948, the Air Force began to consider the possibility that the discs were interplanetary in origin. By the end of 1949, the Air Force had decided there was nothing to the flying saucers that a good dose of ignoring them wouldn't cure. The pesky saucers kept returning, however, and by the fall of 1951, the Air Force was back in the saucer-chasing business once again."

UFOs Beseige Washington, D.C., Orders Given: "Shoot Them Down!"

On July 26, 1952, UFOs were sighted flying over Washington, D.C., in formations of eight to ten craft. It may have been a nervous officer who remembered the secret weapons of the Nazis in World War II who gave the order to "shoot them down" when he spotted the dozens of flying saucers suddenly converging on the nation's capitol.

Several prominent scientists, including Dr. Albert Einstein, protested the "shoot-to-kill" order to the White House and urged that the command be rescinded at once, not only in the name of future intergalactic peace, but also in the name of self-preservation. If Washington was about to host a fleet of extraterrestrial space travelers, it would be prudent to welcome them in peace until their actions dictated otherwise. After all, if these beings had the technological ability to travel through space, they might look unfavorably upon being attacked by primitive jet firepower and they might very well consider such unprovoked aggressive behavior as license to strike back.

> [W]ithin another twenty-four hours, the Air Force was denying that the incredible UFO encounter over Washington, D.C., had ever really taken place.

The shoot-them-down order was withdrawn by White House command by five o'clock that afternoon. That night, official observers puzzled over the mysterious objects observed both on radar screens and by the naked eye, as the UFOs easily outdistanced Air Force jets. However, within another twenty-four hours, the Air Force was denying that the incredible UFO encounter over Washington, D.C., had ever really taken place. They declared that overwrought civilians had mistaken planets and stars for flying saucers.

But it was too late for Air Force officials to declare that the biggest Red Alert since World War II was due to migrating flocks of geese, hallucinations, or laypeople failing to recognize the planet Venus. The national wire services had already sent the word around the world that the large numbers of UFOs over the nation's capitol had made hardened and experienced military officials so jittery that they had issued orders to destroy them.

The accusative cry of "official cover-up" reverberated from coast to coast and around the globe. It was the UFO Red Alert over Washington, D.C., on July 26, 1952, that signaled the beginning of the erosion of confidence in the integrity of the U.S. Air Force to tell the public the truth about the strangers in our skies.

A Rear Admiral Remembers Examining UFO Fragments

The March 1986 issue of *Just Cause*, published by Lawrence Fawcett and Barry Greenwood, printed the copy of a letter from former Navy Rear Admiral Herbert B. Knowles. In the letter, Admiral Knowles states that he was involved in the examination of fragments of a UFO shot down over Washington, D.C., in 1952. The letter was a result of correspondence between Admiral Knowles and Ohio UFO researcher C. W. Fitch, which followed Fitch's conversation with the Reverend Albert Baller.

In his August 27, 1961, response to Fitch's direct questions, the now-retired Admiral Knowles frankly admitted to having examined a piece of a "small disc" given to him by Wilbert Smith, head of Flying Saucer Research for the Canadian government. To the best of Knowles' recollection, the UFO had been shot down by a jet and had fallen in the "yard of a farmer across the river in Virginia." Several pieces of the UFO had been found. Admiral Knowles described the piece from the flying disc as a "chunk of amorphous metal-like structure, brownish in color where broken, with a curved edge…. The outer surface was smooth, but not polished, and at the broken sections there were obviously iron particles…. I would say that the weight was somewhat lighter than if it were of solid iron, but it was not extremely 'light'." According to Wilbert Smith, a chemical analysis made of the piece yielded identification of iron, but "little if anything else could be identified."

Admiral Knowles admitted his firm belief in UFOs and his opinion that the 1952 object could very likely have been a "remotely controlled observation disc" of a type sighted many times "most often in the vicinity of defense installations."

1952 Saw a Busy Saucer Summer: The CIA Creates the Robertson Panel

"The summer of 1952 brought the greatest UFO wave of all time," UFO researcher Hayden C. Hewes has stated. "Flying saucers were tracked visually and on radar over the White House and the Capitol in Washington. Over three hundred UFO reports were made in the month of July alone.

"About this time the Central Intelligence Agency (CIA) became interested in the UFO business for the first time. In January 1953 the CIA convened a panel of eminent scientists who spent four days pouring over the UFO data then available. Named for its chairman, Dr. H. P. Robertson of Cal-Tech, the Robertson Panel concluded that UFOs *themselves* were not a real problem, but that UFO *reports* might be—perhaps even being used by a potential enemy to clog military communications in time of imminent or actual attack.

"The Robertson Panel subsequently recommended that the Air Force Project Bluebook essentially become a palliative to keep those citizens interested in UFOs 'off the backs' of vital channels of military intelligence. Consequently, Bluebook became more a public relations exercise than serious investigations from about 1953 until its termination in 1969."

UFOs over Detroit in 1953

On a clear winter's day in 1953, Lieutenant Colonel Howard C. Strand, base commander of the Detroit Air National Guard, encountered a number of UFOs while flying over the city. At that time he was on active duty in the Air Force, flying F94-B aircraft and was stationed at Selfridge Air Force Base, Michigan. Prior to that sighting he did not believe in flying saucers.

"Approximately 10:00 A.M. one morning in March 1953, I was scrambled on a routine patrol mission," Strand said when we interviewed him in February 1968. "We were expecting the Navy to try to penetrate our air defenses in the local area for practice purposes. After about twenty minutes of flight, the radar site controlling our flight gave us a target to our left at about the eight-o'clock position. Upon visual checking, my airborne radar operator and I could see tiny specks in the sky which appeared as a ragged formation of aircraft. Our position at the time was approximately thirty miles northwest of downtown Detroit. The targets appeared to be over the city's central section.

"I remember thinking more than once that I should be able to start identifying the aircraft any second—but I couldn't," he said. "Their tails, wings, and aircraft features just didn't seem to 'pop out' as they normally do when you close in on an aircraft to identify its type."

> Strand had estimated the number of unknowns to be between twelve and sixteen. He and his radar operator had expected to see and to identify Navy fighter-type aircraft. But now there was nothing.

"The ground radar had both our aircraft and the unknowns painted as good strong targets," Strand said, "but we were still unable to get any positive identification, and the objects seemed to be getting a little larger all the time. About this time my radar operator started receiving some returns on his scope and thought that he was picking up the targets. I was watching the objects until I looked in the cockpit, trying to inch out a little more speed without going into afterburner. When I looked up again—after no more than two to four seconds-the objects were gone!"

Strand had estimated the number of unknowns to be between twelve and sixteen. He and his radar operator had expected to see and to identify Navy fighter-type aircraft. But now there was nothing. *Every last one of the objects had disappeared from sight.*

Immediately Strand asked the ground radar controller where the mysterious craft had gone. "I was told that the targets were still there—loud and clear! We continued to fly the headings given by the controller, right into the center of the targets. We flew and turned in every direction, but there was still nothing in sight."

Gradually the targets disappeared from ground radar after Strand had continued to fly among them for three or four minutes—as close as two thousand feet, according to radar.

No UFO report was submitted by Strand's aircrew for one basic reason: This was the era when the Air Force denied even the possibility of UFOs, and a concentrated effort was made to portray everyone who made such reports as silly or stupid.

General Twining Assures Citizens that the Best Brains in the Air Force Are Working on the Flying Saucer Mystery

On May 15, 1954, Air Force Chief of Staff General Nathan Twining informed an audience at Amarillo, Texas, that the "best brains in the Air Force" were trying to solve the problem of the flying saucers. "If [the-UFOs] come from Mars," he said, "they are so far ahead of us that we have nothing to be afraid of."

High-ranking officers in all military branches were beginning to demand a wider exchange of information regarding the UFO controversy, and important senators and

In recent years, more military personnel have spoken out regarding the interference by UFOs with base radar, aerial maneuvers, and missile silos. (*Art by Ricardo Pustanio*)

congressmen were applying pressure to end the Air Force's policy of secrecy toward flying saucers. The Air Force's strange response to these demands was to issue the controversial Air Force Regulation (AFR) 200-2 to all Air Force personnel on December 24, 1959. Briefly stated, AFR 200-2 made a flat and direct statement that the Air Force was definitely concerned with the reporting of all UFOs "as a possible threat to the security of the United States."

In the controversial Paragraph 9 of the regulation, the secretary of the Air Force gave specific instructions that Air Force personnel were to release reports of UFOs only "where the object has been definitely identified as a familiar object."

More Attacks on Pilots
Suggest that Some UFOs Have Hostile Intent

An informant told us a grim story that he had discovered when he served in the Air Force:

There were no names or dates listed in the report, but I figured that the incident probably occurred around 1952. According to the report an F-86 jet was sent aloft to investigate a UFO that had been hovering over an Air Force base for about an hour. The horrified radar operator saw the two blips come together over the base. Then there was only one blip left, and that one was shooting off the radar screen at an enormous rate of speed. No trace was ever found of the F-86 or its pilot.

A similar case, infamous in the annals of Ufology, and said to be fully documented by the USAF itself, occurred in 1953 when an F-89 jet interceptor was hijacked over Kinross Air Force Base in Michigan. As in the previous incident with the F-86 fighter, while air defense radar watched helplessly, the two blips merged into one—and the UFO soared away toward Canada. Nothing was ever found of the jet or its two-man crew.

UFO researcher Tom Camella managed to catch Master Sergeant D. Hill from the Air Force's Project Bluebook in several moments of candor when he asked him about UFOs and our disappearing military aircraft. "I must confess to you that it is true," Master Sergeant Hill answered.

Hill also relayed an account of the 1955 UFO kidnapping of a transport plane with twenty-six persons aboard. The transport was being carefully tracked by a radar station and maintaining constant radio communication with the base when the radar operator suddenly discovered a second blip on his scope. He immediately radioed the pilot of the transport and advised him to be cautious of an unidentified object that was rapidly moving toward the aircraft.

In the words of Master Sergeant Hill: "The UFO was traveling at a high rate of speed, about 2,500 miles per hour. It jumped about on the radar scope like a tennis ball. All of a sudden the mysterious blip headed straight for the transport plane and before the radar operator could warn it, the two objects had united into one on the radar screen. The one remaining blip sped straight up at a terrific rate of speed."

The transport plane had completely disappeared. A surface search of the water in the area did not reveal even an oil slick. The only evidence of the transport's previous existence was the discovery of a general's briefcase floating on the surface of a nearby lake.

Civilians Witness Flying Saucer Attacks on Military Planes

Around that same time in 1955, a civilian pilot and his friend were doing some prospecting above the Agua River near Prescott, Arizona. The two men swore that they saw two brightly luminous UFOs attack a military plane by directing "some kind of strange beams" at the craft that caused it to explode.

Even worse, according to the pilot and his prospector friend, when the airmen jumped free of the burning craft in their parachutes, the UFOs swung back and seared the survivors with the same deadly rays.

On October 3, 1955, a B-47 bomber crashed near Lovington, New Mexico. One of the crew survived and said that something had struck their plane in midair. A witness said that he had seen a "ball of fire" near the plane before it crashed.

Later that same month another B-47 crashed, this time in Texas. Once again a witness had spotted a ball of fire near the craft.

A UFO Landed, Took Off at Holloman Air Force Base

Strong circumstantial evidence exists to support the allegations that on April 30, 1964, a "force from outer space" landed at the Holloman U.S. Air Force Base near the White Sands Proving Grounds in New Mexico.

According to Terry Clarke of KALG radio in Alamogordo (nine miles east of Holloman), he received a telephone call from an informant who claimed to have monitored the testing range radio communications that day. As he tapped into their frequency, he heard the loudspeaker at Main Control on the Holloman Air Force Base/White Sands Proving Ground Integrated Test Range blare the electrifying words: "I've got a UFO!"

The voice of the man who claimed to have encountered a UFO belonged to the pilot of a B-57, who had been flying a routine mission in the vicinity of Stallion Site, a few miles east of San Antonio, New Mexico.

"What does it look like?" the controller asked.

"It's egg-shaped and white," the B-57 pilot answered. Minutes later, after the big B-57 had made its turn and come in over the area where the UFO was first seen, the pilot contacted Main Control again and shouted excitedly: "It's on the ground! The UFO is on the ground!"

Then, according to Clarke's information source, photo crews were asked to stand by—and then all radio communications ceased. Follow-up telephone calls to the base indicated that a major security clampdown was in effect. Rumors soon buzzed throughout the area that a UFO had been captured on the ground and was being kept in a Holloman Air Force Base hangar under heavy guard.

"The story was essentially true," one of our informants, a former Air Force officer, told us not long ago. "The problem was, though, that the UFO landed at Holloman of its own accord. It wasn't 'captured' at all. The aliens were following their own secret agenda."

Three UFOs Buzz Naval Station near San Diego

On December 16, 1966, three UFOs were spotted over the Naval Auxiliary Air Station near San Diego, California. The objects were observed for nine minutes by fourteen persons. Ensign John Schmidt, a helicopter pilot at Ream Field, reported that he and some friends were leaving through the main gate when they first spotted the UFOs at 9:30 P.M.

"There were three of them," Schmitt said. "They were bright, round yellow objects up about fifty thousand feet and flying in a triangular formation. They looked to be about the size of a quarter from where we were." With the helicopter pilot were Ensign David Coghill, a pilot at Miramar Naval Air Station, and Ensign David Conklin, a North Island Naval Air Station pilot. "We didn't know what they were," Schmitt admitted, serving as spokesman for the trio. "But none of us had ever seen anything like them.

"We agreed that they couldn't be meteors. They would hover, then go forward, then to one side. They were traveling at speeds from about the maximum speed of a bomber to about five times that.

"A fourth one came over the horizon from the east at a terrific speed. It came up to the group of three, stayed near the formation for a minute, then headed east. It dropped to a lower altitude, and the magnitude of its speed increased. It dropped what appeared to be two spheres of light, which disappeared, then it headed west, and we lost sight of it.

"The other three objects suddenly disappeared. They flew in formations and moved in different directions. We had these objects in sight for about nine minutes."

Hillenkoetter, Former Head of CIA, Warns: Flying Saucers Serious Business

On February 27, 1960, Vice Admiral Roscoe Hillenkoetter, USN, Retired, former head of the Central Intelligence Agency, stunned the Air Force when he released to the press photostatic copies of AFR 200-2, which warned Air Force Commands to regard the UFOs as "serious business." Because Killenkoetter was an alleged member of the controversial MJ-12 group, some researchers suggest that Hillenkoetter's conscience had got the better of him and that the press release was his way of alerting the public to certain elements within the Air Force who were playing a dual role in the UFO controversy.

Along with an explanation of the details of AFR 200-2, the press release stated that "unidentified flying objects sometimes treated lightly by the press and referred to as 'flying saucers' must be rapidly and accurately identified as serious USAF business.... The phenomena or actual objects comprising UFOs will tend to increase with the public more aware of goings-on in space, but still inclined to some apprehension. Technical and defense considerations will continue to exist in this era.... What is required is that every UFO sighting be investigated and reported to the Air Technical Intelligence Center at Wright-Patterson Air Force Base and that explanation to the public be realistic and knowledgeable. Normally that explanation will be made only by the OSAF Information Officer...."

> "We agreed that they couldn't be meteors. They would hover, then go forward, then to one side. They were traveling at speeds from about the maximum speed of a bomber to about five times that."

Across the planet curious individuals read the details of Hillenkoetter's press release, and even UFO skeptics had to ask themselves why such a dramatic statement about an unknown phenomenon would be made by an organization that had repeatedly claimed that "flying saucers" were nonexistent, and that anyone who saw one was hallucinating or was abysmally ignorant of natural phenomena.

An intelligent reader could only peruse the contents of the press release about AFR 200-2 and conclude that the Air Force was obviously very much aware of the physical reality of UFOs and was actively investigating their origins—regardless of official dismissals and denials.

A Fleet of UFOs Returns to Washington, D.C., in 1965

Deputy Dempsey Bruton, chief of Satellite Tracking on NASA's base at Wallops Island, Virginia, was standing in front of his house on January 5, 1965, waiting for the appearance of an artificial Earth satellite, when he sighted a bright object over the southwest horizon. It traveled at tremendous speed and gave off a yellowish-orange glow as it streaked through the sky. Several residents near the Wallops Island base confirmed Bruton's sighting by independently reporting it to the NASA installation.

At 4:20 P.M. on January 11, 1965, six Army Signal Corps engineers looked out of the windows of their offices in downtown Washington, D.C., and watched a number of strange, disclike objects zigzagging effortlessly north to south across the sky toward the Capitol building. Suddenly two delta-wing jets burst onto the scene and began chasing the unidentified aircraft, but the discs easily evaded their pursuers.

The flying saucers had returned to Washington, D.C. Would they attempt to land on the White House on this visit?

Although it turned out that the engineers were not alone in their observation of the UFOs, the Defense Department issued an official press release denying that such an incident had occurred. An irate newspaper in the city published the headline: "PENTAGON CAN'T SEE SPOTS IN THE SKY."

A man who was serving as a radar operator on board an aircraft carrier at the time told us that he had seen far more than spots on that date—and so had a number of his senior officers. According to our informant, he had watched the mystery objects approach their vessel, carefully plotting their course, until they dropped too low to be monitored. He had wondered where the UFOs could have gone so quickly: "Their proximity to our carrier had been so near that I almost feared a collision as I watched their approach."

Later that day he heard a remarkable account from some of his buddies who had been on deck with a number of officers. "According to them," he told us, "they had all watched the UFOs drawing nearer and nearer our vessel—until the objects seemed to pass right through us! The officers swore all the men to strict secrecy, and said there would be a court-martial for anyone who made a UFO report."

Project Bluebook Closes Its Pages: "UFOs Pose No Threat"

In December 1969 Project Bluebook closed its pages and issued its official conclusions regarding the mysterious objects that continued to traverse the skies overhead:

1. No UFO has ever given any indication of threat to the national security of the United States

2. There is no evidence that UFOs represent technological developments or principles beyond present-day scientific knowledge

3. There is no evidence that any UFOs are extraterrestrial vehicles

According to many of our informants—some of them former officers in military intelligence—the official conclusion that was released to the public outlined what a secret branch of the government and MJ-12 wanted everyone to believe. These informants have told us that there is no threat to the national security because a deal has already been made with the aliens. There has been a type of peace treaty that has been signed and UFO technology was already being developed in 1969 in several underground bases.

The accounts that were being published were creating a "war of the worlds" mentality and the secret government wanted it to die down. They wanted the masses to stop thinking about the threat of extraterrestrial invaders. Our informants cited films like *Close Encounters of the Third Kind* and *E.T.* as propaganda to popularize the idea of friendly aliens because, they tell us, extraterrestrials will soon emerge openly on the planet.

Aliens and the U.S. Presidency

In the summer of 2010, UFO researcher and Exopolitics proponent Michael Salla reported that Henry W. McElroy, a former representative to the New Hampshire House of Representatives, had released a video statement revealing that he saw a secret brief to President Eisenhower concerning extraterrestrial life. In his statement, recorded on May 8, 2010 in Hampton, Virginia, McElroy claims that the brief revealed that extraterrestrials were present in the United States, that they were benevolent, and that a meeting could be arranged for Eisenhower.

A Republican, McElroy served on various committees during his time in the New Hampshire state legislature and is best known for sponsoring a new Gold Money bill in 2004 that aimed to restore the use of gold and silver coins in the Granite State. He most recently ran for and won the Republican primary for state representative to the 2008 elections, but did not win re-election.

By claiming to have seen this "secret brief" to President Eisenhower, McElroy gave rebirth to one of the most persistent rumors in the history of alien-human interaction—that Eisenhower witnessed UFOs on the ground on a U.S. Air Force base. Some high-ranking military and civil authorities have sworn that it is the "gospel truth," while others have doubted its authenticity.

President Eisenhower Meets Aliens at Edwards Air Force Base

According to alleged eyewitness accounts, President Dwight Eisenhower, who at that time (May 30, 1952) had only recently resigned as the supreme commander of Allied Forces in Europe, inspected a variety of alien space vehicles at Edwards Air Force Base in California. Interestingly the evidence of the supposed incident continues to grow, with new proponents of its historical validity and additional eyewitnesses who claim to have been present at the shattering review of superior extraterrestrial technology.

Dated April 16, 1954, a letter was written by Gerald Light, a writer, lecturer, mystic, and metaphysical community leader in Southern California, to Meade Layne, the late director of Borderline Sciences Research Associates, describing the incredible meeting between a United States President and representatives of an alien world:

I have just returned from Muroc (Muroc Dry Lake, located at Edwards Air Force Base, California). The report is true, devastatingly true! I made the journey in company with Franklin Allen of the Hearst papers and Edwin Nourse of Brookings Institute [President Harry S. Truman's financial advisor], and Bishop McIntyre of L.A. I had the distinct feeling that the world had come to an end.... For I have never seen so many human beings in a state of complete collapse and confusion, as they realized that their own world had indeed ended with such finality as to beggar description. The reality of "otherplane" aeroforms is now and forever removed from the realms of speculation and made a rather painful part of the consciousness of every responsible scientific and political group.

During my two days' visit, I saw five separate and distinct types of aircraft being studied and handled by our Air Force officials—with the assistance and permission of the Etherians. I have no words to express my reactions. It has finally happened. It is now a matter of history.

President Eisenhower, as you may already know, was spirited to Muroc one night during his visit to Palm Springs recently. And it is my conviction that he will ignore the terrific conflict between the various "authorities" and go directly to the people via radio and television.... From what I could gather, an official statement to the country is being prepared for delivery about the middle of May.

I will leave it to your own excellent powers of deduction to construct a fitting picture of the mental and emotional pandemonium that is now shattering the consciousness of hundreds of our scientific "authorities" and all the pundits of the various specialized knowledges that make up our current physics. In some instances I could not stifle a wave of pity ... as I watched the pathetic bewilderment of rather brilliant brains struggling to make some sort of rational explanation which would enable them to retain their familiar theories and concepts.... I shall never forget those forty-eight hours at Muroc!

A British Pilot Also Witnesses the Interplanetary Meeting

The Earl of Clancarty, a member of Great Britain's House of Lords, who treated the subject of UFOs with extreme seriousness for decades, repeated the testimony of a British pilot who had been vacationing in Palm Springs in February 1954 and was summoned to the base by U.S. military officials. According to the pilot—whom Lord Clancarty respected as a gentleman of greatest integrity—the aliens disembarked from

In 1952 a fleet of UFOs were spotted over Washington, D.C., and Capitol Hill. Radar sightings verified the materiality of the craft, and interceptor jets were scrambled to meet the potential threat. Such luminaries as Albert Einstein urged that the Air Force not fire upon the objects. High-ranking officers later filed reports of the incident. (*Art by Ricardo Pustanio*)

their space vehicles and approached President Eisenhower and a small group of political and military figures.

The aliens seemed able to breathe the air of Earth without the need of a helmet with breathing apparatus, and the pilot described the aliens as basically human-like in appearance, about the same height and build as an average man, perhaps around five-foot eight or nine. However, their features were, in his opinion, somewhat misshapen. The aliens spoke English, and the thrust of their dialogue centered on their wish to begin a program of education for the people of Earth that would make all of humanity aware of their presence.

The British pilot recalled that Eisenhower was not in favor of such a program. In a very forthright manner, he told the alien representatives that he didn't believe the people of Earth were ready for the sudden revelation that an alien race was on the planet. Such an announcement, in Eisenhower's assessment, would only cause widespread panic.

The aliens appeared to understand the president's point of view, and they agreed not to put in motion their proposed program of widespread earthling awareness of their presence. However, they informed Eisenhower that they would continue to contact isolated humans until more people got used to their being on the planet. The president agreed with a program of limited contact, but he urged the aliens not to do anything that would create panic and confusion among the people of Earth.

Next, they demonstrated a number of their incredible technical advances. Eisenhower was very uncomfortable when the aliens displayed their ability to become invisible. It was indeed eerie, the British pilot agreed. For although the humans assembled for the exhibition knew the aliens were really there, they could not see them.

After the demonstration of controlled invisibility, the aliens boarded their craft and left the air base. Those who had witnessed the historic meeting were sworn to maintain complete secrecy.

Lord Clancarty made it clear that the pilot had kept his vow; he did not disclose the remarkable events at Edwards Air Force Base until he believed that all the principals who were present in 1954 were deceased.

Provocative rumors persist that presidents, beginning with Harry S. Truman, have hosted alien ambassadors at the White House. President Eisenhower was said to have been given a command performance of the advanced technology of the alien visitors. (Art by Ricardo Pustanio)

A Young Dutch Sailor "Spied" on the Event

Dr. Hank Krastman of Encino, California, revealed in *Unexplained* magazine (Vol. 4, No. 2, 1993) that he had been present that day in 1954 at Edwards Air Force Base as a young sailor in the Royal Dutch Navy. Krastman was trained for internal services dealing with matters concerning the NATO pact and CIA affairs, and at nineteen years of age he was serving as an adjutant to Mr. Rob, the ship's commander.

Krastman remembered that on February 19, 1954, they were briefed about a top security meeting that would take place the following day. The next morning they left Long Beach Navy Base in a van with a military police escort, and they arrived at Edwards Air Force Base at 10:00 A.M.

Escorted to a hangar at the far west side of the base, Krastman recognized the president of the United States, Dwight D. Eisenhower, and, among others, Albert Einstein, Wernher von Braun, Victor Schauberger, and Howard Hughes.

Krastman wondered what the "two Nazi war criminals" were doing there. To the young Dutch sailor, von Braun, with his work on the V1 and V2 rockets, and Schauberger, who was involved in

Hitler's secret V7 flying discs, were two scientists who had been responsible for the deaths of many of his countrymen.

Krastman heard someone tell his commander that there were five alien ships in the other hangar, and that some of the alien pilots would demonstrate the capabilities of the craft. Krastman was not allowed to enter the hangar that contained the aliens and their spaceships. When his commander returned, he was very pale and would not give Krastman any information regarding what he had seen.

In 1959 Krastman returned to the United States as an immigrant, and he continued to dig into the true meaning of his peculiar experience in February 1954.

A Press Conference Never Called

We all know that President Eisenhower never called the press conference that Gerald Light had been so certain would take place. Perhaps Eisenhower's rationale for not revealing the truth about flying saucers to the people of Earth was that he truly feared, as Light put it, "a state of complete collapse and confusion" a "mental and emotional pandemonium" … "pathetic bewilderment" … as humankind realized that the world it had known and charted had ended with "such finality as to beggar description."

Three Witnesses to Seeing Aliens at Edwards Come Forward

Elaine Douglass, associate editor of the *Right to Know Forum*, presented an account of three witnesses who telephoned a radio call-in program on KPFA-FM in Berkeley, California, in April of 1991 to report having seen aliens at Edwards Air Force Base and the China Lake Naval Weapons facility. Apparently either some aliens had remained at the base after the president inspected their craft, or an arrangement had been made to allow them to arrive and depart on a prearranged schedule. One other possibility existed: some aliens had never left Edwards and continued to work among the humans stationed there.

One of the speakers identified himself as a Vietnam veteran, a former Green Beret, a military medal-holder, and a licensed general contractor who had worked on projects at China Lake and at Nellis, Scott, Edwards, and Andrews Air Force bases. He identified the construction projects in which he participated as being "mostly underground," very extensive, and "definitely not normal military structures," with four-foot-thick concrete walls and electronically controlled oval doorways.

In one building at Edwards, it took over five minutes to get from the top to the bottom by elevator—a depth, he estimated, to be thirty stories.

It was here that he saw his first alien. "He was … I'd say between eight and ten feet tall. He was wearing a lab jacket and talking to two [human] engineers. This [being's] arms were almost down to his knees. It threw me into shock!" At that point security personnel spotted the witness and told him to leave. The next day he walked off the job.

When the witness was asked if the being he saw could have been an abnormally tall human, he answered: "Definitely not. He had big slanted eyes. A big head. Greenish skin. And his fingers were extremely long."

The witness reported that he and a number of his coworkers had also encountered smallish "grays" when they were working at the China Lake naval facility. According to his account, one night they were staying late to finish a particular job when one of his coworkers told them to follow him. He had found something that he had to show them.

"We looked in the window and there were these four little gray guys about three feet tall," the witness said. "Right then security saw us and they told us, 'We thought you guys left.' And they escorted us and said, 'You're not allowed around this hangar. This hangar is off-limits to everybody. You'll get yourselves shot.'"

The construction worker said that the sight of the four smallish entities "messed" with his friend's mind so much that he kept sneaking onto the base to observe them: "He finally got caught and was kicked off the base. About three months later they found him dead under mysterious circumstances in Orange County."

The witness admitted that his friend's death had "kind of put a scare" into him. He said that he knew when not to mess with something.

"I know what's going on at Edwards is real," he said. "Somebody's playing games with us."

Is Phobos, the Martian Moon, Really an Alien Satellite?

Dr. Michael Salla and other researchers have pointed out that additional information regarding alien civilizations were received during the Eisenhower administration. On March 1960 Dr. S. Fred Singer, special advisor to President Eisenhower on space developments, issued a statement that the Martian moon Phobos, generally accepted as a celestial body, actually might be an artificial satellite launched long ago by an advanced Martian race.

In his published opinion, Dr. Singer supported a claim first made by the Soviet astrophysicist Iosif Shklovsky that Phobos was a hollow, artificial satellite. Shklovsky suggested that this discovery proved the existence of a Martian civilization and set off heated arguments among astronomers. Shklovsky was not the only astronomer who had noticed Phobos' peculiar orbit. The Russian scientist's claim, together with those of earlier astronomers, seemed to prove that Phobos cannot possibly be an ordinary moon.

Though Dr. Singer said the figures still had to be proved, he stated that he would be very disappointed if Phobos turned out to be solid. "If the figures are correct," he stated, "then Phobos undoubtedly is a hollow, artificial satellite."

According to certain UFO investigators, there was an interesting assessment of Mars given during a space briefing presented at an Eisenhower cabinet meeting. The briefing, by Eisenhower science advisor Dr. James Killian, was given March 14, 1958.

In 1963, Raymond H. Wilson Jr., Chief of Applied Mathematics at NASA, joined Shklovsky and Dr. Singer in their Martian conclusions. He stated that "Phobos might be a colossal base orbiting Mars." He also stated that NASA itself was considering the possibility, and was planning for special probes that would answer the question.

JFK Sights a UFO over Hyannisport

There was a report that President John F. Kennedy had sighted a UFO in 1963, while boating off Hyannisport on Cape Cod. The object was "disc-shaped, about sixty feet in diameter, with a gray top, and shiny bottom." It hovered above the water for forth seconds, emitting a low-pitched humming sound. Then it flew straight up in the air and was gone. Kennedy swore those present to keep the incident secret.

After His UFO Sighting
President Carter Promises Disclosure

In October 1969, future U.S. president Jimmy Carter described his UFO sighting: "It was the darndest thing I've ever seen. It was big and bright. It changed colors, and it was about the size of the moon. A red and green orb radiated as it hurtled across the southwestern Georgia skies. We watched it for ten minutes, but none of us could figure out what it was. One thing's for sure, I'll never make fun of people who say that they have seen UFOs in the sky."

During his presidential campaign in 1976, Carter promised that if he became president, "I'll make every piece of information this country has about UFO sightings available to the public and scientists. I am convinced that UFOs exist, because I have seen one."

Unfortunately, President Carter was unable to keep his well-intentioned promise.

Dr. Alfred L. Webre, Stanford Research Institute, former senior policy analyst, has said that he worked on a 1977 Carter White House Extraterrestrial Communication Project. He was led to believe that the project for creation of central and regional databases under independent control had been approved.

"When I arrived back at my offices at SRI, I learned that the project was to be terminated," Webre recalled. "They had received direct communication from the Pentagon that if the study went forward, SRI's contracts would be terminated.... The senior Pentagon liaison stated that the project was terminated because, 'There are no UFOs.' Here we have a President of the United States who came to the office under a pledge to open up the UFO issue and an open study at the White House, and that was squelched."

> "I'll make every piece of information this country has about UFO sightings available to the public and scientists. I am convinced that UFOs exist, because I have seen one."

French Minister of Defense Finds Frequency of UFO Reports "Disturbing"

M. Robert Galley, French Minister of Defense, was interviewed by Jean-Claude Bourret as part of the radio broadcast of a UFO debate on February 21, 1974. On that date, Galley commented, "I must say that if listeners could see for themselves the mass of reports coming in from the airborne gendarmerie, from the mobile gendarmerie, and from the gendarmerie charged with the job of conducting investigations, all of which reports are forwarded by us to the National Center for Space Studies, then they would see that it is all pretty disturbing.

"I believe that the attitude of spirit that we must vis-a-vis this phenomenon is an open one, that is to say that it doesn't consist in denying a priori, as our ancestors of previous centuries did deny many things that seem nowadays perfectly elementary."

President Reagan Asks If the Alien Threat Is Already among Us

In June of 1982, Steven Spielberg screened his soon-to-be released motion picture *E.T., The Extraterrestrial* to President Ronald Reagan at the White House. After the movie had ended and the lights had been restored, Reagan confided to Spielberg, "You know, there aren't six people in this room who know just how true that really is."

Before the president could elaborate, their conversation was interrupted by well-wishers at the screening.

Three years later, in December, 1985, while addressing Fallston, Maryland, high school students, Reagan again mentioned the subject of space beings.

Recalling his recent conversation with Soviet leader Mikhail Gorbachev, the president said: "I couldn't help but say to [Gorbachev], how easy his task and mine might be if suddenly there was a threat to this world from some other species from another planet outside in the universe. We'd forget all the little local differences ... and find out once and for all that we really are all human beings here on this Earth."

Then, again, in September, 1987, in a speech before the United Nations General Assembly, Reagan remarked: "Perhaps we need some outside, universal threat to make us recognize the common bond that unites all humanity. How quickly our differences worldwide would vanish if we were facing an alien threat from outside this world. And yet I ask you, is not an alien threat already among us?"

> "Mikhail Gorbachev was the first and the last national leader who acknowledged the issue of unidentified flying objects in Russia."

Gorbachev and Yeltsin Were Kept Informed about UFOs

The president of the Academy for Applied Ufology, Academician Vladimir Azhazha, is considered to be the founding father of Russian UFO research. Azhazha shared his knowledge of aliens with Mikhail Gorbachev and Boris Yeltsin.

It goes without saying that the traditional science does not treat Ufology seriously. Vladimir Putin once said that he never believed in extraterrestrial beings.

"Mikhail Gorbachev was the first and the last national leader who acknowledged the issue of unidentified flying objects in Russia," Azhazha said recently, "We established the public UFOlogical center during his rule under my supervision. Thousands of UFOlogists were working for me from 1990 to 1995. We collected tons of

Gabriel Green became a write-in candidate for president of the United States in 1960 and 1972 on the Flying Saucer ticket. Green's credentials included contact with the Space Brothers in the 1950s, who invited him to accompany them on an orbit around Alpha Centuri. Green founded the Amalgamated Flying Saucer Clubs of America in 1957. (*Art by Bill Oliver*)

information to prove the existence of UFOs. There are other civilizations in the universe, no matter if we want it to be so or not."

Azhazha added that the term "extraterrestrial" may not be quite correct. "There is no evidence to prove that aliens come from other planets," he said. "No one knows where they come from. It is not ruled out that they come from a civilization of parallel worlds, or from the ocean. Modern science knows very little about what's happening at ocean's depths."

Gorbachev Gave Credence to Alien Invasion

In a speech entitled "Survival of Humanity," presented on February 16, 1987, Russian leader Mikhail Gorbachev lent some credence to the future "UFO alien" extraterrestrial invasion:

At our meeting in Geneva, the U.S. President said that if the earth faced an invasion by extraterrestrials, the United States and the Soviet Union would join forces to repel such an invasion. I shall not dispute the hypothesis, although I think it's early yet to worry about such an intrusion. It is much more important to think about the problems that have entered in our common home.

As the heads of state for the most powerful nations in the world at that time, Gorbachev and Reagan laid the concept there may be a future "UFO alien" invasion, mutually creating the economic market for a space-based weapons arms race that has dominated the twenty-first century thus far.

Japanese Prime Minister Toshiki Kaifu Says UFOs Must Be Taken Seriously

On June 24, 1990, Toshiki Kaifu, the prime minister of Japan at that time, wrote a letter to Mayor Yoshiko Shiotani of Hakui City, endorsed an upcoming Space and UFO Symposium.

"First of all, I told a magazine this past January that, as an underdeveloped country with regards to the UFO problem, Japan had to take into account what should be done about the UFO question, and that we had to spend more time on these matters. In addition, I said that someone had to solve the UFO problem with far-reaching vision at the same time. Secondly, I believe it is a reasonable time to take the UFO problem seriously as a reality.... I hope that this Symposium will contribute to peace on Earth from the point of view of outer space, and take the first step toward the international cooperation in the field of UFOs."

Billionaire Rockefeller Pressures President Clinton to Reopen Super-Secret Roswell Files

The August 24, 1995 issue of the *New York Daily News* stated that billionaire philanthropist Laurance S. Rockefeller, a personal friend of President Bill Clinton, was pressuring the nation's leader to open the files on the Roswell case. Rockefeller had long been known as an avid UFO buff. Along with his niece, Anne Bartley, the stepdaughter of Winthrop Rockefeller and the then-president of the Rockefeller Family Fund, Laurance Rockefeller established the UFO Disclosure Initiative in 1993, and he was hoping that he could convince Clinton to put an end to flying saucer secrecy and reopen super-secret government files on the world's most baffling UFO incident.

Rockefeller and a host of UFO experts believe the government covered up a UFO crash in 1947 near Roswell, New Mexico, from which alien bodies were recovered. "Many are convinced that Roswell marks the beginning of government secrets about UFO's" says Rockefeller in a letter to the White House obtained through the

Freedom of Information Act. "Whatever the truth of Roswell, a definitive statement about it from the government would be very important."

According to the *Daily News*, Rockefeller hosted President Clinton at his western ranch during the chief executive's vacation in Jackson Hole, Wyoming "and insiders believe he bent Clinton's ear about the UFO issue. He also wrote to President Clinton's science advisor, John Gibbons, to urge that all UFO-related information be released."

In his letter to the White House, Rockefeller suggests that a cover-up may very well have been imposed by jittery bureaucrats. "While much in the public sector has been written about it, the government ... has had nothing to say about it." says Rockefeller. He called on the President to "promise there would be no persecution for those coming forward and revealing their eyewitness accounts of the New Mexico incident.... In addition to lifting classification about Roswell, consideration should be given to granting amnesty on an individual basis to allow those with knowledge about the incident to speak without fear of prosecution: There is a reason to believe that there are individuals who would provide information about the incident under that circumstance."

Clinton did produce an Executive Order in late 1994 to declassify numerous documents in the National Archives, but none of them referred specifically to UFO-related files.

Podesta Says Americans Can Handle the Truth about Aliens

John Podesta, former chief of staff to President Bill Clinton, obviously agreed with Mr. Rockefeller. On October 21, 2003, he said to the National Press Club, Washington, D.C.: "I think it's time to open the books on questions that have remained in the dark on the question of government investigations of UFOs. We ought to do it, because the American people quite frankly can handle the truth, and we ought to do it because it's the law.

"It's time for the government to declassify records that are more than twenty-five years old and to provide scientists with data that will assist in determining the real nature of this phenomenon."

Astronauts and Aliens

"For many years I have lived with a secret," said Mercury and Gemini astronaut Colonel L. Gordon Cooper in an address to the United Nations in 1985. "It is a secrecy that is imposed on all specialists and astronauts. Every day our radar instruments capture objects of form and composition unknown to us. And there are thousands of witness reports and a quantity of documents to prove this—but nobody wants to make them public."

In his memoirs, *Leap of Faith: An Astronaut's Journey into the Unknown* (2000), United States Air Force Colonel L. Gordon Cooper (Retired) provides his readers with many stories of chasing UFOs over Germany in his F-86.

Cooper stated that he had neither flown in a flying saucer nor met the crew of such a vehicle. But in 1951, while serving in Europe, he had the occasion to sight many flights of the mysterious aircraft. For two days, Cooper and his men sighted many UFOs, which were varied in size, flying in formation, generally east to west. "They were at a higher altitude than we could reach with our F-86 jet fighters of that time," he said.

Cooper stated that they sighted groups of metallic, saucer-shaped craft flying at great altitudes over their base. "We tried to get close to them," he said, "but they were able to change direction faster than our fighters."

Later, while flying with several other USAF pilots over Germany in 1957, Colonel Cooper said that they sighted numerous "radiant flying discs above us." None of the pilots could determine how high the UFOs were, because their planes could get nowhere near the altitude of the flying discs.

When he was a captain stationed at Edwards Air Force Base on May 3, 1957, Cooper learned of a metallic saucer-shaped object that had landed and was filmed by a technical film crew that had been on assignment some fifty yards away.

"The camera crew filmed the landing of a strange disclike object that flew in over their heads and landed on a dry lake nearby," he recalled. When the camera crew

Many astronauts have spoken out about having observed dramatic examples of advanced alien technology while they were on space missions. (**Art by Ricardo Pustanio**)

approached the flying saucer, Cooper said "it rose up above the area and flew off at a speed faster than any known aircraft." Although the UFO had zoomed out of sight when the startled photographers attempted to move closer for a better camera angle, Cooper was ordered by Pentagon officials to have all the film developed—but not printed—and to ship it off to the appropriate officials at once. Cooper writes that he obeyed orders, but he also admits that he peeked at some of the negatives and confirmed that the film crew had most certainly captured a flying saucer on celluloid.

Cooper goes on to tell of an Air Force master sergeant friend of his who was assigned to a recovery team to retrieve a crashed UFO in a canyon in the Pacific southwest. According to his friend, they found two very human-looking beings sitting atop a metallic, disk-shaped piece of wreckage, smiling at them. The alien pilots were hustled away, and Cooper's friend told him that he never found out what had happened to them. In his opinion, Cooper said, there is no question that UFOs exist and that the "truly unexplained ones are from some other technologically advanced civilization."

"Deke" Slayton Chased a UFO over Minneapolis

In a 1951 interview, Mercury astronaut Donald Kent "Deke" Slayton said that he was testing a P-51 fighter over Minneapolis at about ten thousand feet when he spotted an object. At first, he thought it was either a kite or a balloon. When he got closer, he could plainly see that it was neither. It was a disc-shaped object.

"There I was," Slayton said, "running at about three hundred miles per hour ... and then all of a sudden the damn thing just took off. It pulled about a forty-five-degree climbing turn, accelerated, and just flat disappeared."

Laika, the First Astro Dog, Was Followed by a UFO

According to author-researcher John A. Keel, a month after the Russians sent the dog Laika into orbit in November 1957, astronomers in Venezuela photographed not only *Sputnik 2* but another unexplained object that was closely following it.

Astronomers Track a UFO Trailing Soviet Sputniks

The *London Times* for November 7, 1957, carried the story of four astronomers at the Commonwealth Observatory near Canberra, Australia, who had been visually tracking both *Sputnik 1* and the recently launched *Sputnik 2* when a *third* object suddenly came into the view of their telescopes. The unknown aerial vehicle was a vivid pink and remained in view for two minutes while it seemed to be trailing the Soviet satellites.

"Since the two Russian satellites were the only known vehicles in orbit in 1957 (America's first satellite went up in early 1958) and since both Sputniks had passed by, it could not be argued that the Australian astronomers had mistaken one of the Soviet satellites for the mystery object," Otto O. Binder said. "It was a genuine unknown, for which the U.S. Air Force already had a response waiting, labeled 'deny, damn, and deride'."

Mystery "Satellite" Pursues *Discoverer-5*

Binder stated that the authorities could hardly deny the mystery satellite spotted in late 1959 and 1960, because the Navy tracked it with their SPASUR (space surveillance) radars, which had often assisted NASA in monitoring Earth-launched satellites.

"The most sensational aspect of this unknown satellite was its polar orbit, which neither Russia nor the United States had thus far used in its space program," Binder said. "A big public furor resulted, and the Pentagon was forced to explain the unknown away by stating that they had somehow lost track of the capsule of *Discoverer-5* and it had somehow shifted its orbit to cross directly over the poles.

"There was one big problem with the Pentagon's fairy tale," Binder stated. "On August 23, 1960, a tracking camera of the Grumman Aircraft Company at Bethpage, Long Island, had obtained definitive photos of the mystery satellite and estimated its weight as at least *fifteen tons*. The *Discoverer-5* capsule weighed 1,200 pounds."

Colonel Glenn May Have Discounted the "Fireflies" but He Believes Some Flying Saucers Are Real

The first U.S. astronaut to successfully orbit Earth, Colonel John Glenn, sent an eerie radio message to Earth during his historic mission on February 20, 1962. In it he described the thousands of greenish-yellow "fireflies" that had approached his space capsule. Although the "fireflies" were later identified as tiny pieces of frost catching the light of the sun, Glenn was quoted as saying that he believed "certain reports of flying saucers to be legitimate."

Test Pilots Are Paced by Flying Saucers

While lecturing at a conference in Washington on May 11, 1962, the famous X-15 pilot Joe Walker said that he had photographed UFOs while he was in flight. Walker described the five or six objects as cylindrical or discoidal and reported that he had photographed similar objects on a previous flight. Le Matin of Paris quoted the pilot as admitting that he was given an assignment to detect UFOs.

A few months later, on July 17, 1962, Major Robert White was flying the X-15 at an altitude of 314,750 feet when he sighted a gray-white object that suddenly appeared alongside his craft and began to pace him. White was astonished when the UFO shot out of sight, for his X-15 was doing 3,832 miles per hour at the time.

The control tower heard Major White shouting excitedly into his radio: "There are things out there! There absolutely are!"

An Unintelligible Language Cuts in on NASA's Transmission

During astronaut Gordon Cooper's fourth pass over Hawaii on May 15, 1963, his transmissions to ground control were abruptly interrupted by an "unintelligible foreign language." NASA officials were both angered and baffled by the unidentified "someone" who had the technology to cut in on the VHF channel reserved for space missions. Language experts were unable to categorize the speech patterns into any known dialect or make any sense of the message that NASA technicians had recorded.

Curiously, it was on that same mission in May 1963 that astronaut Cooper had sighted a glowing greenish disc with a red tail closing in on his space capsule. Cooper was passing over Australia at the time, and personnel at the Muchea Tracking Station scurried outside to take a look. Over two hundred persons clearly saw the object, which was apparently much bigger than Cooper's little space capsule. His description of it was broadcast worldwide on radio and television, but when he returned to the ground he refused to discuss it.

In a later interview astronaut Cooper commented: "As far as I am concerned, there have been too many unexplained examples of UFO sightings around Earth for us to rule out the possibilities that some form of life exists out there beyond our own world."

Were Aliens Responsible for Buzzing Cape Kennedy and Destroying a Thirty Million Dollar Radar System?

On December 5, 1964, at 11:06 P.M., just a little more than a week after NASA had launched *Mariner IV*, UFOs were spotted over Cape Kennedy. Earlier that year, four UFOs locked in on an unmanned Gemini capsule on April 8, 1964, and paced it for one complete orbit around the planet.

A month later, on January 5, 1965, the thirty million dollar radar system at Eglin Air Force Base—at that time the only one of its kind in operation—was destroyed by a "mysterious fire" that burned out of control late at night. The unique radar system, constructed by Bendix and turned over to the Air Force on trial, provided an "eye on space" that could have been used to detect, track, and identify objects coming in from outer space. The primary function of the costly radar system was to view all orbiting bodies at least twice a day and to detect UFOs.

Flying Saucers Harass *Voskhod 1*

The world was amazed on October 12, 1964, when the large Soviet spacecraft *Voskhod 1*, with its three-man crew, came back to earth in Central Asia after only sixteen orbits and twenty-four hours aloft. The Soviet press had boldly proclaimed that the spacecraft would be engaged in a "prolonged flight." What, then, had brought about an abrupt end to the voyage of the *Voskhod*?

The official word from Moscow was enigmatic. The cosmonauts were quoted as stating that they greatly regretted being brought down so soon, because they had seen "many interesting things and wanted to investigate them more fully."

Some witnesses claim that they have knowledge that contact with alien intelligences has been made by NASA officials. (*Art by Ricardo Pustanio*)

What may have been the truth was printed in an account in a German newspaper. The author, S.R. Oilinger, claimed that his Moscow sources told him that *Voskhod 1* "was repeatedly overtaken by extremely fast-flying discs which struck the craft violently, shattering blows with their powerful magnetic fields."

After Astronaut Leonov's Successful Walk in Space
Voskhod 2 Crashes to Earth after Attack by Unknown "Satellite"

On March 18, 1965, Lieutenant Colonel Alexi Leonov stepped from *Voskhod 2* to become the first man from Earth to "walk" in space. Then, for several hours, the Soviet spaceship lost all contact with its control stations on the ground.

Later the downed *Voskhod 2* was found in deep snow near Perm, 873 miles northwest of the area where the cosmonauts had been scheduled to land. The world press carried stories of the spacecraft hurtling toward Earth enveloped in flames, its outside antennae burned off, its two-man crew barely escaping with their lives.

A carefully controlled press conference was held with the cosmonauts on March 27. They persistently avoided questions asking them to confirm reports that they had been harassed by a UFO. They admitted having sighted "an unmanned satellite" about a half mile from their spacecraft at 5:12 A.M. on March 19. They also admitted that they had not been able to identify the object and that it had seemingly appeared shortly before they lost contact with their control stations.

McDivitt and White Sight Egg-Shaped UFO over China

UFO investigator John A. Keel has written of the June 1965 flight of U.S. astronauts James McDivitt and Edward White: "They sighted what they termed 'a mysterious object in space' as they orbited over China. Millions heard them describe it live on radio and TV. McDivitt and White reported it as 'a glowing, egg-shaped thing with arms or projections sticking out of it.'"

Keel went on to say that the two astronauts had also reported another UFO over Hawaii during the same mission. Later McDivitt had commented to the press: "I don't know what it was and so far no one else does either."

At an October 5, 1965, press conference in Dallas, McDivitt confirmed that he and his crewmen had sighted three UFOs on their June 5 orbital flight—and that he had photographed one of them. Later a NASA spokesperson stated that the object remained unidentified.

"They are there without a doubt," McDivitt stated. "But what they are is anybody's guess."

Strange Music Invades Sound System of *Apollo 7*

During the *Apollo 7* flight in October 1968, the astronauts were treated to an unscheduled musical program that featured a wide variety of selections, including "Where Angels Fear to Tread."

This invasion of the astronauts' frequency appears to have been a complete impossibility. The frequencies used to communicate with the *Apollo 7* mission were in the S-Band, which is located around two thousand megacycles—far away from any terrestrial radio station's standard AM and FM broadcasting bands. In addition, the receivers on the *Apollo* were too sensitive to receive random signals, and the reflecting layers of the ionosphere would have blocked such signals from ever reaching the spacecraft in the first place.

Although there are some very talented HAM radio operators out there, the cost to any individual or group of radio hobbyists amassing such high-tech sophisticated equipment would be astronomically prohibitive. Some specialist at NASA figured out that to have jammed the astronauts' frequency with a bizarre selection of music would have required a worldwide tracking system, a fifty-foot moveable dish antenna, the combined knowledge of a few Ph.D.s, and the budget of the average billionaire—if he could have managed to get long-term financing.

Russian Scientists Monitoring *Apollo 11* Moon Landing Sighted Alien Spaceships Observing the Event

Three Russian scientists, Dr. Vladimir Azhazha, Professor Alexandr Kazantsev, and Dr. Sergei Bozhich insisted that Soviet intelligence monitored the historic Moon landing of the *Apollo 11* lunar module on July 20, 1969, and observed that alien space-ships were present to witness the U.S. space mission firsthand.

According to Soviet intelligence reports, Neil Armstrong relayed the message to Mission Control in Houston that two large UFOs were watching the module land on the lunar surface. Buzz Aldrin took pictures of the UFOs from inside the module to support Armstrong's verbal report. The UFOs set down near the lunar module, but flew away just minutes before Armstrong emerged from the craft on July 21 to make his history-making comment: "That's one small step for [a] man … one giant leap for mankind."

The three Russian scientists charged that NASA censored Armstrong's verbal report of the two UFOs on the Moon's surface and placed Aldrin's motion picture film in a top-secret repository after the astronauts returned to Earth on July 24. Dr. Bozhich said that he was of the opinion that the two alien ships that monitored Armstrong, Aldrin, and Michael Collins were there as a backup, in case something should go wrong with the U.S. Moon landing.

In 1979, Maurice Chatelain, former chief of NASA Communications Systems, went on record confirming the claims that the Russian scientists had made concerning alien spaceships. "The encounter was common knowledge in NASA," he said. "When the *Apollo 11* module landed at the bottom of a Moon crater, two alien space-craft appeared at the rim."

Chatelain stated that on the third day of the *Apollo 11* mission, a strange object appeared to the three astronauts. It looked like something made of interconnecting rings. Collins expressed his opinion that the UFO was shaped like a large, hollow cylinder. Aldrin, puzzling over its bizarre dimensions, thought the object resembled a gigantic, half-open book.

Although NASA deliberately interrupted *Apollo 11*'s radio transmissions to Earth to censor the astronauts' reports of the UFO, Chatelain stated that there were a number of other weird interruptions that had nothing to do with Mission Control at Houston. "The astronauts heard noises similar to a train whistle, fire engine siren, or power saw on their radio," Chatelain said. "These sounds were thought to be some sort of code."

Observatories throughout Europe Sight UFOs Following *Apollo 12*

On Friday evening, November 14, 1969, observatories all over Europe sighted two bright, flashing UFOs near the path of *Apollo 12*, which had been launched to place the United States' second team of astronauts on the Moon. As startled astronomers watched through huge telescopes, one UFO appeared to be following the U.S. spacecraft, while the other moved in front of it. On Saturday, November 15, astronauts Pete Conrad, Dick Gordon, and Alan Bean reported to Mission Control in Houston that they had spotted two bogeys tagging along with them *132,000 miles* out.

After exchanging several theories back and forth between the spacecraft and Mission Control, "no definite agreement" could be reached concerning "what the crew might have sighted."

"With ground-elapsed time at only thirty-six hours, forty minutes into the flight, the *Apollo* team had been jolted from what had been scheduled as a 'matter-of-fact' flight," UFO researcher Timothy Green Beckley stated. "Far from being routine, this was to be one of the most bizarre—and scientifically revealing—expeditions to date.

"Several times, as the craft sped toward the lunar surface, scientists monitoring the chatter of the command module were stunned to hear unexplainable sounds that were not emanating either from the ground or from the capsule itself. At one point it was suggested that the astronauts must be talking to somebody strange."

Astronauts Conrad and Bean Heard Weird Sounds on Moon's Surface

At 6:45 A.M. on Wednesday, November 19, in the midst of the astronauts' limbering-up exercises on the surface of the Moon, Conrad and Bean told Ground Control that they were receiving weird background noises.

Bean: I keep hearing a whistle.

Conrad: That's what I hear, okay.

Ten minutes later Dick Gordon in the mother ship orbiting the Moon reported to Houston that he kept hearing a constant beeping sound in the background.

Houston, Mission Control: That's affirmative. We've heard it now for about the past forty-five minutes.

Gordon: That's right, so have we. What is it?

Ground Control admitted that it was unable to isolate the source of the mysterious beeping sounds.

Cernan Thinks UFOs Come from other Civilization

When asked in 1973 by a reporter from the *Los Angeles Times* for his opinion about UFOs, Commander Eugene Cernan, *Apollo 17* Mission, responded by stating that he had been asked that question many times: "I been asked about UFOs, and I've said publicly that I thought they were somebody else, some other civilization."

Cosmonaut Afanasyev Is Convinced Extraterrestrials Have Visited Earth

In April 1979, Russian cosmonaut Victor Afanasyev sighted an alien craft while in space. "I think we are not alone, something of extraterrestrial origin has visited Earth," he said later. "The alien craft turned towards ours, followed us, and flew formation twenty-five to twenty-nine meters away. We photographed the metallic engineering structure that was forty meters long. The film was later confiscated."

Sphere-Shaped Craft Visits *Mir* Space Station

Gennadij Strekhalov, a cosmonaut on the *Mir* Space Station, admitted that on the last two flights he saw something very strange. "During the flight of 1990, I called Gennadi Manakov, our commander, to come to the porthole, but we did not manage to put film in the camera quickly enough. We looked down on Newfoundland. The

Russian scientists monitoring the *Apollo 11* historic Moon landing on July 20, 1969, insist that NASA censored the fact that alien spaceships were present to observe the U.S. mission. (*Art by Ricardo Pustanio*)

atmosphere was absolutely clear. Suddenly a kind of sphere appeared—beautiful, shiny, and glittering. I saw it for ten seconds before it disappeared."

When Strekhalov was asked how large the object was, he replied that there was nothing he could compare it with, but he added that it was a perfect sphere.

Make No Mistake, Dr. Mitchell Says: Roswell Happened

On October 25, 1998, astronaut Dr. Edgar Mitchell, astonished both UFO believers and skeptics alike when in London's *The People* he first issued a statement that he has since made many times: "Make no mistake, Roswell [the alleged crash site of an alien craft in July 1947] happened. I've seen secret files which show the government knew about it, but decided not to tell the public."

When Will Buzz Aldrin 'Fess Up?

On July 13, 2008, advertising teasers for the *Larry King Live* on CNN had every UFO enthusiast hoping that Astronaut Buzz Aldrin would finally admit that the *Apollo 11* crew had sighted an unknown craft during the July 20, 1969 Moon landing. The

UFO encounter had been reported, denied, and debated for decades. When Aldrin began to describe what many believed would be a culture-altering sighting, he started to ramble for so long that even King got impatient and urged the astronaut to tell what he had seen.

To the UFO community's complete disappointment, Aldrin maintained his same old story that the "unknown" that the *Apollo* crew had sighted was only a panel from the rocket's large upper stage, which was about six thousand miles away.

Not at all satisfied with Aldrin's explanation, former Lockheed Skunkworks (the official alias for Lockheed Martin's Advanced Development Programs [ADP]) engineer Don Phillips said that during the *Apollo 11* landing, Neil Armstrong remarked on the size of the UFOs that the astronauts were observing during the Moon landing. Armstrong expressed his feelings that it seemed obvious to him that the mysterious objects did not like the astronauts being there. Phillips said that while he was with the Skunkworks, everyone was required to sign an agreement with the government to keep quiet about what the *Apollo 11* astronauts had seen. The encounter was, according to Phillips, common knowledge at NASA.

Dr. Mitchell, *Apollo 14* Astronaut, Declares that It Is "Way Past Time" to Inform the Public of the Facts of Alien Visitations

D r. Edgar Mitchell, an *Apollo 14* astronaut, has suggested in a number of interviews that perhaps we cannot say that the current U.S. government is really covering up the truth about aliens. He feels it is possible that most of those in official positions in the government and military intelligence over the last fifty years don't know what is going on any more than the public. Dr. Mitchell said that he relies upon the testimony of the "old-timers" who have been involved with UFO investigations for decades.

"We are way, way past time for bringing this information to the public," Dr. Mitchell said. The facts, such as they are known, about the aliens must be acknowledged and discussions must be conducted at the highest levels of Congress and intelligence groups. "Events are moving so very rapidly that no one is really on top of the UFO enigma. If we don't get to the bottom of things soon, we are not going to have an opportunity forever."

Aliens and the
Space Program

In 1954, in the May issue of *The American Weekly*, Dr. Hermann Oberth, the father of modern rocketry said: "UFOs are conceived and directed by intelligent beings of a very high order, and they are propelled by distorting their gravitational field, converting gravity into useable energy. There is no doubt in my mind that these objects are interplanetary craft of some sort.... They probably do not originate in our solar system, perhaps not even in our galaxy. It is my thesis that flying saucers are real and that they are space ships from another solar system."

A Non-Terrestrial Source Has Been
Carefully Observing Our Space Program

For at least the past sixty years, there has been a space program originating from somewhere other than the known terrestrial space centers. It has been placing satellites in orbit around our planet and transmitting bizarre messages, which have led to speculations and conspiracies to hide their existence from the general public. Some researchers have theorized that the unknown orbiting vehicles (UOVs) are probably launched from bases on the Moon or Mars.

It has been over forty years since NASA's successful manned spacecraft landing on our Moon, but those of us who research the subject matter of UFOs and aliens recall the vast number of mysterious events that have always been an undeclared aspect of the space program. There appears strong evidence that dates back decades before the Moon landing that human progress has been under close surveillance by another intelligence, either extraterrestrial or multidimensional. Some would say this intense surveillance began shortly after human scientists successfully harnessed nuclear energy and began to travel out beyond the parameters of our planet. Although textbooks of every nation credit *Sputnik 1*, a Soviet space vehicle launched into orbit on October 4, 1957, as the first artificial Earth satellite, mysterious objects launched by neither the United States nor the USSR have been detected since 1949.

Captain Edward J. Ruppelt, head of the USAF's Project Bluebook from 1951 to 1953, related an account of a sighting on April 24, 1949, when Commander R. B. McLaughlin, USN, and his crew were preparing to launch a Skyhook research balloon at the White Sands Missile Range in New Mexico.

Suddenly their tracking telescope caught the image of an elliptical object moving at fantastic speeds across its field of view. Computations showed that the object was fifty-six miles high and traveling at a velocity of seven miles per second, which translates to eighteen thousand miles per hour, i.e., orbital speed—eight years before *Sputnik 1*.

Did UFOs Try to Land on the White House Lawn in 1952?

In July 1952 the Pentagon had become so shaken over a UFO invasion of Washington, D.C., which set off a Red Alert, that a systematic sky search by telescope and camera was ordered and placed under the direction of Dr. Clyde Tombaugh, the famous astronomer who had discovered the planet Pluto. The avowed purpose of Project Skysweep was to search for tiny *natural* satellites of Earth that might be used as platforms in a future space program. At the same time, Skysweep personnel were advised to keep an eye out for UFOs.

According to science writer Otto O. Binder, "Sometime in 1953 it leaked out that two unknowns had been spied far out in space, circling Earth. They were called 'moonlets' as if they were natural satellites of our planet, but other astronomers failed to verify any such permanent and age-old bodies.

"This discovery really put the Pentagon in a corner, and they never officially admitted that two non-natural satellites had been observed for a short period of time. The mere fact that the unknown satellites later disappeared proved they had moved out of orbit and were therefore powered craft."

Three Mystery Objects Tracked by NASA, Goddard and NORAD

Later in 1960 three mystery objects were tracked not only by NASA's space track system at Goddard Spaceflight Center, but also by NORAD, the antimissile defense radar network established by the Pentagon with central headquarters at Offutt Air Force Base in Nebraska. As fate would have it, it was a leak through NORAD that led journalists to the story and forced NASA to confess that it had also tracked the unknown objects.

Quick to cover its suddenly exposed backside, NASA insisted that two of the mystery satellites were just bits and pieces of space debris, parts of broken-up satellites and launchers. Only one of the three objects, they maintained, was a respectable size, perhaps comparable to the *Telstar* communications satellite.

UFO contactees state firmly that aliens have had bases on the Moon for centuries. They also add that the aliens have taken them there to visit. (*Art by Ricardo Pustanio*)

But other data leaks from NORAD indicated that the authorities were once again playing cover-up-and that all three of the unknowns were mammoth.

And since the three mystery satellites remained in orbit, the International Satellite Authority (centered in France), which grants official designations to all satellites launched by any nation on Earth, had no choice other than to add the three unknowns to their list and provide them with catalog numbers.

A UFO Chases a Polaris Rocket from Cape Kennedy

On January 10, 1961, a UFO suddenly appeared from nowhere and took after a Polaris rocket launched from Cape Kennedy. The radar station at the space center locked on to the object by mistake and clearly plotted its mysterious course.

Four UFOs Pace Gemini Capsule for a Complete Orbit

Four UFOs locked in on an unmanned Gemini capsule on April 8, 1964, and paced it for one complete orbit around the planet.

UFOs Keep an Eye on Cape Kennedy

On December 5, 1964, at 11:06 P.M., just a little more than a week after NASA had launched *Mariner IV*, UFOs were spotted over Cape Kennedy.

Massive Object Hounds Lovell and Borman

When astronauts James Lovell and Frank Borman were orbiting aboard GT-7 on December 4, 1965, a massive spherical object slowly crossed in front of them.

When Borman radioed ground control that they had a "bogey" at ten o'clock high, control technicians suggested that the astronauts might be sighting their booster rocket.

"We know where the booster is," Borman said coolly. "This is an actual sighting."

Engineer at Huntsville Sights Formation of UFOs

On August 26, 1966, B.F. Funk, an aerospace engineer employed at the Huntsville, Alabama, Aero-astrodynamics Laboratory of the Marshall Space Flight Center, spotted a formation of UFOs near Fort Payne. En route with his wife from Atlanta, Georgia, to Huntsville, Funk spotted the bright objects approaching, with one of the UFOs moving back and forth inside the triangle formed by the other three.

The aerospace engineer reported that the UFOs changed in color from white to orange, were moving at a fantastic rate of speed, and made absolutely no sound as they made a sweeping turn and passed out of sight. Unlike a layman who would have had to make a guesstimate, Funk said that according to his mathematical calculations, the objects were flying at an altitude of three thousand feet and that they were thirty feet in diameter.

Funk told the *Huntsville News* that he "knew very well what they [the objects] were. They were no ethnical aircraft."

Dr. Richard F. Haines, retired NASA senior research scientist, Ames Research Center, remarked that what he had found in his observation of UFOs was "compelling evidence that most of these aerial objects far exceeded the terrestrial technology of the era in which they were seen. I was forced to conclude that there is a great likelihood that Earth is being visited by highly advanced aerospace vehicles under highly intelligent control."

Three Hundred-Foot UFO Suspended above Placitas

On June 23, 1966, Julian Sandoval, a flight engineer associated with the Apollo Space Project, sighted a UFO in northwestern New Mexico. Sandoval stated that the object appeared to be suspended above Placitas, a small town north of Albuquerque. He estimated the UFO's length at about three hundred feet and said that it disappeared after it increased its speed to a high velocity.

There have been assertions made that NASA has received strange transmissions of alleged alien voices, music, and messages that have been recorded during various space missions. (*Art by Ricardo Pustanio*)

NASA Officials Unable to Identify Object
Sighted by Astronauts Aboard *Gemini 10*

During the *Gemini 10* space flight in July 1966, astronauts Michael Collins and John Young reported UFOs that were summarily identified and dismissed as fragments of an earlier vehicle. Later during the same space mission, Collins sighted another UFO over Australia that was moving north to south. NASA officials were unable to identify the object and no further comment was made.

When Space Experiment Releases Huge Cloud,
Angry Response from UFOs

On Wallops Island, Virginia, on September 23, 1966, a space experiment sent a huge multicolored cloud hundreds of miles across the sky. As if the colored cloud had been a red flag waved before a group of angry aliens, the skies were suddenly filled with UFOs from Virginia to Chicago. In the Windy City, four pilots at O'Hare International Airport filed a report with the control tower.

Based on Seven Thousand Reports, Atmospheric Physicist with NASA Concludes UFOs to Be Extraterrestrial Probes

On June 7, 1968, when we talked with Lee Katchen, an atmospheric physicist with NASA—who was careful to emphasize that he was speaking as a private citizen—he stated that on the basis of the seven thousand reports that he had examined, he believed UFOs to be extraterrestrial probes.

"UFO sightings are now [1968] so common, the military doesn't have time to worry about them—so they screen them out," Katchen said. "The major defense systems have UFO filters built into them, and when a UFO appears, they simply ignore it."

When asked for specifics, Katchen particularly singled out the radar network employed by SAGE (semiautomatic ground environmental system), the North American tactical air defense system, which tracks all aircraft flights. "The filters cut out all unconventional objects or targets and make no record of UFOs," he said.

Speaking during the Cold War, Katchen noted, "Unconventional targets are ignored, because, apparently, we are interested only in Russian targets, possible enemy targets. Something that hovers in the air, then shoots off at five thousand miles per hour, doesn't interest us because it can't be the enemy," he said. Katchen added that at that time the only system left that was doing any recording of UFOs was the U.S. space tracking system.

"UFOs are picked up by ground and air radar, and they have been photographed by gun cameras all along," he stated. "There are so many UFOs in the sky that the Air Force has had to employ the special radar network to screen them out."

Upsilon Bootes Contacts Earth through Robot Satellite

In 1974 British astronomer Duncan Lunan startled both academic and lay communities when he announced that he had deciphered a message that had been sent to Earth by entities from another solar system. What is more, Lunan made his startling claim in *Space Flight,* the journal of the prestigious British Interplanetary Society.

Lunan's theory postulated that an unmanned "probe" robot satellite, which was placed in orbit around our Moon between thirteen thousand and fifteen thousand years ago, has been transmitting a particular message at intermittent periods since the 1920s. According to the British astronomer, the satellite had been placed near Earth by dwellers of a planet orbiting a star called Upsilon Bootes in another solar system. Lunan translated the message as follows:

> Start here. Our home is Upsilon Bootes, which is a double star. We live on
> the sixth planet of seven, counting outward from the sun, which is the
> larger of the two. Our sixth planet has one moon. Our fourth planet has

NASA has not been able to explain away all astronaut sightings of UFOs as merely discarded space debris. (Art by Bill Oliver)

three. Our first and third planets each have one. Our probe is in the position of Arcturus, known in our maps.

The executive secretary of the British Interplanetary Society, Leonard Carter, said that Upsilon Bootes is about 103 million light-years from Earth. The robot probe referred to in the message is only about 170,000 miles from Earth, near the Moon, and was placed in orbit about 11,000 B.C.E.

"Lunan plotted the echoes on a graph," Carter explained. "Oddly, they seemed to make up a series of dots outlining the known constellations, but they were slightly distorted. However, Lunan has gone in to the question of this distortion and alteration. And the dots related to the constellations as they were about thirteen thousand years ago."

Professor Ronald N. Bracewell, one of the leading radioastronomers in the United States, said that in spite of certain reservations regarding Lunan's interpretation of the signals, he would not discount them altogether. In fact, he advocated a similar theory to explain radio echoes noted in 1927, 1928, and 1934.

Our Conversations with Scientific Whistle Blowers

We have always been rather skeptical about claims that alien scientists have collaborated with our own technological experts to accelerate our spy planes and our space programs. But we have been approached so often after our lectures and seminars by individuals who say that they have something to share with us that we would find extremely interesting. In every case, when we have asked these "whistle blowers" for identification, they have been quick to provide documents that certainly appeared authentic. On one occasion when our informant claimed to be a scientist employed by NASA, he produced a variety of ID cards that appeared to be official. In addition, he pulled out a number of photographs showed him posing with several of the more recognizable and well-known astronauts.

Once we had satisfied ourselves that our informants seemed to be who they said they were, we felt nonplused when they claimed that they and numerous other scientists at NASA and other secret underground bases were working side by side with extraterrestrials in advancing our space program. As difficult as it may have been for us to comprehend in the past, we began to change our attitudes when we heard time and again that these physicists, engineers, technicians, and nuclear scientists had worked with alien intelligences.

"Some are tall, blond, and blue-eyed," one of our informants said. "The 'nordics,' we call them. Others are the small ones that most of us refer to as the 'grays.' We would never have been able to get to the Moon by 1969 if it hadn't been for the technological assistance of the extraterrestrials who are working among us at NASA."

Other individuals told us some very disturbing claims that a "global shadow government" did in fact make a deal with extraterrestrial intelligences to swap various mineral rights and the freedom to experiment on humans in exchange for advanced alien technology. When we learned about the agents of a secret branch of government giving the aliens *carte blanche* to abduct certain humans for experimental purposes of investigating the viability of creating a hybrid race—and in some cases permission to take both livestock and humans to supplement their food supply—it seemed to us that the aliens had not been all that generous in assisting Earth's space program. Unless a secret U.S. government group such as the controversial MJ-12 has their own covert space program operating from some hidden underground base, it would appear that the UFO intelligences have actually been rather busy harassing our space flight centers, as if it is their concerted plan to keep all earthlings bound to the ground—or, at the very least, to keep our space program under close scrutiny.

"Astronauts such as McDivitt and others may have been guessing about the true identity of the UFOs," one of our informants who claimed to have been a NASA scientist stated, "But those few of us privy to the machinations of MJ-12 and the deal made with the aliens knew exactly what the astronauts were seeing up there." He had to admit, though, that a number of NASA scientists who had been working with the aliens had become more than a little irritated by what seemed to be occasions of deliberate interference by the aliens in our space program.

"They were supposed to help us conquer space so that we could join them on a more-or-less equal footing," he groused. "Sometimes it really seemed as though the aliens actually wanted to keep us earthbound and were deceiving us about our becoming true allies." While it was undeniable that the aliens had given them a lot of help

> "Sometimes it really seemed as though the aliens actually wanted to keep us earthbound and were deceiving us about our becoming true allies."

with the propulsion system and some of the metal alloys during the early days of the space program, the scientist told us, after a certain point the aliens began to limit their cooperation with providing the more advanced technology that they were supposed to be sharing with us.

UFOs Filling the Night Skies over the Midwest

Dr. Paul Czysz is a professor of aeronautical engineering at Parks College in St. Louis. He spent eight years in the Air Force at Wright-Patterson Air Force Base, and another thirty years working for McDonnell-Douglas in the field of exotic technologies. While at Wright-Patterson Air Force Base, he was involved in tracking UFOs over Missouri, Ohio, and Michigan.

One of the more interesting nights Dr. Czysz had at Wright-Patterson was when he was the assistant to the head officer-of-the-day over at Patterson Field. He remembers the night well:

"We had 151 phone calls come in regarding unidentified objects flying down U.S. 40—then turning at Columbus and going up to Detroit. These [calls] were [from] state policemen, … doctors that worked late at night, all kinds of people reported seeing this. We had radar tracks on them and had airliners call in that they had seen them. It was very, very interesting. These guys gave very clear descriptions of what they saw." In Dr. Czysz's opinion these UFOs weren't imaginary; whatever these people saw was real, he felt.

Dr. Czysz recalled that one night near St. Louis, there was a fairly large triangular object seen: "It traveled the distance down to south St. Louis. In some of its sightings, it was moving relatively benignly, but then it literally jumped about twenty miles in a couple of seconds."

He received a lot of phone calls from the local newspapers and TV stations, asking how such a seemingly impossible transport could be possible. Dr. Czysz answered that he didn't know "unless you explain it through something like a quantum physics explanation of time and space and relationships…. Other than that, there's no way to do it. And, this object made no sound at all. It starts out at hover, and it literally almost disappears and pops over here—so it's not like a cartoon where it goes 'whoosh.' It's almost like it disappears and comes up over here, according to the descriptions that some of the police officers gave."

Back-Engineering UFOs at the "Skunkworks"

When Don Phillips, a former employee of the Lockheed "Skunkworks" (the official alias for Lockheed Martin's Advanced Development Programs [ADP]) spoke at a meeting of the Disclosure Project, he said that all employees of the famous Skunkworks had to sign an agreement with the government to maintain strict silence about their work. He knew that anti-gravitation research was being conducted, and he learned that there were some captured alien spacecraft from the famous crash at Roswell in 1947. Phillips said that the scientists were able to back-engineer from the downed craft and that the knowledge they had of these technologies came from the craft that was captured at Roswell. Phillips made it clear that he did not see the craft, nor did he see the bodies, but he certainly knew some of the people who did. In Phillips' mind, there is no question that there are beings from outside our planet.

He went on to point out that if the aliens were hostile, "with their weaponry they could have destroyed us a long time ago. We got handheld scanners that scan the body and determine what the health condition is. We can also treat from the same scanner. I can tell you personally that we have been working on them. And we have ones that can diagnose and cure cancer."

One of the purposes that Phillips had for founding his own technology corporation in 1998 was "to bring forth these technologies that can clean the air and can help get rid of the toxins, and help get rid of the need for so much fossil fuel."

Asked about the *Apollo 14* Moon landing, Phillips told the audience that the "UFOs were huge and they would just come to a stop and do a sixty-degree, forty-five-degree, ten-degree turn, and then immediately reverse this action." Phillips repeated what Neil Armstrong had said when he sighted the alien craft: "They're here. They are right over there ... and look at the size of those ships. And, it is obvious they don't like us being here."

A number of longtime researchers who have heard Phillips speak have been reminded of the remarkable comment made by the colorful Ben Rich (d. 1995), the former head of the Skunkworks from 1975 to 1990: "We already have the means to travel among the stars, but these technologies are locked up in black projects and it would take an act of God to ever get them out to benefit humanity.... Anything you can imagine we already know how to do."

In his foreword to *The UFO Cover-Up* (1984), Dr. J. Allen Hynek, astronomer and former scientific advisor to the Air Force's Project Blue Book, commented: "For the government to continue to maintain that UFOs are nonexistent in the face of the documents already released and of other cogent evidence ... is puerile and in a sense an insult to the American people."

Underground and Undersea Alien Bases

Recently, Russian oceanographer and former naval captain of the first rank, Vladimir Azhazha revealed: "Fifty percent of meetings with UFOs are connected with the ocean, and fifteen percent with lakes." Forty-four percent of cases have been recorded in the Atlantic Ocean, sixteen percent in the Pacific, ten percent in the Mediterranean Sea.

Naval intelligence expert and captain for the first rank Igor Barklay noted that the unidentified objects were most often spotted in deep water off the Bahamas, Bermuda, Puerto Rico and the east coast of the United States—close to areas where military forces are concentrated. Underwater craft have been termed "USOs," or "unidentified submarine objects."

Underground UFO Bases Have Already Seen Interplanetary Warfare in 1969

Although we have been informed since the 1950s that there are underground bases in Nevada, Arizona, California, Wisconsin, Colorado, and many other areas, the alleged underground facility outside Dulce, New Mexico, is by far the most notorious. According to many UFO researchers and to men and women who claimed to have worked there side by side with the "grays," the principal research at Dulce is the study of human genetics and the possibility of crossbreeding the two species and/or developing mutations.

A frequently heard account about Dulce concerns a 1969 confrontation that broke out between the human scientists working there and the aliens. In order to guarantee extended cooperation from the secret government, the grays took a number of human scientists as hostages. Crack troops from our Delta Force were sent into the

For centuries there have been legends of intelligent beings inhabiting an inner-earth network of caves and underground bases. Some of these beings are described as reptilian or hominid/human hybrids. (*Art by Ricardo Pustanio*)

vast underground tunnels to rescue our scientists, but they proved to be no match for the aliens. Estimates of sixty-six to several hundred humans were killed during the violent confrontation.

Because of the sudden realization that the grays had their own agenda and could not always be trusted, the representatives and employees of the secret government withdrew from all joint projects with the grays for about two years. Eventually there was a reconciliation, and the alliance between the aliens and the members of the secret government was once again back on course.

It has been said that some of the aliens who work in the underground bases consider themselves to be native earthlings, for they are the crossbred descendants of a reptilian humanoid species—who many thousands of years ago in our planet's prehistory accomplished genetic engineering with early members of *Homo sapiens*. While some of these crossbred reptilian-human "terrans" are loyal allies, others of their group have proven to be untrustworthy mercenary agents for the draco, an extraterrestrial race that is returning to Earth—a planet they consider their ancient outpost.

The grays are most often described as being under four feet tall, with a disproportionately large head and large slanted eyes. Some of their species appear more sophisticated than others, but they all seem to worship technology at the expense of artistic and creative expression. They also seem devoid of emotion and appear indifferent to the general well-being of humans.

In addition to a number of reported "hairy dwarfs" and exceedingly tall alien lifeforms, the most commonly mentioned aliens next to the grays are the so-called "nordics," essentially human in appearance, mostly blond-haired and blue-eyed. Cast in an angelic kind of role in the "alien v. human" drama, they cannot be expected to violate the intergalactic law of noninterference and interfere with the grisly machinations of the grays. But they would intervene, of course, if the grays finally go too far and begin to upset the larger picture of universal balance and order.

The Controversy over a Research Scientist's Claims

Controversial research scientist Paul Bennewitz claims to have been repeatedly harassed and intimidated by the military after he provided government investigators with proof that he had filmed a formation of UFOs flying over the Manzano

Weapons Storage Area and the Coyote Canyon Test Site (where nuclear materials are stored), all part of the Kirtland Air Force Base facilities in Albuquerque, New Mexico. Bennewitz said he saw four saucer-shaped objects lined up beside the outside fence of the air base.

Bennewitz's investigations led him to Dulce, where he spoke with a woman who was kidnapped by aliens after she and her son had witnessed them mutilating a cow. According to the abductee, she and her son were taken inside the Dulce underground base and witnessed horrible experiments in which organs and blood were being removed from animals to create a new species of humanoids through gene splicing.

A number of UFO abductees have reported memories of being taken by reptoid aliens to underground laboratories to undergo physical examinations. (Art by Ricardo Pustanio)

Son of Aviation Pioneer Lear Is Shocked When He Learns the Government Has Made a Secret Pact with Aliens

John Lear is the son of the famous aviation pioneer William Lear, who established the Lear Aircraft Company. John himself has earned a well-deserved reputation in aeronautical circles. He has test flown over 150 aircraft and has won numerous awards from the Federal Aviation Administration.

Before he heard a friend relate a UFO encounter that had taken place in England, Lear had absolutely no interest in such way-out matters. However, as he began to check out various accounts relayed to him, he found to his astonishment that there were mountains of evidence proving that UFOs are real and quite likely from outer space. Pursuing the subject with his contacts in the CIA and his informants in military intelligence, Lear ascertained that the first UFO crash occurred in Germany shortly before World War II. The Nazis used the technology obtained from the wreckage to initiate the rocketry program that destroyed much of Europe and blitzed the British Isles.

Later, Lear was told, a flying disc crashed near Roswell, New Mexico, and one of the injured aliens on board was kept alive for a short period of time in Hangar 18 in what is now Wright-Patterson Air Force Base.

What shocked Lear was that the government had made secret deals with the aliens, actually exchanging humans for advanced technical data. By 1987 Lear had discovered that the aliens were putting together what he called a sort of "Frankenstein Army—part alien, part human" in underground facilities in Nevada and New Mexico.

Lear's painstaking research yielded grisly evidence that humans and cattle had been mutilated by the aliens as early as 1956. An Air Force major had witnessed the abduction of a sergeant early one morning at the White Sands Missile Test Range. When his body was found three days later, his genitals had been removed, his rectum cored out in a surgically precise plug up to the colon, and his eyes had been removed. His corpse had also been drained of all blood.

"From some of the evidence," Lear said, "it is apparent that such surgery is accomplished in most cases while the victim is still alive."

Information provided Lear by informants concerning the Dulce underground base detailed "large vats with pale meat being agitated in solutions" and large test tubes "with humans in them."

In Lear's assessment the abduction scenario seemed to have at least three purposes: (1) insertion of a tiny probe, approximately three millimeters in size that would monitor and program the abductee; (2) posthypnotic suggestions to prepare the abductee for a future mission; and (3) genetic crossbreeding between aliens and humans.

Hamilton Learns of the "Cosmic Top Secret"

William Hamilton, author of *Cosmic Top Secret*, first received news of the existence of the secret underground bases in 1979 when an acquaintance who was a government worker revealed the details of military and alien participation in monstrous genetic experiments. When his employers discovered that the man had stolen photographs depicting these experiments, his wife and children were "taken into custody" by federal agents as an effective means of regaining the classified material that had been "misplaced."

Hamilton's friend told him that the base at which he had been employed had at least seven subterranean levels. On level four, for example, advanced research in mind control was being conducted. At level six, genetic experiments on animals and humans were in progress. Humans were kept in cages and drugged for some nefarious purpose on level seven.

Hamilton's informant had originally been told a false story that the government was conducting special secret tests to cure insanity, but when he realized at last that aliens were actually behind the torturous experiments, he left his post and went into hiding.

In recent years, Hamilton points out, an uncomfortable dilemma has arisen. A small number of abductees have reported surveillance, intervention, or abduction by people they truly believe to be military personnel. "At first glance, the claims of abductees seem outrageous and paranoid," Hamilton admitted. "But are we to dismiss all of these reports as fabrications of deluded minds? Has the military found itself confronting superior intelligence and technology? What if some aliens are friends and others are foes?"

Hamilton feels that the military's role in the UFO controversy seems to argue that we are dealing with actual biological entities and real spacecraft that pose a

Those who accuse a secret agency of the government to have made an agreement with extraterrestrials insist that after the deal had been made to exchange advanced technology for certain of Earth's planetary resources, reptilian aliens constructed huge underground and undersea facilities to house test centers and military bases. (*Art by Ricardo Pustanio*)

potential threat to our way of life. Cautioning against panic, however, Hamilton states that "the aliens have been around a long time and have not taken any mass offensive against us to date."

Hamilton maintains that his greatest concern "is the fact that excessive secrecy [on the part of the government] can lead to a breakdown in our cultural cohesiveness. It can lead to wild rumors and freewheeling speculations. It can lead to ignorance and the disintegration of our society."

A Cheshire Cat from an Unknown Wonderland

In mid-February 1942, Lieutenant William Brennan of the Royal Australian Air Force (RAAF) was on patrol over the Bass Strait south of Melbourne, Australia, on the lookout for Japanese submarines or long-range German U-boats. Fishermen in the area had reported mysterious lights bobbing on the sea at night, and after the

Japanese attack on Darwin on February 19th, the Allied High Command was urging the strictest vigilance.

About 5:50 P.M. on a sunny afternoon the air patrol was flying a few miles east of the Tasman Peninsula when a strange aircraft of a glistening bronze color suddenly emerged from a cloud bank near them. The object was about 150 feet long and approximately fifty feet in diameter. Lieutenant Brennan saw that the peculiar craft had a dome or cupola on its upper surface, and he thought he saw someone inside wearing a helmet. There were occasional greenish blue flashes emanating from its keel, and Lieutenant Brennan was astonished to see, "framed in a white circle on the front of the dome, an image of a large, grinning Cheshire cat."

The unidentified aerial craft flew parallel to the RAAF patrol for several minutes, then it abruptly turned away and dived straight down into the Pacific. Lieutenant Brennan emphasized that the mysterious vehicle made a dive, not a crash, into the ocean. He added that before the craft left them, he noticed what appeared to be four finlike appendages on its underside.

Keep Your Bathyscaphes to Yourself!

In 1948, Professor Auguste Piccard brought his unmanned bathyscaphe (deep sea submersible) up from a record descent of 4,600 feet under the surface of the ocean.

Professor Piccard and his crew were so excited by their successful mission that it took them a moment to become aware of a very peculiar thing. Although the bathyscaphe had suffered no actual damage from the intense pressure of the record descent, its aluminum radar mast had been neatly removed, as if a skilled underwater mechanic had accomplished a clean theft.

Mystery Submarines Elude the Argentine Navy

Early in February 1960, the Argentine navy, with the assistance of U.S. advisers, attacked submarines thought to be lurking at the bottom of Golio Nuevo, a forty-by-twenty-mile bay separated from the South Atlantic by a narrow entrance. The Argentines alternately depth-bombed the craft and demanded their surrender and, on a number of occasions, declared that they had the mystery submarines trapped. Once, they even announced that they had crippled one of the unidentified subs.

There were at least two mystery submarines, and they both had peculiar characteristics. They were able to function and maneuver in the narrow gulfs for many days without surfacing. They easily outran and hid from surface vessels. And in spite of the combined forces of the Argentine fleet and the most modern U.S. sub-hunting technology, they were able to escape capture and destruction.

Skeptics of the bizarre undersea chase accused the Argentine navy of timing a dramatic search for mystery submarines so that it would likely influence the evaluation of the new navy budget by the Argentine Congress. However, UFO researchers enumerated the many reports of strange vehicles seen entering and leaving the sea off the coast of Argentina. In their opinion, the unknown objects were underwater alien craft rather than terrestrial submarines.

Six USOs Pursue Russian Sub, then Soar Off into the Sky

Vladimir Azhazha was the captain of the experimental submarine *Severyanka* in the 1960s, and he has recounted his underwater experiences with unidentified objects in dozens of books and articles on UFOs. He has reported an incident in which a Russian submarine was pursued by six unidentified underwater objects in the Pacific Ocean. Later, after the submarine surfaced to evade them, the USOs emerged from the water and took flight.

Rear Admiral Beketov Encounters Objects that "Exceed Ours Significantly"

Former rear admiral and nuclear submarine commander Yury Beketov has gone on record describing events that occurred in the infamous Bermuda Triangle. "We repeatedly observed that the instruments detected the movements of material objects at unimaginable speed, around 230 knots (400 km per hour [250 mph]). It's hard to reach that speed on the surface—only in the air [is it readily possible].... The beings that created those material objects significantly exceed us in development."

Some researchers have expressed their conclusions that alien beings established underwater bases in the oceans of Earth in prehistoric times. (Art by Ricardo Pustanio)

Invading New York City's East River

At 3:00 A.M. on July 15, 1960, the 24,000-ton Panamanian flag tanker *Alkaid*, with a full cargo of crude oil, was struck by a USO as it passed under the Williamsburg Bridge in New York City's East River. The collision tore a massive gash in the starboard side of the big ship, forcing the captain to beach her near the United Nations building. Later, the *Alkaid*, on the verge of capsizing, was towed off to a dock.

After two days of Coast Guard hearings and an investigation by the Army Corps of Engineers, whose job it is to keep the harbor waters clean, no explanation could be found for the *Alkaid*'s mysterious collision with a USO. Nor could any object be found in the harbor that would have been capable of piercing the tanker's steel hull.

USOs Harass and Sink Shrimp Boat

For many years now we have received regular reports from shrimpers of USO harassment. Ira Pete, owner of the *Ruby E.*, a sixty-seven-foot shrimp boat, had his vessel sink under mysterious circumstances in the first week of July 1961. His account is considerably more serious than the reports of USOs surfacing beside the shrimp boats or buzzing around the crews.

Divers in various parts of the ocean have described encountering strange beings with large clawlike appendages. They were certain these were not ordinary crabs or lobsters, but creatures of extraordinary size and apparent intelligence. (Art by Ricardo Pustanio)

According to Pete, he was fishing in the Gulf of Mexico off Port Arkansas with his two-man crew when something hooked into the boat and ripped off its stem. Fortunately for the three shrimpers, there was another fishing vessel close by.

Australian and New Zealand Warship Maneuvers Interrupted by USO

On November 14, 1961, Australian and New Zealand warships were conducting naval exercises off Sydney Heads when a large unidentified submarine object interrupted their maneuvers. There was no visual sighting of the craft, and the interloper eluded the fleet with speed and ease until contact was lost.

The official response to those who had questions about the mysterious intruder was that it was an "unidentified object."

Yacht Rammed by USO off California

On February 5, 1964, the 105-foot yacht *Hattie D.* was rammed by an underwater object near Eureka, California. Ten men and one woman were lifted from the fast-sinking yacht in a dramatic Coast Guard helicopter rescue.

The survivors all agreed that the *Hattie D.* had been damaged by something big made of steel. When crewman Carl Johnson was informed that no submarines were reported in the area and that the yacht had sunk in 7,500 feet of water, he adamantly replied that he didn't care how deep it was in that area—and he knew that whatever "holed" the yacht had been a very long piece of steel.

Undersea Camera Captures Photo of Strange Artifact

The U.S. ship *Eltanin*, owned by the Military Sea Transportation Service, was specially designed for use in the National Science Foundation Antarctic research program. On August 29, 1964, the *Eltanin* was a thousand miles west of Cape Horn, and its crew of highly trained specialists were busily engaged in photographing the ocean floor, which reaches a depth of 13,500 feet in that area. A uniquely designed camera, housed in a metal cylinder, was being pulled along by a cable.

Later that day, when darkroom technicians developed the exposed film, they found that the camera had captured the image of a bizarre device jutting out of the muck of the ocean floor. A central mast supported four series of cross rods, which made the object look like a cross between a television antenna and a telemetry antenna. The cross rods were spaced at ninety-degree angles and showed white knobs on their extremities.

Although scientific logic argued against such an assessment, the mysterious object appeared to be manmade and definitely seemed out of place in the anticipated natural environment of the ocean floor. The *Eltanin's* specially designed camera had been built to bounce along the seabed and to take photographs at regular intervals. It was only a fortunate, albeit puzzling, accident that the peculiar artifact had been photographed.

When the *Eltanin* docked at Auckland, New Zealand, on December 4, 1964, a reporter questioned Dr. Thomas Hopkins, senior marine biologist on board, about the eight-by-ten prints of the underwater anomaly. Dr. Hopkins estimated the object to be about two feet high and specified its point of discovery as being on the forty-five-thousand-mile fault line rift that encircles the planet. He went on to comment that the device could hardly be a plant, for at that depth there is no light. Without light, of course, there can be no photosynthesis and plants cannot live. For obvious reasons, Dr. Hopkins was reluctant to declare the object to be of human manufacture.

When asked if the thing might be some strange coral formation, Dr. Hopkins replied that if it were, it was of a kind unknown to any of the experts on board the *Eltanin.* Again, he expressed his reluctance to pronounce the object to be manmade, for that would bring up the problem of how it got there.

Superfast USO Travels the Gulf Stream

On July 5, 1965, Dr. Dmitri Rebikoff, a marine scientist making preparations to explore the depths of the Gulf Stream, found himself faced with a most unusual challenge when he detected and attempted to photograph a fast-moving undersea USO on the bottom of the warm-water stream that flows from the Florida Keys to Newfoundland and onward to northern Europe. Dr. Rebikoff told Captain L. Jacques Nicholas, project coordinator, that the object was pear shaped and moving at approximately three-and one-half knots.

The peculiar object was moving beneath various schools of fish, and at first, judging from its size, Dr. Rebikoff thought it to be a large shark. As he monitored it, however, he noted that the direction and speed of the USO were too constant for a shark. The marine scientist theorized that the object was mechanical and running on robot pilot, but since they were unable to receive any signal from the USO, he admitted that he really had no idea what it might have been.

USO Easily Travels "Impossible" Coastline

On January 12, 1965, Captain K., an airline pilot on a flight between Whenuapai and Kaitaia, New Zealand, spotted a USO when he was about one-third of the way across Kaipara Harbour. As he veered his DC-3 for a closer look at what he had at first thought to be a stranded gray-white whale in an estuary, it became evident to him that it was a metallic structure of some sort.

Captain K. saw that the object was perfectly streamlined and symmetrical in shape. He could detect no external control surfaces or protrusions, but there did appear to be a hatch on top. Harbored in no more than thirty feet of water, the USO was not shaped like an ordinary submarine. Captain K. estimated its length to be approximately one hundred feet with a diameter of fifteen feet at its widest part.

Later, the New Zealand Navy stated that it was impossible for any known model of submarine to have been in that particular area due to the configuration of the harbor and coastline. The surrounding mudflats and mangrove swamps would make the spot in which Captain K. saw his USO inaccessible to conventional undersea craft.

The Shag Harbor Sizzling USO Evaded Royal Canadian Navy

On October 3, 1967, the main topic of conversation among the residents of Shag Harbor, Nova Scotia, was the sixty-foot-long object with a series of bright portholes that had been observed gliding into the harbor and submerging into the ocean. The sizzling USO had been seen floating about a half mile offshore, then submerging beneath the surface of Shag Harbor. Within twenty minutes, several constables of the Royal Canadian Mounted Police were on the scene, attempting to reach the spot by boat.

A Coast Guard boat and eight fishing vessels joined the constables in time to observe a large path of yellowish foam and bubbling water. Divers from the Royal Canadian Navy searched the area for two days, but found no physical evidence of any kind.

The Halifax *Chronicle–Herald* quoted Squadron Leader William Bain of the Royal Canadian Air Force as commenting: "We get hundreds of [USO] reports every week, but the Shag Harbor incident is one of the few where we may get something concrete on it."

The Mysterious USO Emits a Blue and White Glow

Captain Julian Lucas Ardanza of the Argentine steamer *Naviero* was some 120 miles off the coast of Brazil on the night of July 30, 1967. The time was about 6:15 P.M., and the *Naviero* was running at seventeen knots. Captain Ardanza was enjoying his evening meal when one of his officers, Jorge Montoya, called him on the intercom to report something strange near the ship.

According to reports in the Argentine newspapers, Captain Ardanza emerged on deck to view a cigar-shaped shining object in the sea, not more than fifty feet off the *Naviero*'s starboard side. The submarine craft was an estimated 105 to 110 feet long and emitted a powerful blue and white glow. Captain Ardanza and the other officers could see no sign of periscope, railing, tower, or superstructure on the noiseless craft. In his twenty years at sea, Captain Ardanza said that he had never seen anything like it.

Chief Officer Carlos Lasca ventured that the object was a USO with a brilliant source of illumination. The seamen estimated the craft's speed at twenty-five knots, as opposed to the *Naviero*'s seventeen.

After pacing the Argentine steamer for fifteen minutes, the unidentified submarine object suddenly submerged, passed directly under the *Naviero*, and disappeared into the depths of the ocean, glowing all the while it dove deeper and deeper.

Is There a USO Base in the Depths of Lake Baikal?

As reported on the Russian website Free Press, in 1982, the Russian Navy reported unexplained activity in Lake Baikal, located in the south of the Russian region of Siberia, between Irkutsk Oblast to the northwest and the Buryat Republic to the southeast. Russian divers on a training exercise suddenly encountered unidentified swimmers in silver outfits with no visible breathing apparatus. They were at a depth of fifty meters (164 feet). Three people with high quality diving equipment died trying to pursue the mysterious swimmers.

Interestingly, not only is Lake Baikal the second most voluminous lake in the world, after the Caspian Sea, but it is the deepest, clearest, and the oldest lake in the world. At twenty-five million years old, the lake is home to more than 1,700 species of plants and animals, two thirds of which can be found nowhere else in the world.

What a perfect place to establish an underwater alien base. With an average depth of 2,442 feet, Lake Baikal contains roughly twenty percent of the fresh water on the surface of the Earth.

Although some of the frightening entities described in various close undersea encounters seem products of the witnesses' worst nightmares, certain UFO investigators suggest that these are instances of alien lifeforms who are adapting to the environment of our oceans. (*Art by Ricardo Pustanio*)

Some Researchers Believe UFOs/USOs May Come from Ancient Hidden Civilizations Here on Earth

Almost immediately following sighting of UFOs and USOs in the modern era, researchers have spun numerous theories. Some have identified the mysterious aerial vehicles that streak across our skies or glide through our lakes and oceans as originating from underground or undersea bases here on Earth. Others have suggested that the inhabitants of these hidden worlds might well be the descendants of the survivors of Atlantis. Among the theories most often cited are the following:

- The UFOs and USOs are piloted by an ancient humanoid race that antedates *Homo sapiens* by at least a million years. Their withdrawal from the surface world survives in the collective human unconscious as the legend of Atlantis.

- Atlantis was an actual prehistoric world that created a superscience and destroyed itself in civil war. The Surviving Atlanteans sought refuge from radioactivity by retreating under the Earth's crust or seas. They have continued to monitor the new race of surface dwellers and accelerated their observation after the detonation of the first atomic bombs.

- Extraterrestrial beings established a colony on Earth about 50,000 years ago when *Homo sapiens* was establishing itself as the dominant aboriginal species. They gave primitive humankind a boost up the evolutionary ladder, then grew aghast at the earthling's perpetual barbarism and left the surface world to establish underground and undersea bases from which to observe how their cosmic cousins would develop without direct interference and assistance.

The late Ray Palmer, editor of *Flying Saucers* and *Search* magazines, once told us that after decades of research he was personally convinced that the answer to the UFO mystery was to be found on our own planet, rather than outer space:

The more one thinks of the extraterrestrial thesis, the more impossible it is to prove. UFOs have been seen in the skies since man's prehistory, and today there seems to be a virtual traffic jam of objects coming in from somewhere. It seems, to me, difficult to conceive that ours should be the only planet of any interest to extraterrestrial life-forms.

The supposition that the saucers have an Earth base and may be manned by an older terrestrial race brings the cosmic concept down to reality. Geographically speaking, our own atmosphere is a heck of a lot closer than Alpha Centauri!

"A UFO the Size of an Aircraft Carrier Rose Out of the Sea"

As the son of an Air Force officer, William Cooper was reared on Air Force bases all over the world. Because his father was a pilot, Cooper heard stories of UFOs and mysterious crashes of craft "not from here" ever since he was a child.

After he graduated from high school in Japan, Cooper joined the Air Force and finished his basic training at Lackland Air Force Base before being assigned to the Strategic Air Command. During his training as an aircraft and missile pneudraulic technician, Cooper remembered that instructors regaled the new men with tales of alien craft that would swoop down on missile silos, paralyze the men on station, then remove the warhead from the missile and disappear at a fantastic speed. "I met a sergeant who told me that he had been part of a team that had transported a large, crashed disc," Cooper said. "The craft could be moved only at night on back roads, so fences and telephone poles had to be torn down and replaced as the convoy passed."

Cooper listened to all these bizarre stories and wondered what was going on, but he didn't really believe them. When he was discharged from the Air Force in 1965, he decided to continue his adventurous life and immediately enlisted in the Navy. He volunteered for submarines, and he was assigned to the USS *Tiru* (S5-416) at Pearl Harbor, Hawaii.

On a cruise to the Portland-Seattle area, Cooper had his first UFO encounter: "While we were on the surface and I was the port lookout, a UFO the size of an aircraft carrier rose up out of the water and disappeared into the clouds. It descended back down into the water and rose back up into the clouds again several times. It was witnessed by me, the starboard lookout, the officer of the deck, the captain, and the

Witnesses around the world report sighting UFOs entering and exiting underwater bases. (*Art by Bill Oliver*)

chief quartermaster, who took pictures of the UFO. We were told never to discuss the incident with anyone ever."

While Cooper was in the Navy, he claims to have come across some highly classified documents pertaining to an alien/government partnership. These documents revealed the details of a secret treaty that had been made with a group of aliens referred to as extraterrestrial biological entities (EBEs). Though at first the government believed that the aliens had only good intentions, it turned out that they had been responsible for abducting humans, mutilating animals, and conducting weird genetic breeding experiments in deep underground bases. In many instances, Cooper learned, the aliens had actually taken over the underground bases from government agencies, which had built the installations to shelter our president and other high-ranking government officials in case of nuclear attack.

When we asked Cooper about the underground bases during dinner while we were lecturing together with him in Hawaii in July, 1991, he replied: "I saw in highly classified documents that there were extraterrestrial underground bases. Whether there really are or not, I don't know. I do know that Nazi Germany perfected the art of building huge underground installations. When the atomic bomb became a reality, underground military installations became not just a reality, but a necessity. I do know that the bases are real, but whether aliens occupy the bases, I don't know.

"These underground bases exist all over the United States," Cooper pointed out. "There is an actual government-in-waiting to take over this country in these installations. There are factories, military units, agencies—everything—living underground in actual cities; and they're just waiting to take over.

"If extraterrestrials are real, then I am sure the documents that I read when I was in Naval Intelligence were true. Or, as I have stated, if aliens are not real, then it is an elaborate deception. But some of it had to be real in order to make the deception work. One learns very quickly in any intelligence organization that disinformation cannot work unless it contains an element of truth that will make the public believe it.

"It was over twenty years ago when I saw those documents. I found a lot of elements of truth in what I read then. I have also found some things that have either changed over the years or that may have been deliberate disinformation. The thing is, there is no way to know which is which."

Massive USO Rises Next to Oil Rig in the Gulf of Mexico

In December 1997, a massive craft was seen emerging from the sea next to an oil platform in the Gulf of Mexico. According to engineer Jeremy Packer, the sighting was witnessed by 250 oil rig workers.

At about 7:58 A.M., Packer said that everyone got frightened when they heard a rumbling noise that they knew couldn't be the engines that ran the platform bore. Looking toward the west, they sighted twenty-five to thirty helicopters on maneuvers. This was not unusual, Packer said, except that the rig commander said that he had not received the usual alert regarding Coast Guard operations in the area.

Then, according to Packer, they all saw something that totally changed their lives. All of the helicopters stopped in midair and a huge metal cigar-shaped object about the size of the oil platform surfaced beneath them. The massive craft, about as long as two football fields, soared straight out of the water and into the air, where it hovered above the helicopters for about two minutes.

Packer described the object as concave on its underside with four large domes on its bottom. The topside of the cigar-shaped craft was encircled by beautiful lights of every imaginable color. And then, as if someone had turned off a light switch, the giant craft disappeared. One second everyone was studying the object through binoculars or telescopes; then, in the literal blink of an eye, it was gone.

As an interesting side note, Packer said that when they got back to the mainland, the crew noticed that their watches were thirty minutes later than the actual time.

We Witness USOs First Hand in Peru

On an unforgettable night in 1990 spent somewhere not far from the sacred Incan city of Ollantaytambo in Peru, our after-dinner talk turned to a discussion of the reality of UFOs. Our shaman guide said that he would take us to a sacred lake where every night one could see such objects entering and leaving the water.

At first, we were not quite certain if he was joking, but he swore that he was quite serious. He said he had grown to trust our respect for both the old traditions and the sacredness of worlds beyond our own. The only condition was that we had to maintain the secrecy of the location.

So on an extremely dark night, the Incan shaman took us to this secret location, where we did, after a wait of what seemed like hours, indeed, see numerous illuminated UFOs emerge from the lake's surface, descend beneath the waters, and bob around the night sky in their peculiar zigzag flight pattern.

The most fascinating aspect of the evening was when Sherry Hansen Steiger wondered aloud if the globe of light that had just emerged from the lake would respond to her thoughts. When Sherry requested that the object split in two, we were all astonished when the light responded to her request.

Amazed by the apparent communication that passed between them, Sherry next asked the globe to reunite, then move to the left, the right, to soar higher, to descend lower. The ship responded.

This was no hallucination caused by the high altitude of the Andes. We were all watching a strange kind of "dialogue" between the mystery object and Sherry.

As if jealous of the attention one of their kind was receiving from the strange visitors, other balls of light emerged from the water. Encouraged by Sherry's success, other people in our group began to conduct their own communication with the lights and achieved the same results.

In spite of the chill in the night air, there were barefooted villagers walking about in the darkness, carrying grain and water to their families in jars atop their heads. We asked them what they thought these glowing objects that regularly entered and left the lake were. "Spirits of the grandfathers," answered some. "Angels," replied others. "The Old Ones," declared a few.

Among our group of adventurers, the answers were equally varied: "The Space Brothers. Aliens who have a base in the lake. Some really weird natural phenomenon. Survivors of an ancient culture who exist in secret underwater and subterranean bases."

Perhaps each of the Peruvian villagers and each of the seekers of mystery from the United States had a piece of a most complex puzzle.

After such a remarkable demonstration of underwater entities responding to human thought, none of us wished to be dogmatic. What we saw that night could well have been a delightful combination of mysteries that nicely demonstrated the wide range of enigmas that wait to be solved.

Aliens and Secret Societies

There are rumors that the musty pages of records from certain ancient alchemical laboratories contain notes on experiments with photography, radio transmission, phonography, and aerial flight. Throughout the Middle Ages and the Renaissance, it is said, there were many scholars who claimed that they had received late-night visits from mysterious members of a secret society who demonstrated that they had accomplished astonishing feats: the mastery of transmuting metals, the ability to prolong life, the knowledge to see and to hear what was occurring in distant places, and the expertise to travel across the heavens in heavier-than-air vehicles.

Helvetius Receives a Visit from the First Man-in-Black

Helvetius was an alchemist who labored tirelessly to fathom the mystery of the "philosopher's stone," the legendary catalyst that would transmute base metals into gold. One day in 1666 when he was working in his study at The Hague, a stranger attired all in black (as befitted a respectable burgher of North Holland) appeared and informed him that he would remove all the alchemist's doubts about the existence of the philosopher's stone, for he possessed magical powers.

Impatiently, Helvetius decided to disrupt his work long enough to indulge the man, who appeared very simple and modest in his demeanor. The stranger immediately drew a small ivory box from his pocket. The box contained three pieces of metal of the color of brimstone and extremely heavy. With those three bits of metal, he told Helvetius, he could make as much as twenty tons of gold.

The alchemist examined the pieces of metal that were supposed to have such remarkable powers. Seeing that they were very brittle, he took the opportunity to scrape off a small portion with his thumbnail. Helvetius returned the three pieces of

People often think of the Men in Black as a modern organization, but the MIB have roots back at least to the seventeenth century. (*Art by Ricardo Pustanio*)

metal to his mysterious visitor and, understandably, asked him for a demonstration of the transmutation. The stranger answered firmly that he was not allowed to do so. It was enough that he had verified the existence of the metal to Helvetius. It was his goal only to offer Helvetius encouragement in his experiments.

After the man's departure, Helvetius was curious to see if the stranger were mad or relaying a fantastic truth. He procured a crucible and a portion of lead, and when it was a state of fusion, he added the stolen grain he had secretly scraped from the philosopher's stone. He was disappointed to find that the grain evaporated altogether, leaving the lead in its original state. Thinking that he had been made the fool by the mad burgher's whimsy, Helvetius returned to his own experiments.

Some weeks later, when he had almost forgotten the incident, Helvetius received another visit from the stranger. "Please do explain further the process by which you *pretend* to transmute lead," the alchemist goaded the man. "If you cannot do as you claim, then please leave me at once to continue my work."

"Very well, I shall show you that that which you most desire does truly exist," the stranger said, agreeing to perform a demonstration of the philosopher's stone for the skeptical Helvetius. "One grain is sufficient," he told the alchemist, "but it is necessary to envelope it in a ball of wax before throwing it on the molten metal; otherwise its extreme volatility will cause it to vaporize." To Helvetius' astonishment, the stranger transmuted several ounces of lead into gold. Then he permitted the alchemist to repeat the experiment by himself, and Helvetius converted six ounces of lead into very pure gold.

Helvetius found it impossible to keep a secret of such immense value and importance. Soon the word of the alchemist's remarkably successful experiments spread all over The Hague, and Helvetius demonstrated the power of the philosopher's stone in the presence of the Prince of Orange, and many times afterward—until he had exhausted the supply of catalytic pieces that he received from the mysterious burgher.

Search as he might, Helvetius could not find the man in all of North Holland nor find anyone who recognized his description of his strange visitor. And pray as he might, the stranger never again visited Helvetius in his study.

Cosmic Alien Tutors Have Been Teaching Our Scientists

Down through the centuries, very mysterious individuals have appeared at certain moments in human history and provided convincing demonstrations that "impossible" inventions *are* possible. The "respectable burgher of North Holland" appeared "modest and simple" to the alchemist Helvetius. It was his incredible knowledge that startled and inspired the alchemists of Helvetius' day, and though these learned and determined men never did acquire the philosopher's stone that would transmute lead into gold, they did fashion the seeds of the science of chemistry that has accomplished so many transmutations of the human environment and the human condition in the last three hundred years.

Out of the smoky laboratories of the alchemists, Albert le Grand produced potassium lye, Raymond Lully prepared bicarbonate of potassium, Paracelsus described zinc and introduced chemical compounds in medicine, Blaise Vigenere discovered benzoic acid, Basil Valentine perfected sulfuric acid, and Johann Friedrich Boetticher became the first European to produce porcelain. We can but wonder if they, too, received visitations from mysterious black-garbed burghers, the first "Men-in-Black, representatives of secret societies inspired by extraterrestrial or multidimensional alien technologies.

Cooper Found Evidence Indicating Secret Societies
Have Been Interacting with Aliens for Thousands of Years

The late William Cooper (1943–2001), a former Naval Intelligence officer, told us that he had seen certain government documents that proved to him that UFOs are real and that an official cover-up of monumental proportions had been set in motion long ago. In addition, he found subsequent evidence indicating that certain secret societies had been interacting with UFO intelligences for thousands of years.

We had become well acquainted with Cooper, author of *Behold a Pale Horse*, and host of the shortwave radio program *Hour of the Time*, as we quite frequently appeared at the same lecture or seminar events. We would have dinner with Cooper and his family, and sometimes our discussions would go late into the morning hours. Although we may not have always agreed with him, his ideas and thoughts were always provocative. We were saddened to learn of his death in 2001.

"If it is true that UFOs have been visiting Earth for thousands of years now, as history seems to indicate, then they are really in control," Cooper told us on one occasion. "Certain societies behind our terrestrial power structures have been communicating with them and getting their guidance from them. Every major improvement in our culture, our science, our technology … every major turn which we have taken throughout history would have been because of *them*."

Cooper focused a great deal of his research on a hidden society generally known as the Illuminati.

"The Illuminati was a very well-organized group that was supposedly founded in Bavaria in 1776 by a German law professor named Adam Weishaupt," Cooper explained. "But I have been able to trace the history of this group all the way back to the ancient Temple of Wisdom in Cairo, long before the birth of Christ. Weishaupt did not begin the Illuminati. He merely headed one chapter of it.

"The Illuminati exists today under many names and many different occupations. They are extremely powerful, very wealthy men, who believe themselves to be the guardians of the secrets of the ages."

And it would seem that, if such secret societies as the Illuminati have also been carefully guarding certain technological gifts of the aliens, they would have become very powerful, indeed. From time to time, perhaps, the aliens and the hidden society, in alliance, elects to make one of its secret technologies known to the general terrestrial population. Such intervention in the affairs of the "outside world" may be accomplished by carefully feeding certain fragments of research to an "outside" scientist whose work and attitude have somehow made him acceptable to the society.

Did the Aliens and Their Secret Society Allies Show Their Presence in 1897?

After thousands of years of surreptitiously working behind the scenes, the alien-inspired secret societies may have decided to reveal their presence in a clearer, more accurate, more technological manner than ever before in recorded human history.

In the year 1897, it seemed that scientific achievement had gone about as far as it could go, and it was poised confidently on the brink of the twentieth century. Many of the world's most learned men and women were filled with pride over a host of new technological accomplishments.

To list only a few of the most notable inventions and discoveries:

In 1893, Karl Benz and Henry Ford built their first four-wheeled automobiles.

Thomas Edison's Kinetoscope (1889) was among the first practical systems of cinematography, and in 1895, Louis and Auguste Lumière presented the first commercial projection. In that same year, Wilhelm Roentgen discovered X rays, Guglielmo Marconi invented radio telegraphy, and Konstantin Tsiolkovsky formulated the principle of rocket reaction propulsion.

In 1896, William Ramsay isolated helium, Ernest Rutherford accomplished the magnetic detection of electrical waves, and Henri Becquerel discovered radioactivity.

The Royal Automobile Club was founded in London in 1897, and cars were going faster every year.

There were as yet no heavier-than-air aerial vehicles to occupy the efforts and the interests of potential aviators, and a good number of brilliant scientists of great reputation doubted that it was aerodynamically possible to build such a flying machine. The future of balloon transport seemed promising, and gondolas could be attached to carry passengers. With all the other marvels of science, how could anyone bemoan the lack of heavier-than-air flying machines?

And yet, in March of 1897, a bizarre aircraft, often described as resembling a cone-shaped steamboat, was seen flying across the United States and, later, sighted throughout the world. (Readers should be reminded that the German Count Ferdinand von Zeppelin did not build his gas-filled dirigible until 1898, and that Orville and Wilbur Wright did not make their historic flight in a powered airplane until 1903.)

> [I]n March of 1897, a bizarre aircraft, often described as resembling a cone-shaped steamboat, was seen flying across the United States and, later, sighted throughout the world.

Could some anonymous American inventors have beaten Count von Zeppelin to the drawing board with a much more impressive vehicle, a forerunner of the modem passenger plane? Or did the aliens disguise their spacecraft as composite, awkward, bulky terrestrial vehicles and place members of the secret society on board as conventional humans in order to survey the planet undetected? Or was a secret terrestrial society of master magicians once again displaying their superiority over the outsiders?

Suddenly the Airships Were Everywhere

The "airships," as they were called, were first sighted in the skies over various cities in California. They were described as cigar-shaped, apparently metallic objects, with various appendages such as wings, propellers, and fins. At night the airships occasionally swept the ground beneath them with brilliant searchlights.

Although many reliable witnesses, including the mayor of San Francisco, sighted the metallic aircraft at their strange maneuvers, astronomers shrugged off the initial reports and issued official statements that the bedazzled citizenry were no doubt seeing the planet Venus, then unusually bright in the evening sky.

In spite of the scientific debunking of the aircraft, people in California, Washington, and Arizona continued sighting the objects throughout November and December.

Certain students of the UFO mystery are convinced that alien intelligences have provided members of secret societies with knowledge forbidden to the masses for thousands of years. (*Art by Bill Oliver*)

The first two months of 1897 were devoid of airship sightings, but in mid-March reports began coming in from Kansas, Nebraska, and Iowa—all describing the same type of mysterious airship that had baffled Californians four months earlier. From the first week in April until mid-May, nearly the entire area east of the Rocky Mountains appeared to be under the scrutiny of the aerial machines.

Quoting from a newspaper account that appeared in the Algona, Iowa, *Republican*, dated April 7, 1897:

Good reliable citizens of Wesley, Iowa, declared upon their honor that on last Friday evening they saw in the heavens what they supposed to be an airship.... It had the appearance of a cone in shape with window in the side through which shone bright lights.... They were not able to see in what manner the ship was propelled or what sustained it in the air....

When first sighted it did not have the appearance of being more than a few hundred feet above the ground.... It traveled quite slowly at times, and again would move quite fast.... Some had an idea they could hear a noise coming from the ship. Some went so far as to say it was human voices, while others thought it was the sound of machinery.

It has not taken a close reading of current scientific periodicals to note that there is a great deal of activity among inventors in the line of practical aerial navigation, and that the old notion is wrong that man is by laws of nature ... to be ... confined strictly to the surface of the globe.... So it is entirely possible that the brief glimpses such as the Wesley people have had, are practicable.

Two farmhands from Springfield, Illinois—Adolph Winkle and John Hulle— came upon a landed airship two miles north of Springfield on April 15. Three occupants, appearing to the farmers as two normal human men and a woman, explained that they had landed to repair their electrical equipment and their searchlight. They went on to inform the astonished Winkle and Hulle that their airship had flown from Quincy to Springfield, a distance of approximately ninety miles, in thirty minutes (roughly a speed of 180 miles per hour).

As if the claim of such speed wasn't enough to boggle the farmhands' minds, Winkle and Hulle must have been left completely baffled by the occupants' claim that they were on a mission to free Cuba from the Spanish and that they would be making a complete report to the government upon the successful completion of their assignment. The Spanish-American War over Cuba did not erupt until the following year in 1898—and unless Winkle and Hulle were astute students of political events in the making, it is unlikely that they would have the slightest idea why the airship would be flying to Cuba in the first place. This is but one of many incidents in which the aliens seem slightly "out of sync" with events occurring in linear time.

"We Are from Anywhere"

When John Barclay of Rockland, Texas, was awakened by his barking dog and a peculiar whining sound, he went to the door of his home to see what was creating such a disturbance at eleven o'clock at night.

Barclay saw "an airship ... with a peculiar-shaped body, oblong-shaped, with wings and side attachments of various sizes and shapes. There were brilliant lights, which appeared much brighter than electric lights.... It seemed perfectly stationary about five yards from the ground."

Barclay watched the airship gradually descend to the ground in a pasture near his house, then he picked up his Winchester rifle and went down to investigate.

The Texan was met by an ordinary appearing man who identified himself as "Mr. Smith," who requested that Barclay run an errand for him. He handed Barclay a ten-dollar bill and requested that he purchase some lubricating oil, a couple of cold chisels, and some bluestone.

When the obliging Texan returned with everything on the shopping list except the bluestone, Mr. Smith thanked him and asked him not to follow him back to the vessel.

"But where are you from … and where are you going?" Barclay called after his mysterious visitor.

The airship occupant replied: "We are from anywhere, but we will be in Greece the day after tomorrow."

Once the stranger was back on board the airship, Barclay stated, "It was gone … like a shot out of a gun!"

A Senator Learns of the Scientist Who Conquered Gravity

Once the stranger was back on board the airship, Barclay stated, "It was gone … like a shot out of a gun!"

The April 23, 1897, edition of the Harrisburg, Arkansas, *Modern News*, provided the details of the otherworldly experience of former state senator Harris.

Awakened about one o'clock in the morning by an unfamiliar noise, Harris was astonished to observe an airship settling down just a short distance from his home. By the time he went to investigate, Harris surprised the crew taking on a supply of fresh water from his well.

The crew was composed of a man with jet-black eyes who appeared elderly, yet whose waist-length whiskers were dark and almost silken, and two young men and a woman who hurried back on board the airship without uttering a sound.

Once the bearded man recovered from the surprise of "finding anyone out at such an hour of the night," he revealed the secret of the airship to Mr. Harris, "everything, except how the effect is produced."

His uncle, so declared the occupant, was a brilliant scientist who had conquered the laws of gravity. He had received offers of huge sums of money from syndicates in New York City, Paris, and London—but he refused them all and managed to lock his secrets alway in a vault shortly before becoming violently ill and dying.

According to the mysterious bearded man, it had taken him another nineteen years before he had been able to decipher his uncle's formula and to devise an airship that was almost perfection. Almost, but not quite—which was why the inventor and his crew traveled mainly at night, to avoid being detected.

For Inventors Protecting Their "Secret Invention"
the Airship Pilots and Crew Seemed to Want to Show-Off

Although the airship was always portrayed by its occupants to be a secret invention, its crew seemed eager that as many people witness its activities as possible. It is also interesting to note that whenever the occupants—most often described as an elderly man with a long dark beard, a young man, and a woman—chose to make verbal contact with a witness, that individual was invariably characterized in the local press as being a person of "undoubted integrity." The airship occupants seemed particularly to single out judges, senators, constables, sheriffs, and prominent farmers and ranchers to hear their story of a brilliant inventor with his secret factory in Iowa (or Texas), who promised to have the airships "in general use around the country" within a year.

Throughout most of the summer of 1897, airship reports continued from places such as: Reynolds, Michigan; Belle Plaine, Iowa; Carlinville, Illinois; Flint, Michigan; Atchison, Kansas; and Hot Springs, Arkansas.

The Airship Leaves the U.S. for Other Countries

On July 17, 1897, a small town in Sweden sighted the airship, describing it as resembling some kind of balloon with drag ropes and a net. One occupant was visible in the object's "gondola."

On August 13 a mysterious airship was reported over Vancouver, British Columbia, and at three or four different points in Manitoba and the other Canadian "territories" as the vessel traveled eastward—terminating its flight, or so it would seem, off the coast of Norway, where the crew of the steamer *Kong Halfdan* spotted it. If it was the same airship that was sighted in these widely separated reports, the craft was traveling at a great rate of speed.

The airship was sighted over Ontario, Canada, once again on August 16, then made what seems to have been its final appearance for that particular flap on September 26 over Ustyug, Russia. There, at 2:30 A.M., an engineer sighted the object moving rapidly southeast over the town of Yakolevskaya. He described the unknown craft as having an electric or phosphorescent sheen.

The Mysterious Craft Disappears Until 1909

The mysterious inventor did not make good his promise to have the wonderful airships available to the general public by 1898.

To the contrary the remarkable aerial vehicle seemed to disappear from the skies completely until March 23, 1909, when Constable P. C. Kettle in the town of Peterborough sighted a "mysterious airship."

On May 18 Mr. C. Lethbridge of Cardiff, Wales, came upon the airship while traversing Caerphilly Mountain. Other citizens of Cardiff also spotted the strange nocturnal visitors, and the Cardiff *Mail* described the object as "very large, with two lights, one at each end."

About the same time residents of Dublin, Ireland, reported a large, cigar-shaped craft "with two clear lights in front and traveling at a considerable pace across the sky."

The London *Weekly Dispatch* listed twenty-two locations where the airship had been reported during the week preceding May 23, plus nineteen earlier reports during March and May.

By July 1909 the residents of New Zealand were visited with a six-week airship flap.

On July 24 a brightly lighted object was seen zigzagging in the direction of D'Urville Island across the bay until it appeared quite close to Motueka, then it changed its course and traveled in the direction of Farewell Split.

Other sightings were reported during the first week in August over Otago, North Auckland, Hawkes Bay, Kaihu, and Clive. The New Zealanders dubbed their mysterious airborne visitor an "Aerialite."

After Touring the South Seas, the Airship Visits New England

Although a mysterious aerial light was reported in the New England area on September 8, 1909, the airship sightings in the United States did not really resume regular flights until December. Although this time the majority of the sightings occurred in the northeastern states, there were a few notable excursions to Arkansas, one of the areas most favored during the 1897 aerial displays.

Thousands of people in various cities throughout Rhode Island and Massachusetts saw an airship grace their skies on the evening of December 22. Witnesses estimated the vehicle was traveling at speeds up to forty miles an hour, and at the same time "sweeping the heavens with a searchlight of tremendous power."

> Thousands of people in various cities throughout Rhode Island and Massachusetts saw an airship grace their skies on the evening of December 22.

On Christmas Eve so many people filed reports of the awesome airship that the Providence *Journal* was led to comment that its readership was obviously suffering from severe attacks of " airshipitis," wishing every star to be an airship, every light in the sky to be an airplane.

The airship was seen over Huntington, West Virginia, early on the morning of December 31, 1909, then seemed to go into seclusion for a few days.

The Airship Disappears Forever in January 1910

At 9:00 A.M. on the morning of January 12, 1910, the mystery aircraft was sighted over Chattanooga, Tennessee. Thousands saw the vehicle and heard the sound of its engines. Later that same day it was seen over Huntsville, Alabama, traveling at a great rate of speed.

On the morning of January 13, it was back over Chattanooga, this time around 11 A.M. The airship crossed the city about ten times, and witnesses spotted an occupant on board the craft before it disappeared into heavy fog along the Tennessee River.

The last reported airship sighting before the occupants decided to return to the secret factory in Iowa, their base on the Moon, or "anywhere," appears to have been logged on January 20, when a number of witnesses saw a craft over Memphis, Tennessee. The airship was said to be high in the air and was traveling quickly. Witnesses stated that it crossed the Mississippi River into Arkansas, veered slightly to the south, then rapidly disappeared.

Did the Mystery Craft Inspire a New Age of Aviation?

Whatever the mysterious airship of 1897 was, and whoever was actually piloting the craft, the fact remains that the reported vehicle was many years in advance of the

The Illuminati is a secret society often suspected of working in concert with alien intelligences. (*Art by Bill Oliver*)

known terrestrial science of the day. On the other hand, many aspects of the enigmatic airships make them appear to be terrestrial in origin. Their engines made a whirring noise, for example; or in some cases sounded like motorcars. Could they really have been the inspired product of some technological genius who manufactured the aeroplanes in his secret factory?

It seems unlikely that such a technological advance could have remained undeveloped and unexploited if, in fact, some eccentric inventor in Iowa or Texas had mastered antigravity and fashioned some remarkable propulsion system in 1897.

But what if the terrestrial inventor belonged to some secret society, perhaps one that had been in touch with aliens—or their records and artifacts—for thousands of years? And what if its principal purpose was to inspire conventional Earth scientists to go beyond the many technological triumphs of 1897 and to enter a new age of aviation?

Or Was It All a Hoax? At Least the Wright Brothers Weren't Laughing

Some UFO researchers have gone back over the list of the "witnesses of integrity" to the 1897 airship sightings and suggested it was all a hoax of gigantic proportions. In a couple of cases, according to some investigators of the airship phenomenon, descendants of those senators, judges, mayors, and law enforcement officers—who gave such vivid accounts to the newspapers in 1897—confessed in their later days that they had told fibs, jokes, and lies.

Perhaps some of those "witnesses of integrity" may have possessed some dubious motive for hoodwinking their peers and constituents with remarkable tales of flying machines. And maybe some of those prominent gentlemen, deciding they had had enough of pomp and propriety, thought they would obtain some relief from all those years of prim and proper behavior by perpetrating one devilishly good hoax before senility set in. On the other hand, maybe some of their descendants are embarrassed by a grandfather's or an uncle's "wild story" and have decided to confess for them.

We don't know. None of those witnesses are alive today to confirm the validity of their sightings or to admit to having pulled the legs of their friends and neighbors.

But if they were telling fibs, then we can wonder about the motives of these respected and generally wealthy men for having done so, and we can speculate as to their possible motives for engineering an international hoax at this particular time in world history.

Or Was the Airship of 1897 a Seed Implanted by the Secret Society that the Aliens Were Here?

If, indeed, such a secret society as the Illuminati does exist and if it has been slowly feeding our scientists technology according to its own hidden agenda—then as long ago as 1897 it may well have been to the society's advantage to begin to promulgate a "war of the worlds" mind-set among the outsiders on planet Earth. If the society's long-range purpose is to establish a New World Order with its own hierarchy in control of world governments, then the society would have done well to have begun the threat of alien invasion at the beginning of the twentieth century, so that they might be in the ultimate positions of power for the advent of the millennium.

The Time for World Domination May Be Now!

The disturbing part of the theories of such researchers as William Cooper is the suggestion that perhaps this secret society of illumined ones is no longer content with merely coexisting with other overt societies. Perhaps they have decided that the time is now to begin to set in motion their plans for world domination.

As Cooper told us, "Whether the extraterrestrials are real or not, their alleged existence is being used to help bring about a one-world government. The menace of extraterrestrials provides the existing governments of Earth with the 'external threat' that will force a one-world government to come into existence.

"It seems as though there is evidence to suggest that extraterrestrials are real, but the alleged threat of aliens could also be the greatest hoax ever perpetuated in the history of the world in order to bring us all together to fight the alleged invaders from outer space and make us all dupes for the so-called 'illumined ones' to place completely under their domination."

And, of course, it may be that the illumined ones, this secret occult society, made their deal with the alien Overlords centuries ago.

And if this secret society is as powerful as some investigators believe it to be, then its ideas and concepts have infiltrated every level of our own larger society. It is interesting to review former president Ronald Reagan's 1987 remarks to the United Nations concerning how advantageous it would be to the various governing bodies of the world if there could be a threat of an invasion from an external, extraterrestrial source. Was President Reagan inadvertently leaking information concerning the deal already made by our government with alien representatives? Or was he being used to propose a concept that had been set in motion by "witnesses of integrity" in 1897?

Nazis and the Aldebaran Aliens

The Coming Race (1871), a novel by the occultist Edward Bulwer-Lytton, was set in the Earth's interior, where an advanced civilization of giants thrived. In this story, the giants had built a paradise and discovered a form of energy so powerful that they outlawed its use as a potential weapon. This force, the Vril, was derived from the Black Sun, a large ball of "Prima Materia" (prime matter) that provided light and radiation to the inhabitants of the Inner Earth.

The symbol of the Black Sun is suggestive of the Norse myth in which our golden sun will be swallowed by the great wolf Fenrir at the beginning of the Wolf Age. Like many secret groups, there appears to have been more than one order—those who followed the Golden Sun and those who followed the Black Sun. The Black Sun, like the swastika, is a very ancient symbol. While the swastika represents the eternal fountain of creation, the Black Sun is even older, suggesting the very void of creation itself. The symbol on the Nazi flag, in fact, is the Thule *Sonnenrad* (Sun Wheel), not a reversed good luck swastika. The Black Sun can be seen in many ancient Babylonian and Assyrian places of worship.

The Old Ones, The Elder Race, That Came to Earth Long Ago

There are persistent legends in nearly every culture that tell of an Elder Race that populated the Earth millions of years ago. The Old Ones—who may originally have been of extraterrestrial origin—were an immensely intelligent and scientifically advanced species who eventually chose to structure their own environment under the surface of the planet's soil and seas. The Old Ones usually remain aloof from the surface dwellers, but from time to time throughout history, they have been known to visit some of Earth's more intelligent members in the guise of an alchemist or a mysterious scientist. In these cases, they offer constructive criticism and, in some cases, give valuable advice about areas of the material sciences.

The Buddhists have incorporated a subterranean empire called Agharta into their theology, and fervently believe in its existence and in the reality of underworld supermen who periodically surface to oversee the progress of the human race. According to one source, the underground kingdom of Agharta was created when the ancestors of the present-day cave dwellers drove the Serpent People from the caverns during an ancient war between the reptilian humanoids and the ancient human society.

By the 1840s, the legend of Agharta had already been widely circulated among mystically minded people in Germany. According to this ancient tradition, the Master of the World already controlled many of the kings and rulers of the surface world by exercising his occult powers. Soon this Master and his super race would launch an invasion of Earth and subjugate all humans to his will.

Secret Societies in Germany Wanted to be Found Worthy for the Alien Masters of the World

The secret societies formed in Germany in the late nineteenth and early twentieth centuries wanted desperately to prove themselves worthy of the super humans that lived beneath the surface of the planet. They also wished to be able to control the incredibly powerful Vril force. This ancient force had been known among the alchemists and magicians as the Chi, the Odic force, the Orgone, the Astral Light.

In 1919, Karl Haushofer, a student of the Russian mystic George Gurdjieff, founded the Brothers of the Light Society in Berlin, and soon changed its name to the Vril Society. The Vril Lodge believed that those who learned control of the Vril would become master of himself, those around him, and the world itself, if he should so choose. The members of the Vril Society were well aware of the Astral Light's transformative powers, creating supermen out of ordinary mortals. Such members of the Lodge as Adolf Hitler, Heinrich Himmler, Hermann Göring, Dr. Theodor Morell (Hitler's personal physician), and other top future Nazi leaders, became obsessed with preparing German youth to become a master race so the Lords of the Inner Earth would find them worthy above all others when they emerged to evaluate the people of Earth's nations.

As Haushofer's Vril grew in prominence, it united three major occult societies, the Lords of the Black Stone, the Black Knights of the Thule Society, and the Black Sun. The Vril chose the swastika, the hooked cross, as its symbol of the worship of the Black Sun. While these societies borrowed some concepts and rites from Theosophists, Rosicrucians, and various Hermetic groups, they placed special emphasis on the innate mystical powers of the Aryan race. Theosophist Mme. Helena Blavatsky listed Six Root Races—the Astral, Hyperborean, Lemurian, Atlantean, Aryan, and the coming Master Race. The Vril and its brother societies maintained that the Germanic/Nordic/Teutonic people were of Aryan origin, and that Christianity had destroyed the power of the Teutonic civilization.

Medium Maria Orsic Contacts
Aryan Aliens from Aldebaran

It was in 1921, while the Vril Gesellschaft (as the Vril Society was now called) was meeting at an old hunting lodge near Berchtesgarden, that the mediums in the society received remarkable news. Maria Orsic (Orsitch), who led the *Vrilerinnen,* a group of beautiful young women psychics in the society, began to receive messages from Aryan aliens on Alpha Tauri in the Aldebaran star system. Maria and a sister medium named Sigrun learned that a half billion years ago, the Aryans, also known as the Elohim or Elder Race, began to colonize our solar system. The aliens spoke of two classes of people on their world—the Aryan, or master race, and a subservient planetary race that had evolved through mutation and climate changes. On Earth, the Aryans were identified as the Sumerians until they elected to carve out an empire for themselves in the hollow of the planet.

Maria, Sigrun, and other members of the *Vrilerinnen* named Traute, Gudrun, and Heike, began to receive transmissions that dictated diagrams and blueprints of advanced flying machines, complete with the mathematics and physics to go with them. Contrary to the style of that time to wear short hair, the mediums grew their hair long to serve as better receptive antennas for the alien messages.

Alien Transmissions
Help to Build a Flying Saucer

By 1921, some say that a working model of what would one day be called a "flying saucer" had been built. Working in underground bases with the Aryan alien intelligences who had chosen the German people as their earthly successors, the Vril Gesellschaft mastered antigravity space flight, established space stations, successfully traveled through time, and developed their spacecraft to move at warp speeds.

In 1922, members of Thule and Vril Gesellschaft claim to have built the *Jenseitsflugmaschine,* the Other World Flight Machine, based on the psychic messages received from the Aldebaran aliens and channeled through Maria, Sigrun, and the other mediums. W.O. Schulmann of the Technical University of Munich was in charge of the project until it was halted in 1924, and the craft was stored in a hangar at the Augsburg location of German aircraft manufacturer Messerschmitt.

Gudrun was a member of the *Vrilerinner,* a group of female mediums associated with the Vril, a secret society that included Adolf Hitler, who later became the dictator of Germany. (**Art by Ricardo Pustanio**)

Hitler was a member of the Vril Society, which chose as its symbol the swastika, or hooked cross. (**Art by Bill Oliver**)

German Scientists Become Fascinated with Rockets

The fascination with rockets by conventional German scientists who were not associated with (or perhaps even aware of) the Vril Gesellschaft began in 1923 with Dr. Hermann Oberth's book *By Rocket to Interplanetary Space*. There were many other books that advanced the cause of spacecraft development that appeared in Germany in the mid-1920s.

In 1927 the *Verein für Raumschiffahrt* (Society for Space Travel) was organized; Wernher von Braun and Willy Ley were counted among its members. The VFR produced the world's first rocket-powered automobile, the Opel-Rak I, with Fritz von Opel in 1928. Further experiments were conducted with railway cars, rocket sleds, crude vertical takeoff and landing aircraft. Some successful rocket launches were made from the *Rakentenflugplatz* (rocket airfield) near Berlin.

When Adolf Hitler seized power in Germany in 1933, the Nazi party took over all rocket and aircraft development, and all astronautical societies were nationalized. In 1937 the Peenemuende group was formed under the direction of Walter Dornberger and Wernher von Braun.

Hitler Authorizes the Construction of Flying Discs

Hitler authorized the construction of the *Rundflugzeug*—the round, or disc-shaped vehicle—for military use and for spaceflight. A few years later, the Führer officially abolished all secret societies, but sources indicate that the Vril Gesellschaft continued its work unabated in the strictest secrecy.

The Third Reich's Expedition to Discover Inner Earth

In April, 1942, Nazi Germany sent out an expedition composed of a number of its most visionary scientists to seek a military vantage point in the hollow earth. Although the expedition of leading scientists left at a time when the Third Reich was putting maximum effort in their drive against the Allies, Göring, Himmler, and Hitler are said to have enthusiastically endorsed the project. Steeped in the more esoteric teachings of metaphysics, the Führer had long been convinced that Earth was concave and that a master race lived on the inside of the planet.

The Nazi scientists who left for the island of Rügen had complete confidence in the validity of their quest. In their minds, it would be a real coup to discover the opening to the Inner World. It would not only provide them with a military advantage. It would also help to convince the Old Ones of the superiority of the German people. This could persuade the masters of the Inner World to mix their blood with the Germans and create a hybrid master race for the surface world.

Some maintain that Hitler had a dramatic encounter with a Vril master. Rather than a late-night visitor like the respectable burgher who had appeared to the alchemist Helvetius, Hitler was shaken by the incident. According to Hermann Rauschning, governor of Danzig, Hitler declared that the "new man" was already living among them and that he was "intrepid and cruel." The Führer admitted that he was afraid of him.

Aliens Help Nazis Master Antigravity Space Flight

UFO researcher Vladimir Terziski firmly believes that an "alien tutor race" secretly began cooperating with certain German scientists from the Thule, the Vril, and the Black Sun societies in the late 1920s. With help from extraterrestrial intelligences, Terziski postulates, the Nazis mastered antigravity space flight, established space stations, successfully traveled through time, and developed their spacecraft to move at warp speeds. At the same time, the aliens "spread their Mephisthophelean ideas" into the wider German population through the Thule and Vril societies.

Terziski maintains that antigravity research began in Germany in the 1920s with the first hybrid antigravity circular craft, the RFZ-l, constructed by the secret Vril society. From 1942 to 1943 a series of antigravity machines culminated with the construction of the giant 350-foot-long, cigar-shaped Andromeda space station. It was built in old zeppelin hangars near Berlin by the research and development arm of the SS.

Shortly before the Third Reich collapsed in 1945, Wernher von Braun, Hermann Oberth, and about eighty other top scientists were smuggled out of Nazi Germany by the Allies. The Allies also captured various documents, files, plans, photographs, and designs. However, one specific file containing discoid-shaped aircraft, disappeared.

However, according to some sources, the one specific file containing discoid-shaped aircraft disappeared before the Allies could lay their hands on it. Other sources state that the plans were taken by Nazi scientists aboard one of the submarines headed for an Antarctic base. Still others maintain that the plans were taken by those "liberated" Nazi scientists who were secretly taken to the United States in the Project Paperclip operation. There is also the persistent rumor that the plans are kept in the secret vaults of the Illuminati or some other secret society.

Giant Underground Launch Pads Are Built by Slave Labor

In 1938 Martin Bormann, an aide to Hitler, had ordered the careful mapping of all mountain passes, caves, bridges, and highways and began selecting sites for underground factories, munitions dumps, and food caches. Giant underground workshops and launching pads, known as "U-plants," were established in which top German scientists would be assigned the task of creating secret weapons. A slave-labor force of 250,000 was required to complete work on such fortresses. Networks of tunnels and assembly plants were fashioned in Austria, Bavaria, and northern Italy.

Allied intelligence had learned of work at the Luftwaffe experimental center near Oberammergau, Bavaria, to create Project *Feuerball* (Fireball), an aerial device designed to confuse Allied radar and interrupt electromagnetic currents. Efforts were accelerated to perfect the craft in 1944, but then work seems to have been shifted to the development of the *Kugelblitz* (Round Lightning), a round, symmetrical airplane, quite unlike any previous flying object known in terrestrial aviation history.

De Havilland Aircraft Made a Nazi Saucer Fly—For Awhile

A friend of ours who once worked as a design engineer at the De Havilland aircraft plant in Canada told us that Canadian intelligence had taken plans for an advanced circular aircraft that had been found at Peenemuende, site of the Nazi rocket experimental complex from 1937 to 1945, and presented them as a challenge to the scientists at De Havilland.

"We actually made the 'flying saucer' fly—for a while," our friend said. "We never mastered the complete techniques of the propulsion system to keep the bloody thing in the air for very long at a time."

Nazi Space Scientists Are Scooped Up by Operation Paperclip

Before the smoke had barely cleared from the final resistance in Nazi Germany, Major General Hugh Knerr, Deputy Commanding General for Administration of U.S. Strategic Forces in Europe, acknowledged that the U.S. was "alarmingly backward" in many areas of research, and he ordered the U.S. occupation forces to seize both the "apparatus and the brains" that had created the advanced scientific accomplishments

According to many eye witnesses, the Nazis perfected an aerial war machine based on the channeled messages of Maria Orsic and other members of the *Vrilerinnen*. (*Art by Bill Oliver*)

of the Nazi scientists. He believed without this strategy the United States would remain several years behind.

While it was agreed that the United States should scoop up as many German scientists as possible, the occupation forces faced a dilemma since it was illegal for a former member of the Nazi Party to immigrate to America. Of the 1,600 scientists and their dependents who had been assembled for immediate relocation to the United States, a superficial inquiry revealed that at least 1,200 of them had been avowed Nazis. Informed of this, President Harry S. Truman decided that it was in the national interest of the United States to gain technological superiority, and the U.S. allowed the scientists to declare that they had been "nominal Nazis" and had not actively supported Nazi military efforts.

The relocation of the scientists still had to be conducted in utmost secrecy, for the war had been costly and many American lives had been lost. It was assumed, therefore, that the U.S. public would not respond favorably if they found out that many of these scientists had worked in laboratories that had been constructed by Nazi slave labor and occupants of the death camps. The scientists and their family members who were selected by the Joint Intelligence Objectives Agency had their immigration papers specially prepared by having their scientific papers attached to the standard forms. This process came to be known as "Operation Paperclip."

As we stated in our *Conspiracies and Secret Societies: The Complete Dossier* (Visible Ink Press, 2006), Operation Paperclip was not made public until after the first astronauts had set foot on the Moon in 1973. The eminent Dr. Hubertus Strughold, the "father of space medicine," was one of the prominent physicians who entered the United States under Operation Paperclip. In 1977, the Aeromedical Library at the USAF School of Aerospace medicine was named after Dr. Strughold.

Among those allowed entrance to the United States under Operation Paperclip were: Reinhard Gehlen, Nazi Intelligence mastermind, who helped Allen Dulles restructure the Office of Strategic Services (OSS) into the Central Intelligence Agency (CIA); Klaus Barbie, the "Butcher of Lyon"; Otto von Bolschwing, infamous for Holocaust abuses; and the SS Colonel Otto Skorzeny. In 1984, Arthur Rudolph, who had been awarded NASA's Distinguished Service Award in 1969, left the United States rather than face charges for Nazi war crimes.

Von Braun Tells Press that "Powers" Knocked the *Juno 2* Rocket off Course

Long before Operation Paperclip was finally disclosed, the general public was well aware that the success of the U.S. space program had depended greatly upon participation of such individuals as Dr. Wernher von Braun and Dr. Hermann Oberth, who was widely recognized as the "father of modern rocketry."

Late in 1958, after the peculiar malfunction of the *Juno 2* rocket, von Braun was quoted in West German newspapers as saying that the rocket had gone off course in a strange manner, as if it had been "deflected." On January 1, 1959, he told a reporter for *Neues Europa* that "we feel ourselves faced by powers which are far stronger than we had hitherto assumed.... More I cannot say at present. We are now engaged in entering into closer contact with these powers and in six or nine months' time it may be possible to speak with more precision on the matter."

Who were the far stronger "powers" von Braun blamed for the malfunction of the *Juno 2*? Had he been, after all, familiar with the interactions of the Vril and other German secret societies with the Aryans from Alderberan?

Dr. Oberth Admits that Germans Were Helped by Aliens from Other Worlds

Von Braun's enigmatic reference recalls an earlier comment made by his mentor, Dr. Oberth. Oberth protested the accolades given to the Germans for their brilliant accomplishments in pioneering rocket designs by stating: "We alone cannot take the credit for our record advancement in rocket technology. We have been helped by people from other worlds."

Just who were these mysterious people "from other worlds" who had served as the tutors that enabled Nazi scientists to create a technology unparalleled on Earth?

Canadian and U.S. Failures to Create Flying Saucers from Rocket Base Plans Seems to Prove that the Nazis Had Help from the Aliens

On February 16, 1953, the Canadian Minister for Defense Productions released information to the Canadian House of Commons that Avro-Canada, a Canadian aircraft manufacturing company, was engaged in developing plans for a "flying saucer" that would be able to lift up and descend vertically, and fly at 1,500 miles an hour. Avro projected that their proposed vehicle would make all other forms of supersonic aircraft obsolete.

It was no secret that the Canadians had retrieved some of the research from the German rocket base at Peenemuende. It was there that Walter Dornberger and Wernher von Braun had directed the production of the *Vergeltungswaffe*, the V-2 rocket that ravaged London. The announcement by the Canadians seemed clear evidence that they had been successful in assembling one of the Nazi's secret craft.

It seemed the United States was not to be outdone by the Canadians. On February 15, 1955, the Air Technical Intelligence Center, together with the Wright Air Development Center at Wright-Patterson U.S. Air Force Base in Dayton, Ohio, revealed that the Air Force proposed building jet-propelled "flying saucers" under the code name of Project Silverbug.

Circular, saucer-shaped, like the classic UFOs that civilians had been sighting since at least 1947, the largest of the proposed saucers would weigh twenty-six thousand pounds and would be powered by radically advanced jet engines that would be able to lift the craft to an altitude of 36,090 feet in about one minute and forty-five seconds. The cruise speed of these remarkable vehicles would be Mach 3.48 and the operating ceiling would be up to 80,600 feet. By way of comparison, today's F-15 fighter jet has a similar performance range, and it was developed more than twenty years after the proposed saucers of Project Silverbug.

For some UFO researchers, this rare disclosure from the Air Force seemed proof that the German occult Vril Society really had made contact with extraterrestrials who had given the Nazis their technological advantage at the onset of World War II. Others believe that the Nazis discovered a downed UFO and employed German scientists and engineers, who worked intensely to reverse-engineer the alien spacecraft.

A large number of UFO researchers remain convinced that the U.S. Air Force continued to develop the saucer-shaped superships at Area 51 in Nevada and that many of the huge "motherships" sighted in the skies recently have been our very own flying saucers, which were built from the specifications of the alien-inspired craft first constructed by the Vril Society.

In 1921, Maria Orsic (Orsitch) began to channel messages from Aryan aliens from Alpha Turi in the Aldebaran star system. Calling themselves the Elohim, or Elder Race, they lived in ancient times among the Sumerians before retreating to bases in Inner Earth. The Aldebarans gave Maria plans for building a master race and for constructing advanced anti-gravity circular aircraft. (*Art by Ricardo Pustanio*)

What Happened to the Mediums Who Channeled the Aldebarans, the Aryan Masters?

Research sources are vague as to the eventual fate of Maria Orsic. Some say that Maria, Sigrun, Traute, Gudrun, and Heike were transported by the *Jenseitsflugmaschine*, the Other World Flight Machine, to live eternally with their extraterrestrial guides on another planet. Another source has Maria escaping to Acapulco where Admiral Wilhelm Franz Canaris had established a submarine base in 1945. Rumors had circulated that the two had had a clandestine love affair. Others maintain that all five of the lovely mediums went with Vril members by submarine to establish a secret base in Antarctica in 1943.

Those who know of Admiral Richard Byrd's claim of finding a "new world" in Antarctica remind us that the Americans, Canadians, British, and Russians did not snatch up all the German scientists. Some point out that as many as 130 scientists who were working on the secret Vril projects disappeared immediately at the end of the war. Simultaneously, a number of German freight U-boats capable of transporting 850 metric tons each vanished from official inventory. And, at the same time, several airliners capable of flying very long distances seemingly disappeared from Tempelhof Air Base. Shortly after these aircraft and submarines had mysteriously vanished, officials noted that tens of millions of marks in gold bullion and precious stones were missing from the Reichsbank.

A Strange Meeting with German Scientists and Their Alien Friends

A most intriguing question that may always remain unanswered is whether or not the Vril Society divided its membership after contact was established with the Aldebarans and sent some of its alien-inspired scientists to the United States.

In 1969, Brad was living in Chicago, and he tells of an incident from that time:

I received a telephone call from Ray, an executive in a large advertising agency who asked me to appear as a consultant at a meeting. This meeting was going to bring together an executive from a major airline, some investment counselors, and a group of people who claimed to be a secret group of German scientists who had been working with extraterrestrials—or non-Terrans, as the aliens preferred to be called. The scientists claimed that they were now willing to share their secrets to a number of inventions that the larger Earth society could use: a powder that transformed common tap water into smokeless, non-pollutant, no-knock fuel, and a liquid that would totally fireproof any surface upon which it had been sprayed. Ray wanted me to attend and advise him and his friends because he really couldn't figure out just who the hell these "people" were who claimed to be German scientists.

For the first meeting I asked my friend Glenn, a former detective, to accompany me. We met in a private home not far from O'Hare Airport. There were three principals:

- Ray, the advertising executive. I had met Ray before; he was a former jet pilot who had chased UFOs in Korea and had been on their trail ever since.

- Bill, an executive with a major airline. Bill was dedicated to solving the UFO enigma and able to travel anywhere at a moment's notice to investigate any UFO report firsthand.

- The member of the secret society who had been chosen to negotiate and explain the fuel base and the fireproofing solution.

I was never really introduced to any of the others who, apparently, were the investment counselors, and a number of stoic, silent men and women who were apparently members of the secret society of German scientists and their alien or non-Terran allies.

One of the alleged non-Terrans, a tall redheaded woman with very strange, staring eyes, was extremely hostile to me, complaining that in one of my books I had said that some UFOs may not have the most friendly intentions. After a time, she retreated to a corner of the room with the other members of the silent non-Terran/German scientist group.

Did the fuel work?

Yes, Ray said. He had used it in his lawnmower all summer with good results. An attorney used it in his Lincoln Continental for several months, and he had been told by mechanics that the motor was in excellent condition.

A jarful was mixed and handed around the room. There seemed to be little odor. Glenn dipped in a finger and touched it to his tongue. Little taste—maybe a bit like kerosene. We poured a bit out and touched a match to it. Instantly, it ignited into smokeless flame.

Did the fireproofer work?

We were informed that a demonstration of the fireproofer had been arranged at a nearby airfield. I was told that a group of witnesses were astonished as a mixture of oil and gasoline that was consuming an old fuselage was extinguished within seconds with one squirt of the substance.

Ray felt he could get backers to raise the money the group was requesting for the formulas.

Learning the Mysterious Alliance
of the Secret Society and the Aliens

In subsequent late-night meetings with the negotiator for the group, we learned that he had been trained by the German scientists who worked closely with the non-Terrans from Aldebaran. He was a rarity among the group in that he was not of German descent, but was an Italian-American.

According to his account, at the end of World War I, Dr. Rhinelander (as we shall call him) was a member of a secret society in Germany that had been contacted by a group of non-Terrans, the Aryans from Alderberan, and told that he would be given the plans and assistance to build marvelous aerial craft that would run on a propulsion system totally unknown to the earth science of the day. If he wished to receive this information, he must form a group of scientific disciples and immigrate to a certain coal-mining community in the midwestern United States.

> Eventually, through the apparently unlimited funds provided by the non-Terrans, Dr. Rhinelander was able to buy up old mines to convert into spacious laboratories and to employ large numbers of the indigenous community.

Dr. Rhinelander agreed, and as soon as possible, the Germans immigrated to the designated area. It was important to be near these nearly played-out mines, Dr. Rhinelander was told, because the fuel he would need for the crafts would be made from a by-product of coal.

Dr. Rhinelander and his fellow scientists established themselves in the community, beginning their day when the last whistle sounded in the mines. While the other miners trudged to the bars, then went home to have their supper and go to bed, the scientists entered their laboratories and set about to fulfill the time schedule that had been set for them by their mysterious benefactors. Eventually, through the apparently unlimited funds provided by the non-Terrans, Dr. Rhinelander was able to buy up old mines to convert into spacious laboratories and to employ large numbers of the indigenous community.

Those who wished to work for Dr. Rhinelander had to pass a rigorous physical examination and a tortuous, maddening psychological examination. If one was accepted, he was given a special diet and was required to submit to a regular testing of his blood, "to see if it stayed right."

When the first craft was completed in about 1924, Dr. Rhinelander had such confidence in his brilliant daughter's abilities as a pilot that he permitted her to captain the maiden flight of the aerial craft that had been designed according to their tutors' specifications. Although the takeoff occurred without incident, the craft was no sooner free of the Earth's atmosphere than a similar but larger vehicle appeared and literally "caught" the ship piloted by Ms. Rhinelander within its cage-like metallic structure.

The alarmed and confused German scientists were then informed that another group of non-Terrans had objected to the intervention of Dr. Rhinelander's benefactors. They were not eager for *Homo sapiens* to have the secrets of interstellar travel. In fact, they would seek to delay humankind's leap to other worlds as long as possible.

Hostile Aliens Had Not Approved of the Union of Earthlings and Aldebarans

In spite of this interference by a hostile extraterrestrial group, Dr. Rhinelander became determined to master space travel and to negotiate for the return of his daughter. Two more vehicles were lost to the opposing faction of non-Terrans before the Germans perfected a means of avoiding capture. Dr. Rhinelander's daughter and the other crew members were never returned, although the Terrans were assured that these people were being well cared for on another world.

Dr. Rhinelander had finally accomplished space travel in the 1930s, but it seemed to matter little. He grieved over the loss of his daughter and became diverted from his work. Concurrently, the unlimited financial funding that they had enjoyed seemed to be curtailed. Chaos began to permeate their once-splendid structure of efficient order.

At the time of Dr. Rhinelander's death, the group was approaching poverty, so the scientists wished to sell the formulas to the non-pollutant fuel and the fireproofer. Even though they remained in close contact with the non-Terrans in their underwater bases, the scientists had little inclination to attempt more than an occasional foray into the night skies with their two surviving craft.

Encountering Maids from the German Moon Base

I went along on a midnight meeting in some seedy bar where we were to rendezvous once again with the negotiator. It rained so hard that night that it must have kept even UFOs out of the sky, because the man did not show to deliver the formulas.

Ray tried several time to rendezvous with the negotiator and, although the negotiator failed to keep the appointments, it was not long before Ray found himself confronted by attractive young women who claimed that they had gone to school on a base on the Moon that had been established by German scientists in the 1930s. Ray telephoned me and appealed for help. He said that the women could answer any technological question that he, a former Air Force jet pilot, could throw at her, without hesitation.

Excitedly, he told me that he had taken one of the Moon Maids for dinner a couple of nights before in an attempt to ply her with alcoholic beverages to loosen her tongue. She had put away enough drinks to topple a horse without slurring a syllable, without contradicting any previously disclosed aspect of her story, and without once excusing herself to go to the ladies' room.

I turned down the opportunity to come along for the next "for sure" transfer, and I was hardly surprised when Ray told me that our mysterious salesman had not shown on that occasion, either.

Were the strange group of German scientists and alleged aliens that we met that night in Chicago really a splinter group of the Vril Society who had made their spacecraft work in hidden bases in the United States? Or were they clever frauds who tried to exploit the romance of secret societies and extraterrestrial mentors? If they were merely scammers, however, why did they never take the money that was offered to them several times and just leave town? From my point of view at the time, it seemed that the group that had met with us had somehow violated the code of their larger society and had been ordered to break off contact with those outsiders who wished to buy their formulas.

Ray kept in touch for quite some time, and he proved to be extremely determined. He told me of a number of midnight meetings, where the other parties never showed. On occasion, he was "tailed" by three dark men in dark automobiles, who proved to be unshakable.

But he never managed to track down those magical formulas, and he never received another telephone call from the mysterious secret society.

As a footnote, although outlawed in Germany, the Vril society has recently resurfaced in Italy where it is known as Causa Nostra (Our Cause). Membership is restricted to women only, and the principles are said to be those established by Maria Orsic, the original Vril Chefin, and the Vril Gesellschaft of Sigrun, Traute, Gudrun, and Heike. Maybe this time, their extraterrestrial contacts will reveal themselves to the world at large. Or maybe the non-Terrans, the aliens, have been walking among us unnoticed for years now.

Alien Researchers Face Threats and Death

The late Ray Palmer, editor of *Flying Saucers* magazine, was one of the most prominent figures on the UFO scene for nearly thirty years. An editor of pulp magazines in the 1940s, Ray had edited numerous periodicals for Ziff-Davis, including the science-fiction classic *Amazing Stories*. After he and Curtis Fuller cofounded the unique journal, *Fate*, Palmer ran so many articles and covers on flying saucers that an irritated Air Force officer once accused him of having invented the UFO controversy to sell magazines.

During one of our visits with Palmer in the late 1960s in his office in Amherst, Wisconsin, he said that he would never have gone further in exploring the flying saucer controversy if the Air Force had not interfered with a special issue of *Amazing Stories* that he had planned in 1948. "They stepped in and tried to halt publication of the magazine," he told us. "That's where they made their first mistake. They convinced me that there really was something to this fantastic story. We had the magazine all ready to go, when Mr. Ziff, the boss, came into my office and told me to kill the issue. Later I saw him talking to seven or eight Air Force men, one a colonel. It was my first experience with military silencing."

Shortly after Kenneth Arnold had made his historic sighting of flying saucers near Mt. Rainier in 1947, Palmer collaborated with the pilot in authoring *The Coming of the Flying Saucers*, the first flying saucer book. "Almost immediately after the book was released," Palmer said, "Arnold and I were each visited by representatives of the Internal Revenue Service and told that we each owed the government $1,800. There was no room for appeal on our part; we just had to pay the money. Undeclared revenue? No, just their way of letting us know they were unhappy with us."

In later years, Palmer claimed regular visits from nearly every known branch of government intelligence. He was falsely accused of printing pornography in addition to his publications *Search*, *Space World*, and *Rocket Exchange*. Once he was even investigated for using his presses to print counterfeit money.

As reports of space beings continue to proliferate since the Flying Saucer Age began in 1945 with Kenneth Arnold's sighting near Mt. Ranier, an increasingly wide variety of entities has been described. Strange as it may seem to some, many witnesses claim to have interacted with insectoid beings. (*Art by Ricardo Pustanio*)

Ray Palmer did not hesitate to express his opinion that the Central Intelligence Agency had financed a good many of "the more ridiculous" aspects of flying saucers. "This has been an important part of their plan to discredit serious UFO research," he said. "If the CIA were able to establish UFO investigators as akin to cultists and kooks, then all flying saucer researchers would be guilty by association. The crazier a UFO contactee may appear to the general public, the more likely is he to be having his bills picked up by the CIA."

Palmer believed that the Air Force and the government were suppressing knowledge about UFOs, because "the one inescapable fact of history is that the people who are in control want to stay in control."

The Men in Black Visit Oklahoma City

When respected UFO researcher Hayden Hewes and his International UFO Bureau sponsored a symposium on flying saucers in Oklahoma City in 1973, and was gathered with some of the speakers, one of them, a noted lecturer in the field, became very quiet after he received a telephone call.

"In a few minutes, a long black limo pulled up in front of our office and two men wearing dark sunglasses and dressed completely in black came to the door and picked up our featured speaker," Hewes said. "The two guys looked like the Blues Brothers in their dark suits and shades. Anyway, they drove off with our speaker, returned him after a couple of hours, but he never said one word regarding where he went or with whom.

"I don't know if they told him what he could or could not say. I don't know if he was one of them," Hewes commented. "I just know that I physically saw them and their limo—and our speaker never said one word to me about what it had all been about."

At roughly the same time the International UFO Bureau published two booklets authored by Hewes and illustrated by Hal Crawford—*The Aliens* and *The Intruders*—which graphically depicted alien types and UFO shapes. "Shortly after publication I received a visit from a man identifying himself as an officer in Naval Intelligence," Hewes said. "He showed me several UFO photographs of flying saucers fluctuating, as if they were materializing in some kind of force field. You know, like on *Star Trek*, when they are 'beaming up' but haven't quite reached solid form. 'The officer told me, We know what these UFOs are, and we don't want you to give them any publicity.'"

Hewes showed him several photos from his files, and the officer quietly acknowledged them. Then he repeated his request, "Don't give the kind of UFOs in the pictures that I showed you any notoriety, any publicity of any kind whatsoever. We have no problems with your publishing any of the other UFO photographs in your files."

Hewes said that the conversation was approximately two hours long and very low key. "I don't know if those were government UFOs or alien craft that they had identified. I do know that such photographs of that kind of 'fuzzy' UFO never again crossed my desk."

Secret Government Thugs or Alien Toughs?

Since the late 1940s, civilian UFO researchers have complained that witnesses who claimed to have encountered alien entities or sighted UFOs would also say that they had been silenced by men who claimed to be Air Force personnel or members of some secret government agency. In certain instances, the witnesses stated that they had been threatened, even roughed up, by alleged agents of the U.S. government.

Photos of UFOs were confiscated. Debris left behind at UFO landing sites was appropriated. Dramatic accounts of interaction with UFO occupants were silenced. Angry civilians began to complain that the United States was not Nazi Germany or Communist Russia. Military personnel simply could not come into the homes of private citizens, confiscate their personal property and leave them in fear of physical harm.

It has never been within the line of duty of any U.S. government agency to threaten private citizens or to enter their homes without a search warrant. And no government agency is empowered to demand the surrender of private property by any law-abiding citizen.

UFO researchers themselves began to complain that sinister voices had whispered threats to them over the telephone, issuing stern warnings to stop their investigations immediately.

The Air Force Officially Denies Being UFO Silencers

When the complaints against Air Force strong-arm tactics could no longer be ignored, Col. George P. Freeman, Pentagon spokesman for Project Bluebook, issued a formal statement that his office had checked a number of cases in which civilians claimed to have been threatened after their UFO sighting. Their research indicated that "these men are not connected with the Air Force in any way." Colonel Freeman stated that by posing as Air Force officers or as government agents, the UFO silencers—whomever they might be—were committing a federal offense.

Colonel Freeman's official denial had barely been uttered when four bogus Air Force officers assembled the police officers and the civilians who had witnessed heavy UFO activity over the reservoir in Wanaque, New Jersey. Sternly, in no uncertain terms, the people of Wanaque were told that they "hadn't seen a thing," and they were admonished not to discuss their claims of UFO sightings with anyone.

The MIB Phenomenon Begins with Bender in 1953

The prototype of what has come to be known in UFO research as the men-in-black (MIB) phenomenon began with the alleged silencing of Albert K. Bender in September 1953. According to the late Gray Barker, who wrote *They Knew Too Much about Flying Saucers* about the case in 1962, Bender had received data convincing him that he had been given remarkable insights into the truth about the origin of flying saucers. He wrote his thesis, then sent the report to a trusted friend. When three men appeared at his door, one of them supposedly held that letter in his hand.

Bender later told his friends that the three men were "pretty rough with him." He was informed that if people were to learn the actual truth about flying saucers, there would be dramatic changes in all things. Science, especially, would suffer a major blow. Political structures would topple. Mass confusion would reign.

In June 1967 two of Bender's closest friends, Dominick Lucchesi and August C. Roberts, said that Bender had seemed to be a changed man after the three MIB had visited him. "He was scared, and he later suffered from tremendous headaches which he said were controlled by 'them'." Roberts said that Bender dropped all UFO research and went underground, although they knew he was living under another name and managing a motel somewhere in California.

> Experienced UFO researcher John A. Keel set forth his opinion that the MIB were "the intelligence arm of a large and possibly hostile group."

Experienced UFO researcher John A. Keel set forth his opinion that the MIB were "the intelligence arm of a large and possibly hostile group." Keel said that he considered the UFO silencers to be professional terrorists assigned the mission of harassing UFO researchers who became highly involved in investigations that might reveal too much of the truth. Keel said that in his own research he had uncovered some extreme cases of personal abuse in which certain UFO contactees and/or UFO investigators had been kidnapped by three men in a black car. "For some reason," Keel noted, "it is almost always three men." He reports that they subject their victim to some sort of brainwashing that leaves him or her in a state of nausea, mental confusion, or even amnesia—and the condition can last for several days.

Beckley Snaps a Photograph of a MIB

Researcher, author, publisher Timothy Green Beckley has been pursuing the UFO enigma since, at the age of ten in 1957, he and his family and neighbors had a dramatic UFO sighting in New Jersey. Young Tim wrote to the local newspaper to protest the official analysis of the flying saucer as a weather balloon. By the age of fourteen, he was publishing his own newsletter and making media appearances.

When he was still a teenager and working for James Mosley, one of the earliest of UFO researcher-publishers, Tim spotted a "man in black" watching their office from an alley. Tim managed to sneak around and take a photograph of the MIB, long black automobile and all.

"We have to entertain the possibility that some of these MIB reports are of overzealous CIA operatives," Beckley said. "The Central Intelligence Agency is made up of thousands of individual and independent agents. Within the blanket of the agency are darker, more secretive groups. And there are individual rogue agents, no longer under anyone's control."

Beckley has also wondered if some of the MIB might not be representatives of big business or organized religion. "If the complete UFO story should ever be totally revealed, it would have a tremendous impact on all of our civilization—our political structures, religions, business methods. Our social strata and our world would change. And there will always be those who wish to preserve the status quo at all costs."

What Is the True Identity of the UFO Silencers?

Just exactly who comprises the "silence group" that seems so determined to make a sinister battleground of UFO research?

We lost a lot of friends and contacts during 1966 to 1972, which seems to have been a particularly active time for MIB harassment of UFO percipients. Some good people whose friendship we had cherished simply could not endure the disturbances on their telephone lines and the bizarre phenomena that had suddenly intruded into their formerly quiet lives as a result of being our friends or assisting us with some phase of our research.

Sometimes, we encounter angry individuals who accuse us of having conducted UFO investigations in areas where we have never traveled and of having abused, insulted, and threatened witnesses of UFO activity while we were there. In addition, we are frequently told of people who say they have attended our lectures and seminars in small towns and cities we have never visited. And these good folk repeat a lot of strange statements that we allegedly made during those phantom lectures—statements that we never would have uttered.

Even though we were actively moving around the United States and Canada investigating UFO phenomena during that period, it seems that persons posing as us were just as active in a negative—often openly hostile—manner.

Are the UFO silencers horror or hoax?

And, if it is all a hoax, then who is perpetrating it and why?

Are the silencers, in spite of all the indignant official denials, human agents from a top-secret U.S. government agency, one that knows the answer to the UFO enigma and has been given the mission of keeping the truth from the public? In some instances we are convinced that the men who identified themselves as Air Force personnel were, indeed, who they claimed to be—investigating officers who, officially, "weren't there." In certain cases we strongly suspect that overzealous civilian researchers, jealously guarding a "really good UFO case," might have been responsible for making ill-advised threats to UFO witnesses to ensure the exclusivity of their investigation.

But in a great many cases, the nagging question seems to demand the answer that the MIB—as some UFO researchers firmly believe—may be extraterrestrial aliens. If so, they are laboring to spread confusion and fear among those who have witnessed activities subversive to our species, activities that our visitors wish to keep secret.

Or, as other investigators insist, are they agents from some ancient secret society endeavoring to guard its clandestine activities for a while longer?

Or could the UFOs and the silencers be coming from a much older terrestrial race—perhaps extraterrestrial in origin—which has survived unnoticed in some remote region of Earth and which has become more scientifically advanced during its self-imposed isolation?

> [T]he nagging question seems to demand the answer that the MIB—as some UFO researchers firmly believe—may be extraterrestrial aliens.

Do the MIB wish us to remain ignorant of the true facts about the UFO controversy because they realize that the more ignorant we are of the true nature of the dangers that face us, the less able we will be to deal with a future crisis situation of overwhelming proportions? Because the less we are prepared to handle the inevitable confrontation with an alien race, the more rapidly we might allow ourselves to become slaves to a society or a species that considers itself superior to us.

The mysterious silence group may prove to be members of a hostile element within an alien species—or citizens of a secret society no longer content with being obscure and benevolent. Whatever the case may be, a number of UFO researchers learned through tragic consequences that some of these silencers were no longer content to knock on doors and merely harass them. Some researchers may have paid the price of their curiosity with their lives.

The Mysterious Deaths of UFO Researchers

Prof. G. Cope Schellhorn relates the following:

Mysterious and suspicious deaths among UFO investigators are almost as old as the phenomenon itself. In 1971, the well-known author and researcher Otto Binder wrote an article for *Saga* magazine's *Special UFO Report* titled "Liquidation of the UFO Investigators." Binder had researched the deaths of "no less than 137 flying saucer researchers, writers, scientists, and witnesses" who had died in the previous ten years, "many under the most mysterious circumstances." The cases Binder offered were loaded with a plethora of alleged heart attacks, suspicious cancers, and what appear to be outright examples of murder.

Some of the most intriguing deaths in Ufology were those of Dorothy Kilgallen, M. K. Jessup, and Dr. James McDonald—the former an alleged accident, the latter two purported suicides. The details of these deaths, despite official pronouncements to the contrary, are disturbing to say the least. Each of the three individuals seemed to have much to live for, all were successful, and every one of them was deeply immersed in the relatively new field of UFO research.

Dorothy Kilgallen

Dorothy Kilgallen was the most famous syndicated female journalist of her day. People who didn't read her column and articles were familiar with her appearance as a regular on the popular television program *What's My Line?* Living in England from 1954 to 1955, and privy to the highest levels of English society and its secrets, she wired two unusual dispatches, which may have contributed to her death.

The first, sent in February 1954, mentioned a "special hush-hush meeting of the world's military heads" scheduled to take place the following summer.

Her next dispatch, in 1955, barely preceded her death from an alleged overdose of sleeping pills and alcohol. It quoted an unnamed British official of Cabinet rank who stated: "We believe, on the basis of our inquiry thus far, that flying saucers are staffed by small men—probably under four feet tall. It's frightening, but there is no denying the flying saucers come from another planet."

Whatever the source (rumored to be the Earl of Mountbatten), this kind of leak in the Cold War atmosphere of the mid-1950s was an unacceptable breach of conduct. The secret CIA-orchestrated Robertson Panel on UFOs had met in 1953 and issued the Robertson Report, which represented a new hard-line military attitude toward covering up all significant UFO phenomena. The UFO cover-up as we know it today was initiated in that year.

Did Dorothy Kilgallen actually commit accidental suicide? There appears to be an excellent probability that she had help.

Dr. James McDonald

Dr. James McDonald, senior physicist of the Institute of Atmospheric Physics, and professor in the Department of Meteorology at the University of Arizona, died in 1971 purportedly of a self-inflicted gunshot wound to the head. There was no one who had worked harder in the 1960s than McDonald to convince Congress to hold serious, substantial subcommittee meetings to explore the possibility of the existence of UFOs. He was thoroughly convinced of the reality of UFOs and was a thorn in the side of those who maintained the official cover-up.

McDonald, allegedly depressed, shot himself in the head. He didn't die, but he was confined to a wheelchair. Several months after his attempted suicide, he allegedly got in an automobile, drove to a pawnshop, purchased another pistol from his wheelchair, drove to the desert, and killed himself.

Astronomer M. K. Jessup

When astronomer and archaeologist M. K. Jessup allegedly committed suicide in Dade County Park, Florida, in 1959 certain alarm bells should have gone off. There is no doubt the well-known author of such influential works as *The Case for the UFO* and *The Expanding Case for the UFO* had been depressed. Things had not been going well for him. He had, it must be admitted, indicated his gloom to close friends, Ivan Sanderson, the biologist, and Long John Nebel, the well-known New York City radio host. Sanderson reported him disturbed by "a series of strange events", which put him "into a completely insane world of unreality."

But was the reality Jessup was faced with at the time "completely insane" or were there, perhaps, forces driving Jessup to the edge, forces with a plan?

Those were the days of secret government mind-control experiments, which have only recently been uncovered. When researcher Anna Genzlinger thoroughly investigated Jessups's death, her conclusion was: "He was under some sort of control."

> When researcher Anna Genzlinger thoroughly investigated Jessups's death, her conclusion was: "He was under some sort of control."

Certain facts about the Jessup case raise red flags. For example, no autopsy was performed, contrary to the state law. Sergeant Oben-clain, who was on the scene shortly after Jessup's body was discovered, has said for the record, "Everything seemed too professional." The hose from the car exhaust was wired on; and it was, strangely, washing machine hose.

Jessup died at rush hour, with more than the usual amount of traffic passing by. Some say that Jessup had been visited by Carlos Allende (of Philadelphia Experiment fame) three days before his death and, according to his wife, Jessup had been receiving strange phone calls. We know the Navy was very much interested in what he was doing; and we all know it is the Office of Naval Investigations (ONI) that has been in the forefront, from the very beginning, of the UFO cover-up.

And what of particular interest was Jessup investigating at the time? Something that was top secret and would remain so for some time: The Philadelphia Experiment.

Frank Edwards

Frank Edwards, the noted news commentator, author of *Flying Saucers: Serious Business*, died of an alleged heart attack on June 24, 1967, on the twentieth anniversary of the Kenneth Arnold sighting. Was that coincidence?

It so happened that a "World UFO Conference" was being held in New York City at the Commodore Hotel on that very day in June, chaired by UFO publisher and author Gray Barker. Barker stated publicly that he had received two letters and a telephone call threatening that Frank Edwards would not be alive by the end of the conference. It definitely looks like someone was sending a message.

Strange Deaths and Disappearances Haunt Ufology

The annals of Ufology are frighteningly filled with the deaths of UFOlogists from unusual cancers, heart attacks, questionable suicides and all manner of strange happenings. Did former Secretary of Defense James Forrestal really commit suicide as purported by jumping out a hotel window at about the time saucers may have been crashing down in the southwestern desert? Was UFO writer Damon Runyon Jr.'s suicidal plunge off a Washington, D.C., bridge in 1988 really an act of will? What really happened to Dr. B. Noel Opan who, in 1959, after an alleged visit by MIBs, disappeared. And what about the disappearance of Edgar Jarrold, the Australian UFOlogist, in 1960?

Phil Schneider

No one has shook up more of those individuals who have been following UFO facts and rumors than Phil Schneider. Schneider died January 17, 1996, reportedly strangled by a catheter that was found wrapped around his neck. If the circumstances of his death seem highly controversial, they are matched by the controversy over his public statements made not long before his death.

Phil Schneider was a self-taught geologist and explosives expert. Schneider claimed he had worked in thirteen of the 129 deep underground facilities he maintained the U.S. government had constructed since World War II. Schneider reported that gray humanoid extraterrestrials worked side by side with American technicians at the bioengineering facility at Dulce, New Mexico. In 1979, a misunderstanding arose between the aliens and the earthlings, Schneider had said. In the ensuing shootout, sixty-six Secret Service, FBI, and Black Berets were killed, along with an unspecified number of grays. It was during the violent encounter that Schneider received a beam-weapon blast to the chest, which he feels later caused his cancer.

If Schneider is telling the truth, he obviously broke the code of silence imposed on all major black-budget personnel. The penalty for that misstep is presumably termination. Schneider maintained that numerous previous attempts had been made on his life, including the removal of lug nuts from one of the front wheels of his automobile to cause a fatal automobile accident. He had stated publicly that he was a marked man and did not expect to live long.

Some of Schneider's major accusations are worthy of attention:

1. The American government concluded a treaty with gray aliens in 1954. This mutual cooperation pact is called the Grenada Treaty.

2. The space shuttle has been functioning with special metals provided by the aliens. A vacuum atmosphere is needed for the creation of these special alloys, thus the push for a large space station.

3. Much of our stealth aircraft technology was developed by back-engineering crashed alien craft.

4. AIDS was a population control virus invented by the National Ordinance Laboratory of Chicago, Illinois.

5. Unbeknownst to just about everyone, our government has an earthquake device: The Kobe quake had no pulse wave; the 1989 San Francisco quake had no pulse wave.

6. The World Trade Center bomb blast and the Oklahoma City blast were achieved using small nuclear devices. The melting and pitting of the concrete

and the extrusion of metal supporting rods indicated this. (Remember, Schneider's forte, he claimed, was explosives.)

Finally, Phil Schneider lamented that the democracy he loved no longer existed. We had become instead a technocracy ruled by a shadow government intent on imposing their own view of things on all of us, whether we like it or not. He believed many of his best friends had been murdered in the last twenty-two years, eight of whom had been officially declared suicides.

Whatever we think of Phil Schneider's claims, there is no denying that he was of peculiar interest to the FBI and CIA. According to his widow, intelligence agents thoroughly searched the premises shortly after his death and made off with at least a third of the family photographs.

Ron Rummel

We had become instead a technocracy ruled by a shadow government intent on imposing their own view of things on all of us, whether we like it or not.

Another recent disturbing case is the death of Ron Rummel, ex-Air Force intelligence agent and publisher of the *Alien Digest,* on August 6, 1993. Rummel allegedly shot himself in the mouth with a pistol. Friends say, however, that no blood was found on the pistol barrel and the handle of the weapon was free of fingerprints. Also, according to information now circulating, the suicide note left by the deceased was written by a left-handed person. Rummel was right-handed. Perspiration on the body smelled like sodium pentothal—or so it is alleged.

The *Alien Digest* ran seven limited issues, all now almost impossible to acquire. Ron Rummel's magazine was touching on sensitive issues such as the alien-human relationship and the use of humans as food and recyclable body parts. Did Rummel cross a forbidden line? It would seem so. But which line, and where?

Interestingly enough, one of Rummel's friends was Phil Schneider, and the two had been collaborating.

Ron Johnson

Ron (Jerrold) Johnson, MUFON's Deputy Director of Investigations, died in an equally disturbing way. Johnson was forty-three years old and, it would seem, in excellent health. He had just passed a recent physical examination with the proverbial flying colors.

However, on June 9, 1994, while attending a Society of Scientific Exploration meeting in Austin, Texas, Johnson died quickly and amid very strange circumstances. During a slide show, several people sitting close to him heard a gasp. When the lights were turned back on, Johnson was slumped over in his chair, his face purple, blood oozing from his nose. A soda can, from which he had been sipping, was sitting on the chair next to him.

Did Ron Johnson die of a stroke? Possibly. An allergic reaction? Another possibility.

Some of the more outstanding facts of Ron Johnson's life might easily lead a more skeptical person to a tentative conclusion that his death was probably neither accidental nor natural. For instance, his most recent job was with the Institute of Advanced Studies, purportedly working on UFO propulsion systems. He had been formerly employed by Earth Tech, Inc., a private Austin, Texas, think tank headed by Harold Puthoff. It would appear that Johnson held high security clearances, traveled frequently between San Antonio and White Sands, and had attended two secret NATO meetings in the last year or so. One of those meetings, it is rumored, dealt with ET communications. If most of the facts offered above are accurate, one thing seems obvious: Johnson was walking both sides of the street. This in itself was highly dangerous, and he may have paid the ultimate price in an attempt to serve more than one master.

As for the cause of Ron Johnson's death, a number of possibilities beyond natural ones present themselves. It is quite easy in this day and age to induce strokes through chemicals or pulsed radiation. It is just as easy to induce heart attacks and other physical debilitations, such as fast-acting cancers. The best bet is that Ron Johnson was eliminated by a quick-acting toxin, perhaps a nerve agent. As for exactly why he was killed, we will probably never know. The autopsy has been officially classified as inconclusive.

Ann Livingston

Another death that seems very strange is that of Ann Livingston, who died in early 1994 of a fast form of ovarian cancer. Livingston made her living as an accountant, but she was also a MUFON investigator and had in fact published an article entitled "Electronic Harassment and Alien Abductions" in the November 1993 MUFON *UFO Journal*.

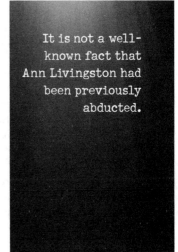

It is not a well-known fact that Ann Livingston had been previously abducted.

Some facts that seem relevant to the case stand out. At 7:15 A.M., December 29, 1992, Livingston's apartment, which was close to O'Hare airport in Chicago, was lit up brightly by a silver-white flash. She was accosted later in the day while in her apartment parking lot by five MIBs, which she described as being almost faceless and carrying long, flashlight-like black objects. She was rendered unconscious.

Assuming her story is true, we feel compelled to ask what was done to her at this time, and why? And did it have anything to do with her later rapidly-advancing ovarian cancer?

It is not a well-known fact that Ann Livingston had been previously abducted. Could genital intrusions from past UFO abductions have poisoned in Ann Livingston's system in some way? Karla Turner (author of *Masquerade of Angels, Taken,* and *Into the Fringe*) had this suspicion had about the breast cancer that preceded her own death during the summer of 1996. Both publicly and privately, Karla Turner contended that her illness was the result of alien retaliation for statements that she had made in print, especially in *Masquerade of Angels*. How much her suspicions were founded in reality we will probably never know.

Danny Casolaro

Danny Casolaro, an investigative reporter looking into the theft of Project Promise software—a program capable of tracking down anyone anywhere in the world—died in 1991 of a reported suicide.

Casolaro was also investigating several UFO cases: Pine Gap, Area 51, and governmental bioengineering.

Brian Lynch

Brian Lynch, young psychic and contactee, died in 1985, purportedly of a drug overdose. According to Lynch's sister, Geraldine, Brian was approached approximately a year before his death by an intelligence operative working for an Austin, Texas, PSI-tech company. Geraldine said they told Brian they were experimenting on psychic warfare techniques. After his death, a note in his personal effects was found with the words "Five million from Pentagon for Project Scanate."

Capt. Don Elkin

In the 1980s, Eastern Airlines pilot Captain Don Elkin committed suicide. He had been investigating the UFO cover-up for over ten years and, at the time, was deep into the study of the *Ra Material* with Carla Rucker. There are reports of negative psychological interferences developing during this latter investigation.

Dean Stonier

Dean was the organizer and promoter of the Global Sciences Congress. Over the years it had hosted many top researchers including Phil Schneider and Al Bielek, who claims to be the sole survivor of the Philadelphia Experiment. Dean died of a heart attack in August 2001, just a few months after a Denver Global Sciences Congress.

Jim Keith

Jim Keith died in 1999. The author of many books, including *Mind Control, World Control,* Jim died while in the hospital during surgery to repair a broken leg he received while attending the infamous Burning Man Festival in Nevada. It seemed a blood clot was released during the surgery and traveled to the heart, causing a pulmonary edema.

Ron Bonds

Ron Bonds published books on unsolved mysteries, unexplained phenomena, and conspiracies—from the Kennedy assassination to the ominous black helicopters of the New World Order. In the subculture of the paranormal, his reputation was such that writers for the television series *The X-Files* used to call him for ideas.

In April 2001, fifteen hours after eating a meal in a Mexican restaurant in Atlanta, Georgia, Bonds suffered an agonizing evening of vomiting and diarrhea. He was taken by ambulance from their home to Grady Memorial Hospital where he died.

During an autopsy, the medical examiner found copious amounts of blood in the bowels, so he sent a stool sample to the Georgia Public Health Laboratory in Decatur. The lab discovered high levels of Clostridium perfringens Type A, a bacterium often seen in small quantities in beef and poultry. When it occurs in larger quantities—anything above 100,000 organisms per gram is considered unsafe—it can release toxins that cause diarrhea, vomiting and, rarely, hemorrhaging. The bacterium figures in 250,000 cases of food poisoning a year, the CDC estimates, only seven of which result in death.

Four days after Bonds ate there, epidemiologists visited El Azteca to collect samples of ground beef from the steam table. When C. perfringens becomes dangerous, it usually has to do with cooked meat being held at too low a temperature. The lab found six million organisms per gram—sixty times the safety threshold.

One obvious question is: Why didn't other people get sick too?

Bizarre Death of Scientists

Certainly nothing is stranger and breeds speculation more quickly than the thirtysome odd deaths associated with SDI (Star Wars) research at Marconi Ltd. in England between 1985 and 1988. Here in capsulated form is a list of a few of the more bizarre deaths:

Roger Hill, a designer at Marconi Defense Systems, allegedly committed suicide with a shotgun in March 1985.

Jonathan Walsh, a digital communications expert employed by General Electric Company (GEC), Marconi's parent firm, fell from his hotel room, November 1985, after expressing fear for his life.

Ashad Sharif, another Marconi scientist, reportedly tied a rope around his neck, and then to a tree, in October 1986, got behind the wheel of his car and stepped on the gas with predictable results.

Trevor Knight, also associated with Marconi, died of carbon monoxide poisoning in his car in March 1988.

Peter Ferry, marketing director of the firm, was found shocked to death with electrical leads in his mouth (August 1988).

Alistair Beckham was found shocked to death in the same month of the same year. Electric leads were attached to his body and his mouth was stuffed with a handkerchief. He was an engineer with the allied firm of Plessey Defense Systems.

Andrew Hall was found dead in September of 1988 of carbon monoxide poisoning.

What, you may be asking, does SDI research have to do with the deaths of UFO investigators?

Theoretically, quite a lot. If, as many investigators have hypothesized, Star Wars research was initiated with the dual purpose of protecting "us" against Soviet aggression and/or the presence of UFO craft in our atmosphere, then several possibilities arise. Most compelling is the idea that the Soviet KGB, realizing that the Western powers were on the verge of perfecting a high-powered beam-weapon that could be used from outer space or atmospheric space against them, marshaled an all-out espionage offensive to slow or destroy the project. If this scenario is true, and the weapon was indeed successfully developed, we have an explanation for the collapse of the Soviet Union ("Surrender or you might be incinerated.").

Other explanations have been offered. For example, scientists working on the project discovered the true nature of the research and the overwhelming stress and guilt led them to suicide. Or they discovered that their real collaborators were aliens or Western politicians working with/for gray aliens.

One thing seems obvious. Something went terribly wrong at Marconi. Scientists usually don't commit the kinds of bizarre, "unscientific" suicides we find here.

One other possibility is that a contingent of unfriendly aliens got wind of what GEC and Marconi and its affiliates were up to and, to protect themselves, created enough psychic trauma within the minds of many of the scientists to drive them to suicide.

But if this is so, why have the deaths stopped? Has the project been shelved?

Highly unlikely. The best bet is that the project was completed in 1988 perhaps, and whatever it is, beam-weapon or something else, it is now operational.

Natural ... or Strange Deaths?

How do we explain the rash of heart attacks that took so many: Frank Edwards; author H. T. Wilkins; Henry E. Kock, publicity director of the Universal Research Society of America; author Frank Scully; and contactee George Adamski? How do we correlate accurately the large number of purported suicides, including: Rev. Della Larson, contactee; author Gloria Lee (Byrd); Marie Ford, UFO enthusiast who discovered Larson's body; researcher Doug Hancock; and, more recently, researcher Feron Hicks? What do we do with the inordinately large number of cancer deaths that pepper the UFO field and burn doubtful holes in our credulity: Canadian researcher Wilbert B. Smith; Brazilian researcher Dr. Olavo Fontes; Jim and Coral Lorenzen. And what about the deaths of biologist Ivan Sanderson and CUFOS founder Dr. J. Allen Hynek, both from rare brain cancer?

> One thing seems obvious. Something went terribly wrong at Marconi. Scientists usually don't commit the kinds of bizarre, "unscientific" suicides we find here.

Certainly not all of these individuals—and many other less prominent researchers—were marked for termination. Many, perhaps most, died natural deaths. But so many of the cases leave doubt; some seem to be branded by the mark of Cain. We now know how easy it is to induce strokes and heart attacks through chemicals, pulsed beams, and microbes. We have learned that the federal government was (and still is) involved in PSI-tech research. An individual's mind is rather easily manipulated, and minds can be subtly shaped like putty into despair and madness.

Ufology is not the safe hobby or pastime some would like it to be. There may be real danger in sticking your nose in places where the powers that be don't want you to be.

What is the cause? Who is the villain? Again, it must be emphasized that the "problem" is complex. Rogue intelligence agencies, negative aliens, freelancing PSI-tech firms, and reactionary cultist groups all seem to play, or to have played, a part in the more nefarious UFO-related events described here. It seems highly likely that sometimes one or more of these agencies may be working together, with or without the knowledge of the other's presence.

What can we do about such a state of affairs? Several things. We can inform ourselves like good democratic citizens. And we can inform others. We can and must raise a hue and cry when we suspect foul play. If we are to protect our very lives and the democratic hopes we say we cherish, then we must not go, silent and ignorant, into the night, pretending innocence.

Certainly the public at large, and even many UFOlogists, seem thoroughly aware of the real risks that UFO investigators run. In fact, those UFOlogists who are aware of the suspicious deaths of some of their colleagues in the 1950s and 1960s, seem to believe that the forces and agencies that were responsible have softened their tactics in the new century. The evidence, as we have indicated, does not seem to support such a conclusion.

This portion of the chapter was adapted from lectures given by Professor G. Cope Schellhorn and from his article in UFO Universe Magazine, *1997.*

Aliens in Earth's Prehistory and Religion

Although an atheist, Francis Crick, the codiscoverer of DNA, wrote a book, *Life Itself*, which subscribed to the theory that our universe was not simply the result of a series of chemical accidents. He believed that primordial life was shipped to Earth in some sort of spaceships.

He states, "Life did not evolve first on Earth; a highly advanced civilization became threatened so they devised a way to pass on their existence. They genetically modified their DNA and sent it out from their planet on bacteria or meteorites with the hope that it would collide with another planet. It did, and that's why we're here."

Our DNA was encoded with messages from that other civilization. The molecules were programmed so that when we reached a certain level of intelligence, we would be able to access their information, and they could therefore "teach" us about ourselves and how to progress.

Genesis II: Those Who Have Come Down from the Heaven to Earth Found the Daughters of Men Fair

Many serious-minded UFO researchers have suggested that if we were to read the creation story in Genesis with our current awareness of genetic engineering, the interaction between the sons of God and the fair daughters of men would assume a rather different interpretation.

The Bible refers to giants, known as the Nephilim, fourteen times. These beings, who were regarded as gods, lived among humans prior to the great flood. As Genesis, Chapter 6, describes them: "And it came to pass, when men began to multiply on the face of the earth and daughters were born to them, that the sons of God saw the daughters of men were fair; so they took them wives of all whom they chose.... There were giants in the earth in those days; and also after that, when the sons of God came in unto the daughters of men, and they bore children to them, and they became giants who in the olden days were men of renown." (Genesis 6:1–4)

If those smitten sons of God were actually extraterrestrial scientists conducting experiments on female members of the developing strain of *Homo sapiens*, rather than decadent heavenly beings sinning with Earth's daughters, they might have been carrying out the directive of the Alien Overlords to provide nascent humankind with a genetic boost.

It seems clear that the ancient Israelites thought the sons of God were godbeings or angels, possessed of supernatural powers. Some contemporary researchers believe that these particular "sons of God" came from another world—not a heaven, but an actual physical place. And that their "coming in unto" the daughters of men to produce the "giants" quite likely refers to genetic manipulation, rather than sexual intercourse.

Later, we learn that the Lord has grown dissatisfied with the human experiment and is grieved in His heart that He had even made man on the Earth (Genesis 6:5–6).

Many individuals who have experienced alien contact report that they continue to sense some form of alien intelligence watching them, as if monitoring their behavior and reactions to their encounter. (Art by Ricardo Pustanio)

Perhaps an assessment was made that the great majority of the apelike beings were not progressing as hoped. Perhaps many of the creatures remained too close to the animal level.

But certain of the Lord's "sons" were not ready to give up on the experiment. They considered the offspring of the daughters of men, the evolving product of their genetic engineering, to be successful in their progress. These offspring only needed more time to eliminate some of the more negative aspects of their primitive nature.

For those UFO researchers who espouse the theory that Earth's humans may well be the "property" of an extraterrestrial species, the biblical Great Flood becomes a symbol of the time when certain alien overlords coldly and dispassionately made the decision to eliminate great numbers of those primitive offshoots of humans. They chose to preserve only the strain that would lead to *Homo sapiens*, modern man from the stars.

The Book of Enoch suggests that Noah himself was a very unusual individual, far different in appearance from his brothers, sisters, and friends. He is described as a person with "a body white as snow, hair white as wool, and eyes that are like the rays of the sun." Passages in the Dead Sea Scrolls reveal that Noah's mother, Bat-Enosh, was suspected of infidelity when the strange baby was born.

The Bible is filled with references to "fiery chariots" traveling across the skies and of prophets being lifted into the heavens. Pillars of illuminated clouds led the Israelites fleeing Egyptian tyranny; Sodom and Gomorrah were destroyed by fire raining down upon the cities; Ezekiel saw a wheel within a wheel and beheld a strange alien creature emerging from an aerial object; "angels" visited tribal leaders, prophets, and kings. (*Art by Bill Oliver*)

In the Book of Enoch, however, Bat-Enosh tells her husband, Lamech, that the child is truly his son. "He is not the child of any stranger, nor of the Watchers, nor of the Sons of Heaven," she insists. The Book of Enoch claimed that the "Watchers" were two hundred fallen angels. Other apocryphal sources state that they were the Georgoroi, other visitors from the heavens.

The Star Gods Demolish Sodom and Gomorrah

The Old Testament also lends credence to the theory that star gods from other worlds may have prompted the destruction of Sodom and Gomorrah. Russian scientist Matest M. Agrest has suggested that the cities were devastated by an ancient nuclear blast.

Moscow's *Literary Gazette* published an account of Dr. Agrest's theories as early as the 1960s, and we were privileged to hear him discuss the matter in person when we lectured together at an Ancient Astronaut Conference. Simply stated, he believed the two cities were fused together under the searing heat of a prepaleolithic atomic explosion.

In Genesis 19:1–28, we are informed that Lot was waiting by the community gate of Sodom when two angels approached him. Some scholars conclude that Lot must have made prior arrangements to meet these heavenly beings. After their meeting, he escorted the entities to his home where they were fed and lodged. Such researchers as Professor Agrest maintain that if these angels were wholly spiritual beings, they would not have been interested in an evening meal, or a bed. Later, when the coarse men of Sodom pound on Lot's door and demand to "know" his visitors sexually, the angels appear to employ some kind of unusual weapon that instantly blinds the Sodomites and blots out their lust.

When Lot is informed by the heavenly representatives that Sodom will soon be destroyed, he chooses to remain in the city. Neither Lot nor other members of his family seem to take the warning seriously. However, when the morning sun rises, the angels urge Lot and his family to flee at once. Those who subscribe to Professor Agrest's theory believe that a nuclear device had been triggered and the "angels" had been assigned to lead Lot and his family away from the blast area.

Perhaps the alien overlords had become concerned with the rampant sin and perversion of their human creations, and they utilized an nuclear bomb as the fastest way of eliminating the transgressors from the "laboratory."

Ancient Hindu Texts Also Tell
of a Great War of Supernatural Beings

Sacred Hindu texts also tell of the wrath of the alien overlords and clearly describe flying machines, advanced technology, and awesome weapons wielded by supernatural beings in ancient times. The Hindu hymns, the *Rig-Veda,* constitute some of the oldest-known religious documents, and tell of the achievements of the Hindu pantheon.

Indra, who became known as the "fort destroyer" because of his exploits in war, was said to travel through the skies in a flying machine, the Vimana. This craft was equipped with weapons capable of destroying a city. These weapons seem to have had an effect like that of laser beams or a nuclear device. Another ancient Indian text, the *Mahabharata,* tells of an attack on an enemy army: "It was as if the elements had been unfurled. The sun spun around in the heavens. The world shuddered in fever, scorched by the terrible heat of this weapon. Elephants burst into flames.... The rivers boiled. Animals crumpled to the ground and died.... Forests collapsed in splintered rows.

Horses and chariots were burned up.… The corpses of the fallen were mutilated by the terrible heat so that they looked other than human."

There are many very old traditions that speak of a war between the forces of light and darkness that raged in humankind's prehistory. Perhaps there were rival extraterrestrial forces that fought for dominance over prehistoric Earth.

Throughout our world there are accounts of desert areas where sand is melted into glass, hill forts where portions of stone walls are vitrified, and the remains of ancient cities where there is destruction by what appears to have been extreme heat—far beyond what could have been created by the torches of primitive human armies. Even conventionally trained archaeologists, when encountering such anomalous finds have admitted that none of these catastrophes could have been caused by volcanoes, lightning, crashing comets, or conflagrations set by prehistoric humans. Some researchers make the point that in this ancient warfare there is little doubt that some of the destructive flying vehicles were piloted by reptilian extraterrestrials.

In Isaiah 30:6 one reads: "From whence come the young and old lion; the viper and fiery flying serpent." Earlier in 14:29 Isaiah writes: "For out of the serpent's root shall come forth a cockatrice, and his fruit shall be a fiery flying serpent."

The Douay Confraternity translation of Isaiah 30:6 calls the flying serpent the "flying basilisk." The Jerusalem Bible refers to the flying serpent of Isaiah 14:19 as a "flying dragon." The New English translation of Isaiah 30:6 speaks of a "venomous flying serpent."

Dr. M. M. Agrest, First Scientist to Suggest that Earth May Have Been Visited by Aliens in Ancient Times

When we were lecturing as featured speakers at the Twenty-fifth Anniversary Conference of the Ancient Astronaut Society held in Las Vegas in 1993, we met Dr. M.M. Agrest of the former Soviet Union. He told us that in 1959—when he became the first scientist to suggest that Earth may have been visited by extraterrestrials in ancient times—he was more highly criticized by his Communist colleagues for having read the Bible and other holy works than for issuing provocative statements about our planet's unknown history.

The diminutive, white-haired, soft-spoken Dr. Agrest pointed out that sacred Hindu texts contain many descriptions of airships appearing in the sky at the "beginning of time." The *Manusola Puma* tells of "an iron thunderbolt," a gigantic messenger of death that reduced the entire race of the Vrishnis and the Andhakas to ashes. The corpses were so burned as to be unrecognizable. Those who survived the initial blast had their hair and nails fall out. Pottery broke without any apparent cause, and the birds turned white. After a few hours all foodstuffs were infected. "The thunderbolt was reduced to fine dust."

In Dr. Agrest's opinion, the above is a poetic, yet explicit, description of an atomic blast with its resultant deadly fallout.

Ancient pictographs suggest the Grays visited nearly every country in the world, including the American Southwest and Peru. (**Art by Ricardo Pustanio**)

Another Hindu text records the destruction of three cities by "a single projectile charged with all the power of the universe. An incandescent column of smoke and flame, as bright as ten thousand suns, rose in all its splendor...."

Prehistoric Cave Paintings of Aliens and Space Craft Found in Remote Area of India

Rajasthan *Times* reported in early 2010 that a group of anthropologists working with hill tribes in a remote area of India made a startling discovery: intricate prehistoric cave paintings depicting aliens and UFO-type craft.

The images were found in the Hoshangabad district of the state of Madhya Pradesh only seventy kilometers from the local administrative centre of Raisen. The caves are hidden deep within dense jungle. A clear image of what might be an alien in a space suit can be seen in one cave painting along with a classical flying saucer-shaped UFO that appears to be either beaming something down or beaming something up, in what might be an ancient UFO abduction scenario. A force-field or trail of some sort is seen at the rear of the UFO. Also visible is another object that might depict a wormhole, explaining how aliens were able to reach Earth. This image may lead UFO enthusiasts to conclude that the images might have been drawn with the involvement of aliens themselves.

Local archaeologist Mr. Wassim Khan has personally seen the images. He claims that the objects and creatures seen in them are totally anomalous and out of character when compared to other, already discovered, examples of prehistoric cave art depicting ancient life in the area. As such, he believes that they might suggest beings from other planets have been interacting with humans since prehistoric times.

Aliens Transported the Eskimos from Central Asia

In the late 1950s a series of excavations conducted in Mongolia, Scandinavia, and Ceylon unearthed artifacts that archaeologists assessed as being very similar to those found among Eskimos. The Smithsonian Institution, sponsors of the study, concluded that ten thousand years ago the people who became Eskimos had inhabited Central Asia, especially the warm, tropical paradise of Ceylon.

One immediately wonders how, in ancient times, people from a veritable Garden of Eden would travel thousands of miles to settle in bleak, northern wastes. One cannot also help wondering *why* they would choose to exchange their lush forests for snow and ice.

The Eskimos themselves, however, have had an answer for generations, an answer that has never received more than a patronizing smile from anthropologists and missionaries. The Eskimo tradition says that they were *deported* to the frozen northland by a flock of giant *metallic* birds.

Communist Officials Banned
Chinese Professor's Work on Alien Stone Discs

In the late 1960s sixteen stone disks were found in a cave in the Bayan-Kara-Ula Mountains on the China-Tibet border. One Chinese expert has theorized that the groove writing found on the disks relates to spaceships that landed there twelve thousand years ago. He believes that the frail tribe of four-foot-tall people who inhabit the area—and who hitherto have defied ethnic classification—are descendants of those space colonizers.

Although official Communist party pronouncements from Peking banned the Chinese professor's paper, Moscow scientists conducted investigations of their own. One leak to the West asserted that hieroglyphics on one of the stone discs told of beings called "Dropas" that came down from the clouds on gliders.

It was also claimed that Russian investigators discovered that the disks contained large amounts

Ancient Indian texts such as the Vedas, including the Mahabharata and the Ramyana, recount the deadly power of such flying craft as the *vimana*. Piloted by warlike "gods," they were capable of destroying cities with aerial bombardments. (*Art by Ricardo Pustanio*)

of cobalt and that they vibrated in an unusual rhythm, as if they carried an electrical charge or were part of an electrical circuit. In nearby caves Soviet archaeologists allegedly found twelve thousand-year-old vestiges of graves containing the remains of beings with huge craniums and underdeveloped skeletons.

Ancient Cities in Peru and Bolivia Were Built by Aliens

Certain excavations indicate that the massive cities located on the high plateaus of Peru and Bolivia were once inhabited by a race of giants who constituted a highly advanced civilization over thirty thousand years ago. Irrigation works and housing accommodations of this ancient culture are built of huge blocks of stone, each weighing as much as forty or fifty tons. The construction of these mammoth, sprawling cities high in the Andes Mountains would quite likely lie beyond the capabilities of modern-day electric turbo-drills or our most rugged machines.

Even those archaeologists who steadfastly refuse to acknowledge the existence of vanished advanced technologies in ancient times are hard-pressed to explain why the known inhabitants of Peru—those Incas who met the Spanish conquistadores—

Evidence of ancient astronauts are found throughout the world, such as in Egyptian hieroglyphs, stone engravings, and in images of various sky gods. (*Art by Bill Oliver*)

had built such an enormous and complex system of paved roads *before* they had invented the wheel.

The Giant Aliens Traversed the Earth

Throughout the Old Testament, the wandering Israelites encountered many gigantic peoples, whom they slew upon "guidance" from the Lord—and with the assistance of the strong sword arms and the sling-shots of such warriors as Joshua and David. In early struggles for "lands of milk and honey," the nomadic tribes of the Middle East, Central Europe, and the Americas might very well have massacred the last of our giant species' ancestors.

On December 2, 1930, the *New York Times* carried an item that told of the discovery of the remains of an apparent race of giants who once lived at Sayopa, Sonora, a mining town three hundred miles south of the Mexican border. A mining engineer, J. E. Coker, said that laborers clearing ranch land near the Yazui River "dug into an old cemetery where bodies of men, averaging eight feet in height, were found buried tier by tier...."

On February 14, 1936, the *New York Times* ran a piece datelined Managua, Nicaragua, which stated that the skeleton of a gigantic man, with the head missing, had been unearthed at El BoQuin, on the Mico River, in the Chontales district. "The ribs are a yard long and four inches wide and the shin bone is too heavy for one man to carry. 'Chontales' is an Indian word, meaning 'wild man'."

The year 1936 must have been a good one in which to find gigantic skeletons. On June 9, the *New York Times* published this item with a Miami, Florida dateline:

> A tale of human skeletons eight feet long imbedded in the sand of an uninhabited little island off Southern Florida was brought here today by three fishermen. They exhibited a piece of one skull containing six teeth.

E. M. Miller, zoologist at the University of Miami, said the mandible was that of a man and was probably several hundred years old. "It is entirely probable that this find might be important," he commented. The men said that the skulls were unusually thick, the jaws protruded, and the eye sockets were high in the head.

Horned Giants in North America

In his book *Forbidden Land*, Robert R. Lyman wrote of two archeological discoveries in Pennsylvania of American Indian giants; in one case the men had the added distinction of horns growing from their heads:

> At Tioga Point ... a short distance from Sayre, in Bradford County, an amazing discovery was made. Dr. G. P. Donehoo, State Historian and a former minister of the Presbyterian Church in Coundersport, together with Prof. A. B. Skinner of the American Investigating Museum, and Prof. W. K. Morehead of Phillips Andover Academy, uncovered an Indian mound. They found the bones of sixty-eight men which were believed to have been buried about the year 1200. The average height of these men was seven feet, while many were much taller. On some of the skulls, two inches above the perfectly formed forehead, were pro-

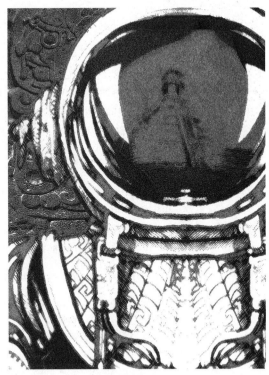

An increasing number of researchers have come to believe that "ancient astronauts" from an extraterrestrial source built the Egyptian and Mayan pyramids. (*Art by Ricardo Pustanio*)

tuberances of bone, evidently horns that had been there since birth. Some of the specimens were sent to the American Investigating Museum....

In December 1886, W. H. Scoville of Andrews Settlement discovered an Indian mound at Ellisburg. When opened, the skeleton of a man was found. It was close to eight feet in length. Trees on and around the mound indicated that burial had been made at least two hundred years before.

Human-like Footprints in the Same Strata as Dinosaurs

Dr. Clifford Burdick spent more than thirty years in a study of what appear to be human-like footprints in geological strata contemporaneous with the age of dinosaurs.

Dr. Burdick first began investigating "footprints in stone" in the early 1950s when the Natural Science Foundation of Los Angeles assigned him to go with four other members to examine strata in and around Glen Rose, Texas, that showed man-tracks as well as dinosaur prints. The committee soon learned that men had been cutting dinosaur and human tracks out of the limestone of the Paluxy River bed near Glen Rose since at least 1938. A Mr. A. Berry gave them an affidavit that stated that in September of that year, he and other men found "many dinosaur tracks, several sabre tooth tiger tracks, and three human tracks" in the river bed.

Dr. Burdick learned that Dr. Roland Bird, field explorer for the American Museum of Natural History of New York City, had also examined the Berry tracks. Describing them in the May 1939 edition of *Natural History* magazine, Bird admitted that he had never seen anything like the tracks, and assessed them as "perfect in every detail." But since the manlike tracks measured sixteen inches from toe to heel, Bird declared that they were too large to be human, although the barefoot tracks did show toes, insteps, and heels in the proper proportions.

Dr. Bird became less enthusiastic about the prints when he saw them in association with dinosaur tracks, because "man did not live in the age of dinosaurs." So his trip would not be a total waste, Dr. Bird dug up several large Brontosaurus tracks and shipped them to the museum.

Humans may not have lived in the age of dinosaurs, but visiting bipedal cosmonauts from other worlds or dimensions may have—and they may well have explored the developing planet Earth.

In his *Footprints in the Sands of Time*, Dr. Burdick describes the find made by Charles Moss of "a sequence of from fifteen to twenty perfect giant barefoot human tracks, each about sixteen inches in length and eight inches in width. The stride was about six feet until the fellow started to run, when the stride lengthened to nine feet, when only the balls of the feet showed, with the toes. Then the series of tracks disappeared into the bank."

Were the Footprints Caused by Alien Visitors or by Evolved Earthly Bipedal Reptilians?

The challenge offered by these remarkable footprints do require a meaningful scientific explanation. Whatever species of creature made these tracks, it was definitely bipedal. The footprints all have about the same length of stride, consistent with that of a man with a sixteen-inch foot. The shapes of the prints are more human-like than those of any other animal known to science.

If the tracks are accepted as being human, then scientists will be forced either to place man back in time to the Cretaceous period or to bring the dinosaur forward to the Pleistocene or Recent period. While orthodox scientists must undergo a weighty struggle to accept either alternative, creationists, who adhere to the Biblical accounts of "giants in the Earth," consider the fossil evidence much less startling.

In referring to the evidence of the Glen Rose tracks, Dr. Burdick stated that the general theory of evolution would be dealt a lethal blow, because the geologic record of human footprints contemporaneous with dinosaur tracks "suggests that simple and complex types of life were coexistent in time past or during geologic ages.... This does not harmonize with the hypothesis that complex types of life evolved from lower or more simple forms.

"Evolution implies that through the geologic ages life has not only become more complex, but has increased in size. If evidence from the man-tracks can be used as a criterion, ancient man was much larger than modern man as an average. This harmonized with most fossil life which was larger than its modern counterpart."

A Prehistoric Bipedal Creature with an Enormous Stride

The April 19, 1883 issue of *Nature* carried an account of an unidentified bipedal creature with a remarkable stride who left human-like footprints. Again, the footprints were found in stratum contemporaneous with prehistoric animals.

The impressions were discovered while building the State Prison near Carson City, Nevada, and were described to the California Academy of Science by Charles Drayton Gibbs, C.E.:

These tracks include footprints of the mammoth or some other animal like it, of some smaller quadrupeds, apparently canine and feline, and of numerous birds. Associated with these are repeated tracks of footsteps, which all who have seen are agreed can be the footsteps of no other animal than man.... The most remarkable circumstance characterizing them is their great size. In one case there are thirteen footprints measuring nineteen inches in length by eight inches wide at the ball, and six inches at the heel. In another case the footprints are twenty-one inches long by seven inches wide. There are others of a smaller size, possibly those of women. One track has fourteen footprints eighteen inches long. The distance between the footprints constituting a "step" varies from three feet three inches to two feet three inches and two feet eight inches, whilst the distance between the consecutive prints of the same foot constituting a "pace" varies from six feet six inches to four feet six inches. In none of the footprints of the deposit are the toes or claws of animals marked.... If confirmed, it is a highly remarkable discovery, especially as connected with the curious intimation so concisely made in the Jewish Scriptures, "And there were giants in those days."

The Mystery of Giant-sized Human Skeletons

Other historical accounts of giant-sized skeletons include the one given by the Abbe Nazari. This venerable cleric noted that a body exhumed in Calabria, Italy, measured eighteen Roman feet. The average weight of the molars was one ounce.

And Hector Boetius, writing in the seventh book of his classic history of Scotland, declares that the bones of a fourteen-foot man, who had been jokingly nicknamed "Little John," were preserved.

In addition to the giant footprints of human-like bipedal creatures discovered throughout the world, there are other indications that a much larger race had inhabited North America in prehistoric times; in Supai Canyon, Arizona, a petroglyph was discovered that depicts a mammoth attacking a man. This primitive work of art was found by Harold T. Wilkins, who determined that the beleaguered man must have been over ten feet tall, according to the perspective employed by the ancient artist. Amerindians in the vicinity stated that the drawings had been made by the "giants of long ago." One finds that particular phrase cropping up repeatedly in this field of research.

> An increasing number of researchers have come to believe that "ancient astronauts" from an extraterrestrial source built the Egyptian and Mayan pyramids.

Do the Cabrera Ica Stones Prove Alien Interference in Earth's Evolutionary Timetable Four Hundred Million Years Ago?

When we called Dr. Javier Cabrera Darquea in his offices in Ica, Peru, in September 1990, he met us in a most gracious manner. A friendly man, impeccably attired in a three-piece suit and tie, complete with pocket handkerchief, he was at first somewhat cautious in explaining his theories.

However, once we had made it understood (through our broken Spanish and the efforts of our interpreter, Sara Lazo) that we would not condemn him for his speculations about a world before our own, he readily told us of his provocative concepts.

Dr. Cabrera's collection of remarkable stones range in size from fist-sized rocks to rather hefty boulders—and they are all covered with weird petroglyphs, or rock engravings. Many of the largest depict bizarre-looking, five-fingered, pointy-nosed people fighting off giant reptiles with what appear to be Viking-style battleaxes.

Dr. Cabrera, a medical doctor who specializes in circulatory ailments by day and conducts archaeological digs by night, claims that he first became interested in the controversial engraved stones of Ica when, in May 1966, a childhood friend, Felix Llosa Romero, presented him with a small specimen that might be used as a paperweight. Intrigued by the notion of what the stone might represent, Dr. Cabrera began to search for the mysterious rocks near Ica on land that his father owned in Sallas. Fortuitously, an earthquake provoked a landslide, which exposed a large deposit of the picture rocks.

Many of his most severe detractors insist that Dr. Cabrera hires Indians to carve the petroglyphs; and to the frustration of his defenders, he refuses to divulge the exact location of the perplexing cache of stones so that impartial experts might examine the site for themselves.

Dr. Cabrera holds fast to his theory that the petroglyphs were fashioned by protohumans who lived near what is now present-day Ica over 230 million years ago, during the Mesozoic Era. Furthermore, he believes that those prehistoric humanoids were genetically engineered by extraterrestrials who first visited Earth as long as 400 million years ago.

In response to questions about supportive data regarding the incredible antiquity that he claims for the stones, Dr. Cabrera produces documents from various geologists and petrologists declaring the stones to be derived from lava flows dating from the Mesozoic Era, characteristic of the zone where they were found.

On April 29, 1975, Josef F. Blumrich, the NASA scientist who developed the design of the Saturn V and participated in the design of *Skylab*, expressed his opinion about Dr. Cabrera's discoveries in these words: "I am deeply impressed by what I have seen here, and I am happy to have found so much direct evidence of what I began to feel and to understand before. There is no doubt in my mind about the authenticity of these stones."

Genetic Engineering of the Protohuman

Several of Dr. Cabrera's most cherished stones portray otherworldly genetic engineers seeking to perfect a progenitor of *Homo sapiens*, using first amphibians, then reptiles, and finally early mammalian life forms to arrive somewhere near where we stand today on the evolutionary ladder.

Dr. Cabrera agrees that the stones represent a most wondrous combination of intellect, and he readily concedes that their existence may stretch the scientific imagination—but he tirelessly and consistently argues that the stones are genuine, not the products of an elaborate hoax.

"We know that Mesozoic rocks date from around 230 million years ago," he told us, smiling as he tapped one of the engraved stones with a metallic pointer. "And although this date of roughly 250,000 years ago is far removed from the accepted date of the appearance of man on Earth, I believe that it is not scientific to dismiss the evidence of these engraved stones which demonstrate the existence of humans in a previous, unknown past."

Medical Marvels Performed by Five-Fingered Surgeons

Some of the most remarkable petroglyphs in Dr. Cabrera's museum appear to depict the five-fingered protohumans conducting brain surgeries, heart transplants, liver operations, and other medical procedures that have no known counterparts. Others portray the protohumans riding horses and pulling wheeled carts and other vehicles.

Strangely enough, the great majority of the petroglyphs show protohumans with no opposing thumbs. Because even the most primitive apes have opposing thumbs—both in the fossil record and in the modern world—Dr. Cabrera seizes upon this anomaly as additional proof that his protohumans predated the apes.

"These entities without opposing thumbs were designed to be as intellectual as their genetic creators," he explained. "They were genetically engineered to be reflective people-scientists, philosophers, artists of the highest order. Those entities who have opposing thumbs were genetically engineered to be the workers, to be assigned to common labor tasks."

The ancient maxim to be "wise as serpents" might have originated from humankind's ancestral memories of a time when benevolent reptilian culture bearers taught people the rudiments of science and the arts. (*Art by Ricardo Pustanio*)

The Genetic Engineers and Their "Reflective Humans" Flee Earth

It is Dr. Cabrera's further contention that great numbers of the prehistoric humanoids were destroyed by a cataclysmic disaster shortly after they had completed many important achievements, including the pyramids of Egypt. The super-science of the extraterrestrially spawned and programmed "reflective humans" enabled them to recognize the signs of approaching cataclysms and to make preparations to return to their ancestral planetary home.

"All that remained on Earth," he explained, "were the majority of the people of lower intellectual capabilities than the reflective, scientific types. The workers and laborers with opposing thumbs were left behind.

"After the great cataclysm, which gave final form to the continents of Earth, a few of these prototypical humans survived; and those few, after a long and difficult path through time and across continents, became the remote, but direct, ancestors of modern humans," Dr. Cabrera commented.

"I think that the fossilized bones, skulls, and skeletons that anthropologists have and continue to find, are, if not these same men, then their descendants, which explains why every day older and older human fossils are being found."

Native Americans Have a Strong Tradition of the Sky People's Visitations

The Native American tribes have a rich and varied tradition of an interaction with the "sky people," or "star people," that is as extensive as fairy lore among the natives of the British Isles. Amerindians, for example, have been aware of "magic circles" left by the star people, just as their British counterparts know of "fairy rings," and the modern UFO investigator examines strange, scorched "circles" left in farmers' fields and meadows.

There are certain risks involved in ascribing "ancient astronaut" motifs to petroglyphs (stone carvings) and pictographs (stone paintings). These may have been inspired by an artistic flight of fancy rather than an alien spaceship. "Domed space helmets" often turn out to be representations of horned headdresses, exaggerated in size to denote a chief's prowess and acumen or a medicine man's power and skill. However, some petroglyphs and pictographs are worthy of examination as a record of Amerindian interaction with the "star people," the extraterrestrial visitors.

Thirty miles northeast of Price, Utah, is the beginning of Nine Mile Canyon, one of the most unusual canyons in the United States. Prior to 1100 C.E, the Fremont culture occupied the canyon, and the records they left in the form of petroglyphs and pictographs comprise the heaviest concentration of rock art in the world today.

The Fremont people developed their own art style, which, interestingly, was typified by horned, trapezoidal-bodied, human-like "anthropomorphs." Were these creatures somehow symbolic of nature spirits? Or did they truly represent visitations by beings decidedly different from the other tribal neighbors of the Fremont people?

In one dramatic petroglyph in Nine Mile Canyon, one may view an unusual depiction of one of these horned anthropomorphic figures (an ancient astronaut enthusiast might say, "antenna-spouting"). In this instance, the creature is standing before a row of upraised human hands, which seem to imply awe, reverence, or fear. To the anthropomorph's left, there is a disc-like object. To the left of the disc left, there is an upside-down anthropomorph faintly etched in the stone.

RICARDO PUSTANIO 2010

The "feathered serpent" Quetzalcoatl, the Mesoamerican deity and culture bearer, may actually have been a reptilian alien who arrived in a spaceship thousands of years ago. (*Art by Ricardo Pustanio*)

Flying Saucer Pictograph Found in Grotto
near Christina Lake, British Columbia

UFO researcher John Magor describes a most intriguing "flying object" pictograph that is located in a natural grotto near Christina Lake, British Columbia. The drawing depicts a white disc with black winglike protuberances, hovering over four figures who appear to have bent their knees in an attitude of reverence. Squiggly lines, perhaps suggestive of rays of light, emanate from the top of the object. Longer, more irregular lines, possibly portraying smoke or fire energy, extend from the bottom of the disc.

Magor points out that although it was a practice of these primitive artists to depict exactly what they saw, they were no doubt limited by their inability to draw in depth. In order to compensate for this lack of perception, the artist may have tilted the object to indicate its discoid appearance. At the same time, he probably retained the winglike rim outline, which no doubt impressed him.

Despite the limitations of painting on rock, Magor feels that the unknown artist showed great skill in conveying the idea of something extraordinary in the air. "Because of its comparative size," Magor says, "it is obviously not a bird. And just as obviously because of its shape (perhaps that is why he retained the winged look) it is not the sun."

Magor feels that the touch of real brilliance on the part of the Amerindian artist lay in the use of the four human figures. "Not only do they lend size and height to the object, but by their suggestion of a worshipful attitude, they create the impression that this was an event of rare spiritual importance."

Perhaps, though, the pictograph is not all that old. Could the Amerindian artist have been depicting his tribe's reaction to the first terrestrial aircraft that paid them a low, over-flight visitation? Magor answers this question by seeking out reference volumes, which date the pictographs in the area as sometime around 1860.

There is another impressive similarity between tribal pictographs and "chariots of the gods" in the cone-shaped, rocketlike objects discovered near Cayuse Creek and Kootenay Lake. Quoting from Alan Jay's article in the *Columbian*:

> Yet another rock painting at Cayuse Creek shows what is clearly a cone-shaped rocket with smoke and flame trailing behind it. And it contains a single humanoid figure apparently holding on to the inner wall of the rocket.

> A pictograph near Kootenay Lake depicts the same kind of enclosed vehicle, also containing a single humanoid figure. The drawing also shows sections resembling the firing stages of a modern lunar rocket and two appendages closely resembling the retractable landing "legs" of a lunar space module.

Aliens: Deceivers or Deliverers?

The November 1993 issue of the *Journal of Abnormal Psychology* contains the results of a study conducted by psychologists at Carleton University of Ottawa, Canada, which states that people who think that they have seen a UFO or a space alien are just as intelligent and psychologically healthy as other people. According to the authors of the report, "Our findings clearly contradict the previously held notions that people who seemingly had bizarre experiences, such as missing time and communicating with aliens, have wild imaginations and are easily swayed into believing the unbelievable."

Dr. Nicholas P. Spanos, who led the study and administered a battery of psychological tests to individuals who claimed to have undergone a wide variety of UFO experiences, said that such people were not at all "off the wall." In fact, he affirmed, "They tend to be white-collar, relatively well-educated representatives of the middle class."

Such comfortable reassurances from academia that one may experience a UFO encounter and not be diagnosed as crazy will come as no small comfort to many students of the phenomenon. Many of them have suddenly found themselves in the midst of a maelstrom of bizarre and unexplainable occurrences. Our own research led us years ago to accept the various manifestations of the UFO controversy as evidence that we humans are part of a larger community of intelligences. And they are a far more complex hierarchy of powers and principalities, a potentially richer universe of interrelated species—both physical and nonphysical—than we could ever imagine.

Supernormal Entities from a Magic Kingdom

In many old traditions, especially in the British Isles and Scandinavia, the fairy folk were supernormal entities that were said to inhabit a magical kingdom beneath the surface of the earth. Fairies were considered to be similar to humans, but they were known to be something more than mere mortals. Reluctant to resign them to the realm of spirit, ancient texts declared fairies to be "of a middle nature, betwixt man and angel."

One factor that has been consistent in fairy lore is a particular annoying attribute of the "middle folk." They seem to revel in meddling in human affairs, sometimes doing good, other times causing trouble.

In tale after tale we learn that the fairies have the power to enchant humans and to take advantage of them. It was often thought that they could cast a spell on a comely lass or lad and have their way with them. From time to time they would whisk a mortal off to the fairy kingdom, where an entirely different system of time seemed to exist. At their nastiest, fairies often kidnapped human children.

On the other side of this bizarre coin, it was said that fairies could materialize to help a poor farmer harvest his crop before a storm or aid a browbeaten housemaid clean up a soiled kitchen. If they so chose, fairies could use their ability to foresee the future as a way to guide humans. They could stand by at the birth of favored human children and guide and protect them for the rest of their lives.

Although some aliens may claim to be angels that have come to deliver humankind from disease, war, and social ills, some may have ulterior motives to deceive and enslave us. (**Art by Ricardo Pustanio**)

As we have seen throughout this book, aliens have been reported to hypnotize or "enchant" men and women in order to make earthlings more malleable. There have been many reports in which people claim that the UFO beings had sexual intercourse with them in what would appear to be an attempt to create a hybrid species. There are numerous cases in which it seems that men, women, and children were abducted and taken aboard UFOs. And aliens have been reported working closely with scientists, doctors, and inventors—aiding, advising, and perhaps sharing their advanced technology.

Fairies, elves, grays, angels—do UFO intelligences resemble any of these? We may not yet have any idea what the UFO intelligences really look like. We suspect they may have the ability to influence the human mind telepathically and project what appear to be three-dimensional constructs. If so, the actual image perceived may depend in large part upon the preconceptions, fears, and hopes that witnesses may have about extraterrestrial or supernatural life or energy forms.

Aliens Accomplish Miracle Healings

Many times, it would seem, aliens assume the role of benevolent healers.

Dr. John Salter Jr., chair of American Indian Studies at the University of North Dakota, and his twenty-three-year-old son, John III, say that they were abducted by humanoid aliens while driving on central Wisconsin's Highway 14 on March 20, 1988.

After being moved off the highway by an unseen force, the Salters found themselves in the company of numerous entities about four to four-and-one-half feet tall, with thin bodies and limbs and comparatively large heads and large slanted eyes. A much taller humanoid guided the father and son through the woods to an alien spacecraft. Communication between the earthlings and the aliens was telepathic.

The senior Salter recalled receiving a couple of injections from the aliens while they were in a brightly lighted room aboard the UFO, but he has nothing negative to say about the results. "My immunity is heightened," he told nuclear physicist and UFO investigator Dr. Franklin R. Ruehl. "Cuts and scratches now clot immediately and heal rapidly. My head hair, fingernails, and toenails now grow at three times the normal rate. Some of my age spots have disappeared, and the wrinkles in my face have faded.

"Also, hair has developed all over my arms, legs, stomach, and chest, which previously had been almost hairless," added the university professor, who was fifty-five at the time of his alien encounter. "For the first time in my life, my beard is so thick and dark that I have five o'clock shadow."

Although John III did not experience the same physical changes as his father, he characterized the alien encounter as "the most extraordinary event of my life."

Dr. John Salter is not alone in reaping of positive benefits from a close encounter with UFO aliens. Over the past fifty years of UFO research, we have gathered other such intriguing accounts of "miracle cures" attributed to aliens. The following are some examples.

A Toothless 80-Year-Old Grows New Teeth after Abduction

In 1973 a toothless, eighty-year-old farmer from Brazil was pleasantly surprised to find that he had new teeth growing in his jaws within two months after his abduction by four small men in a silver, circular-shaped craft.

Healed of an Infection in Her Hand

In 1983 a farmwife from Illinois injured her hand while helping her husband load livestock for sale. Within a few days she developed an infection that necessitated a visit to the family doctor. Although the doctor gave her antibiotics, he said the swollen hand would require several weeks to heal.

The following morning she was walking in a field near their house when she saw a luminous, egg-shaped object that seemed to approach her from the sky. The next thing she knew, she was in a brilliantly lighted room filled with high-tech equipment. Three small creatures surrounded her, each wearing a surgical mask.

The farmwife lapsed into unconsciousness. When she awakened back in the field, she discovered that her hand was completely healed.

Beam of Light Shrinks an Enlarged Liver

A native of Finland had an enlarged liver ever since his birth, and in 1983 he had been told by his doctors that it could never become normal.

Two years later, as he was skiing down a remote slope, he was caught in a white beam of light from an egg-shaped UFO.

Disturbed because he had no recollection of time that had passed during his strange encounter, the man went to a doctor and underwent a complete physical examination. During this examination the doctors found that his liver had been reduced to a normal size.

> He remembered being examined by smallish humanoids who worked on his legs with great care and with emanations of love and kindness.

UFO Entities Restore the Use of His Legs

One evening in 1986 wheelchair-bound Richard T. was enjoying the solitude of a beach near La Jolla, California, when a one hundred-foot long, torpedo-shaped UFO appeared from out of nowhere to hover above him.

Later Richard said that he felt as if he had entered into a light trance, and somehow both he and his wheelchair were lifted into the spacecraft. He remembered being examined by smallish humanoids who worked on his legs with great care and with emanations of love and kindness. Hours later, when an acquaintance spotted him in a more remote part of the beach and came to check on him, Richard remembers waking up with a tingling feeling in his legs. Before his friend's startled eyes, Richard stood up from his wheelchair and managed a few awkward steps before he felt a powerful energy surge flow through him.

Richard still walks with a pronounced limp, but he has no complaints. As far as he is concerned, benevolent beings from "somewhere out there" enabled him to walk again.

The World Is More Than It Seems

"The world is more than it seems," declares Peter Kor in his article, "Myth, Reality, and Flying Saucers" (*Flying Saucers*, October 1967). The classic spiritual epics and the enigma of the UFO all tell of forces and powers beyond the human order of things. "The Realm" that exists beyond the limits of man's awareness, Kor asserts, is "forever active, intruding into the human environment in the form of various transhuman phenomena.

"Historically, encounters with these phenomena generate mystical movements. The movements, conditioned by cultural circumstances, fashion mythological frameworks. The myths help to translate the activity of 'The Realm' into human terms."

Kor cautions us that perhaps humankind has always sought a conventional, physical place for their gods and angels and, now, for the UFOs and the aliens. Contemporary physics is steadily demonstrating that, in the words of Sir James Jeans, "There are other than material ingredients in the world which, although equally as real as the material ones, do not make a direct appeal to our senses. In effect, these ingredients reside outside our space-time experience."

These immaterial elements, which cannot be apprehended by mortal senses include electromagnetic fields, radiations of various energies and intensities (i.e., infrared, ultraviolet, microwave), and space itself. Even that which we conceive of as an absolute vacuum has properties that can be mathematically defined. The so-called physical world, Kor reminds us, is merely that which our limited sensory measuring equipment has defined as reality.

The gods and the UFOs, then, "represent an activity which is normally invisible—an activity which is so subtle with respect to the intense stimuli of our physical world that it registers only in Man's deepest subconscious. The so-called 'collective unconscious' of modern psychology is nothing less than a subliminal doorway to that immaterial domain which the physicists are so busily mapping on a different level!

"The 'gods' and UFOs may visit us more often than we suspect. For they exist only a frequency-difference away in the background of our consciousness, waiting for some triggering condition to bring them into focus. That triggering condition necessarily has something to do with the psychological state of the 'observer'—which is precisely why the 'gods' seem to be selective in their choice of contact, and why subjective elements invariably condition mystical and flying saucer experiences."

Aliens Wish to Teach Us That We Are Not Alone

It is of extreme importance to the UFO missionaries at this time to convince the people of Earth as dramatically as possible that they are not alone in the universe, that there are other planes of existence and other planets in the solar system that bear intelligent life.

According to the UFO contactees, the space beings look upon this as a solar system problem and one that requires a fully integrated, interdimensional, and interplanetary ruling. They say that there is a Hierarchal Board of the solar system, which evolves slowly, methodically, and enjoyably, with thousands of rulers on many grades, who participate in solar system government.

A Time of Transition, Not Doomsday, Awaits Humankind

The UFO contactees have been accused of belonging to the grim category of "Doomsday Prophets." In actuality, those men and women who claim communication with space beings speak more often of a Time of Transition than of a Judgment Day. There is far more contactee channeling regarding the "raising of Earth's vibratory rate" than there are admonitions of repentance before the Apocalypse.

Perhaps, as some contactees have related, there have been many physical group "Judgment Days." Each old age ends with a period of purgation that purifies those who survive the transitional period so that they might become better prepared for the emerging New Age. According to several contactees, these periodic Judgment Days occur approximately every two thousand years. If this is so, then it truly is no coincidence that hundreds of men and women are now claiming contact with entities and intelligences in the same kind of spiritual unrest that characterized the Apostolic era.

Another two thousand years have run their course on some great cosmic calendar, and another transitional "Judgment Day" is at hand. It is once again time for young men and women to see visions, and old men and women to talk to God in their dreams. The transition from one age to another requires a higher level of consciousness than the previous epoch.

It may well be, then, that there is an internal consistency in the ageless messages of revelation. This may at first lead one to consider that the Mind of God might really be some supercosmic transmitter that has endlessly broadcasted the same message to all of the world's saints, mystics, and other inspired men and women of history. But if the prophets of 3000 B.C.E., the apostles of 30 C.E., and the UFO contactees of 2011 have all been receiving essentially the same messages, then might we not conclude that the very repetition of a basic program of spiritual and physical survival may be evidence of the vital relevancy and the universality of certain cosmic truths?

The Essential Messages of the Space Beings

What constitutes the essential messages and admonitions received by the contactees? The space beings are visiting our planet in this present period for two primary reasons. First, the space beings have grave concern about our indiscriminate use and experimentation with atomic energy, particularly in building instruments of war. The space beings' history shows that another planet in our solar system blew itself up when such devices were used in warfare.

This event, listed in the Bible (Exodus 7) during the time that the children of Israel were in Egypt, caused the rivers to turn to blood and the fish to die; due to the falling radioactive dust of a planet that once existed between Mars and Jupiter and which is now seen by our astronomers as the Asteroid Belt. The Bible again refers to this event in Isaiah 4:12: "How art thou fallen from heaven, O Lucifer, Son of the morning?" The planet Lucifer (known to our space brothers as Maldek) was then the morning star of Earth.

For the protection of our people and their people the space beings have interfered with certain nuclear experiments being conducted by both the United States and other countries, which they indicate would have blown up the entire planet, thereby affecting vital elements in the universe if carried out.

Second, our entire solar system is in transit into a new area of space, a new density. This is changing the vibratory rate of the nucleus of every atom in our planet, raising it to a higher frequency. The space brothers point out that all life on our planet—plant and animal and the consciousness of man—is also being affected by the lifting in the vibratory rate that is now upon us.

This change is a particular problem for humans of Earth because they have fallen behind in their spiritual evolution and are not ready for the events that are at hand. For this reason, our brothers and sisters from other worlds have emphasized that every man and woman on this planet must make a choice and that this choice is being presented to them in terms they understand regardless of their special condition in life.

Each and every one of us must decide within the depths of our consciousness, in terms that are real to us, whether we wish to give ourselves in service to our Creator and to our fellow humans, or whether we wish to continue in the ways common to most Earth people and seek the service of ourselves.

Although those who teach the alien gospel of the Space Brothers and Sisters may be sincere in their beliefs, wisdom dictates that one should exercise caution before embracing alleged cosmic requests to surrender one's powers of discernment. (*Art by Ricardo Pustanio*)

Our brothers and sisters from space have stated that they have been sent by the will of our Infinite Creator to help those who choose the path of love and service to raise themselves to a new consciousness. This is the level of consciousness that very soon will be necessary for humans if they are to continue to live and evolve with this planet as it enters fully into the new area of space, which will bring about the period many have called the New Age.

Humans Must Achieve Transitions to Higher Dimension

Aleuti Francesca, "telethought channeler" of the Solar Light Center, has relayed messages from entities that are concerned with humans' abilities to step up their personal frequency. According to "Voltra of Venus":

You will still be yourselves; you will still function as human beings with all the sense perceptions of human beings. But you will be of a more rarefied construction. Transition from physical to fourth etheric substance will take place.

Many of us with whom you speak are of this composition in our bodies and therein has lain much of the misunderstanding among your people as to our nature. We can and do lower the frequency rate of our bodies to become visible to the physical retina of your eyes. We are *physical-etheric*, whereas you are *physical-dense*.

The composition of all matter on your planet is rapidly reaching a point wherein it will either become a finer etherialized structure or will disintegrate....

Our purpose at this time is to educate those of you who will work with us at and after the time of the frequency change.... We once more stress that you will not become ... discarnate beings: you merely step up one level and gain so much by so doing. Your sense perceptions, rather than being eliminated, will only become heightened and an awareness of all that which is of beauty, of love, of eternal nature will become as one with you.

Studies Find Other Possibilities
that Explain Abduction and Contactee Phenomena

In spite of studies that demonstrate the basic psychological soundness of UFO percipients, a good number of psychiatrists and psychologists maintain that there are other explanations for tales of alien abductions and sexual assaults by exploitative extraterrestrials. During an early peak of the abduction "fad" that had been set in motion largely by Whitley Strieber's bestseller *Communion* and Budd Hopkins' *Intruders*, an article by anthropologist Dr. Elizabeth Bird in the April 1989 issue of *Psychology Today* sought to explore other possibilities that might explain the abductees' trauma.

Critical of UFO researchers who use hypnosis to help alleged abductees recall their harrowing experiences, Dr. Bird states that "while hypnosis may elicit remarkably detailed accounts, they are no more accurate than normal memories. Indeed, suggestible people produce notably less accurate accounts under hypnosis."

Perhaps most relevant to the discussion at hand was Dr. Bird's citing of the comparisons made by folklorist Bill Ellis, assistant professor of English and American Studies at Pennsylvania State University. He saw parallels between UFO abduction experiences and the accounts of the phenomenon known in Newfoundland culture as the Old Hag: "A person who is relaxed but apparently awake suddenly finds himself paralyzed in the presence of some nonhuman entity. Often, the sensation is accompanied by terrifying hallucinations—of shuffling sounds, of humanoid figures with prominent eyes. Often the figure even sits on the victim's chest, causing a choking sensation."

Most of the contactees claim an initial physical contact with a space brother or sister, but the operable mechanics of the experience seem very reminiscent of what we have come to see in spiritualism as the medium works with a spirit guide or a control from the "other side." In spiritualistic or mediumistic channeling, the psychic sensitive goes into various depths of the trance state and requests information of the spirit guide, and contacts various spirits of deceased human personalities. In a similar way, the experience of the contactee often seems like going into some state of trance and channeling information from space beings.

George King, George Van Tassel, Gloria Lee, George Hunt Williamson, and several other contactees had been members of psychic development groups before they met their benevolent space being—a fact that many skeptics have attempted to use to discredit their contacts with alleged aliens.

Aliens—Beyond Real and Unreal

In his thought-provoking book, *A Mile to Midsummer*, Michael Talbot refers to such phenomena as UFOs, appearances of the Virgin Mary, fairies, and so forth, as "protean-psychoid." They are "protean" because they are all part of the same chameleon-like phenomenon that changes to react to the belief structures of the time. They are "psychoid" in that they are a paraphysical phenomenon and are related to the psychological state of the observer.

Talbot feels that it is the subjective and paraphysical aspect of UFOs that sheds the most light on their nature. If UFOs appeared to be totally a physical phenomenon, Talbot points out, it would be easier to deal with them as extraterrestrial or even ultra-terrestrial.

"In any case," Talbot says, "three facts remain: (1) People are experiencing UFO phenomena and contacts. (2) The phenomenon strongly suggests an 'objective' nature. (3) The phenomenon also strongly suggests a 'subjective' nature.

"The fact that we have not been able to resolve the conflict between their subjective and objective nature indicates that perhaps the only conflict is in our assumptions concerning experience. Not only must UFOs be considered in both their subjective and objective light; that is, as an 'omnijective' phenomenon, but the categories of 'real' and 'unreal' become meaningless."

For an earlier work, we asked Michael Talbot to prepare an essay, "UFOs: Beyond Real and Unreal," which outlined his theory of "protean-psychoid" phenomena and from which we now quote selected portions:

The subjective nature of protean-psychoid phenomenon and their "mythic origins" can be summed up in seven major points. They are as follows:

1. The "perpetrators" of protean-psychoid phenomena reveal many mythological characteristics.

The men in black bear a marked resemblance to the Brothers of the Shadow in Eastern mysticism. The Virgin of Guadalupe, which miraculously appeared upon the tilma of Juan Diego, stands on the horns of a crescent moon, just as Isis was depicted by the ancient Egyptians as standing upon the horns of a crescent.

However, the most revealing "mythic" giveaway in UFO contactee cases is the delivering of the "cosmic gospel." Many UFO entity encounters (like appearances of

Tim Beckley loaned the authors this photo, which is legendary in the UFO field. It is the first—and to this date only—photo of an MIB.

the Virgin) have the characteristics of divine revelation. The entities' avowed purpose for appearing to the witness is to convey a sort of heavenly message or "orgalogue." In this sense, some protean-psychoid phenomena differ insignificantly from the Pymander of Hermes to the Ahura Mazda of Zoroaster.

2. Protean-pyschoid phenomena have been with us throughout our written history, and most assuredly before. In essence, the phenomenon is changeless—the old gods reappearing in new clothing.

Although it has been suspected by some investigators that UFOs are carrying on a secret war against humanity and that they are possibly after our "orgone" or life energy, this seems unlikely. The mere fact that the "Trojan horse" of protean-psychoid phenomena appears to have been in our midst for centuries and still hasn't revealed its long-awaited coup d'etat indicates perhaps that no coup was ever planned.

In fact, this sort of heaven-hell conflict—the devil after our souls and the aliens after our orgone—has much subtler psychological implications. If we can no longer believe in heavenly hierarchies, extraterrestrial hierarchies will suffice.

3. Protean-psychoid phenomena reveal no overall malevolence or benevolence.

Almost every investigator will agree that UFO entities do not behave in a predictable manner. At times they seem hostile towards humanity; at times they are filled with good will. They follow the rationale of an entity in a dream, and at any moment their nature can fluctuate.

4. Protean-psychoid entities are concerned with sustaining our belief.

In *Apparitions and Precognition* Aniela Jaffe states:

"There is a widespread German legend expressing in an image the independence and dependence of ghosts in relation to humans. The legend says that ghosts have no breath of their own, but breathe and speak with the breath of man (breath = pneuma = spirit). Therefore man himself must have 'the first and the last word'; otherwise the ghost would talk him to death."

This same sort of dependence upon the belief or breath of man can be found in various protean-psychoid phenomena. The entities involved in the great airships of the 1890s, for instance, invariably appeared to reputable witnesses such as well-known lawyers, judges, and senators. The fact that various cosmic gospels or orgalogues are amended or changed with the times also seems to reflect this dependence/independence. All sorts of stratagems and ploys are used—automatic writing ... "spirit guides," "trance communications," "Virgins and Christ figures," and "evangelizing extraterrestrials."

Whether the Virgin of Fatima is imploring her witnesses to "pray, pray much and believe in me," or the UFO entity is preaching the cosmic gospel, the message remains the same. Our desire to find meaning in the universe is reflected in the protean-psychoid entities' concern with sustaining our belief.

5. Protean-psychoid occurrences are filled with archetypal contents.

A close study of the phenomenon reveals many "psychological leitmotifs".

For instance, in Tarot iconography the angel Temperance stands with one foot on land and one foot in the water. This is interpreted as a metaphoric bridging between the symbol for consciousness, the land, and the symbol for the unconscious, the water. Interestingly, just as Leonardo da Vinci painted his Madonna and Child with St. Anne with one foot upon land and one foot in the water, the Virgin of LaSalette appeared to the two children Maximin and Melanie with one foot upon the land and one foot in the water.

Another archetype that occurs frequently in UFO contactee cases is the "androgyne." In many ancient traditions "angelic personages" are depicted as androgynous or bisexual. The Pymander of Hermes preached that a state of spiritual bisexuality (that is, the Hermetic androgyne of alchemical texts) was necessary for contacting higher powers. UFO contactees often describe the entities as being androgynous in appearance.

6. Protean-psychoid occurrences reveal collective anxieties.

For instance, the well-known "interrupted journey" of Betty and Barney Hill is one of the most convincing cases in favor of the "objective" nature of UFOs, except for the fact that the commander of the UFO was dressed like a Nazi. This and other "subjective" giveaways make little sense when the phenomenon is viewed in a strictly objective light.

Similarly, in the 1890s, the rash of Asians in airships was almost a precursor of the Buck Rogers comic strip projection of a world of the future in which the "Asians" and their airships take over the world. There are numerous cases of UFO contactees experiencing encounters that possess every hallmark of being extraterrestrial, except for the fact that the alleged extraterrestrials pose as Germans, Asians, Russians, and so forth. Such flaws in the totally objective explanation seem to indicate the presence of something collectively psychological.

7. Protean-psychoid phenomena are dreamlike.

> According to tradition, a few moments passed in "fairy land" might be equivalent to several hours of normal time.

In *Steps to an Ecology of Mind*, Gregory Bateson points out several aspects of dreams vs. animal behavior that bear a striking similarity to many UFO encounters. Briefly, they both deal in opposites, they both have no tenses, they both have no "not," and they both work by metaphor.

Protean-psychoid phenomenon most strongly resembles dreams in its usage of metaphors and mythic imagery. When the Virgin of LaSalette sits with one foot on land and one foot in the water, the phenomenon is apparently dealing with a metaphor. When the men in black boast the insignia of the triangle with the eye (an almost universal symbol for the eye of god, the third eye, or second sight), the phenomenon is again dealing with a metaphor.

Protean-psychoid occurences also have no tenses. They are suspended in time, much as dream reality is suspended in time ... or what might be called the Rip Van Winkle effect, common in both encounters with fairies and UFO entities.

According to tradition, a few moments passed in "fairy land" might be equivalent to several hours of normal time. Betty and Barney Hill's loss of several hours in their interrupted journey differs little from tales of a traveler falling asleep on an elfin mound. In both visits to the fairy realm and visits aboard flying saucers, time takes on what can only be called a dreamlike sense of timelessness.

In the 1960s, when Warminster, England, was in the midst of a UFO flap and barraged by poltergeist activity, the Warminster "thing" expressed a sentiment of nonhostility in a distinctly dreamlike manner. In early May, 1965, a young woman and her three children had been playing by a stream. A gust of wind suddenly blew up with incredible intensity and power. Its deafening wail convinced the mother immediately that it was the "thing" (the name the citizens of Warminster had given their local poltergeist). It swept her three children off their feet.

In *The Warminster Mystery* Arthur Shuttlewood states: "The boy felt his face rubbed into tough grass above the pathway, neck clamped in a viselike grip. He fought for breath. The seven-year-old was knocked flat on her back, spread-eagled nearby. Pressure was exerted on her forehead and upper lungs in chilling extent; the ground vibrated under her."

To her horror the mother saw her three-year-old sprawling down the bank.

She was about to be drowned by the invisible force.

Suddenly, unseen hands caught the tiny girl as she tottered on the edge of the bank and lifted her away from danger. The child floated gently away from the bank and back onto the footpath.

It was as if the Warminster "thing" was trying to correct its bad reputation.

In summation, the panorama of protean-psychoid phenomena reveals a very "subjective" quality. A large portion of UFO encounters are distinctly paraphysical and related to the psychology of humanity in some strange and possibly collective sense. Many UFO orgalogues appear to be evolved by the same psychological motivations that create both myth and religion; indeed, as notables such as Carl Jung have suggested, UFOs are a modern-day myth in the making.

However, as I have indicated, UFOs also reveal a physical and "objective" aspect. This is the much-cherished structure that the UFOlogical establishment concentrates upon.

UFOs can be tracked on radar; Virgins give their witnesses "real" roses; the men in black make "real" telephone calls; and UFOs and their occupants leave footprints and burnt circles in deserted fields. As I have just shown, the "objective" explanation for UFOs does not explain their paraphysical nature. Similarly, the "folie à deux," or shared hallucination, simply does not explain their physical nature. A "new view" of UFOs must take both aspects into account.

Many of the ancient Sky Gods demanded worship and sacrifice from their followers. Others taught humans to acknowledge only a benevolent universal force. Certain UFO investigators fear that some people today could be deceived by the godlike powers that an advanced extraterrestrial civilization would exhibit and find themselves worshipping a new advent of "Saviors from the Skies." (Art by *Ricardo Pustanio*)

Humanity's emotional need for a cohesive mythic structure, in one sense, generates the UFO phenomenon. The belief that we generate UFOs still entails the categories of real and unreal. In dealing with the concept of omnijectivity, the belief that reality is plastic or ideational must necessarily transcend this notion as well.

Beyond real and unreal, lies an absolute elsewhere that is presently being realized by the two branches of science most concerned with consciousness and reality. In the study of human behavior and quantum mechanics, three "new views" are materializing that will radically affect our position and role in the universe. These are:

- Consciousness and reality are continuum.
- UFOs are part of our "self-reference cosmology."
- All possible realities "exist" in an indefinite number of universes.

Are UFOs The "Grand Deception"?

Norio Hayakawa, author of *UFOs—The Grand Deception and the New World Order* (1993) warns of a global UFO conspiracy linked to a "sinister occult force" that is manufacturing a "Grand Deception."

Hayakawa believes that this worldwide plot is designed to "stage a counterfeit extraterrestrial contact-landing to simulate an extraterrestrial 'threat' of invasion in order to urgently and ultimately bring about a delusive New World Order." In his view the actual guiding force behind the staged global event may be "highly intelligent, but deceptive, ultradimensional negative entities conveniently materializing in disguise as extraterrestrial 'aliens'."

Such a shocking series of global events will place millions of people in "an absolute stupor for weeks," Hayakawa states, during which time "an ingeniously executed, extremely effective 'multi-leveled' mind control program will be activated to calm the stunned populace."

At this point in the scenario envisioned by Hayakawa, while the leadership of the New World Order struggles to assume complete control over the global populace, a "dynamic, charismatic leader" will arise out of the European community (by then known as the United States of Europe), appear in a worldwide television broadcast, and offer a brilliant explanation to sedate the public. Hayakawa believes that this dynamic leader is currently residing somewhere in Western Europe, just waiting to begin his 'official mission'."

Apparently—from what we can ascertain from ancient records—angels and/or aliens were far more open in their terrestrial comings and goings in less technologically sophisticated times. In fact, according to Roman Catholic scholar Matthew Fox, the number one cosmological question in the Mediterranean area in the first century C.E. was whether or not angels were friends or foes.

Today we have accounts of UFO beings making accurate prophecies, performing miraculous healings, and offering benevolent guidance on the one hand, and participating in cruel abductions, conducting genetic experiments, and plotting our planet's destruction or enslavement on the other. UFO researchers in 2011 must ask: Are the UFO entities friends or foes?

The "great UFO cover-up," the "grand UFO deception," has been going on since the first intellectual stirrings of human civilization. Whether the UFOnauts are extraterrestrial or multidimensional beings, they appear to have had our planet under surveillance for millions of years—and they have chosen to conduct their activities in secret for reasons that remain as yet undetermined by the general populace of Earth.

Sometimes it seems as though we are dealing only with multidimensional tricksters who deliberately seek to confuse us and to mislead us concerning their true purpose on our planet. In other instances there appear to be dramatic clues indicating that we are dealing with paraphysical entities that may have always co-existed with us and are somehow participating with us in some grand evolutionary design. Still other fragments of evidence would indicate that we are in occasional contact with superscientists from "somewhere out there" who created our species and many of the other lifeforms on this planet, and who continually hover over their handiwork, shepherding their biological field project.

Sometimes it has seemed to us as though the intelligence behind the UFO controversy has always been provoking humankind into higher spirals of intellectual and technological maturity, guiding us to mental and spiritual awareness, tugging our entire species into the future.

Throughout our history it seems that the UFO intelligence has always been there to show us that the impossible can be accomplished, that the rules of physics are made to be broken. In decades past they have demonstrated the possibility of air flight, radio communication, television, and a host of technological extensions of all of our senses. Today their baffling maneuvers might be demonstrating the possibility of dematerialization, invisibility, and rematerialization. Perhaps they are somehow showing us that the best way of dealing with space travel over megadistances is not to travel through space but to avoid it altogether.

However, an annoying question remains: Has this been for our benefit ... or theirs?

Do We Face a Final War of the Worlds?

Recently, we received an email from Dr. Alfred Lambremont Webre that informed us that a "hyperdimensional UFO in overflight approximately one mile southeast of the White House in Washington, D.C., appears to have fired a ray of light or directed energy beam in the vicinity of the White House.

"The incident, which occurred on July 20, 2010 at 3:18 A.M., was photographed in high-speed, high definition photographs by Wilbur 'Will' Allen, a former White House employee and Air Force One engineer under U.S. presidents Ronald Reagan, George H.W. Bush, and Bill Clinton. Mr. Allen is also a talented professional photographer for major motion picture studios such as Warner Brothers."

According to Allen: "On July 20, 2010 … a relatively short distance from the White House, I imaged a slow-moving UFO pulse through the sky, and then [observed the UFO] fire an energy beam which extended from it."

On July 26, 2010, Allen sent a video to Dr. Webre, and added: "In the ten frames of images [in the video] are other objects … in pursuit of another object … [In] the ten frames the objects mentioned all are perhaps in a tactical posture…. Ironically, it echoes the hyperdimensional UFOs on July 16, 1952/July 16, 2002."

Dr. Webre wonders if the UFO that seemingly fired some kind of plasma beam near the White House was engaged in "(1) horseplay or creative signaling by a hyperdimensional UFO from an interdimensional intelligent source as a consciousness awakener to the public at large … (2) a false flag event from a U.S. or other black ops vehicle; or (3) a 'socially destabilizing' event."

Throughout this book, we have posed the question of whether aliens occasionally engage in "horseplay" with us citizens of Earth or if their actions are deliberately intended to "socially destabilize" us. As we have stated in certain chapters, there are some researchers who are concerned that secret societies on Earth are in league with the aliens.

Have the World's Leaders Made a Deal with Demonic Aliens?

A few years ago, when President George H.W. Bush began speaking about a New World Order to beef up his campaign for re-election, evangelist Pat Robertson, who was briefly a presidential candidate, passionately spoke out, saying that "new world order" was actually a code for a secret group that sought to replace Christian society with a worldwide atheistic socialist dictatorship. He went on to state that aliens will reveal themselves as demonic entities that delight in doing Satan's work. The planet will be in torment and turmoil until Jesus returns to deal the final blow to the minions of evil.

Bush, the conspiracy buffs charged, was a member of one of the world's most devilish and powerful secret societies: the Order of Skull and Bones. What was more, according to these same buffs, Bush was linked to the Bilderbergers and the Trilateral Commission, dangerous elitist organizations.

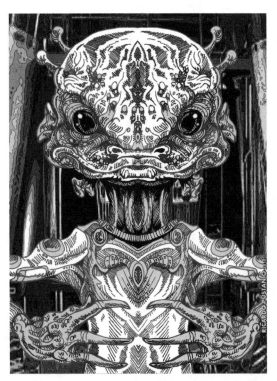

While humans ponder the mysterious strangers in the skies, could alien warlords be biding their time to launch a war of the worlds? (*Art by Ricardo Pustanio*)

At about the same time that President Bush's alleged secret affiliations were being exposed, a number of fundamentalist evangelists began to take their first real notice of the UFO phenomenon and saw the mysterious aerial objects as the "signs in the skies" referred to in apocalyptic literature and in the biblical book of Revelation. It was a short leap for many evangelists to begin to blend accounts of UFOs with stories of the secret societies of top U.S. government officials, politicians, corporate chairmen, international bankers, and many others who sought to bring about the dreaded "New World Order."

According to the proponents of this cosmic conspiracy, when President Reagan gave his famous "alien invasion" speech to the entire United Nations General Assembly in September of 1987, he had already secretly advised representatives of the 176 member nations that the leaders of their respective governments must meet the demands of the technologically superior extraterrestrials or be destroyed.

Furthermore, a plan has been devised by the aliens and the world leaders: shortly before the year 2012, a carefully staged "alien invasion" will convince the masses of the world that a real-life *Independence Day*-type attack is about to begin. People of all nations will believe their leaders who will say that the aliens are a benevolent species and that unconditional surrender to them will be beneficial.

Immediately following the "surrender" to the aliens, the leaders will form a One World Government, a New World Order, thus fulfilling biblical prophecies about a return to the days of Babylon.

New French Report Says UFOs Are Definitely Alien Craft

A new French report released on May 31, 2010 concluded that UFOs are definitely real and quite possibly of extraterrestrial origin. France is the only country where the collection of Unidentified Aerospace Phenomena and its scientific study have been assigned since 1977 to a civilian official organization, the CNES (National Center for Space Studies, the French space agency) through the GEIPAN study group. Our longtime friend and fellow UFO researcher J. Antonio Huneeus, editor of *Open Minds* magazine, translated the French report into English for the August 16, 2010 edition.

Referring to the interaction of UFOs and the conventional aircraft of Earth's air forces, the study group states, "The behavior of these devices during encounters with fighter jets or interceptors—some have participated in real swirling battles in the U.S.—suggests they are controlled, guided or led by particularly sophisticated automation.... [None] of the many interceptions which have been made against them, in the United States for example, have been able to overcome one of these devices."

After outlining a number of characteristics exhibited by UFOs, such as "remarkable accelerations of the craft right after a stationary mode," Huneeus goes on to state that the GEIPAN group concluded: "We feel that we must reject the thesis of a terrestrial origin for all the observations made since World War Two. Indeed, if a nation of the world had been able to secretly develop such an armada of exotic craft, like those observed for more than half a century, the means of analysis and strategic logistics available would have permitted their rapid identification. The illegal overflights which they have been guilty of conducting could constitute a casus belli [cause for war]."

The French study group agrees with so many UFO researchers that what appears to be alien craft "do not seem to belong to an identifiable terrestrial technology at the times when they were observed." And some researchers have made note of the fact that even if the aliens have violated the air space of several nations, and given "cause for war," they have not yet launched an all-out invasion. And, after all these years, why would they do so now?

Chinese Astronomer Declares Extraterrestrials Are Visiting Earth in a Research and Development Mission

Dr. Michael E. Salla informed us that in a speech at a science forum held in the city of Guangzhou on August 23, 2010, "a veteran Chinese astronomer with almost forty years of experience claimed that some UFOs are extraterrestrial spacecraft."

Salla went on to write: "Professor Wang Sichao is a planetary astronomer at the Purple Hills Observatory of the Chinese Academy of Sciences. Based on scientific observations of UFOs over his thirty-nine-year career, he has concluded that some UFOs are powered by antigravity devices." A summary of Wang's speech was reported by a number of Chinese newspapers including the influential *People's Daily Online*. Wang's key points were:

- Some extraterrestrials are visiting Earth in a research and development capacity, and are therefore friendly enough to begin cooperation and mutual exchanges.
- These UFOs are probes manned by robots.
- The craft travel at eighty percent the speed of light.
- These unidentified craft have been seen by the observatory many times at between 150 and 1,500 kilometers above Earth.
- It seems likely that the aliens might use nuclear fusion to propel their craft.
- These craft use Earth's gravity to maneuver and stay aloft.

Wang Sichao told the Chinese newspapers that he disagreed with Stephen Hawkings' recent comments regarding the dangers of making contact with extraterrestrials. In Wang's opinion, the aliens that he has monitored appear peaceful and require nothing materially from us, because they can create their own materials using their advanced technology.

However, Wang stressed, in the event that these aliens do not come in peace, "They are not gods ... they have flaws, and thus we can defend ourselves."

Discovering Above-Top Secret Documents

Some UFO researchers, who have served in the armed services, state that they have seen certain Above-Top Secret documents and witnessed alien activity that suggests a very sinister and sobering reality. If, indeed, there is to be a "war of the worlds," Earth will be very much the desperately overmatched underdog.

Bob Dean, a retired Army Command sergeant major, told us during an exclusive interview in the early 1990s that he became involved in the UFO field "through the back door." A veteran of twenty-seven years in the Army, Dean was Infantry Unit commander in combat in Korea, Laos, Cambodia, and North Vietnam. He was also with Special Forces attached to an outfit in South Vietnam known as MAC-V-SOG, or Military Advisory Command Vietnam Special Operations Group.

In the summer of 1963, Bob Dean was assigned as an intelligence analyst to Supreme Headquarters, Allied Powers, Europe (SHAPE) in Paris. One of the requirements for Bob's assignment was a top-secret clearance, the highest given at the North Atlantic Treaty Organization (NATO).

Dean, a master sergeant, was assigned to the Operations Division-Supreme Headquarters Operation Center. Dean learned that this was basically a "war room." He explained that "SHAPE was the Central Headquarters Command for all Allied forces throughout Europe—from the northern border of Norway clear down to the southern border of Turkey. All the NATO countries with military forces had representation—[fifteen countries] at the Paris headquarters."

Soon after beginning his new assignment, Dean became aware of a secret UFO study that had begun in 1961. This study had been triggered by an incident in February 1961 involving about thirty to fifty enormously large, circular, disc-shaped, metallic objects flying in formation over Central Europe. Similar circular objects had been sighted many times before, especially throughout the late 1950s. On this particular occasion, however, these UFOs almost caused the Soviets and the Allies to start shooting at each other—each suspecting the other of invading their territory.

These craft would mysteriously appear flying out of the Eastern zone, over Soviet Russia and the Warsaw Pact nations. Flying very high and extremely fast, these objects were apparently under intelligent control. Not only were they physically visible, but they were tracked by every radar installation and station in the area.

For some time the Allied forces and the Soviets each believed the mysterious new type of craft to be some military breakthrough by the other side. Dean explained to us that many military personnel at that time did not have a background on UFO information.

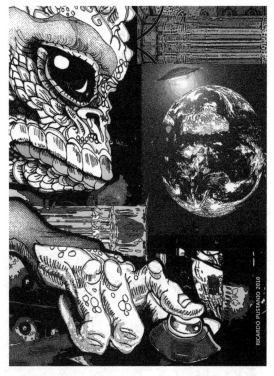

Ever since Orson Welles frightened North America with his "War of the Worlds" radio broadcast on October 30, 1938, a large portion of the human psyche has feared that some alien overlord has his finger on the button that would bring about mass destruction. **(Art by Ricardo Pustanio)**

A huge circular, metallic disc thirty meters wide crashed near the Baltic Sea in a little German town called Timmensdorfer, which was in the British zone. "The Brits put a perimeter around it and somehow figured out how to get inside the disc craft where they found *twelve little alien bodies*," Dean told us. "The beings were very strange looking. They were smallish and gray in color. All of the information I have ever run across indicates that no other UFOs have ever crashed other than those manned by the little gray entities."

Continuing his account of the alien corpses, Dean said that one of the things about the autopsy report that intrigued him the most was the determination that all twelve bodies were absolutely identical. "In fact, they looked so much alike that when they were lined up on the autopsy tables one of the doctors commented that they looked as if they were cut from the same pattern," Dean said.

The autopsy report revealed that the extraterrestrial entities were apparently "living systems." Each one possessed a lung system, a heart system, a blood circulatory

Small towns and villages would not escape the alien invasion. (*Art by Ricardo Pustanio*)

system—yet they had no indication of being either male or female. There was no reproductive system.

The Deputy Supreme Allied Commander at the time was British Air Marshall Sir Thomas Pike. He was the equivalent of a five-star ranking general and was directly under Bob Dean's boss, four-star American Army General Lyman Lemnitzer, who later became Supreme Allied Commander in Europe (SACEUR). Sir Thomas Pike had tried repeatedly to get information from both London and Washington, D.C., on UFOs. "Every time he tried, he was completely stonewalled," Dean said. Finally, Air Marshall Pike decided to order an in-house (NATO/ SHAPE) study to assess the situation involving these incidents of the circular discs and related matter. The study, known first as *An Assessment*, was later named *The Assessment: An Evaluation of a Possible Military Threat to Allied Forces in Europe*.

"By speaking out about what I saw in the Assessment, I'm violating my National Security oath," Dean admitted. "I'm not an unpatriotic soldier by any means. I've never divulged any of my security secrets—but the implications of everything I saw in the Assessment has caused me for the past thirty-some years to wrestle seriously with my conscience until I'm at the point where I am now. I feel that not only the people in this country—but the people on the entire planet—are being lied to. And I mean that there is a massive cover-up.

"In this particular matter, I feel that not only does everybody have the *right* to know—but to use a military term—they have a *need* to know what is really going on. The Cold War is over now, but so many things have developed—and come through my own research since the Assessment—that show me that this is a deep, ongoing matter about which everyone needs to know the truth."

The knowledge that Bob Dean gained in reviewing the Assessment over and over prompted him to develop an obsession with studying and researching history, philosophy, religion, anthropology, archaeology—everything that might fill in the pieces and add to his understanding of the evolutionary, and various other, implications of UFOs and extraterrestrials on our planet.

The Assessment: An Evaluation of a Possible Military Threat to Allied Forces in Europe

According to Dean, The Assessment, the main document, is an inch and a half thick. The Annex, or the support information to the Assessment material, is over eight inches thick. The official report took three years to complete, and there were only fifteen copies published—one copy for each of the NATO allied countries. Dean told us that the study ended in 1964 with the following conclusions drawn by the researchers involved:

1. Our planet Earth and its inhabitants, the human race, have been under extensive, detailed, in-depth surveillance.

2. This surveillance or monitoring has been going on for a long time—for hundreds or even thousands of years—and was a possible threat to our Allied forces.

3. However, because of the high level of demonstrated technology, whoever or whatever is behind these circular, metallic discs must not be a real danger. By now, if these beings were hostile or malevolent, they could have easily destroyed us. We have virtually *no defense against their advanced technology*. We can only conclude that they must be watching or observing us.

4. There seems to be enough evidence that some kind of a procedure or process—some "plan" on the part of the aliens—seems to be developing. The sightings, landings, and abductions appear to be growing. The visitors seem to be *increasing contact with us in the gradual unfolding of a plan in which they eventually interact with Earth's inhabitants*.

Four alien races are visiting Earth:

Group 1: Referred to as the "grays," biological androids or clones

Group 2: Humanoids or human-like in appearance

Dr. J. Allen Hynek made a cameo appearance in a scene from Steven Spielberg's *Close Encounters of the Third Kind,* for which he served as scientific advisor.

Group 3: Taller grays—about six feet tall with human-like heads, but without the big wrap-around eyes

Group 4: Reptilian in appearance—some kind of reptilian connection, with lizardlike skin and eyes with vertical pupils

The researchers determined that if these four groups weren't working together, they at least seemed to be cognizant of what the other groups were doing and were aware of one another's presence.

Dean remembered that what really intrigued the generals the most was that one of the extraterrestrial species looked human. They looked so much like we do, in fact, that if one of them sat next to anyone of us in a restaurant, dressed as we are, no one could ever possibly tell the difference. That fact so affected the generals that they wondered if these extraterrestrials could be walking the halls of SHAPE—or anywhere else for that matter—totally undetected.

There seemed to be no conclusion in the Assessment about the place of origin of any of the four extraterrestrial groups. Dean did not recall seeing any reference at all to planets, galaxies, or areas of the universe where these extraterrestrial species came from. Nor did Dean recall reading that there was any kind of "official" contact or interaction between any of the alien species with any of our government officials or military officers.

Working with the "Galileo of UFO Research"

Newsweek hailed Dr. J. Allen Hynek as "the Galileo of UFO research" and the world's ranking expert on the science of Ufology. *Time* said that, "he was the scientific community's most outspoken investigator of UFOs." Dr. Hynek, as we have noted before in this book, served in the official capacity of scientific advisor for Project Bluebook, the twenty-year top-secret United States Air Force study of unidentified flying objects.

Dr. Hynek, who was responsible for categorizing UFO sightings (sightings of the first kind, second kind, third kind, and fourth kind), was technical advisor to Steven Spielberg's *Close Encounters of the Third Kind.* Dr. Hynek and Spielberg corresponded frequently, and the movie was based on composite cases from the files.

Dr. Hynek was so dedicated to trying to find an answer to the UFO controversy that when the Air Force's Bluebook study was terminated, he founded the nonprofit Center for UFO Studies based in Evanston, Illinois, and in the last few years of his life, with the promise of funding, he founded a second office, the Center for UFO Research, in Scottsdale, Arizona.

Dr. Hynek investigated over eighty thousand reports of unidentified flying objects from over 161 countries worldwide. Sherry was honored to have worked closely with Dr. Hynek during the last years of his life, serving as his publicist. Through her work with Dr. Hynek, Sherry was privy to much information and obtained great insight into the incredible and often bizarre field of Ufology. Any doubt she might have had as to the possibility of conspiracies and cover-ups was quickly put to rest.

Hynek told Sherry that the UFO reports that came into Project Bluebook that seemed to have the most substantial information were taken from his hands. As a matter of fact, he was sometimes ordered to concoct cover-up stories to steer the public away from any UFO suspicions. In some cases, such as the famous "Michigan" sighting, such a flurry of facts had already leaked out to the press that Dr. Hynek was ordered to go on record at a press conference to tell the public that all the strange occurrences were attributed to "swamp gas."

Of the eighty thousand cases in Bluebook files, over ten thousand were "actual UFOs." Or in other words, phenomena that could not be explained away to the public as weather balloons, aircraft, or natural phenomenon—they were true unidentified flying objects.

> Dr. Hynek was impressed by the caliber and sincerity of the people who reported the cases he investigated firsthand.

Dr. Hynek was impressed by the caliber and sincerity of the people who reported the cases he investigated firsthand: "Worldwide, people who report UFOs have *definitely* seen something, but the fact remains that more people do not report what they have seen or experienced for fear of ridicule."

But Dr. Hynek was always quick to point out that with the information available, no one has been able to prove whether or not the sightings were alien spaceships or some unknown earthly phenomenon. "The sightings and descriptions display a strange universal consistency that adds to the mystery," Hynek told Sherry.

She recalls that she witnessed hundreds of drawings made of aliens by witnesses from nearly every country on the planet. By far, the majority of the drawings were of the dark-eyed, large-headed gray, regardless of where the sighting originated. She reminds the reader that this was before the day of Internet and instant international communication.

Canadian Government Declares UFOs "Top Secret"

In a Canadian Department of Transport memo dated November 21, 1950, Wilbert B. Smith, senior radio engineer, forwarded a proposal to the controller of telecommunications suggesting certain formal studies, for example, the use of Earth's own magnetic field as a possible energy source. The subject of UFOs came up in Smith's memo. According to Smith, he made discreet enquiries through the Canadian Embassy staff in Washington, D.C., who were able to obtain the following information:

a. The matter is the most highly classified subject in the U.S. Government, rating even higher than the H-bomb.

b. Flying saucers exist.

c. Their modus operandi is unknown but concentrated effort is being made by a small group headed by Vannevar Bush.

d. The entire matter is considered by the U.S. authorities to be of tremendous significance.

The Smith memo itself was classified top secret.

A Sudden Flurry of Strong UFO Reports in the Mid-1980s

In 1985 a mysterious sequence of events unfolded in Dr. Hynek's life that raise some puzzling questions: the promised funding for the new center did not materialize, and top officials promised nuts-and-bolts proof about alien bodies and volumes of classified, and top-secret files that were to be released into his hands.

Once Dr. Hynek was in Scottsdale, Arizona, intense discussions ensued between Hynek and military and government officials at the highest level. Hynek asked Sherry to join him in some of the conference calls, and she soon learned that the calls also involved representatives from a number of foreign countries. These discussions had to do with the likelihood of the imminent release of the largest batch of classified top-secret files regarding unidentified flying objects that had ever been amassed. If they were released, they would be given to none other than Dr. Hynek himself. Because of Hynek's high standing and reputation, he was considered the person most worthy of this trust.

Promises were made to Hynek, telling him he could "view" the alleged bodies of aliens and extraterrestrial spacecraft whenever he was ready. After his intensive pursuit of this goal over the years, Hynek wondered: Why now? Sherry said that this offer made Dr. Hynek very nervous. He didn't know if he was being set up to be made the fool or if this was at last the real thing.

At the same time, a great deal of information was coming to Hynek regarding several UFO cases on videotape, as well as thousands of substantial witness accounts. Dr. Hynek asked Sherry to view and discuss the videos sent to him and to help him interview witnesses. One of these cases is referred to as the Westchester or Hudson Valley incident, which took place in upstate New York. The other was the Woodbridge/Rendlesham Forest incident, more commonly referred to as the "Bentwaters Case," which occurred over a shared U.S. and U.K. NATO base boundary in Great Britain.

The Hudson Valley Sightings

There were so many reports in the Hudson Valley sightings that investigators could only concentrate on the "close encounters" where the object came within five hundred feet of the witnesses. A conservative estimate was that over five thousand people saw a triangular or boomerang-shaped object as big as a football field. Sometimes the object shot straight up and disappeared instantly. At times it hovered. Sometimes it shot down beams of light. At other times, there were different colored lights or, often, no lights at all. Some people reported telepathic communication from the object, some were terrorized; others heard a voice saying, "Don't be afraid." As the reports were more closely investigated, many people claimed to have "missing time" or reported abductions. There were so many sightings that the Taconic Parkway and switchboards were jammed for many hours, endangering emergency vehicles, calls, and reports.

The FAA denied any craft in the area and said there were absolutely no clearances given for landing or take-off at the time of all the activity. So, what was it? The Stealth Bomber became public knowledge not too long after that; but no jet could duplicate the strange behavior of the unidentified craft, and certainly the Stealth Bomber is not the size of a football field.

If aliens from an advanced extraterrestrial civilization were warlike and bent on conquering Earth, it is likely that they would have terrible weapons of mass annihilation at their disposal, such as death rays. (*Art by Ricardo Pustanio*)

The Remarkable Woodbridge-
Bentwaters Case

The Woodbridge-Bentwaters case is perhaps one of the most documented close encounters between the military and extraterrestrial intelligence to this date.

In 1980, on Christmas Day, just after 9:45 P.M. (Greenwich Mean Time), several mysterious lights were sighted in the skies of northern Europe. The lights passed from northern Portugal toward Germany and the southern English counties of Kent and Sussex.

Radar base operators tracked an unidentified flying object that crossed the coast and "landed" near the Rendlesham Forest, where tracking was lost. They phoned facilities in the area to see if any other radar site had tracked the object. They discovered that the object had been seen from the Bentwaters and Woodbridge bases, and these bases were told to retain their radar records for future investigation.

Intelligence officers from the USAF visited the base a few days later, taking these records and telling the staff at the Royal Air Force Station Watton that a UFO had come down near Woodbridge Air Base and had been observed by senior military personnel.

Author-researcher Jenny Randles spoke with the radar officer at the base who was present when the intelligence officers visited, and removed the evidence. One radar officer told Jenny that the altitude from which the UFO descended was far above any aircraft's ceiling—so high, in fact, that he could not tell her the altitude because it would reveal details of the radar's limitations, strictly prohibited under Britain's Official Secrets Act.

In spite of "official denials" on the behalf of both the U.S. and British governments, over twenty-five eyewitnesses were found and interviewed. Many of the first-hand witnesses experienced ongoing problems dealing with what happened to them during those nights in 1980 and were troubled with nightmares and anxiety.

Several tapes regarding the Bentwaters landing case were sent to Dr. Hynek in 1985 and 1986. Sherry said that within these tapes there was discussion that there had been actual photographs, recordings, and video of the UFO and its alien occupants, as well as soil samples, radioactive readings, etc. All the main evidence had been taken from the officers on duty by an unmarked black jet, to be whisked away for "official analysis."

Public Pressure Demands Investigation of UFO Reports

There were so many credible witnesses to these cases that the government was pressured by attorneys and citizens for answers. It appeared that the Freedom of Information Act and the dedication of those in pursuit of truth was about to pay off—but it didn't happen. Instead, some disruptive events took place, and Dr. Hynek died of a brain tumor in April 1986.

Whether or not a conspiracy of sorts had taken place to set up Dr. Hynek with false promises and throw him off guard—as many suspect—cannot be proven. Perhaps these "officials" were legitimate and sincere, but the intended release of documents never took place because of the untimely death of Dr. Hynek.

In the meantime, in 1983 *Omni* magazine had run an article describing a small craft moving in and out of the trees at Bentwaters and escaping the pursuing USAF. Several witnesses came forward shortly after the publication of the article. One of these witnesses was Larry Warren. In 1983 Warren approached Citizens against UFO Secrecy (CAUS).

CAUS received a copy of the report submitted by the Bentwaters base to the British Ministry of Defense in London, after using Warren's testimony and the American Freedom of Information Act.

The Freedom of Information Act Gains Official Statement Regarding the Woodbridge-Bentwaters Case

The document was signed by Lieutenant Colonel Charles Halt, then deputy base commander (later promoted to full base commander). Halt and Don Moreland confirmed the strange encounter was real—as did the Defense Ministry in London—after hiding it for several years.

Copy of Lieutenant Colonel Halt's letter, dated 13 January 1981:

SUBJECT: Unexplained Lights
TO: RAF/CC

1. Early in the morning of 27 Dec 1980 (approximately 0300L), two USAF security police patrolmen saw unusual lights outside the back gate at RAF Woodbridge. Thinking an aircraft might have crashed or been forced down, they called for permission to go outside the gate to investigate. The on-duty flight chief responded and allowed three patrolmen to proceed on foot. The individuals reported seeing a strange glowing object in the forest. The object was described as being metallic in appearance and triangular in shape, approximately two to three meters across the base and approximately two meters high. It illuminated the entire forest with a white light. The object itself had a pulsing red light on top and a bank of blue lights underneath. The object was hovering or on legs. As the patrolmen approached the object, it maneuvered through the trees and disappeared. At this time the animals on a nearby farm went into a frenzy. The object was briefly sighted approximately an hour later near the back gate.

2. The next day, three depressions 1 1/2" deep and 7" in diameter were found where the object had been sighted on the ground. The following night (29 December 1980) the area was checked for radiation. Beta/gamma readings of 0.1 milliroentgens were recorded with peak readings in the three depressions and near the center of the triangle formed by the depressions. A nearby tree had moderate (.05–.07) readings on the side of the tree toward the depressions.

3. Later in the night a red sunlike light was seen through the trees. It moved about and pulsed. At one point it appeared to throw off glowing particles and then broke into five separate white objects that moved rapidly in sharp angular movements and displayed red, green and blue lights. The objects to the north remained in the sky for an hour or more. The object to the south was visible for two or three hours and beamed down a stream of light from time to time. Numerous individuals, including the undersigned, witnessed the activities in paragraphs 2 and 3.

[signed]
CHARLES I. HALT, Lt. Col., USAF
Deputy Base Commander

This document clearly establishes that there was more than one significant encounter and further clarifies some areas that caused confusion surrounding the testimonies. Although the sightings of alien beings suspended or floating in a beam of light coming from the craft are not mentioned, the document reveals the following.

A team of security police had gone into the forest in response to sightings of an object crashing (in the early hours of December 26, 1980) and pursued a strange craft through the trees before it outran them and left.

RICARDO PUSTANIO 20-10

Some researchers are convinced that we could soon see massive motherships looming over all the major cities of the world. (*Art by Ricardo Pustanio*)

Ground traces (three indentations in the earth forming a triangle) and excess radiation found inside these holes were discovered at dawn by investigating officers.

The additional witness statements tied in with Warren's testimony. A team of USAF personnel in the woods the next night, December 27, investigated the strange lights that created a disturbance among local farm animals, also witnessed by Halt.

In October 1983 banner headlines in Britain's top-selling newspaper, the *News of the World*, reverberated around the world and provoked questions of the British Parliament. Ralph Noyes, though retired at the time of the Bentwaters incident, headed the British department and received UFO data from air bases and police. Noyes made the statement, "We now have evidence, I blush to say of my own Ministry of Defense, that they have lied about this matter—they have covered it up."

Lord Peter Hill-Norton, a brilliant military tactician and former head of Britain's naval fleet, was briefed about the UFO case by respected investigator-author Tim Good. (See Tim Good's excellent book *Above Top Secret*.) Insisting that this incident *did* indeed have defense significance, Lord Hill-Norton pursued answers, but finding out only that "the Ministry of Defense was content that the Rendlesham [Forest] incident was of no defense significance, because whatever was witnessed was not apparently hostile."

We question, however, how so many high officials can be so certain that whatever was witnessed was not hostile. Several of the witnesses said they saw high-ranking officers working side by side with "the aliens" to repair the UFO. If this is so, then it seems there was previous contact with the aliens in order to be so sure they were nonthreatening. Could the "secret deal" with the aliens be true?

The UFO Invasion of Mexico

Beginning in July of 1991, thousands of UFOs have been sighted over Mexico City. Some believe this to be the largest, most-documented UFO sighting in history—the beginning of an alien invasion predicted more than three thousand years ago by Mayan shamans.

The sightings began on July 11, 1991. On that date there was a total eclipse of the sun and Mexico City was one of the best places to view the eclipse. Thousands of people had their home video cameras pointed at the sky, poised to capture the total eclipse on film.

It's not surprising that modern scientists and astronomers know the exact date that a total eclipse will occur. What might seem surprising to some though, is that, three thousand years ago, ancient scientists predicted the exact date for this eclipse in the Mayan calendar. They also predicted that on the date of the eclipse, a new Age of Enlightenment would begin. It is referred to as the "Prophecy of the Sixth Sun."

Archaeologist Armando Nicolau, of the University of Mexico, says, "The legend of the sixth sun, the eclipse that occurred on July 11, 1991, signified what the legend refers to as the opening of knowledge. The sixth sun legend speaks of precisely the very moment of its arrival."

Hundreds of home video cameras—aimed to capture the eclipse—got something quite unexpected on their cameras—UFOs. Reports of more than 110 video films were verified to contain footage of unexplained, unidentified craft. Thousands of people from all walks of life recorded wave after wave of UFOs hovering in the sky. One of the first to come forward was a respected dentist. He felt that people actually seemed to like the idea of UFOs and these appearances could actually benefit Earth. Once the first videotapes were publicly released in Mexico City, more and more people came forward with their videos, sightings, and photographs.

Many television cameras and crews, reporters, and investigators from all over the world have launched their own invasion of Mexico City to evaluate the mass sightings. It is believed by many that the UFOs could be alien spacecraft from an unknown planet or from a civilization that visited here long ago and these entities are returning at this time—according to the Mayan prophecies—from their enlightened civilization to enlighten ours.

Who or What Are the Aliens—and What Do They Want with Us?

We have endeavored throughout this book to reveal a record of alien-human interaction from prehistoric times to the present day. Many questions exist.

Do they come in peace, to guide us to higher levels of technology and a higher standard of living?

Or do they come as conquerors, to use and to exploit us as they wish?

Did they long ago come to Earth to become our "gods," our creators, through genetic engineering, and continue to be concerned about our well being?

Or did they come in prehistoric times merely to begin a biological experiment and have now become impatient and uncertain of its value to the workings of the universe?

Do they feel love and concern for us as a developing species, their "little brothers and sisters" to nurture and to oversee our path into our future?

Or are they devoid of feelings and quite indifferent to our overall welfare and future, perhaps regarding us as no more than primitive animals—and at times, as livestock?

Do they come from some as yet undiscovered planet in a galaxy beyond our science?

Or do they come from another dimension of time and space, an alternate universe that may be completely incomprehensible to our present definition of reality?

Although we have spent a good portion of the past fifty years researching the alien/UFO mystery, we freely confess that we have no final answers. Alas, we have only more questions than when we began.

Each reader will have to discover a definition of the aliens that best satisfies himself or herself. Our final caution would be that people do not invite the experience of an alien encounter until they first answer the question: Are the aliens deliverers or deceivers?

BIBLIOGRAPHY

Adamski, George. *Behind the Flying Saucer Mystery (Flying Saucers Farewell)*. New York: Paperback Library, 1967.

Adler, Bill, ed. *Letters to the Air Force on UFOs*. New York: Dell Publishing, 1967.

Asimov, Isaac. *Is Anyone There?* New York: Ace Books, 1967.

Barker, Gray. *They Knew Too Much about Flying Saucers*. New Brunswick, NJ: Inner Light, 1992.

Beckley, Timothy Green. *Subterranean Worlds*. New Brunswick, NJ: Inner Light, 1992.

———— *Jimi Hendrix: Starchild*. New Brunswick, NJ: Inner Light, 1992.

————. *The American Indian UFO-Starseed Connection*. New Brunswick, NJ: Inner Light, 1992.

————. *The UFO Silencers*. New Brunswick, NJ: Inner Light, 1990.

Binder, Otto. *What We Really Know about Flying Saucers*. New York: Fawcett, 1967.

————. *Flying Saucers Are Watching Us*. New York: Tower, 1968.

Bowen, Charles, ed. *The Humanoids*. Chicago: Henry Regnery, 1969.

Brownell, Winfield S. *UFOs Key to Earth's Destiny*. Lytle Creek, CA: Legion of Light, 1980.

Bryant, Alice, and Linda Seeback. *Healing Shattered Reality: Understanding Contactee Trauma*. Tigard, OR: Wild Flower Press, 1991.

Chester, Keith. *Strange Company: Military Encounters with UFOs in World War II*. San Antonio, TX: Anomalist Books, 2007.

Clark, Jerome. *The UFO Book: Encyclopedia of the Extraterrestrial*. Canton, MI: Visible Ink Press, 1997.

Clark, Jerome, and Loren Coleman. *The Unidentified*. New York: Warner Paperback Library, 1975.

Clarke, Arthur C. *Voices from the Sky*. New York: Harper and Row, 1965.

Commander X. *Nikola Tesla-Free Energy and the White Dove*. New Brunswick, NJ: Inner Light, 1992.

———. *Ultimate Deception*. New Brunswick, NJ: Inner Light, 1992.

———. *Underground Alien Bases*. New Brunswick, NJ: Inner Light, 1991.

Condon, Edward U., project director. *The Scientific Study of Unidentified Flying Objects*. New York: Bantam Books, 1969.

Constable, Trevor James. *The Cosmic Pulse of Life*. Santa Ana, CA: Merlin Press, 1976.

Cooper, Milton William. *Behold a Pale Horse*. Sedona, AZ: Light Technology, 1991.

Crystal, Ellen. *Silent Invasion*. New York: Paragon House, 1991.

David, Jay, ed. *The Flying Saucer Reader*. New York: New American Library, 1967.

Dennett, Preston. *UFOs Over New York: A True History of Extraterrestrial Encounters in the Empire State*. Atglen, PA: Schiffer Publishing, 2008.

Downing, Barry H. *The Bible and Flying Saucers*. New York: Avon, 1970.

Drake, W. Raymond. *Gods and Spacemen in the Ancient West*. New York: New American Library, 1974.

Edwards, Frank. *Flying Saucers—Serious Business*. New York: Lyle Stuart, 1966.

———. *Flying Saucers Here and Now*. New York: Lyle Stuart, 1967.

Erskine, Allen Louis. *Why Are They Watching Us?* New York: Tower, 1967.

Esoteric Publications. *I Am Ishcomar*. Cottonwood, AZ: Esoteric Publications, 1978.

Evans, Hilary. *Visions, Apparitions, Alien Visitors*. Wellingborough, Northhampshire, England: Aquarian Press, 1984.

Fawcett, George D. *Quarter Century of Studies of UFOs in Florida, North Carolina and Tennessee*. Mt. Airy, NC: Pioneer Printing, 1975.

Fawcett, Lawrence, and Barry J. Greenwood. *Clear Intent: The Government Coverup of the UFO Experience*. Englewood Cliffs, NJ: Prentice Hall, 1984.

Fry, Daniel. *The White Sands Incident*. Madison, WI: Horus House, 1992.

———. *To Men of Earth*. Elsinore, CA: El Cariso, 1973.

Fuller, John. *Incident at Exeter*. New York: G. P. Putnam, 1966.

———. *Aliens in the Sky*. New York: Putnam/Berkley, 1969.

Good, Timothy. *Above Top Secret—The Worldwide UFO Coverup*. New York: William Morrow, 1988.

———. *Alien Contact: Top-Secret UFO Files Revealed*. North Yorkshire, England: Quill, 1994.

———. *Need to Know: UFOs, the Military, and Intelligence*. New York: Pegasus Books, 2007.

———. *The UFO Report*. New York: Avon, 1989.

Ginsburgh, Irwin. *First Man, Then Adam!* New York: Pocket Books, 1978.

Gladden, Lee, and Vivianne Cervantes Gladden. *Heirs of the Gods*. New York: Rawson, Wade, 1978.

Goldsen, Joseph M., ed. *Outer Space in World Politics*. New York: Frederick A. Praeger, 1963.

Greene, Vaughan M. *Astronauts of Ancient Japan*. Millbrae, CA: Merlin Engine Works, 1978.

Hamilton, William F. *Cosmic Top Secret*. New Brunswick, NJ: Inner Light, 1991.

Hayakawa, Norio F. *UFOs—The Grand Deception and the Coming New World Order*. New Brunswick, NJ: Civilian Intelligence Network/Inner Light, 1993.

Huyghe, Patrick, and Harry Trumbore. *The Field Guide to Extraterrestrials*. New York: Avon Books, 1996.

Hynek, J. Allen, and Jacques Vallee. *The Edge of Reality*. Chicago: Henry Regnery, 1975.

Hynek, J. Allen, and Philip J. Imbrogno, with Bob Pratt. *Night Siege*. New York: Ballantine, 1987.

Imbrogno, Philip J. *Interdimensional Universe: The New Science of UFOs, Paranormal Phenomena and Otherdimensional Beings*. Woodbury, MN: Llewellyn Publications, 2008.

Jacobs, David M. *Secret Life: Firsthand, Documented Accounts of UFO Abductions*. New York: Touchstone, 1999.

Jung, C. G. *Flying Saucers: A Modern Myth of Things Seen in the Sky*. New York: New American Library, 1967.

Kean, Leslie. *UFOs: Generals, Pilots and Government Officials Go on the Record*. New York: Crown, 2010.

Keel, John A. *Strange Creatures from Time and Space*. New York: Fawcett, 1970.

———. *The Mothman Prophecies*. New York: Saturday Review Press, 1975.

Kent, Malcom. *The Terror above Us*. New York: Tower, 1967.

Keyhoe, Donald E. *Flying Saucers from Outer Space*. New York: Henry Holt, 1953.

LaViolette, Paul A. *Secrets of Antigravity Propulsion: Tesla, UFOs, and Classified Aerospace Technology*. Rochester, VT: Bear and Company, 2008.

Lewis, Richard S. *Appointment on the Moon*. New York: Viking Press, 1968.

Ley, Willy. *Missiles, Moonprobes and Megaparsecs*. New York: New American Library, 1964.

———. *Rockets, Missiles and Men in Space*. New York: Viking, 1944.

Lorenzen, Coral, and Jim Lorenzen. *Encounters with UFO Occupants*. New York: Berkley, 1976.

Lovell, A. C. B. *The Individual and the Universe*. New York: Harper and Brothers, 1958.

McWane, Glenn, and David Graham. *The New UFO Sightings*. New York: Warner Paperback Library, 1974.

Menger, Howard. *From Outer Space to You*. New York: Pyramid, 1967.

Michel, Aime. *The Truth about Flying Saucers*. New York: Pyramid, 1967.

Palmer, Raymond A. *The Real UFO Invasion*. San Diego: Greenleaf, 1967.

Pawlicki, T. B. *How to Build a Flying Saucer and Other Proposals in Speculative Engineering.* Englewood Cliffs, NJ: Prentice Hall, 1981.

Randle, Kevin D. *Invasion Washington: UFOs over the Capitol.* New York: HarperTorch, 2001.

———. *Case MJ-12: The True Story behind the Government's UFO Conspiracies.* New York: HarperTorch, 2002.

Randle, Kevin D., and Donald R. Schmitt. *The Truth about the UFO Crash at Roswell.* New York: M. Evans, 1994.

Randles, Jenny. *Out of the Blue.* New Brunswick, NJ: Global Communications, 1991.

Redfern, Nick. *On the Trail of the Saucer Spies: UFOs and Government Surveillance.* San Antonio, TX: Anomalist Books, 2006.

———. *The NASA Conspiracies: The Truth behind the Moon Landings, Censored Photos, and the Face on Mars.* Pompton Plains, NJ: New Page Books, 2011.

Rimmer, John. *The Evidence for Alien Abductions.* Wellingborough, Northamptonshire, England: Aquarian Press, 1984.

Romanek, Stan. *Messages: The World's Most Documented Extraterrestrial Contact Story.* Woodbury, MN: Llewellyn Publications, 2009.

Ruppelt, Edward J. *The Report on Unidentified Flying Objects.* New York: Doubleday, 1956.

Sagan, Carl, and Thornton Page. *UFOs—A Scientific Debate.* Ithaca, NY/London: Cornell University Press, 1972.

Sagan, Carl, and Shklovskii, I. S. *Intelligent Life in the Universe.* New York: Dell, 1968.

Santesson, Hans Stefan. *Flying Saucers in Fact and Fiction.* New York: Lancer, 1968.

Saunders, David R., and R. Roger Harkins. *UFOs? Yes! Where the Condon Committee Went Wrong.* New York: New American Library, 1968.

Schellhorn, G. Cope. *Extraterrestrials in Biblical Prophecy and the New Age Great Experiment.* Madison, WI: Horus House, 1990.

Science & Mechanics, eds. *The Official Guide to UFOs.* New York, Ace, 1968.

Shapley, Harlow. *The View from a Distant Star.* New York: Dell, 1967.

Sitchin, Zecharia. *The 12th Planet.* New York: Avon, 1978.

Stanton, L. Jerome. *Flying Saucers: Hoax or Reality?* New York: Belmont, 1966.

Steiger, Brad. *Alien Meetings.* New York: Grosset & Dunlap, 1978.

———. *Atlantis Rising.* New York: Dell, 1973.

———. *The Fellowship.* New York: Doubleday, 1988.

———. *The Gods of Aquarius: UFOs and the Transformation of Man.* New York: Harcourt Brace Jovanovich, 1976.

———. *Mysteries of Time and Space.* Englewood Cliffs, NJ: Prentice Hall, 1974.

———, ed. *Project Bluebook.* New York: ConFucian Press/Ballantine, 1976.

———. *Strangers from the Skies.* New York: Award, 1966.

———. *The UFO Abductors.* New York: Berkley, 1988.

——— and Hayden C. Hewes. *UFO Missionaries Extraordinary.* New York: Pocket Books, 1976.

——— and Sherry Hansen Steiger. *The Rainbow Conspiracy.* New York: Kensington/Pinnacle, 1994.

——— and Sherry Hansen Steiger. *Starborn.* New York: Berkley, 1992.

——— and Sherry Hansen Steiger. *Super Scientists of Ancient Atlantis and Other Unknown Worlds.* New Brunswick, NJ: 1993.

——— and Sherry Hansen Steiger. *UFO Odyssey.* New York: Ballantine, 1999.

———, Sherry Hansen Steiger, and Alfred Bielek. *The Philadelphia Experiment and Other UFO Conspiracies.* New Brunswick, NJ: Inner Light, 1990.

——— and John White. *Other Worlds, Other Universes—Playing the Reality Game.* New York: Doubleday, 1975.

——— and Joan Whritenour. *Flying Saucers Are Hostile!* New York/London: Award/Tandem, 1967.

——— and Joan Whritenour. *Flying Saucer Invasion: Target Earth.* New York/London: Award/Tandem, 1969.

——— and Joan Whritenour. *New UFO Breakthrough.* New York/London: Award/Tandem, 1968.

Stevens, Wendelle. *UFO Contact from the Pleiades.* Tucson: UFO Photo Archives, 1982.

Stonehill, Paul. *Soviet UFO Files: Paranormal Encounters behind the Iron Curtain.* Barnsbury, Guilford UK: Quadrillion Publishing, 1998.

Story, Ron. *The Encyclopedia of Extraterrestrial Encounters.* New York: New American Library, 2001.

Stranges, Frank E. *My Friend from Beyond Earth.* Van Nuys, CA: I.E.C., 1960.

——— *UFO Conspiracy.* Van Nuys, CA: I.E.C., 1985.

Strieber, Whitley. *Communion.* New York: Beech Tree/William Morrow, 1987.

Sullivan, Walter. *We Are Not Alone.* New York: McGraw-Hill, 1964.

Trench, Brinsley Le Poer. *The Flying Saucer Story.* New York: Ace, 1966.

Tyler, Steven. *Are the Invaders Coming?* New York: Tower, 1968.

Vallee, Jacques. *Messengers of Deception: UFO Contacts and Cults.* Daily Grail Publishing, American Edition, 2008.

Velikovsky, Immanuel. *Worlds in Collision.* New York: Dell, 1967.

Von Daniken, Erich. *Twilight of the Gods: The Mayan Calendar and the Return of the Extraterrestrials.* Pompton Plains, NJ: New Page Books, 2010.

Walton, Travis. *The Walton Experience.* New York: Berkley, 1978.

Warren, Larry, and Robbins, Peter. *Left at East Gate: A First-Hand Account of the Rendlesham Forest UFO Incident, Its Cover-up, and Investigation.* New York: Cosimo Books, 2010.

Watkins, Leslie. *Alternative 3*. London: Sphere, 1978.

Weldon, John, with Zola Levitt. *UFOs—What on Earth Is Happening?* Irvine, CA: Harvest House, 1975.

Wilkins, Harold T. *Flying Saucers Uncensored*. New York: Pyramid, 1967.

Wilson, Clifford. *UFOs and Their Mission Impossible*. New York: New American Library, 1974.

Woodrew, Greta. *On a Slide of Light*. New York: Macmillan, 1981.

———. *Memories of Tomorrow*. New York: Doubleday, 1988.

INDEX

Note: (ill.) indicates photos and illustrations.

A